The Journals of George M. Dawson: British Columbia, 1875–1878

D1739349

The Journals of George M. Dawson: British Columbia, 1875~1878

Volume II, 1877~1878

Edited by Douglas Cole and Bradley Lockner

University of British Columbia Press

Vancouver 1989

ISBN 0-7748-0286-3

Canadian Cataloguing in Publication Data

Dawson, George M., 1849-1901.
  The journals of George M. Dawson
  (Recollections of the pioneers of British Columbia)

  Includes bibliographical references and index.
  Contents: v. 1. 1875-1876—v. 2. 1877-1878
  ISBN 0-7748-0276-6 (v. 1).—ISBN 0-7748-0286-3 (v. 2)
  1. Dawson, George M., 1849-1901 – Diaries. 2. Geologists –
Canada – Diaries. 3. Geology – British Columbia. 4. Indians of
North America – British Columbia. 5. British Columbia –
Description and travel. I. Cole, Douglas, 1938- II. Lockner,
Bradley John, 1950- III. Title. IV. Series.
  FC 3817.2.D39 1989 917.11′043 C88-091648-6 F1087.D39 1989

This book has been published with the help of a grant from the
Social Science Federation of Canada, using funds provided by the
Social Sciences and Humanities Research Council of Canada.

The Journals of George M. Dawson, 1877–1878

Dawson's 1877 Route

18-27 MAY: Travelled by steamer *Enterprise* from Victoria to New Westminster, river steamer *Royal City* to Yale, and coach to Spence's Bridge. Then continued by stage to Savona (Savona's Ferry) Ferry and lake steamer to Kamloops. Travelled by steamer up the North Thompson to junction with the Clearwater and returned to Kamloops.

29 MAY-17 JUNE: Travelled south past Stump Lake, taking side trip up Nicola River to Douglas Lake. Continued south past Quilchena (Hamilton's)[1] Creek, Clapperton's near Nicola Lake, to the junction of the Coldwater and Nicola rivers. Travelled south on the Hope Trail, along the Coldwater, until mouth of Boston Bar Creek (the west branch of the Coquihalla River) and southwest down the Coquihalla Valley to Hope.

11-12 JUNE: At Hope.

13-26 JUNE: Eastward to junction of Similkameen and Nicola trails, then followed Sumallo River east, across Allison Pass, and on to junction of the Similkameen and Tulameen rivers at Princeton (Hayes). Moved east following Similkameen River, past Hedley Creek (20 Mile Creek), Ashnola River, Keremeos Creek (Kerremeoos Brook) and Price's farm to north end of Osoyoos Lake.

1.   Current topographical names are given, with Dawson's most frequent usage in parentheses.

26 JUNE–6 JULY: Side trip to south end of Osoyoos Lake and back, then travelled north along the Okanagan River, along the west side of Skaha (Du Chien) Lake, and the east side of Okanagan Lake to Mission Creek. Took a side trip up Mission Creek to see gold mines, then moved north past Wood (Primeewash) and Kalamalka (Long) lakes to Vernon's Coldstream Ranch.

7–18 JULY: Side trip five miles up Coldstream Creek to "Nelson's," and then travelled east up Coldstream Creek to junction of Cherry Creek and Shuswap River, then returned to Vernon's.

19–25 JULY: Travelled northwest past Round Lake to Westwold (Ingram's), moved north along Monte (Pringle's) Creek to Duck's Roadhouse on the South Thompson River, and then by stage west to Kamloops.

26 JULY–15 AUGUST: Returned east up South Thompson River to Monte Creek (Duck's) and Chase (Chase's Farm) at the southwest end of Little Shuswap Lake. Canoed along the south shore of Little Shuswap Lake, the north shore of Shuswap Lake, north up Seymour Arm, and then through Cinnemousun Narrows and down southwest shore of Salmon Arm. Returned by Anstey Arm, through Cinnemousun Narrows, and back along the south shores of Shuswap and Little Shuswap lakes to Chase and Kamloops.

16–29 AUGUST: Up the North Thompson River to the North Thompson Indian Reserve and coal deposits south of Chu Chua. Returned by same route to Kamloops, where, after climbing Mount Paul (Mt. St. Paul), canoed west along the north shore of Kamloops Lake, travelled three miles up Tranquille River (Creek), and returned to Kamloops.

30 AUGUST–13 SEPTEMBER: Travelled along the previous route south to Stump Lake, east across the Plateau Trail to Chapperon Lake, and then along the Salmon River northeast to Westwold. Continued southeast along Salmon River to O'Keefe's Ranch at the head of Okanagan Lake, down the west side of Okanagan Lake to Allison's, and then travelled southwest on plateau to Princeton.

14–23 SEPTEMBER: Moved north along Allison and Quilchena creeks to Nicola Lake, and the mouth of the Coldwater River, then west across the mountains along Spioos Creek to Boston Bar.

24 SEPTEMBER-10 OCTOBER: Travelled north along the Fraser to Lytton, Lillooet, Fountain and Pavilion, east along Marble Canyon, Hat Creek, north along Bonaparte River, and northeast via wagon road to Clinton. Took a side trip to Kelly Lake, then back south along the Bonaparte to Cache Creek and up the Semlin Valley to Savona (Savona's Ferry).

11-19 OCTOBER: Followed the Thompson southwest past Ashcroft (Cornwall's), southeast along the Nicola, north up Guichon (Ten Mile) Creek, north across the plateau to a wagon road, and finally Kamloops.

20-27 OCTOBER: Travelled by trap and stage to Cache Creek, Lytton, Boston Bar, and Yale, and then by steamers to New Westminster and Victoria.

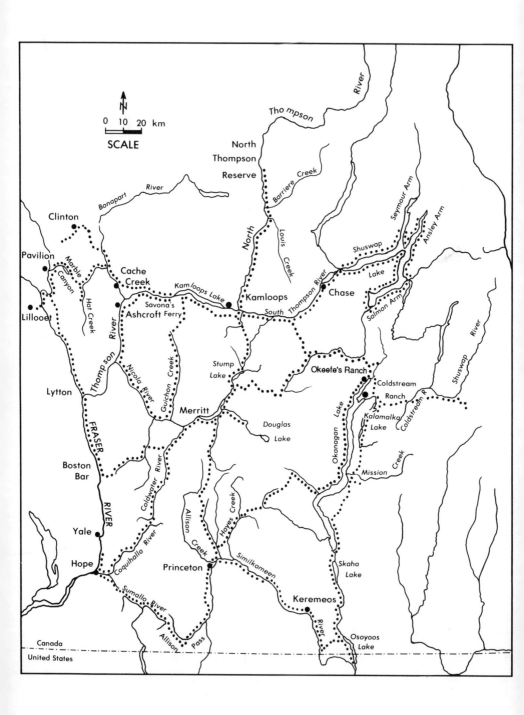

II

1877

[Dawson left Montreal by train on 24 April 1877, bound for the west coast via Chicago, Omaha, Provo, and northern California. That trip, Dawson's overland voyage north, his stay in Victoria, and preparations in Kamloops until 27 May 1877, are all recorded in a small pocket diary. Omitted in the present edition are entries for the trip to Victoria and loose journal material such as calling cards and newspaper clippings.]

May 10 up at 4 A.m. starting for Victoria in Str North Pacific at 5 a.m. Called at Ports Gamble Ludlow, Townsend & one other place, & got to Victoria about 3.30 P.m. Put up at Driard House, where find some of the Surveyors. Cambie* went up country last week. Gamsby* is at Burrard Inlet, & Bell*, Perry,[1] & McMillan* leave tomorrow morning.

Day overcast & cloudy, preventing view of Mountains in Crossing from the sound. Unpacking & getting settled here.

May 11. Unpacking, making various arrangements. Called at Liut Governors[2] in P.m. & received several visits. Wrote short note home. Day remarkably fine.

---

1. C. E. Perry, an engineer in charge with the CPRS.

2. Albert Norton Richards (1822-97) had been appointed to the position on 20 July 1876. Earlier, Richards practised law in Brockville, Upper Canada, before sitting in the House of Commons from 1872 to 1874. Richards was appointed police magistrate in Victoria in 1888.

G. M. Dawson to Margaret Dawson*, 11 May 1877, Victoria

I arrived here Safe & well last evening after journeying sixteen days from Montreal. The direct mail by Steamer closes shortly, & I sit down after having unpacked my things, merely to announce the fact that I am here.

Some of the Railway survey parties have already gone into the interior, two having left last friday, & two more this morning Tomorrow or next day when my Plans are somewhat matured I hope to write at greater length, & give you some account of my trip, which has been on the whole a very pleasant one.

May 12   Making various arrangements. Afternoon went boating up the arm with the Creases*, returning after dark.
May 13 Sunday Reading, writing, & in the afternoon for a walk.

G. M. Dawson to Anna Lois Harrington*, 13 May 1877, Victoria

As already announced in a short note to Mother, I arrived here on Thursday Evening last, my previous movements should also have been pretty well defined if the post cards dropped from time to time have all reached Safely.

I suppose you will expect to receive some Short account of my journey, which occupied sixteen days, & so will try to give you a few notes. — The time occupied would have been just 14 days but for two days of forced rest, one at Roseburg on a Sunday, the second at Seattle on "the Sound" waiting for the steamer, which only makes two trips a week each way.

At Port Huron I got safely through the hands of the Customs officers, without any Particular trouble, & proceeded on to Chicago in the regular course. Thence changing cars, & {after} waiting about an hour onward to Omaha, arriving there in a great storm of wind & rain — by no means pleasant as two changes have to be made, the first into the Bridge transfer Cars, & then after Crossing again into the Pullman on the U.P. Ry.[3] In the western states, & at Omaha every thing was green, somewhat in advance of Montreal, willows being in flower &c., but on going a few miles further west, vegetation being at about the same stage, we got into a snowstorm, which continued with little intermission till we reached the Summit at Sherman. Several miles befor Sherman we got into quite deep dry drifted snow-banks & had some difficulty in getting through with three engines & a snow Plough. On leaving Omaha people know that they are

3.   Union Pacific Railway.

bound to spend a few days together as on a short sea voyage & in Consequence at once become more conversational & friendly. There were two Pullmans on the train & some very pleasant people most of whom I forget already. I had a seat with a Mr Wise, connected with the Ry. office at Ogden Utah who proved intelligent. Near at hand was an Americanized Dutchman appointed as Postmaster to some remote district, & travelling with his daughter a not too ugly girl but too modest to speak. There was a Mrs Lawrence from Washington going out to join her husband, a doctor in Arizona. Also another lady who soon became a chum of hers but got off to go to Gold Hill in Nevada, where her husband is something in mines — Also a number of other people, including several young ladies all of whom with the exception of one were sufficiently plain looking & common place in every respect. The one was returning to Oakland in California from a visit East, with her mother & other members of the family — she was extremely good looking to say the least of it & clever also — but as I can just imagine you running your eye along the next line to see all about it I shall pull up here without telling you her name or anything else. We had a small Cabinet organ on one of the Pullmans, & the musical portion of the community continued to enliven the journey with songs till we lost the music box in changing cars at Ogden. About the only tune everybody seemed to know was *Hold the Fort*, so this & some others of M. &. S. series[4] were favourites. Disgusted with the loss of our instrument we solaced ourselves by sitting out on the platforms & steps waiting for sunrises, sunsets, meridian passages & other astronomical phenomena — watching them, & then going back indoors to shake bushels of dust out of our clothes, & wash pebbles out of our eyes. One sunset over the Great Salt Lake was very satisfactorally observed. We also observed antelope which appeared to reciprocate in most cases, & from time to time several people would dash themselves violently against a window to see a Jack rabbit which never could be seen. In the Salt Lake Valley we found apples, peaches & &c. in full bloom & everything like early Summer, but soon ran into the wastes of the Humboldt Valley, & thence Crept up to the summit of the Sierra Nevada where the appearance was that of very early spring with plenty snow lying about. From the summit {which} you attain in the very early morning, you run down to San Francisco in one day, arriving there in the evening. As we slid along, — the only use of the engine now being to keep the train from running too fast — we Passed down through the foot hills now green & beautiful with flowers to the wide Sacramento

---

4. Moody and Sankey. Dwight L. Moody (1837–99) and Ira D. Sankey (1840–1908), American evangelists, published sacred songs and gospel hymns which were widely used in North America and the United Kingdom.

Valley, & found ourselves in Summer, haying going on strawberries ripe & all the trees in full foliage. At Roseville Junction near Sacramento I reluctantly left the comforts of the Pullman, & in five minutes found myself alone & forlorn kicking my heels in as dull a little country waiting room as you ever saw. I had several hours to do it in & so did not hurry, but tried reading & walking & having some dinner, & at last four o'clock Came & with it the train for Maryville, surcharge with hot local passengers intersprinkled with babies. At Marysville I had to get a new ticket, telegraph for a place on the stage, get luggage rechecked & supper within 20 or 25 minutes — which being fulfilled we jogged on to Reading, stopping at all Sorts of little stations by the way, but finally pulling up at the terminus at about 1 a.m. After going to bed we got up at half past four to breakfast for the stage starting at five. The first view of the stage was not very reassuring as the inside was half filled with mail matter, & a miscellany strapped all over the back top. For Passengers we had a stout Great grandfather & his wife going up to Oregon to see their children, an Americo-German Jew buying skins & furs, an attorney to something & a non-descript man also with a wife. We gradually settled as the stage moved on, those at first occupying the honourable but incommodious position of keystones, finding themselves on the seat in the course of half an hour. The great grandmother would have kept plenty of room in her corner had she been strong enough, but fortunately years had done their work & she was'nt. Various kalidescopic changes occured as we went along which even to remember would be tedious. We lost some passengers & gained others, till finally the losses preponderating I found myself alone with the driver on arriving at Roseburg. From Reading we drove on for three days & two nights, the longest stop we made being at Yreka for two hours. The roads were execrable having just hardened after the winter rains, & being composed of ruts & hard intervening ridges, in most places so narrow that it is with the greatest difficulty a place can be selected for two coaches to pass. Though not passing along sheer cliffs as on the Frazer River, this road cut out for long distances like a shelf on steep grassy hill sides & with almost impossibly steep hills to ascend & descend, is really far more dangerous. At one place near the north line of California you ascend the Siskiyou Mountain — a sort of pass — over 2000 feet high by means of a system of most involved doubling too & fro. On the top, you at once begin to descend again by a road very like the ascent I suppose though I dont' know much about it as it was pitch dark. I only heard the brake shrieking against the wheels as we went bumping along, & saw the horses (six of them) apparently dancing on the edge of an abyss as we flew round the curves. However we reached the bottom at last & I dont' particularly want ever to see that hill again. One begins to get sleepy too about the third day. You are admiring the scenery — paying the greatest *possible* attention to it — when all at once you relapse into a state of temporary insanity with the most absurd dreams rushing through your head till ⟨all at once⟩ {suddenly} you wake just on the point of jolting forward among the horses. When at last we stopped I found myself all covered with contusions & tender spots, hands brightly polished with holding on to the iron rails, & head nearly sawn off by the edges of my collar, but still in a capital condition for a good night's sleep. Next day we went on again in the stage till about 3 P.m. when we reached Roseburg. Thence to Portland Ogn. by rail, thence on the Willamette & Columbia by steamer to Kalama, thence by rail to Tacoma, thence by steamer to Seattle & finally thence by steamer here. On reaching, at last, the Pacific at the lower end of the Sound they presented us among other delicacies with clams. I proposed to eat some of these in honour of the occasion & began on one, but finally concluded I would try Something else as we had only half an hour for supper. I cannot enter into detail however with the various gastronomic struggles experienced during the journey, or the varying consequent forms of indegestion. It would be too sad a subject to close with. I find too I have not said anything about the scenery which was the chief object of the letter at the outset, also that my record of the weather has been prematurely brought to a close about page 2. both of which circumstances you will no doubt deeply regret. Some of the country is really very pretty, & it is all well worth seeing once. You pass in Northern California within a few miles of the base of Mt Shasta a wonderful snow clad volcanic mountain over 14,000 feet in height, & almost isolated. Then the Valley of the Rogue River, & those of the Shasta, Klamath, & Umpqua are remarkably beautiful. The country is generally mountainous but with little rock showing, bare grassy slopes rising steeply from the valleys to heights of 1000 or at least several hundred feet, scattered clumps & groves of fine well grown & rounded oaks, maples, & tall firs. The whole giving the effect of a perfectly kept park, with wide fertile fields in the flat bottom-lands of the valleys, all at this season beautifully green. The climate too is probably as fine as any in the world, with scarcely anything that we would call winter, less rain than on the actual coast, & an Italian Summer admitting of the easy cultivation of grapes on the large scale. It being Sunday I may be allowed to characterize it in the words of the psalmist as a region "Where every prospect pleases, but only man is Vile" for really I never heard so much concentrated bad language before as during the last ten days.

The Steamer from San Francisco is expected in hourly & by it I hope to hear from home & to know that your convalescence has been complete. I feel already as if I had been journeying forty years in the wilderness since leaving Montreal, but hope to enter into the Promised Land via New

Westminster about next Friday. I fear I have written a great deal of non-
sense & so shant read it over to see. I address to McGill as I have forgotten
your number please send it to me on a slip.

May 14. Making purchases & arrangements about outfit &c. Evg. called at
Robsons*. Jennings* & other engineers arrive from the East.
May 15   Wrote to Bowman* offering him $60 a month with the option of
Staying only 3 months if he pleases & Promising to keep the place open
for him till noon tomorrow.
May 16. Did not hear from Bowman* or find anyone else Suitable for the
place. Morning packing, afternoon Called at Creases*, evening dined at
Duponts* returning late
May 17. Paying bills, arranging for money at bank, comparing barom-
eters, packing &c.
May 18   Started at 730 Am for New Westminster 〈....〉 in steamer
Enterprise with a very heavy freight & great number of passengers Strong
tide against us all day preventing our getting in till after 6 P.m. Saw Trew*
about leaving the specimen of Anthracite in Montreal. Returned platinum
& Indian bread to museum. Wrote home, Selwyn*, Bernard*, Boscovitz*.

G. M. Dawson to Margaret Dawson*, 18 May 1877, New Westminster

My intension was to have written two long letters before leaving
Victoria, one giving some account of my Journey there, the other of
occurrences there & plans. The first has been accomplished & addressed to
Anna*, the second has fallen through, but here on my way up the country
I must send back some account of my movements.
  Though a week in Victoria I feel as though I accomplished little there,
one really gets into lazy loafing habits in travelling so long, & the things I
had to look after left me with broken fragments of time as they went
slowly but not without attention. You must give me credit for doing my
duty when I tell you that the day after my arrival I Called on the Lieut
Governor, & made also several other Calls during my stay. Last Saturday
the Creases* asked me to a boating party, which not having any excuse to
refuse, I accepted. Several people did not turn up at the last moment, & I
found myself in for taking an oar, though not an adept in rowing. We got
along however, going up to the head of the Arm[5] — about five miles —
when the excursion resolved itself into a Picknick. The second part of the
party came overland on horseback, & we had a combined spread, rowing
back again during twilight & after dark. The weather was charming & on

5.   Probably through the Gorge to Portage Inlet.

the whole the trip was very enjoyable. People in Victoria are very kind & I was obliged to decline several invitations on account of business connected with my departure.

I am now on my way up to Kamloops which will probably ⟨by⟩ be my centre during a great part of the summer. A number of the Railway people are also on the steamer, most of them not going so far as Kamloops & some of them further. Mr Cambie* I hope to see on the way or at Kamloops, & from Mr Selwyn* I have heard that I may depend on the same assistance in the way of transport & supplies as formerly. I will probably write again before leaving Kamloops telling my route &c. more particularly.

Please thank Rankine* for his post card & letter, the latter enclosing stamps.

I sleep on board the steamer tonight to avoid going to hotel & having to get up very early in the morning. There is noise & confusion on board & I am tired & must postpone writing at greater length

May 19. Slept on board the str. Royal City which started at 7 a.m. with a heavy freight & many passengers. Rival steamer Glenora off at same time & racing going on all day. our boat fastest but having to stop at many landings. Tied up after dark a short way above Hope.

May 20. Sunday Arrived at Yale 5 A.m. Part of Survey parties go off at once but Some wait for the regular stage on Monday Morning. Reading & walking about Yale & on the waggon road. Rain most of day yesterday & during night Showers all day today & Mountains clouded up. Found an indian Chipped tool under about 5 feet of fine bedded yellow Sand which included layers of charcoal here & there. The implement at a height of about 25 feet above present high flood level, but evidently beds formed by flood water of river when it rose higher or before it cut its bed down so low. This near the old toll house about a mile above Yale.

May 21 Start about 7 a.m. & drive on to Boston Bar Thence go on with Steve Tingley[6] in a buggy to Spence's bridge, arriving there about 9.30 P.m. A very pleasant drive, but extremely Sleepy at last. Turned in at once.

May 22 Found Cambie* here on getting up, & talked over plans with him. Stage arrived about 8 a.m. Went on to Cache Creek arriving about

---

6. Stephen Tingley (1839–1915), a stage driver, was known throughout the British Columbia interior. He came to Victoria in 1861, spent several seasons in Barkerville, then established a harness shop in Yale. Tingley was a partner in the F. J. Barnard & Company and British Columbia Express Company, before becoming sole owner of the latter.

1.30 Off again at 3 P.m for Savona's ferry[7] in an extra arranged for to take Wallace[8] to his party at Kamloops. Found the little steamer waiting at the ferry, & after getting supper Started for Kamloops. A beautiful moonlight Sail on the lake which almost perfectly calm. Engine power small & some difficulty in getting up the river near Kamloops but at last arrived at 1 A.m. Cambie* had suggested a trip on the steamer up the N. Thompson, which finding everyone agreeable, & that delay in fitting out pack train likely to arise — decided to make. Write to Ross* telling him what I will need & requesting him to do what possible in the matter before my return. Got bunk on board & turned in.

May 23. Steaming up the N. Thompson all day against the strong current. The stage of the water at present however good, being neither too high nor too low. Made a remarkably good days work tying up at dark at Mosquito Flat about 15 miles from the Clearwater.

May 24 Early this morning the timbers below the boiler furnaces were found to be on fire, & owing to the difficulty of reaching the place, some time was employed in getting it put out. Made a rather late start in consequence but reached the Depot at junction Thompson & Clearwater by about 10 A.m. All hands at work soon unloaded the stuff, & the party after having dinner on board began to arrange packs for moving 5 miles to camp before night. Started in steamer at 1 P.m. & raced down the river, finding, owing to the stage of water no trouble in any of the bad places. Stopped once for wood & twice to take on grain & tied up at the Saw mill[9] after dusk in a heavy shower of rain.

At the Fish Trap 'rapid' saw An old indian sitting at his fire cooking something in a pot, with two or three half dried fish on a pole near him & a dog. He sat in a crouched attitude with his back to the river, intently stirring his pot, & though we passed almost within a Stones throw of him never turned, nor indicated in any way that he noticed the steamer at all!

Found quite a number of ripe strawberries on the sunny side of a bank near the C.P.R. depot At Clearwater.

The valley of the North Thompson runs nearly due north. Its Sides are formed by hills which appear to follow in their direction the length of the valley, but are probably to be regarded as the escarpments forming the edges of the plateau above, which has been cut into by the river valley. The height of the hills may average from 1500 to 2000 feet above the river

7.   Savona.

8.   A. Wallace, a leveller with the CPRS.

9.   Probably the sawmill constructed by J. Jamieson and his partner Charles Petch in 1871, situated about fifteen miles above Kamloops. Lumber produced by the mill was rafted downriver to Kamloops.

in its lower portion, becoming somewhat higher northward, & near Clearwater even showing some summits which still hold snow. A mountain mass in the fork of the rivers is in great part Snow clad. The Country to the west I am told averages from 3500 to 4000 feet & forms in the main a rolling partly open plateau over this the Howes Sd. line to Clearwater[10] was run. It probably represents the Green Timber &c. plateau. The river is bordered generally on both sides, but always on one by flats, extending out from the base of the steep side hill or higher benches. The river now appears like most streams to be gradually cutting down to lower levels & forming wide swampy sand flats which are first covered with Cottonwood. It is not however excavating its rocky channel which must — from analogy — lie far below somewhat thus. [*Illus.*] Like the Fraser Below Hope the N. Thompson as far as Clearwater appears to be backed up either by relative change in altitude of its mouth & source, by damming up or some other cause. The valley resembles that occupied by the various long lakes of the country but the blocking up has not been complete as in other cases.[11]

Terraces appear in many places but usually more or less Completely weathered away. The highest distinctly seen probably not over 1000 feet above the river

The gravel drift in the banks about Clearwater mouth is composed in great part of volcanic materials, many pebbles being of a pale vesicular rock.[12] There are also many of mica schist — grey & silvery, & of grey granite. Also of compact greenish grey rock perhaps of same series as the vesicular In one place, near Meridian bend,[13] a bank shows a face of what appears to be true boulder clay. It is overlaid by stratified sands & gravels. Higher up on the river some banks show white material not unlike that of the 'White Silts' & in one place holding here & there large angular stones.

---

10. A reference to the explorations of Joseph Hunter of the CPRS. "In 1873 he took a pack train up from the head of Howe Sound, up the Cheakamus River through to Lillooet River — along the route of the present P.G.E. — and explored the country between the Cariboo wagon road and the Clearwater River" (*Victoria Daily Colonist*, 9 April 1935).

11. The North Thompson River from Kamloops to McLure is probably on the site of an infilled lake, judging from the rate of infill of Kamloops Lake. See C. H. Pharo and E. C. Carmack, "Sedimentation Processes in a Short Residence-time Intermontane Lake, Kamloops Lake, British Columbia," *Sedimentology* 26 (1979): 523–41. The section from Louis Creek to Clearwater could also have been a lake, separated from greater Kamloops Lake by a shoal at Fishtrap Rapids infilled by North Thompson River sediment. Glacial scour, rather than damming, could also have been responsible for the upstream lake.

12. Volcanic rock with small spherical or ellipsoidal cavities produced by bubbles of gas trapped during the solidification of the rock.

13. At the confluence of the North Thompson and Clearwater rivers, where the North Thompson bends at a right angle.

This however not very far from a steep rocky bluff which might have supplied them.[14]

The Coal Said to occur near the Indian Reserve[15] is probably the same as that about which told by old miner at Victoria. Indians keep the place Secret, but it is probably in the valley of the brook entering about 3 miles above the Indian houses on the same — east — side. Cannot tell much about the rocks as they seldom appear on the river & then do not show their natural colours being weathered. Saw no columnar basalt or horizontally bedded traps like those of some regions. Nor any sign of sandstones or lignite clays. Inclined to believe that the character of the rocks somewhat varied, though may be all be volcanic up to Assiniboine Bluff as Mr Selwyn* seems to suppose.[16] The lower part of the valley is thinly timbered like the Kamloops Country & with much open hillside & flat. This runs up for perhaps 30 miles when with evidence of increased rainfall the timber becomes thicker & when Clearwater is reached becomes quite dense. The P. ponderosa continues to occur abundantly on all suitable places about ⅔ way up. The Cedar then begins to appear & before Clearwater is quite abundant. There are a good many farmers — perhaps altogether about 15 — on the lower part of the river. Irrigation is here necessary but further up, toward the Clearwater would probably not be required.[17]

May 25. Taking on lumber at the mill for some hours. Arrived at Kamloops about 11.30.[18] Saw Ross* & in the evening rode up to C.P.R. Camp to look at the Animals. Find the 7 remaining mules Crippled & useless & so decide to get pack horses in addition to the riding animals Ross*

14. Dawson was describing terraces cut, at least in part, into late glacial lake silts. The Clearwater River valley contains Quaternary basaltic lava and this, or even more so, the Raft River to the east, brings down micaceous sediments. See Fulton, "Silt Deposition."

15. The deposit, located in the gorge of Newhykulston Creek about three quarters of a mile from its mouth, was later worked by the Chu Chua Coal Company. For a description of the coal deposits and workings of the company, see W. L. Uglow, "Geology of the North Thompson Valley Map-Area, British Columbia," in Geological Survey of Canada, *Summary Report, 1921, Part A* (1922), 92-98. The Indian Reserve is now North Thompson Reserve One.

16. Selwyn had noted in his published report that the northeastern boundary of the Volcanic Series is "about sixty or seventy miles above Kamloops" (Selwyn, "Journal and Report," 57).

17. A sketch of a paddlewheel steamer on the river, dated 24 May 1877, is on the last page of the journal entries.

18. In his published report, Dawson places the date of his Kamloops arrival as 23 May. See George M. Dawson, "Preliminary Report on the Physical and Geological Features of the Southern Portion of the Interior of British Columbia, 1877," Geological Survey of Canada, *Report of Progress for 1877-78* (Montreal: Dawson Brothers, 1879), 2.

had already purchased. Got well drenched in a storm on the way up to Camp.

May 26. Went over to Indian Reserve to see about buying horses. Saw several   Found the chief Louis[19] in a sweat house with a friend & held a conversation with him through the blankets. He promised to bring some horses now in the mountains over in the evening. Packing stuff & making arrangements.

May 27 Sunday Packing. Adjusting sextant &c. at dusk the horses from Sullivans[20] on north River[21] arrived completing the outfit. Reading &c.

G. M. Dawson to J. W. Dawson, 27 May 1877, Kamloops*

I hope to leave here tomorrow morning on my way Southwards, with a few pack & riding animals & three men, a Packer, an Indian, & a white man called Douglas.[22] There are so many routes through this open & lightly timbered country that I am Scarcely able to say exactly how I may go. At present, however, my plan is to visit the Nicola Valley & make a somewhat careful examination of the rocks there, with those of the Douglas Valley which opens eastward from it. Next to go southward towards Similkameen & Hope, making the latter place my turning point, & returning to the Nicola Valley by another trail. Thence I may go down the Nicola Valley, striking the Waggon Road at the junction of the Nicola & Thompson & from there possibly going north as far as Marble Cañon & Clinton before returning to Kamloops. Much is of course, provisional, & I may change the route if by doing So I can cover the ground better. It will be at least a month before I get back to Kamloops, which will be my centre during the summer. There are then two other expeditions to make, one towards Okanagan, & the second, by Canoe, on the South Thompson &

19. Chief Louis or Hli-hleh-kan (1828–1915) was the leader of the Kamloops Indians from about 1855 until his death. He guided his people through the difficult transition stage when the region was settled by large numbers of Euro-Canadians. Louis represented British Columbia Indians several times in Ottawa and also went to England as a delegate to Queen Victoria. See Mary Balf, "Chief Louis Earned Respect," *Kamloops Daily Sentinel*, 19 July 1971.

20. Michael Sullivan (b.1838) arrived in British Columbia in 1863 and worked as a Cariboo freighter until 1870 when he pre-empted land on the east bank of the North Thompson River. Sullivan sold his land in 1889 and moved to the Shuswap Lake area, returning to the North Thompson a short while later.

21. North Thompson River.

22. Although here and below Dawson refers to his assistant as "Douglas," in the published report he describes his party as consisting of "a Mexican packer, Lillooet Indian, as packer's assistant and cook, and D. McFarlane as general assistant" (Dawson, "Report on the Southern Portion," 2).

Shushwap Lake. These may probably occupy the remainder of the
summer, as I do not intend to hurry along where there is anything of interest to examine. During my first trip I will be in the vicinity of Settlements
or scattered Settlers. There are now seven parties scattered along the proposed C.P.R. route from Burrard Inlet to Tete Jaune Cache, by the Fraser
& Thompson Rivers, & a complete location line will be surveyed before
autumn, which there seems much probability will be the one ultimately
selected.

   I met Mr Cambie* going down to Victoria, when I was on the way up.
He is going in a few weeks up the coast to the Mouth of the Skeena &
Nasse Rivers, & will go thence inland by Canoe to Skeena Forks & then
explore Southward to François Lake. The object is to exhaust the possible
railway routes by an examination of this, the only one now remaining
unsurveyed. It is supposed that the result both as to harbour & route will
be unfavourable, & that it will not be thought worthwhile ⟨....⟩ to make
any instrumental survey of the route.

   When we met ⟨mr⟩ Mr Cambie*, we found him very anxious that
Wallace*, on of the Surveyors on the Stage, should get up at once to join
his party, which was waiting at Kamloops for him, & the instruments he
was conveying. Arrangements had been made for an "extra" from Cache
Creek to the lower end of Kamloops Lake, & a remarkably dimutive little
steamer familiarly known as "the Pup"[23] was waiting there to take him
up to Kamloops. Glad to escape the usual delay at Cache Creek I availed
myself also of the "extra" & on arriving at Kamloops at 1 A.M. we found
the Party (*W.* Party) all on board the larger steamer,[24] & ready to start at
any moment. Hearing that there was likely to be some difficulty in provid-
ing me with animals, I wrote a note to Ross*, in charge of commisariat
here, & decided to go up the N. Thompson in the steamer & return. The
steamer only makes occasional trips as business requires so the Chance
was not likely to occur again. I did not get a chance of ⟨doing more than⟩
examining the rocks but saw the general character of the River up as far as
Clearwater Mouth, which is practically the head of navigation. There is a
deposit of Coal about forty miles up the river which If I get time I must try
to visit before autumn.

   The weather is very fine here now, Summer-like but not excessively
warm.

---

23. In 1872 the CPRS had a small, twelve-ton sidewheeler named *Kamloops*, built to take
    supplies from Savona to Clearwater. This, presumably, is the "Pup." See Mary Balf,
    Kamloops: A History of the District up to 1914, 2d ed. (Kamloops: Kamloops Museum
    Association, 1981), 22–23.

24. The *Marten* was an HBC steamer which ran aground in 1877 and had to be scrapped.

[Dawson's personal journal entitled, "Diary & General Note-Book British Columbia. 1877. George M. Dawson." begins here and continues until 26 October 1877, when he reverts to a small pocket diary which is appended to the main 1877 volume. A number of rough notes at the end of the journal have been omitted.]

May 28. 1877. Monday. Animals all ready early this morning. Rigging fitted, packs made up & various other little matters attended to & train off by 11 A.m. Stayed in Kamloops for lunch & then rode on, overtaking packs before they reached camp. Accompanied as far as 'Packers Camp' (3 m.) by Ross*. Camp near a little Lake at Shumway's[25] ⟨(?spelling)⟩ Ranch. The distance called about 10.m.

Party consisting of self, Jacinto (my packer of last summer) A Lytton Indian, & Douglas, recommended by Ross* as a sort of general assistant.

Met a shower on the way over the high lands.

The season a remarkably early one here as elsewhere. Probably two weeks in advance. Geum triflorum past flowering. Chokecherry nearly past, Amelanchier in most places with fruit formed. Viola Canadensis in thickets by water.

May 29. Up early & off at good hour. Travelled till about 3 P.m. when camped near farmer's, abreast of the lower end of Stump Lake & about a mile from it. Hot in the middle of the day, but cooler toward evening when scattered thunder-storms floating about & occasional gusts of wind. Tried to get a photo. of the valley after camping but I fear the attempt not a success owing to unfavourable state of weather.[26] Collected a few plants & pressed them.

May 30 Rode over to lower end of Stump Lake to try if possible to learn cause of its production. Follow pack train down trail to Crossing of Nicola River, or Big Creek[27] & camp. After Lunch rode out up the valley towards Douglas Lake, about six miles, & after making sketch of it & examining rocks by the way return.

Weather of same general character as for nearly a week past. Calm & moderately clear in the morning, clouding up towards noon & in P.m. developing massive cumulus clouds which seen trailing fringes of rain with them here & there. When one of these approaches it brings a gust with it.

25. Ammi Warren Shumway (1832–89) was an American who came to British Columbia as a packer on the Cariboo Road in the 1860's. Shumway pre-empted land on the lake south of Kamloops that now bears his name, largely to provide a wintering ground for his pack animals. Shumway later leased his land upon retirement in 1886.

26. See "Photographs," 29 May 1877, GSC155–C1 (PA 152394).

27. Nicola River.

Rain seems to fall but sparingly, & in many cases the precipitation seems to be dried up before reaching the earth.

Stump Lake is rather a puzzle. A large sheet of water, which along the edges shows many stumps now submerged, some of them charred. Told that these can be seen not only on edges but far out in the Lake, & that the Indians say that some now living can remember when no lake there. Told also that at one time within memory of settlers, which can only be a few years ago, water ceased to flow from the Lake, or did not flow at all, & that a drought threatening the *clay* &c stopping it up was removed. Now a good sized stream, say 10 feet wide by 2 deep with a gentle current, near the Lake.

The stream near the lake holds stumps of the ordinary pine[28] which can never have grown in the water, but must have grown when the present channel was merely one of these little hollows with gravelly bottoms, quite dry except on special occasions, where they often now flourish. The lower end of the lake is shallow & reedy, but is well rimmed round by mounds & ridges of drift material — considerably worn — on all sides but that now giving issue to the stream, showing that no former channel in different direction possible. The stream on leaving the lake proper winds for less than 100 yds through marshy land, in a rather deep channel part of which is evidently artifically deepened, as above said. The current is pretty swift even between the clay banks, however, & if the whole of the gravel & clay was removed the lake would be perhaps 2 or even 3 feet lower than at present, before the ledge of solid rock, over which the stream next falls in a cascade of about 10 feet, would form the actual dam. There is no stream at hand to carry in gravel or clay, nor the least appearance of movement in the surrounding country. No evident marks of old high-water lines surround the lake. The large brooks now entering the head of the lake must always have taken their course into the wide hollow now filled by it, & on the whole can scarcely see any feasible explanation but that of a subterranean outlet, through which the water passed away, but which was subsequently blocked.

The valley of the Nicola above the bridge continues wide & open, though the river itself flows in a deep gorge with lateral branches. The hills are covered with rounded masses of somewhat modified drift & terrace deposit,[29] which still in some places preserves its perfectly terraced

---

28. Ponderosa pine, *P. ponderosa*.

29. The terrace deposits mentioned by Dawson were shoreline and deltaic or locally incised lake-bottom sediments. The locality is the site of a series of former ice-dammed glacial lakes. These glacial lakes, which covered the Nicola drainage basin at different periods, are described in Robert J. Fulton, *Glacial Lake History, Southern Interior Plateau, British Columbia*, Geological Survey of Canada Paper no. 69–37 (Ottawa: Queen's

character, the bench marks being at very many different elevations, but some fully 600' above the river. The lower end of Douglas Lake is surrounded by flat land, through which the Nicola flows out, & another stream coming from S or SE enters.[30]

May 31. Rain commencing about 9 Pm. last night, continued till 9 this morning. Hearing the pattering on the Tent did not get up till after 5 a.m., & delayed start. On appearance of clearing get packed up & off, reaching Hamiltons Creek[31] about noon. Had intended riding up the creek valley several miles but being too late devoted myself to taking a few photographs (3) under considerable difficulties from wind & rain,[32] & examining the limestone & adjacent rocks. Massive clouds hanging round all afternoon & passing showers with squalls.

When at supper about 7 P.m. an Indian messenger appeared with the mail, sent by Ross* from Kamloops. Gave him $5 as Ross* wrote he had promised, & some supper before he left.

June. 1. Made paced Measurement & examined section from the limestone exposure down to Clapperton's[33] at lower end Nicola Lake. Day quite warm after the sun well up. Still a few heavy clouds hanging about, but general appearance of more settled weather. After arriving at camp, which pitched before we came in at the bridge, examined rocks of vicinity, & got photo looking down the valley, with Iron Mountain.[34]

The Mountains on the N Side of Nicola Lake are much higher than those on the south, & probably in places rise over 2100' above the water. The are apparently composed of rocks similar to those of section measured, & appear to decrease in height northward.

The lake is probably held in by the gravel & boulders of a great fan[35]

Printer, 1969), 4–5.

30. Spahomin Creek.

31. Quilchena Creek.

32. See "Photographs," 31 May 1877, GSC156–C1 (PA 152388); GSC157–C1 (PA 51044); and GSC158–C1 (PA 152389).

33. John Thomas Wilson Clapperton (1835–1913), along with Edwin Dalley, pioneered settlement at the foot of Nicola Lake in 1868. Clapperton attained an influential position in the region, assuming a wide variety of positions including justice of the peace, government agent, and first postmaster. Clapperton was also an enterprising and wealthy businessman and farmer who operated a grist mill and developed several mining properties. Clapperton later sold his interests and retired to Victoria. See Patrick A. Dunae, "Jottings of a Gentleman," *British Columbia Historical News* 15, no. 4 (Summer 1982): 19–21.

34. See "Photographs," 1 June 1877, GSC159–C1 (PA 152390).

35. Most alluvial fans such as the ones at the foot of Nicola Lake began deposition immediately after the disappearance of the ice from the glacial period. For a detailed

which extends across the valley from the N side. The river now flows out at the extreme southern edge of the flat bottom land, & a short distance below the lake falls over a rocky barrier about four feet. It is probable however, that the stream originally found exit on the other side, & this is no proof that the basin is rock rimmed. Just above the outlet of the lake a second large fan protrudes into it from the S side, & about half way up the NSS reach a large fan stretches in from the north more than half across the lake. It will eventually no doubt divide it in two. The production of these fans depends in most cases on the abundant soft material & gravel of the drift & benches, which thus indirectly responsible for the formation of lakes &c. In other cases however, mainly or entirely due to crumbling of solid rocks of mountains, which first form rock slides & are then washed down.

June 2. Moved from Bridge to Coldwater opposite the Coal exposure. Packs followed the road, while self & Douglas* scrambled along the face of the mountains on the north side of the valley trying to define the edge of the Coal formation. Reached camp hot & tired at 12.30. Afternoon took a photo.[36] reading &c. one or two showers some of them heavy & after sundown cloudy. Saw Charters[37] & found out all I could about the coal, & iron in a neighbouring mountain.

Eleagnus argentea in full flower & the air heavy with its scent in some places. Saw a good many ripe strawberries.

June 3. Sunday Off at 8 Am with Douglas* &, Robt. Charters* to examine ⟨coal⟩ Iron ore in the mountain east of Coldwater. Ride down the Hope Trail about six miles to An Indian camp, & after a little trouble Secure a youngster to guide us to the spot. Ride laboriously up to the summit of the Mountain, gaining eventually an altitude of about 5200 feet. owing to the Ignerance of our guide see only some smaller seams of the ore, & not the main lead. Get however some very interesting *glacial* facts finding foreign boulders & ice marked surfaces to summit.[38] Fine views in various

description of fan construction and structure in southern British Columbia, see J. M. Ryder, "The Stratigraphy and Morphology of Para-glacial Alluvial Fans in South-central British Columbia," *Canadian Journal of Earth Sciences* 8 (1971): 279–98.

36. See "Photographs," 2 June 1877, GSC160–C1 (PA 51043).

37. Robert Charters (1837–1904) was an early Nicola region settler.

38. Dawson further noted in his published report that "the summit of this mountain rises to an elevation of 5,280 feet above the sea, or 3,500 feet above the valleys at its base. It has been heavily glaciated, and its projecting rocky masses worn into ridges parallel to the direction of ice movement, still preserve striated and polished surfaces, both horizontal and vertical" (Dawson, "Report on the Southern Portion," 136). Dawson's discovery of glaciated features at such a height provided additional support for the prior existence of a thick ice sheet covering the region. In fact, at its greatest development, glaciation during the so-called Fraser Advance period covered the highest mountains of the

directions, the impression from the summit being that many peaks & ridges in {the} different bearings reach about the same altitude as that now in question, which as it has no other name may be called Iron Mountain.

On the summit the aspens are just opening their leaves & some other bushes, willows &c. are yet scarcely at all in leaf. Note *Pinus Albicaulis*,[39] with *P. contorta* & abundance of Douglas fir. P. ponderosa disappears between 3000′ & 4000′ & with it the bunch grass, a "sour" grass & peavine replacing it, with evidence of greater moisture. Pachystima myrsinites[40] 1000′ (about) below summit.

Indian food. The women now busily engaged gathering the wild onion[41] which will soon burst into flower. They wander about in the woods with basket on back, & a crutch like stick in hand, with which the plants are uprooted, & then tossed over the shoulder. On arriving at Indian camp this morning, find the family in a rather large wigwam with large central opening, composed of poles & rush mats. Their property of various Kinds being in trees around out of reach of dogs &c. On one tree many bundles of the onions, very neat & clean looking, & some strings or wreathes of the same which were cured. These looked quite black, & more like seaweed than anything else, & had been steamed in holes in the ground with hot stones. After this they are dried, & so kept for future use. The process is said to render them quite Sweet

June 4   Drizzling rain all morning & light showers in the afternoon. A gale of wind & clearing towards evening. Engaged all day examining the Coal rocks across the river. First visiting the different outcrops with some of the people of the vicinity, then getting some of them scarped down with pick & shovel. Devoted most of afternoon to investigating a bed below the main seam which proves to hold some insect remains! of these quite a number obtained though indifferently preserved

June 5 Very high wind in the night, making me fear for the tent. Morning overcast & rain soon began. Showers all day though now clearing, with a resumption in the afternoon of the S.W. gale. The trees hereabouts, especially the pines I notice have a lean to the N.E. showing the present wind to be the prevailing one. At work from early morning till 1 P.M.

Nicola-Kamloops area. The ice, which moved generally in a southeasterly direction, left fluted (drumlinoid) terrain and striated bedrock surfaces, as well as boulders, some of which can be identified with northerly or northwesterly sources. See Robert J. Fulton, *Quaternary Geology and Geomorphology, Nicola-Vernon Area, British Columbia*, Geological Survey of Canada Memoir no. 380 (Ottawa: Information Canada, 1975), 36.

39. Whitebark pine, *P. albicaulis*.

40. Oregon boxwood, *Pachistima myrsinites* (Pursh) Raf.

41. The "wild onion" was the nodding onion, *A. cernuum*, a very common species favoured by the Indians. See Turner, *Food Plants of Interior Peoples*, 68–72.

connecting the coal crops by pacing, & getting some more of them scarped down. Find unexpected complication in the arrangement of the beds. Afternoon writing up notes & getting specimens packed, the wind threatening to take away the tent at any moment, & much dust drifting in. Make sketch map of the vicinity to fix topography.

June 6. Off early & travelled about 18 miles to the 57 mile post from ⟨of⟩ Hope. Spent the afternoon in searching for the coal which had been reported as occurring here, but could find nothing but coaly streaks in sandstone. The coal may be covered by the water of the river (?) though not now excessively high. Day as a whole bleak, with one or two light showers, as usual. Soon after camping, a small band of Cattle (Cows Calves &c.) passed on their way to Nicola, from Sumass. Two very young calves, dropped by the way, were tied up in gunny sacks, all but their heads, & one fore leg each, which projected. Thus secured, they were hung one on either side of a Mexican Saddle.[42] The drover said he had killed two calves already as unable to travel, but that the cows always wanted to go back, & so he found it less trouble to carry them on thus. The horse seemed in no wise embarrassed by his strange load, but when the drove stopped strayed about feeding quite unconcerned. Not so the anxious mothers who followed the horse, lowing loudly, & looking earnestly at their calves as though they did not exactly know what to make of it.

The valley of the Coldwater continues wide, with extensive flats or gentle slopes. Its average width is probably about a mile, though the greatest extent of level ground in any one place, generally lies fifty, a hundred feet or more above the river. From what they tell me on Nicola summer frosts probably render the otherwise cultivable flats of this river useless except for the hardier grains, & perhaps precarious for even these. Summer frosts occasionally nip potatoes even in the Nicola Valley, & seem to be very inexplicably distributed, some spots always escaping, while others almost the same in situation are nearly always affected. Continued evidence of greater rainfall in following up the valley. Timber thicker. *P. ponderosa* now very scarce, & only in particularly dry situations. A douglasi increasingly abundant. P. contorta appears & is now very abundant. Noted *pachystima* at this camp, also *Epilobium latifolium*? along the river, a *frittillaria* probably the same as collected near Victoria.[43] Also. [*Illus.*] The bunch grass in its range nearly follows P. ponderosa. It is now

---

42. A Mexican pack saddle or aparejo. See 27 September 1875.

43. The *"pachystima"* was Oregon boxwood, *P. myrsinites*; *"Epilobium latifolium"* was the broad-leaved fireweed, *Epilobium latifolium* L.; and *"frittillaria"* the chocolate lily, *Fritillaria lanceolata* Pursh.

almost entirely replaced by *pine grass*,[44] forming however pretty good feed, & in some places tangled with pea vine.

The hills bordering the valley maintain their height with considerable regularity, & probably average from 1500 to 2000′ above it.

June 7 Horses having strayed away start not quite so early as usual. Moved on 9 miles to bridge, having been warned not to go further late in the day. Day fine throughout, though with the usual complement of heavy clouds in the afternoon, & a little wind in gusts. On camping, examined rocks of vicinity, Collected a few plants, pressed them & changed all the papers. Got a photograph,[45] & endeavoured to get sextant into working order. A large band of cattle coming up behind us nearly ran over our Camp, which unfortunately directly on the trail. River valley today in many places narrow & gorge like, though not deserving the name of a canon, as the rocks bluffs do not occur on the different sides simultaneously. Continued evidence of change of climate. *P. ponderosa* appears to be quite lost. The woods much thicker. *Populis tremuloides* abundant on slopes, & not as before confined to Creek valleys &c. See *Smilacina*, the large species, *Actea, Sambucus, Viola pubescens* (? see specimen) *Cornus canadensis* & other similar plants. Also at evening Camp the first "balsom" *Abies lasiocarpa*[46]

Opposite camp a very high bluff with little waterfall coming down over the summit.

June 8. off early. Went ahead of packs & paced some miles, & ⟨then⟩ rocks then seeming to become scarce, reckoned rest of day's work by time. As it happened no rock was seen in place from end of pacing to near evening camp, the trail passing most of the way through dense woods of trees of fair to large growth, & the surface being composed of drift. MacKintosh[47] had told me that at some swamps reached by a little trail

44. Pinegrass, *Calamagrostis rubescens* Buckl.

45. See "Photographs," 7 June 1877, GSC161–C1 (PA 152391).

46. "*Actea*" was baneberry, *Actaea rubra* (Ait.) Willd.; and "*Sambucus*" red elderberry, *S. racemosa*. "*Viola pubescens*" was an eastern Canadian species. The most probable violet in the Nicola region was the yellow prairie violet, *Viola nuttallii* Pursh. The "*Abies lasiocarpa*" was the alpine fir, *A. lasiocarpa*.

47. James McIntosh (1842–1901) came to British Columbia in 1862 and worked as a miner and packer in the Cariboo before arriving in Kamloops in 1865. In 1867 he pre-empted land above the Tranquille River and two years later opened a sawmill and grist mill in partnership with William Fortune. After selling his interests to Fortune, McIntosh pre-empted 100 acres immediately east of the Hudson's Bay Company post at Kamloops, then subdivided that land to form the old town of Kamloops. In the 1870's, McIntosh became a profitable contractor, building a new Hudson's Bay Company store, the first jail and court house, and many roads in the Kamloops area, then founding the extremely profitable Shuswap Milling Company at Kamloops. He was also active in

between the 35 & 34 mile posts, feed could be found. Did not see the trail however, & came to the conclusion that the feed to be found in any swamps would be of no value, besides being dangerous from the "poison weed"[48] which abounds & has caused the death of cattle here. The little swamps near the trail, with the surface of the country generally about evening camp (33 ½ miles from Hope) has quite the aspect of early spring, with a somewhat alpine flora. The surface is wet, & looks as though Snow not very long gone. The dense shad of the large trees will in a measure account for this, but they themselves appear here owing to some climatic cause, which if not excessive rainfall, may be due in great measure to heavy snow fall. The mere altitude being insufficient to account for the facts.

During todays march *A lasiocarpa* becomes abundant, *P. Monticola* appears & becomes common, growing to a great height with tapering form & a tuft loaded with its large cones at the summit. *A. Menziesii* a variety with cones like those got last year at Bute Inlet, but even smaller — common. Hemlock & Cedar also appear, & about camp the Devil's Club is just expanding its tufts of leaves, while the great *veratrum* is pushing up through moss in swamps, & the little yellow thick-wood violet[49] is abundant & in flower. The fact that some of the above trees found here at much lower altitude than further north shows clearly their dependence on rainfall more than temperature. P.m. determined index error of sextant, & prepared to take ob. on polaris, but day heretofore fine towards evening became cloudy & it now rains gently but persistently. The horses tied by their halters to a long rope stretched between two trees stand disconsolately in the wet, with their thoughts no doubt, poor things, on bunch grass, or the flesh pots of Egypt in some other form.

June 9. Travelled on about 14 miles, camping on a flat about ½ mile beyond the mouth of the W. branch of the *Coquihalla*.[50] Soon after leaving morning camp, among the woods of the summit, began to descend into the canon of the Coquihalla R, which followed to evening camp. on reaching the bottom of the Canon, get at once into a country of large Cedars, & other accompanying coast & warmer climate plants. Magnificent scenery, wooded or nearly bare mountains & cliffs rising abruptly from the river to a great height, with beautiful cascades pouring down over them in many places. The river itself working toward the Sea in

community affairs.

48.   False hellebore, *Veratrum viride* Ait.

49.   "*A. Menziesii*" was Douglas-fir, *P. menziesii*; "great *veratrum*" false hellebore, *V. viride*; and "yellow thick-wood violet" probably the yellow wood violet, *V. glabella*.

50.   Boston Bar Creek.

the bottom of the valley with a steady roar, beyond the sound of which you never get in all the windings, & ascents & descents of the trail. Mountains & cliffs not unlike those of the similarly situated part of the Fraser, but the valley considerably narrower, & more tortuous giving additional grandure to the scene. See several places where years ago great snow slides have descended the mountains, sweeping a broad clearly defined [veld?] completely clear of timber, the trees being smashed off so close to the ground that scarcely even any prominent stumps remain. At the foot of the slope the trees are piled in tangled splintered mass, of the most confused character, & giving the idea of almost irresistable force. The W. branch enters by a perpendicular-sided Canon with walls 200' to 300' high composed of slaty rocks ⟨like⟩ the trail crossing by a bridge not far above the water, gets down to that level by a complicated series of zig zags.

Much burnt timber in this part of the valley, & after making evening camp find a huge partly rotten tree with a decided lean over my tent. After turning in in the evening a little wind getting up, I though it advisable to carry my blankets out, & slept accordingly on the windward side of the rampike. Very little feed for the animals about here

June 10. Up again about 30.15 & off early, making Hope before 2 P.m. a distance of 18 miles. The trail pretty hilly, & with many mud holes, now poached up by the passage of the cattle ahead of us. Valley opens out a little, showing flats generally, wide or narrow, on one side or other. Timber increasing in size *Vine maple* & *Yew* appear, with the salmon berry, skunk cabbage, bracken, yellow mimulus,[51] sallal, (now in flower) & many others.

Find it necessary to buy feed for the animals here, there being none uninclosed.

A remarkably dull little place. Cannot even get any fresh beef without telegraphing to Yale to have it brough down by the steamer in the morning.

June 11. Occupied writing up notes, packing specimens, arranging for supplies, & writing letters. Examined rocks near the sawmill, & took a couple of photographs[52] of Silver peak & associated mountains. Day fine, but warm, & with a strong wind blowing up the river. This I am told is the usual thing every day from pretty early in the morning to sundown.

---

51. The "*Yew*" was the western yew, *Taxus brevifolia* Nutt.; "salmon berry" the salmonberry, *Rubus spectabilis* Pursh; "skunk cabbage" the western skunk cabbage, *Lysichitum americanum* Hultén & St. John; "bracken" the bracken fern, *Pteridium aquilinum* (L.) Kuhn; and "yellow mimulus" probably the common monkey flower, *Mimulus guttatus* DC.

52. See "Photographs," 11 June 1877, GSC163–C1 (PA 51042) and GSC164–C1 (PA 51041).

June 12. Started with Yates of HB Co,[53] & An Indian man, & woman in a canoe up the river to Murphy's,[54] about two miles to see a vein, said to contain copper & silver, & a deposit of limestone. Saw the vein, but found the other brother not at home, only, knows about the limestone, which though we looked for it, we could not find. Visited an Indian village[55] almost opposite Murphy's*, which very neat, with pretty little whitewashed houses, & small garden patches, fields & orchards! surrounding them. The Indians of all this region are fast becoming more industrious & agricultural. Yates* tells me however, that while a few years ago probably 250 Indians between the Fraser Mouth & Yale, belonged to the Ch. of England, there are probably now not over 60, the rest having gone over to the Catholics. This is on account of shabby treatment of the converts by the Ch. of England Missionaries, according to Yates*.

Murphy*, who mines for gold in the flat near his house, tells me that from time to time he comes across Indian relics, some of which he gave me. They occur under the sand filling the flat, & on the surface of the gravel below, some ten ⟨of⟩ or fifteen feet below the surface, on which trees fully 100 (Murphy* says his brother counted one 400) years old are growing. The pay dirt is at about the same level with the Indians tools, which are chisels, hammers, &c. of the usual type. one of the peculiar mortars,[56] elsewhere before seen, was among the relics. It represents perhaps a bird; or imaginary Creature, & has the bowl of the mortar cut out on its back. M. also finds on the surface of the gravel below the layer of sand, Stones arranged in little circles where fires have been confined, the pieces of stone still retaining their position.

Salmon. The second run of small fish, & the hump backs,[57] late in the summer go up the Coquihalla as far as the mouth of Boston Bar Creek, 18 m. from here. This is their limit.

---

53. William Yates (1832–1917) began his service with the Hudson's Bay Company in 1849 at York Factory. Later he moved to New Caledonia and, in 1854, came to the British Columbia coast. In 1856 he assumed his position at Fort Hope where he was in command for many years.

54. The Murphy brothers, James and Charles, lived two miles above Hope on the opposite side of the Fraser River. In the late 1870's they struck gold in paying quantities on Union Bar Flat near their residence.

55. The village was Iwa'was, sometimes called Union Bar. Although only a few people live there today (actually a little down river, at Ay-wa-wis Reserve), the village had always been an important settlement.

56. Some carved stone mortars are treated in Wilson Duff, *Images Stone B.C.: Thirty Centuries of Northwest Coast Indian Sculpture* (Toronto: Oxford University Press, 1975), although none approximate Dawson's description here.

57. Pink salmon, *Oncorhynchus gorbuscha* (Walbaum).

Left box with Wm. Yates* H.B. Company to be forwarded to Victoria

G. M. Dawson to Margaret Dawson*, 12 June 1877, Hope

As this is a place of some importance, & to be found on the maps I suppose I need not begin by explaining where I am. We arrived here two days ago, & tomorrow leave again this time going eastward to the Similkameen River & Okanagan. There is a good well travelled trail all the way, I believe, which is a comfort.

I have worked my way down to here from Kamloops, *via* Nicola, & the Coldwater & Coquihalla Rivers, most of the way through a fine open bunch grass country, but for the last forty or fifty miles through Cañons & gorges of the Coast Range. The trail is good all the way, however, being constantly used ⟨for⟩ in driving Cattle down here for the Victoria market.

I dont' know whether I have yet given you a detail of my party — it is as follows. Self, Jacinto Mexican Packer, the same man I had last year, Douglas* a second white man recommended to me at Kamloops, & a Lytton Indian of the usual name *viz* Johnny. Johnny does the cooking & Assists the packer, while Douglas* Carries rocks & hammers, attends to my horse, puts up tent & generally makes himself useful. He is a very quiet man of a mild disposition, but does very well, & saves me much trouble.

On arriving at Kamloops I found that animals were scarce, & all that were any good had already been sent out or apportioned to the Various C.P.R. Parties. It was found necessary in consequence to purchase some horses to complete the outfit, & I have now with me four riding animals & five Packs, forming a very good working complement & not necessitating heavy packing. While in the Nicola Valley, I had one mail sent in to me by an Indian, from Kamloops, giving me dates a week later than those received before leaving Victoria. Since then I have had no home news, & do not expect to get any till my return to Kamloops, where letters &c. are now accumulating. I may get back there in about a month, *via* Okanagan, & it is more than probable that I will have no chance of writing home again for about that time, so you must not feel anxious if it should prove so.

If my memory serves, I wrote a long letter last time to Anna*, & so, as there is nothing much to say, I will not write again to her by this mail. I send by post however a book which I have been reading at spare moments, which I think is a pretty good story, on the whole, & worth reading.

Hope is a very picturesque place, on the bank of the Fraser River, a triangular flat, through which the Coquihalla issues, bounded on every side by high & very abrupt mountains, some of them snow-clad. There may be altogether some twenty-five white people here, with a larger, but variable number of Indians. A place of some importance in early mining days, it has now dwindled down, & become one of the quietest places on the face of the Earth. The steamer calls twice a week each way, & constitutes the only relief to the monotony of life. There are two stores, one belonging to the universal H.B. Company, A small saw mill, & two "hotels". How they live I cant make out. I have been making some purchases of supplies of the H.B. Co, & in so doing have made the acquaintance of an old man Called Yates* who is in charge here, & has lived here without once returning to Victoria for some thirty years. Naturally he is posted on the history of the place, & gives you all the dates of events with as much importance as though he spoke of the history of an empire. Hope, I think, occupies about 270 degrees of his horizon. He has been in the H.B. Company's service all his life, & before taking root here has travelled to & lived at nearly all the posts in B. Columbia. He is an orkney man & a type of a class of Amiable Hudson Bay fossils, specimens of which are scattered all over the north-west.

Pray remember that no news is good news for some weeks to Come, though if I get a chance of dropping you a line sooner I will do so.

G. M. Dawson to J. W. Dawson*, 12 June 1877, Hope

I received a couple of weeks ago quite a budget of correspondence readdressed by you, & felt quite ashamed that you should have so much to do for me, especially when there is nothing I can do for you in return, in this part of the world.

Tomorrow morning early I start for Similkameen &c. as more fully explained in my letter to Mother. So far nothing very startling in a geological point of view has been found, though some additional facts as to general relations of formations obtained. In connection with the Nicola Coal formation (Tertiary) I found a few more insects, beetles, which may perhaps be all referable to a single species, however. I also ascended Iron Mountain at the Junction of the Coldwater & Nicola, about 5200 feet high (altitude possibly subject to some correction) Benches occur a long way up, & rounded erratics & drift to the very summit, which is also heavily glaciated across in a direction not far from N.S. magnetic.

The relations between the different volcanic series are very puzzling, & there are whole masses of rocks which cannot be certainly placed at present, however I hope that as the work progresses Additional facts may be obtained

So far the weather has not been unpleasantly warm, in fact we have had light showers almost every day, it appears however to be taking a turn towards heat now.

I thought I had a great many things to write about when I sat down, but now feel like nothing so much as going to sleep, & so must bring this unsatisfactory note to a Close.

June 13. Off early, & rode back 4 ½ miles to junction of Similkameen & Nicola Trails, this part of route being over diorite & granite, probably intrusive, & of no particular interest. At junction began pacing survey & got along fast, as exposures few, & following parallel to strike. Some miles on before overtaken by packs, then gave Jacinto directions to camp at the 14 m. house. He misunderstood them however, & went on fully six miles further, giving me a great deal of additional work. Finally about four oclock, marked point, & rode ahead, being pretty sure from the tracks that packs still ahead, & not passed by any accident. Found them at last, just camping in a dense grove of large & tall cedars, with stupendous cliffs fully 1500 feet high almost appearing to overhang the little flat. Turn in early, being tired.

The valley passed through, serves first as the Channel of the Nicolome, then of the [blank] a tributary of the Skagit.[58] The intermediate region, between these two rivers holds a little string of lakes & swamps. It not only follows the strike of the rocks pretty closely, but is parallel to the main direction of the Cascade range. It must have been in most places, especially about the summit, worn out & cleared to a much greater depth at one time, either by ice or water or both. It now forms a Cañon, with perhaps an average width of ¼ mile from the foot of the slopes on either side, which rise in cliffs or very abrupt slopes to an average altitude of perhaps 2000′ above the trail. Higher snow covered mountains are seen through gaps occasionally. The original chasm, about the Summit, appears to have been filled in with huge masses of rock broken down from the cliffs.

June 14. Up early & off by 5 A.m. two & a half miles back on the trail to point where left pacing yesterday. Morning cold, but soon warmed up, becoming oppressively hot at noon. The packs went ahead with orders to stop at the 28 m.p.[59] or near it, where feed said to be. Stopped near the 27

58. The "Nicolome" was the Nicolum River; and the "tributary of the Skagit" was the Sumallo River. This valley was occupied by a southeasterly flowing meltwater stream at the end of the last ice age, when ice was still blocking the lower Nicolum River. Gravels laid down by the meltwater stream were buried by a major landslide about nine thousand years ago and this, in turn, by the Hope Slide of 1965 A.D. See W. H. Mathews and K. C. McTaggart, "The Hope Landslide, British Columbia," *Proceedings of the Geological Association of Canada* 20 (1969): 65–75. Probably both ice and water contributed to the deepening of the valley.

59. Mile point.

where little or no feed to be seen, but Jacinto in searching round came on a small patch of grass. Got into camp before noon, with some fossils! of the Tatlayoco L. Group from the rocks near by. Wrote up notes, & then went back on the trail to collect some more fossils.

The scenery remarkably fine today, butting cliffs on the [blank][60] near where we leave it. Then pass over a well marked stony bench, on which *rhodadendrons* are abundant, in full bloom & with magnificent heads of pink flowers. Get a view up a valley to the north, & another down the valley of the Skagit to the south, revealing tier upon tier of snow clad mountains, though none of them excessively high, or going up much beyond the timber limit. Looking back, down the valley of the E. branch of the Skagit,[61] from the hillsides near where we are camped a wonderful scene of mountains, with the river, a mass of foam, winding along below.

Yesterday afternoon & today see a few specimens of *P. Monticola* & *A. Menziesii*. The thickets of Salmon berries passed through on the Nicolome soon disappeared, & the large spiræa seems to have vanished here. The white flowering raspberry still abundant. *Lonicera involucrata* & another red flowering & beautiful species, in flower.[62]

June 15. Travel on from Cedar Flat, where camped last night, to the foot of the steep ascent to the summit, just beyond the 38 m.p. & near the last crossing of the Skagit, now only a good sized brook. Pass Wardle[63] the Kootenay Mail carrier on his way west, with an Indian & two or three pack Animals, Find *Bristol*[64] a man in charge of the trail near our evening camp, with a pack horse & a couple of Indians.

Rapidly ascend during latter part of day's march, & where we now are the branch of the Skagit — probably the main branch — which we have been following splits up into a many little streams, which all rise not far off among the mountains. Got a photo.[65] from hills above Camp, of view

60. The cliffs of the Sumallo canyon are meant.

61. Probably Skaist River.

62. The "large spiræa" was hardhack, *Spiraea douglasii* Hook.; "white flowering rasp-berry" probably the wild raspberry, *Rubus idaeus* L.; and the "red flowering species" possibly the western trumpet honeysuckle, *Lonicera ciliosa* (Pursh) DC.

63. James Wardle was a Cariboo miner who had also mined in the Columbia River and Similkameen regions. After 1871, Wardle received the contract for carrying mail from Hope to Wild Horse Creek, near Fort Steele. See James Wardle, "Reminiscences," unpublished typescript, PABC.

64. "Captain" William Yale Bristol, who farmed on Bristol Island west of Hope, also oper-ated an express canoe mail and passenger service between Yale and New Westminster for some twenty years. See Allison, *Pioneer Gentlewoman*, 157.

65. The "photo." referred to is listed in neither Dawson's Field Notebook nor in the National Photography Collection, PAC.

looking down the valley.

About camp, with an elevation of about 4300' (see bar obsn.) Vegetation very luxuriant in burnt ground, & on open slopes. Valerian (?) very abundant, with heads of pink-white blossom. Mountain ash Just coming into flower. Two species of currents, in flower. Pachystima Amelanchier in flower. Elder, red Castilleja, Lonicera involucrata, & the pale yellow-white lonicera[66] found last year near Salmon R, — in flower

June 16. Left camp at 5.30 climbing the long ascent to the summit, & measuring a fine section of Cascade Cryst rocks by the way. Packs caught up just at summit,[67] where got camera off & took three photos,[68] of the panorama of snowy peaks & bare rocky hillsides, which stretches out, the valleys all concealed, & the general prospect perhaps much like that of the usual surface of the country many degrees further north.

Cloudy with some wind, & cold on the summit, so business completed, glad to descend. Continued on to "Powder Camp"[69] near the 49 m.p. where propose to stay for Sunday as good feed.

Wrote up notes & stayed up late getting an observation of Polaris. Much of the Country East of the summit has been burnt over a few years ago, & while the feed improved, the dead & bleached sticks the picture of desolation

[verso]

Memo of obsns.[70] Powder Camp June 16–17

66. The "Valerian" was valerian, *Valeriana* spp.; "two species of currents" sticky currant, *Ribes viscosissimum* Pursh, and swamp gooseberry, *Ribes lacustre* (Pers.) Poir.; and "yellow-white lonicera" possibly the Utah honeysuckle, *L. utahensis*.

67. Allison Pass.

68. Only two photographs remain. See "Photographs," 16 June 1877, GSC165–C1 (PA 51040) and GSC166–C1 (PA 51039).

69. "Powder Camp" or "Powder Flat" was located in the Whipsaw Creek valley, seven miles east of the summit on the Hope-Princeton trail. According to Susan Allison, "we called it Powder Flat from the circumstance that one time [when] my husband and his partner were packing out the camp caught fire and there was a rush to throw the blasting powder into the creek" (Allison, *Pioneer Gentlewoman*, 22).

70. In his published report, Dawson explains the presence of the many and detailed observations in his 1877 diary. Because of a lack of a good map for the southern interior region, "it was therefore necessary to keep a careful running survey during the entire summer, in which bearings from point to point, or approximate average bearings were taken, and the distances generally estimated by the time occupied in travel. Where circumstances appeared to warrant the additional expenditure of time, these were replaced by paced surveys. The whole being arranged so as to form a loose net-work of lines over the region under examination, and being tied in at known points, or fixed in latitude, from time to time, by sextant observations. Having been unable to secure the services of a suitable scientific assistant, the whole of this work devolved upon myself" (Dawson, "Report on the Southern Portion," 3).

June 16. Polaris 10 h 10 m. pm by watch sextant alt uncorrected 96° 29'
10″

June 17. obsn for time.

Time by watch	2h 13m 30 s	Sun 109° 1' 30″
"	2 16 00	" 108° 21' 00
"	2 18 57	S 107° 35' 00

(Assume lat & long to calculate time for correction of lat by pole)
[end verso]

June 17 Sunday. did not move camp. Rode some miles back this morning
to satisfy myself about junction of the C. Cryst, & green rocks, on which
we now are. The latter appear to dip here conformably under the former.
Returned in time for obn. of sun at noon, but clouds prevented. P.m.
Changed all plants finished writing up notes, packed specimens. observed
for time & tried working out the obsn.

Day cool & showery with many heavy clouds floating over from W.

June 18. Heavy rain early this morning delaying our start. Left Camp at 7
Am. & was soon overtaken by packs, as discovering a fossil in black shales
associated with the problematical green igneous series, had to ascend a hill
at the side of the valley to get altitude, & search for more specimens,
though unsuccessfuly. Morning showery, & told Jacinto to go twelve
miles, but if turning to heavy rain to camp at 5 m. A few heavy showers
frightened him into camp, where we find ourselves at 10 a.m. Got lunch, &
off at noon, pacing on about 4 ½ m. to a small stream, where found fossil
plants of the Tertiary in some abundance Stayed here some time & collected a number, & then rode back to camp, getting there at 6.15. Tired &
hungry. Wrote up notes & turned in

Do volcanic products occur in the Cret. rocks of the Skagit valley distinctly,[71] & if so can these be supposed to represent any part of the green
or Nicola Lake series,[72] supposing the latter to be also Mezozoic?

Bunch grass & pinus ponderosa resume a mile or two below this
evening's camp. Blue Lupins[73] abundant from the summit, (& beyond)
now make the hillsides gay. Found a peculiar & very beautiful bright red
flower — unknown —

June 19. Horses having strayed far, made a rather late start, & even then

71. Some volcanic detritus is indeed present in the Cretaceous (and detritus and minor lava
    in the associated Jurassic) sediments of the Skagit and Skaist valleys. Its source could be
    in the rocks of the "Nicola Lake" (now the Upper Triassic Nicola Group) series to the
    east, but Jurassic volcanoes could also be a source.

72. First named by Dawson in 1877, the Nicola Lake Series was also correctly dated by
    Dawson to the Triassic. Now known as the Nicola Group, it is a volcanic rock with
    minor argillite, quartzite, and limestone.

73. Lupine, *Lupinus* spp.

without my horse & Douglas'* which had ⟨....⟩ gone ahead. Rode Jacinto's horse to brook where left pacing survey yesterday, & then paced on about four miles, Camping at small brook just before the 61 m.p. Lunched, & then rode off to the S.E. to find the coal locality on the S. fork of the Similkameen.[74] Told that it four miles off the trail, & direction for finding it given, being to follow down an old water ditch. Found the distance off the trail not much more than a mile, all down hill. Found & examined the coal,[75] & made quite a little collection of fossil plants from rich layer above it.[76] Got back to camp about 4.30. Had a nap; wrote up notes & packed specimens.

After leaving 9 mile, or fossil Creek,[77] where pacing stopped yesterday, travel all the way over broad benches, covered with mixed bunch grass & "pine grass", & lightly timbered with P. ponderosa. The material of the benches mostly travelled, & not of the Tertiary rocks underlying. Soil on some of the benches good, others sandy & stony.

S Fork of the Similkameen a fine rapid river, scarcely fordable in its present stage, & full of clear greenish water

Fire has lately passed over much of the country hereabouts, destroying the grass, & many trees as well; whether set accidentally or otherwise do not know.

June 20 Paced on 5 miles to Hay's[78] (Princeton of maps) beyond the crossing of the N Fork of the Similkameen,[79] & near the junction of the two forks. Hay's* being out, & wishing to take photo &c. decided to camp. Got photos[80] looking up & down the river. Got the sun at noon. Read papers brought in from Victoria by Costen[81] (seen before at Hope) Go fishing unsuccessfully, but get a good bath. Change & dry plant

---

74. Similkameen River proper.

75. Actually lignite. See Dawson, "Report on the Southern Portion," 130.

76. The bed of "perfectly preserved plants" represented a shallow Tertiary pool, ibid., 130. J. W. Dawson described them at 186–87.

77. Lamont Creek.

78. Hayes was an American who came to Princeton in the 1860's. Shortly thereafter he became a partner of John Fall Allison in a cattle ranching venture but the partnership dissolved in 1879 after a dispute. Margaret Ormsby notes in *Pioneer Gentlewoman*, 160, that though directories of the period refer to Hayes as J. Hayes, Susan Allison calls him S. W. Hayes. For Dawson's further comments on Hayes see below 14 (really 13) September 1877.

79. Tulameen River.

80. Only one of the photographs mentioned remains. See "Photographs," 20 June 1877, GSC167–C1 (PA 152392).

81. Possibly Richard Lowe Cawston (1849–1923) who came to the Okanagan in 1875 and later, in 1884, purchased a large amount of land in the Lower Similkameen region.

papers. Talked to Hay's* on his return & got some little information on the country, trails &c. Morning quite hot but soon clouded over & became temperate, now looks almost as though gathering up for rain.

Native Copper found in small (occasional) pieces in Similkameen also native silver, gold & platinum? the latter chiefly obtained from the workings visited yesterday on the S. Fork.[82] Most of the gold here very fine, the platinum about similar in size. At one place, about 16 m. down the river from here, a red streak Crosses the valley, & just here, Hays* thinks connected with said red streak, a good deal of gold got at one time, pieces small but not flat, & gold of fine quality & peculiar.[83]

Quite a camp of Indians about a mile up the N Fork, now living on nothing in particular but waiting for something to turn up. Own a good many horses, & some cattle.

Hay's* says frosts every month in the year here, so that though tried, ⟨....⟩ found impossible to raise squashes, beans, cucumbers &c. other harder Crops of course do well. Soil of benches however for most part sandy & poor. Fine cattle ranges to the N. & N.E. Hays* is a partner of Allison*, whose head quarters near the Mission on Okanagan Lake.[84] The cattle driven up here for summer range, taken back there in winter.

Note the Cactus in flower today for the first time.

Hay's* a main man, full of talk, who has been in California, Australia, & here since 1860. His first question whether you will not take something to drink, which being declared he urges to "take a glass of milk, take something" The glass of milk being agreed to, a small tumbler produced from a cupboard, with dried traces of former milk. Washed in a bucket & rinsed, & then filled up with milk, which certainly good.

Saw two fine deer[85] this morning, but could not approach them
[verso]
June 20. Princeton. Hay's*. Sun at Noon 127° 30′ 3″
June 21. At Same place 6.04 A.m. Mag. bearing of sun = N54E.
[end verso]
June 21. Delayed a little in starting by the horses, which though hobbled had strayed several miles off in the open country Got off at 7 A.m. &

---

82. The diggings are described in the published "Report on the Southern Portion," 156, which adds that "a few Chinamen were working here at the time of my visit."

83. For a description of placer deposits in the Similkameen region, see H. M. A. Rice, *Geology and Mineral Deposits of the Princeton Map-Area, British Columbia*, Geological Survey of Canada Memoir no. 243 (Ottawa: King's Printer, 1947), 57–64; and, on platinum, especially 59.

84. At "Sunnyside," now Westbank on Okanagan Lake.

85. Mule deer, *Odocoileus hemionus hemionus* (Rafinesque).

travelled till 1.20 making about 13 miles. Day overcast & disagreeably showery throughout

Wrote up notes, examined granite of vicinity, which probably a great intrusive mass,[86] &c. Devoted an hour or so to fishing in the river which *looks* a beautiful trout stream, but result only two very small trout.

The river valley which was noticed to open out so remarkably on the onset of the Tertiary on Whipsaw Cr, narrows in again equally markedly on the resumption of the "green series" & Granites, which intrusive in the latter. Now tortuous with narrow bottom, & only occasionally flats of any size.

Note Cedar again along the bank of the river at evening Camp, Also for the first time (though it may have escaped notice before) the seringa (mock orange)[87] at home among rocks on the hill slopes.

The granite above mentioned, owing to its jointing, has fallen in many places, down in huge blocks which cumber the sides of the valley.

June 22. Waited half an hour this morning for showers to pass over, & started with appearance of clearing, but showers & squalls continued to come up from the west all day, making it very uncomfortable. Finding a very interesting series of exposures about the time the packs caught up, decided to camp on 20 m. Creek[88] Spent afternoon in examining rocks getting photo[89] (in very adverse circumstances of weather) &c.

The boundary mountains are increasing in height as we descend the river, one ahead now down the valley, shows still a little snow.

June 23. Paced on about 12.m. Camping below the junction of the Ashanola (?) river.[90] Collected a few plants, wrote up notes &c. in p.m. Rocks very puzzling & provoking. All in slides at the bases of the mountains, & nothing to be seen of bedding up above. Shakes faith in all previously fixed formations to find these apparently so much jumbled together. Must be a huge mass of quartzites.

---

86. Dawson was describing Coast Intrusions, in which "intrusions of pre-upper Lower Cretaceous age form batholiths, stocks, and associated sills and dykes. They are far more widely spaced and diversified than those of later age, and represent nearly a third of the bedrock of the area. The principal component is granodiorite, presumable belonging to the general family of the Coast Range batholithic rocks, with associated more basic and more alkaline phases" Rice, *Geology and Mineral Deposits*, 33.

87. Mock orange or syringa, *Philadelphus lewisii* Pursh.

88. Hedley Creek.

89. While Dawson mentions only a "photo" in the journal, he obviously took three views. See "Photographs," 22 June 1877, GSC168–C1 (PA 152393); GSC169–C1 (PA 51073); and GSC170–C1 (PA 801500).

90. Ashnola River.

Showery & windy weather as usual, wetting note book &c. from time to time, but fine & cool. Indian tells us that many rattlesnakes hereabouts, & onward, & Jacinto killed one when out looking after animals, to confirm the statement.

Notice *Amelanchier* berries beginning to turn colour, also *raspberries* ripe. Noted cactus in flower for first time at Hay's*.

Alkali begins to be abundantly seen on the soil in places, & is accompanied by its indicative "rye grass"[91] Note *Artemesia trifida*[92] forming a large bush, for the first time.

June 24. Sunday & a doubtful looking day, with high wind & masses of heavy clouds. Decided not to move Camp, but started at 6 a.m. & paced down to Price's[93] beyond Kerremeoos Brook,[94] about six miles. Interviewed Price*, an Englishman, with a good house & everything very comfortable about him, & then rode back, getting to Camp at 11.30. Write up notes & read on to the end of P Schmidt's essay on Descent & Darwinism,[95] which contains a great deal of information, but written in an ill tempered & intolerant spirit which renders it to some extent repulsive.

Still cloudy & windy this evening, with occasional drops of rain, & withall chilly. Have not yet experienced the hot weather which I thought to find in this southern interior — it may be coming. Price* calls the distance from his place to Osoyoos 25 miles.

June 25 rode down to Mr Price's* & thence carried work on about ten miles; camping on the bank of the river on a dry spot {sparsely} covered with *Plantago patagonica*,[96] now very common. *Echino spermum Leppula*, & a little *A. frigida* & bunch grass. Examined rocks of vicinity, Got a photo[97] looking down valley, & including some fine mountains, wrote up notes, fought mosquitoes & turned in.

Still showery today, with occasional squalls, with lucid intervals of great heat, now, however, looking more settled than it has done for some time.

91. Ryegrass, *Elymus cinereus* Scribn. & Merr.

92. Three tip sagebrush, *Artemesia tripartita* Rydb.

93. Barrington Price moved to Keremeos in 1873 when he sold the store in Osoyoos he had owned and operated since 1871. Price established a prosperous farm by pre-empting 640 acres in 1873 and adding more in following years.

94. Keremeos Creek.

95. Oscar Schmidt, *The Doctrine of Descent and Darwinism* (London: H. S. King & Co., 1875).

96. Woolly plantain, *Plantago patagonica* Jacq.

97. See "Photographs," 25 June 1877, GSC171–C1 (PA 801501).

The valley expands greatly about Prices*, (below Keremeoos Stream) & from there on shows much flat, bottom land, probably averaging nearly a mile wide, & some of it likely so low & damp as to be capable of raising crops without irrigation. Told that not only wheat &c. succeeds here, but tomatoes, Corn, beans & other tender plants. No outside market, however, for anything but cattle & horses. Price* is putting up a small steel flour mill.[98] This is a very thickly populated country — one can hardly put ones foot down without treading on a large black beetle, small do — do — or an ant. The grasshoppers which are in great abundance & variety nimbly keep out of the way of the feet, but occasionally dash themselves violently in ones face, coming on stern first under all sail in a good breeze. All these miscellaneous 'Critters' & many others too numerous to mention are racing & tearing about over the hot surface, in the shade (pretty thin) of the plants above mentioned, like clerks in a city — though the streets are not very well defined. They all appear to be looking for something ? what.

These green rocks have slipped in again without proving their connexion with the quartzites properly, or their right to appear at all

> Oh! for a fossil, Some poor shell.
> That died upon that ⟨olden⟩ {lovely} shore
> But yet in whispered voice can tell,
> — Last hollow throbbing of a bell —
> Of ⟨that⟩ {the} old oceans roar.

June 26. Travelled on to Osoyoos Lake, about fourteen miles, with a good deal of up & down hill. Hot in the morning, & heavy rain with Cold wind after noon for about half an hour. On coming down into the wide Osoyoos Valley expected to see settlement of some sort, but could see nothing & did not even know which way to take. On the point of camping at a little stream when discerned a house, & steering toward it, soon saw another establishment. Find that the families resident here are two in number. "Judge" Haynes[99] the customs officer &c. & a German Called

98. The water-powered grist mill built by Price on Keremeos Creek had a ten to twelve foot diameter wheel driven by water diverted from further up Keremeos Creek and brought along a flume cut into an embankment. Price operated the mill for about eight years then sold it. For a description of the mill, which still stands today, see Carolyn Smyly, "The Keremeos Grist Mill," in Okanagan Historical Society, *Forty First Annual Report* (1977), 23–28.

99. John Carmichael Haynes (1831–88) emigrated from Ireland to British Columbia in 1858 and joined the British Columbia Police as a constable. In 1860, he became deputy collector of customs at Rock Creek then, in 1862, took charge of the district and moved to Osoyoos. Haynes grew to be a powerful regional figure, later becoming assistant gold

Kreuger.[100] The valley a huge wide flat bottomed trough, with no timber, scanty bunch grass &c. & open thickets of ragged looking "Chaparaal"[101] giving it a weird & strange aspect. Finding these places with so few people in them, seems to make the whole country appear much more lonely than when camped apart in the heart of the forest.

Saw a fine deer this morning swim across the Similkameen River. It took a narrow channel to an island or gravel bar, stood on the bar a few moments, while I was trying to get out my revolver, then dashed into the wider & swifter current, & notwithstanding a random shot at about 300 yards, got out in safety & bounded into the thicket.

June 27. Heavy rain & wind in the night, & continued rain till about 11 a.m. Kept to tent, writing & reading. Afternoon rode down to outlet of lake, about 5 miles, the last three south of the 49th parallel. There is a fence, roughly built, with a pound of movable bars, forming the gateway of British Columbia in this direction. It stretches between a rocky bluff & the shore, & is to prevent Cattle & horses leaking out into the United States. Accepted Mr Haynes* invitation to dine with him, & had a capital dinner off a table & clean table-cloth. Vegetables in plenty from his little garden patch, which is near the lake shore, & where with plenty water he finds he can raise everything. A packer called Newman[102] arrived this evening *en route* from Walla Walla to Kamloops. Took chance to write to Kamloops to have mail forwarded to Okanagan,[103] also to scribble a line home. He brings news of an Indian rising south of the Columbia in W.T.[104] Vague & indefinite but apparently true. The Indians south of the

commissioner and magistrate, then county court judge and member of the British Columbia Legislative Council. Haynes also possessed major land holdings covering some twenty-two thousand acres. See Hester E. White, "John Carmichael Haynes: Pioneer of the Okanagan and Kootenay," *British Columbia Historical Quarterly* 4 (1940): 183–201.

100. Theodore Kruger (1829–99) came to British Columbia as a miner in 1858. After a time in the Cariboo, Kruger settled in the Osoyoos Valley and bought the former Hudson's Bay Company store. Like J. C. Haynes, Kruger amassed large land holdings in the southern Okanagan. See Chrestenz Kruger, "Early Days at Osoyoos," in Okanagan Historical Society, *Sixth Annual Report* (1936), 76–80.

101. Antelope-bush, *Purshia tridentata* (Pursh) DC.

102. Probably B. Newman of Kamloops, enumerated in the voters' list as a stock grower.

103. The post office was located on Cornelius O'Keefe's ranch, at the head of Okanagan Lake near Vernon.

104. Dawson's reference (he means Oregon, not Washington Territory) is to the conflict of Chief Joseph and the Nez Percé Indians over their traditional lands in the Wallowa Valley in northeastern Oregon. Joseph's people resisted resettlement on a reservation. Only after a valiant fighting retreat of seventeen-hundred miles did the Nez Percés finally concede defeat to General Oliver Howard on 5 October 1877, in northern

line it appears have been talking of fighting for some time, saying that the whites are going to take all their land from them.

Cattle on the Similkameen & Osoyoos to S. end of Okanagan Lake. Mr H gives me the approximate number at 4550 in all.

Settlers on the Similkmeen. 7 in number, none with families.

Miners at Rock Creek[105] perhaps about 15 now. All Chinamen, making about wages. perhaps $1.50 per diem.

Osoyoos Lake & Valley. The valley strikes one in entering it as being entirely different to anything seen between here & Hope. A wide flat bottomed trough, averaging here probably 2 miles in width ⟨from⟩ between the bases of the rocky slopes. The bottom of the trough formed by clean washed & rounded, generally rather fine gravel, & sand; the sides of rock, sometimes almost naked, but generally with more or less remnant of drift covering, often in the form of degraded benches, which rise in places to a height of at least 300 feet above the lake. The lake itself is about 9 miles in length, & averages probably a mile in width. It is said to be deep, but is remarkably divided near its centre, by two bars or spits.[106] The northern of these is at Kreuger's*, just opposite the custom house, & must be shaped somewhat thus. [*Illus.*] It so nearly divides the lake that a rough bridge has been easily built, & below this a strong current flows, — the Okanagan R. The second spit is about a mile further South, & has also a narrow Channel cutting through it, this time near the E. end. These spits are quite different in character from the 'fans', several of which are seen elsewhere, but always in evident relation to entering streams, which these are not. The material is as far as seen chiefly fine gravel & sand & the surfaces of the spits do not rise far above the water level. There is little to show that they might be remnants of moraines. The material would probably be coarser if So. They may be *Eskers*.[107] The lower terraces & gravel

Montana. For a detailed account of the incident, see Alvin M. Josephy, *The Nez Perce Indians and the Opening of the Northwest* (New Haven: Yale University Press, 1965), 485-633.

105. Gold was discovered at Rock Creek in 1859, and a large contingent of miners soon arrived and worked at a frantic pace throughout the season. By 1861, however, the area was almost completely abandoned as miners moved on to richer paying areas. See L. Norris, "The Rise and Fall of Rock Creek," in Okanagan Historical Society, *Second Annual Report* (1927), 37-40.

106. The spits could mark the sites of shoal areas or low islands of unconsolidated sediment left when the glacial ice retreated. Wave action in postglacial time could then have redistributed the sediment to form the spits.

107. A glacial deposit in the form of continuous, winding ridges of sand and gravel, unrelated to the surrounding topography.

deposits round the lake,[108] are not regularly flat topped, but full of large hollows & depressions some of which hold swamps &c. The material is also very generally arranged in long boat bottomed ridges, generally pointing up & down the valley, & the whole appearance is as if the action of powerful currents, when the water stood at an elevation of say 50 feet above the present, & as it lowered to its new level. When higher than this these may also have been currents, though not nearly So strong.

This valley being so low, must have formed an important strait or channel at one stage of the glacial submergence[109] (get actual height by comparative readings) & may have been one of the great channels for a current bearing glaciating ice from the north. The rocky sides are decidedly moutonée[110] everywhere, though the original surface generally obliterated. The appearance is that most powerful or exclusive glaciation from N. to S. Where the original surface remains, it is not fluted & deeply parallelly scored as near Victoria e.g. but polished with little trace of striation, reminding one of action of Hinds* Labradoor "Pan ice".[111] It would seem clear that at least the last glaciation has been here by water borne ice. The mountains bordering the valley do not I believe rise in any place to 2000′ above it, & generally are comparatively low, showing to some extent a primitive, or very ancient general slope of the surface hereabouts toward the great valley. An interesting further question is as to the original formation of the valley, which here certainly has the appearance of being an older & more important eflux of the country than the Fraser, the canon of the latter having nothing on this part of the former at all comparable with it. Will the levels allow the supposition that this valley in pre-glacial times

108. The terraced gravels and sand west of Osoyoos Lake are pitted with kettles and were laid down amid stagnant blocks of ice from the dwindling ice sheet.

109. Once again Dawson introduces the now abandoned concept of floating ice. Recent research indicates an ice cap rising at its climax above the eight thousand foot contour, sloping and flowing southward to central Washington. Most deposits, terraces, meltwater channels, and so on, date to the retreating stages of the ice cap when high ground was exposed and masses of ice were left to melt away on the valley floor. See Hugh Nasmith, *Late Glacial History and Surficial Deposits of the Okanagan Valley, British Columbia*, British Columbia Department of Mines and Petroleum Resources Bulletin no. 46 (Victoria: Queen's Printer, 1962).

110. *Roches moutonnées* are glacial erosion features consisting of asymmetrical mounds of rocks of varying size, with a gradual smooth abraded slope on one side and a steeper and rougher slope on the other.

111. The so-called "pan ice" is "derived from Bay ice, floes and coast ice, varying from five to ten or twelve feet in thickness" which rises "over all the low lying parts of the Islands grinding and polishing exposed shores, and rasping those that are steep-to" (Henry Youle Hind, "Notes on Some Geological Features of the North Eastern Coast of Labrador," *Canadian Naturalist and Quarterly Journal of Science*, n.s., 8 [1878]: 229–30).

drained a great part of the interior of B.C.? May it have been drift blocked at that time, & if so where? The present level of the river & lake is not of course at all that of the bottom of the valley, which, following the analogy of other rivers in the country should be nearly v—shaped. What depth would be the supposed old channel have, taking a width of say only 1 ½ mile; sides sloping down at average of Say 15° or 20° (?) thus. [*Illus.*] A question however if any important block occurs in this channel between here & the Columbia.[112]

The lower end of Osoyoos Lake,[113] is continued by low swampy land for some distance, & there is no apparent reason for its ending where it does in the form of a rocky or other substantial barrier. A wide old 'fan' coming in from the E. side probably has something to do with it.

There is a considerable area of flat land in the valley about here, but it is all light gravelly & sandy soil, & morover there are scarcely any streams coming down into the valley, now large enough to irrigate a wide area. The bunch grass is said to have been much better in 'early days' than now, the stock having increased so much.

June ⟨July⟩ *28.* Should have been off early this morning, but the horses having wandered away, were delayed for some time. Took a topographical sketch looking N. then tried the spoon in the lake, & caught one fine large trout. Light rain commenced as we left, continued & constantly grew heavier, with strong wind, till finding it impossible to continue work satisfactorally, camped at noon, only 6 m. from the Custom House. Rain soon after ceased, & with only a few showers, the afternoon has been fine. Writing up notes &c. occupied nearly all time, tried for gold in the brook, but with poor luck, scarcely getting a Colour. Johnny & Jacinto going down to the river caught about two dozen fair-sized "white fish".

Trail via Ft Shepherd to Kootenay.[114] Has not been travelled for some years, but Mr Haynes* thinks could be traversed with a little chopping without much difficulty. Poor feed a drawback. The trail *impassable* by ⟨way⟩ reason of the man crossings of rivers, at high water. August or September would be most favourable time.

112. Some combination of river and glacial erosion carved the Okanagan Valley into the southern part of the Thompson Plateau. See Stuart S. Holland, *Landforms of British Columbia: A Physiographic Outline*, British Columbia Department of Mines and Petroleum Resources Bulletin no. 48 (Victoria: Queen's Printer, 1964), 71–72. The axis of the valley at the end of the last glaciation was below the present river level, which has been elevated to varying degrees by infill with glacial outwash, glacial-lake sediments, and alluvial fans, or is covered by open water.

113. Osoyoos Lake seems to be held up in Washington by two fans: Tonasket Creek from the east, and the Similkameen River from the west.

114. The eastern portion of the Dewdney Trail, on which Dawson had been travelling the western end from Hope, was constructed by Edgar Dewdney in 1865.

June 29   Left Camp at 5.45 & actually experienced a fine day, with scarcely a drop of rain from morning to night! Travelled on till about noon, when striking the southern outcrop of the Tertiary, & wishing to examine it, we camped near a small stream fringed with aspens & willows, on the northern edge of a wide upland valley. A pretty peacefull looking spot. Many herds of Cattle feeding around. After lunch got horses & went back to Tertiary crop, returning to Camp after five. Wrote up notes, took evening observation & went to bed. Had some difficulty notwithstanding minute directions, in following trail, so many & so well worn Cattle tracks.

Saw a flock of about 12 or 15 *Recurvirostras*[115] this morning, hopping about in the grass & screaming at us, evidently aware that no gun. Put up two prairie chickens, saw some ducks in ponds, deer tracks in great abundance, & the skin (shed) of a large rattlesnake.

Additional evidence with regard to glaciation & Currents &c. The little Mountain opposite us {at morning camp} shows the moutonee appearance well, & is fringed below with streaked off current benches. A diagram of its appearance about thus — [*Illus.*] A few miles above camp (morning) the valley open out, Considerably, & further up again becomes much narrower, with steeper walls. A current flowing from the north has, loosing its velocity in entering the wide reach, deposited a great Carapace-like broad mound of gravel &c., which is now in great part cut away by the river working at a lower level.[116]

Near evening Camp (approx elevation 1800′) on the highlands W. of the Okanagan Valley, a good illustration of S. flowing current. The W base of a synclinal of hard igneous (Tertiary) rocks has opposite it a wide shallow depression occupied by a saline lake[117] with neither outlet nor any important inlet. There is no cause for the excavation of the hollow, without outlet, nor could it well have been formed & an outlet filled. There is no appearance of this. A strong current sweeping round the point, there increasing its speed has cut more deeply. [*Illus.*]

---

115. The American avocet, *Recurvirostra americana* Gmelin. Common on the Canadian prairies, avocets are only very occasionally seen in southern British Columbia. Given their easily identifiable markings and Dawson's familiarity with the species in his previous work with the Boundary Commission, it was unlikely Dawson was mistakenly identifying the bird. His sighting of a flock is thus very noteworthy.

116. The gravel "Carapace" was probably deposited by flooding outwash streams flowing between the valley wall, and a body of ice along the centre of the valley, and not in a wide ice-free stretch of the valley as we see it now.

117. The site described by Dawson is clearly White Lake, a local basin along a meltwater stream flowing southward and southeastward. The hollow is partly filled by deltaic and outwash sediment.

Johnny has just given us a remark on a bird singing on a tree near by. He says it "wa-wa all same Siwash la langue"[118] & says do not steal, or words to that effect. The curious part of it is though that the Lytton, Kamloops, & Similkameen dialects are somewhat different, & the bird he affirms & really believes, speaks in each locality the dialect there spoken by the Indians.

[verso]

The Lower end of Okanagan L. is separated from the upper of Du Chien L.,[119] by what appears from a height to be a broad strip of flat land. Both Lakes lie in the same great valley. It is found, however, that the separation is really due to coalesced flat fans,[120] probably of subaqueous origin, & formed by the large streams coming in here on the opposite sides of the lake, one at the Indian village, the other at Ellis'.[121]

[end verso]

June 30   Up at 3.30 & off early, pacing about a mile in Continuation of yesterday's survey, & then sedimentary rocks giving out, & packs overtaking, mounted, & kept distance by time. Obliged to remain near the packs, as many trails & much danger that Jacinto with his wooden head, would go wrong. Came about 11 A.m. to Indian Village,[122] which, taking for Mr Ellis's* or Penticten[123] (? spelling) got packs put off a brook, wishing to learn about trail &c. Found mistake but stayed for lunch before

118. A mixed bit of Chinook and French presumably meaning, as Dawson words it, "the bird speaks in each locality the dialect spoken there by the Indians."

119. Or Lac du Chien. Later it was called Dog Lake and then officially, since 1930, Skaha Lake. "Skaha" is the Shuswap word for "dog."

120. "Penticton, Ellis, and Shingle Creeks have built alluvial fans graded to the present lake level, and these fans are sufficiently extensive to coalesce and divide the formerly continuous lake into the two lakes Okanagan and Skaha. The present Okanagan River follows a sinuous course between the fronts of the fans from Okanagan to Skaha Lakes, and it carries sand brought down by Shingle and Ellis Creeks to Skaha Lake, where wave action distributes the sand along a broad beach extending across the north end of Skaha Lake" (Holland, *Landforms of B.C.*, 23).

121. Thomas Ellis (1844–1918) was another powerful south Okanagan rancher and land owner. Ellis landed in Victoria from Ireland in 1865 then travelled into the Okanagan Valley, settling at the south end of Okanagan Lake. Along with his friend, Andy McFarland, Ellis bought some land from the nearby Indian reserve and opened a trading post and store in 1866. Ellis gradually expanded his holdings until his ranch covered an enormous area. See Kathleen W. Ellis, "Tom and Mina Ellis," in Okanagan Historical Society, *Fourteenth Annual Report* (1939), 98–109; and Margaret A. Ormsby, "Thomas Ellis Describes an Irish Wedding," in Okanagan Historical Society, *Forty-first Annual Report* (1977), 92–96.

122. The village was located on what became Penticton's Huth Avenue. It is now the site of a power station.

123. Penticton was the Indian name used by Thomas Ellis for his ranch when he settled in the region in the 1860's.

going on. Ellis's* about a mile further & on opposite bank of Okanagan River, which Crossed by a good bridge. Found Elliss* farm home, & that neither fresh meat nor butter could be had for the simple reason that there was none. Continued on four or 5 miles up the lakeshore, travelling on benches between the lake & the mountains. Met many Indians on the way home from a great potlatch which has been for some time in progress at the head of the lake. Family parties Camped on a small stream about 1000′ from the lake, but high above it. A romantic looking little spot, with tall pitch pines, & flat shelving gneiss rocks.

In riding ahead to recanoitre the Indian village, Came suddenly on a brook in which an Indian woman was sitting in a state of nature, engaged in ablutions. She seemed a little put out at being caught thus, but wisely sat still. On looking up a little further saw paterfamilias & a whole brood of children occupied in the same way. Retiring a little I called to the gentleman, who obligingly put on his unmentionables & came over to answer questions about trail &c.

Johnny's "Hilo Capswallow"[124] bird caused some amusement today To cook lunch he took a bar off the Indians fence, & shortly afterwards the moral bird perched on a tree near us kept reiterating his advice not to steal. On calling Johnny's attention to the fact he was vastly amused, & a little conciense struck; but eventually he called it a "Cultus Chicken"

An old Indian passing on the trail Came into Camp with his horse all hung over, like a butcher's shop, with the various parts of a large deer. To this imposing display of fresh meat, he riding on top, formed the imposing apex, & imposed on us to the extent of a dollar for a hind leg!

July 1. Sunday. Did not move camp. Wrote up notes &c. Got photographs[125] looking up & down the lake. Examined silty deposits & gneissic &c. rocks of neighbourhood. Changed plant papers & unsuccessfully endeavoured to correct sextant for collination by sun & moon, clouds continually obscuring the latter till too late. Had a good bath in the lake, under the patronage of a water snake[126] about a yard long, who swam up & looked at me. A brown fellow with dark spots, very graceful & pretty. Read a little, but bothered by a slight headache all day. This Okanagan Lake a truly beautiful sheet of water.

Rocks about camp would make good Laurentian[127] in some places but

124. Or "Halo Kapswalla," a Chinook Jargon expression meaning "not to steal."

125. See "Photographs," 1 July 1877, GSC174–C1 (PA 51074) and GSC175–C1 (PA 51066).

126. Probably the three-lined garter snake, *Thamnophis sirtalis trilineata* Cope, which is sometimes called a "water snake" because of its aquatic habits.

127. A name that is widely and confusingly used for granites and orogenies of Precambrian age in the Canadian Shield.

cannot allow lithological characters to cross the mountains.
July 2. Up at 3.10 A.m., but rain commencing almost immediately delayed start till 6. Took half an hour's sleep after breakfast, & then, weather apparently clearing, got off, & travelled till 2 P.m., making about 14 miles on a very crooked trail, leading most of the way, after leaving the lake, through wooded Country Camp at an elevation of over 4000′ by the barometer. Made an examination of the rocks of the vicinity. At about 5.30, the fine spell came to an end & heavy rain set in, which still continues, with dull leaden sky & Calm. our camp among thick growth of dense scrub pines, beside a swamp & pool with *nuphar*[128] reminds of some of last summer's dreary spots. Great boulders strew all the neighbourhood, project from & almost replace the soil.

Immediately after beginning to ascend from the Okanagan valley, the vegetation begins to change. bunch grass & Pinus ponderosa lost, douglas fir prevails, then "sour grass" & scrub pine, with a return of many familiar plants. Linnea, now in flower. Spiraea betulifolia, the little common slender trailing blush astragalus, lonicera involucrata, also the red Skagit lonicera, the little Turk's Cap lilly. Noted also a few small trees of larch, the first seen this season. Also a very beautiful *Cypripedium*, nearly pure white, Nuphar polysepolum in pools, roses here still in good blossom though more or less pasee below. A white speranthes (not ceruna) Epilobium not in flower, Heraclum in flower[129] &c. &c.

Motto "If this is a *dry* climate let me try a wet one". It was probably raining when 'the man' cut out this terribly Crooked trail, he then fell back on his recollection of the position of the North Star.

Are the boulder heaps here of the nature of moraines, or exaggerated boulder clay due to great abundance of masses of decomposing 'granitic' rocks (?)[130]
July 3. Crept out of camp under a dull leaden mist, which brightening occasionally gave promise of clearing. bushes & trees all loaded with moisture, & the lower parts of trail very muddy between the boulders. Heavy showers from time to time all day, with some thunder, now apparently

---

128. The yellow pond-lily, *N. polysepalum*.

129. The "Linnea" was northern twinflower, *L. borealis*; "red Skagit lonicera" the western trumpet honeysuckle, *L. ciliosa*; and "Turk's Cap lilly" the tiger lily, *Lilium columbianum* Hanson. The "*Cypripedium*" was the mountain lady's slipper, *Cypripedium montanum* Dougl.; "speranthes" hooded ladies' tresses, *Spiranthes romanzoffiana* Cham. & Schlecht.; and "Heraclum" cow parsnip, *H. lanatum*.

130. Dawson answers his own question later in his published report: "the summit is strewn with large granitic boulders which appear to be of the rock of the country, broken down and weather-rounded nearly in place" (Dawson, "Report on the Southern Portion," 55).

clearing up. Camped near "the store", after crossing mission Creek, a very rapid ford, above the horses belly, but with good bottom. A wide stretch of good country, with some fine crops about here. Some seventeen families in all settled here, & along the road within about ten miles.[131] Made enquiries as to what supplies can be obtained, possibility of getting canoe &c. &c.

In descending from the mountains, when the lake & flats of Mission Creek first sighted, a very pretty effect. A dense grey fog hung over us on the higher country, while beneath the edge of this, between it & the hollowed bottom of the valley we were descending, the bright blue of the lake first seen, without any surroundings. soon after the broad open & cultivated flats of the Mission with groves of trees &c., all in full sunshine & looking yellow & warm in the dull cold surroundings.

July 4. Started about 6 a.m. for the Mission Creek mines,[132] about 7. m. from here, having a lad to guide us as to the trail. Forded the creek in very strong water about ¾ mile below the mines. Examined the deposits, rocks, &c. & bought a small specimen of the Gold. Had dinner in a miner's Cabin & got back to camp in the afternoon. Rode down to the lake shore, about a mile, to get elevation of camp. Mr C. Vernon[133] arrived about dark, on some business connected with land grants. Had a talk with him.

Drenching heavy rain this evening

This valley appears to be a sort of Arcadian retreat. The first settler, called Laurence[134] came here about 18 years ago, & others have been here nearly as long. Mostly seem to be half-breeds, speaking french, but some french people from old france besides the two priests at the mission. They

---

131. Modern day Okanagan Mission. "The settlement dates from about eighteen years back," wrote Dawson, with most of the families being francophone half-breeds. "A considerable proportion of the land is under cultivation, with fine-looking crops. The farm buildings are in some cases substantial, there is a school with about twenty scholars, and a church and mission buildings under the care of two French priests" (ibid.).

132. "The locality worked is situated about seven miles from the mouth of the stream, where it is found issuing from a narrow rocky gorge, into a wider valley. Some years ago mining was carried on in the bed of the Creek, and very good pay got for a time, in a reach of about half a mile below the gorge above mentioned. Two or three ounces of gold were obtained *per diem* to the hand in some instances. No remunerative ground was found above the gorge or cañon" (ibid., 157).

133. Charles Vernon (1840–1906) came to the Okanagan Valley with his brother Forbes and Charles Frederick Houghton in the early 1860's. The Vernons eventually acquired a large amount of land that formed the nucleus of the Coldstream Ranch. Along with his interest in the ranch, Charles Vernon also engaged in mining activities and merchandising, and for a number of years served as gold commissioner, land commissioner, and justice of the peace.

134. Cyprian Laurence was a French Canadian who pre-empted land at Okanagan Mission in 1860.

seem to be comfortable enough in their way, & some of them have much land under cultivation with fine looking crops, & good farm buildings &c. There is a school with about 20 scholars {all half breeds} some of whom we met on our way to the mines, with lunches & books, neatly dressed. There are about 17 families in all, graduating through various breeds down to Indians, with whom cordial relations of course subsist. A little log church with a tinkling bell, which gives out a few notes every evening. Land with some improvement probably not worth more than $5 per acre, & plenty still to be had by preemption or bought of the govt. for $1 an acre. Mail once a month.

"The tumult of the times disconsolate
In inarticulate murmers dies away"

July 5. Slight shower this A.m. early, but day otherwise fine, & pretty warm. Camp at S end of Primeewash Lake[135] of the map, about half a mile off the road, a pretty but mosquito-haunted spot. Afternoon rode across to Okanagan L. & round on the hills looking at the rocks. Difference between Primeewash & Okanagan Lakes 133 feet, the latter lower.

A fine grazing country, open or dotted with P. ponderosa everywhere & much good flat land, on which water can be got with little trouble from the Mission to the first lake.

Saw two half breed women on the trail today. One middle aged & about ¾ Indian, the other pretty fair, & younger. Both with gay coloured handkerchiefs round their heads. The younger woman with three children. The eldest, perhaps three years old, riding a little horse tied securely to the saddle. Two younger ones, one sitting behind the mother, & the other in front, on the Same horse. both women riding straddle The one with the children going to her husband at Cherry Creek.

July 6. Left Camp at 5 a.m. but after getting a few miles found a good point of view for "the Railway" separating Primeewash & Long Lakes,[136] & stayed till arrival of pack train to get the camera off & take a view of it.[137] Then on again, travelling till nearly 3 P.m, & Camping at Vernon's* Coldstream.[138] Added about a mile to journey by mistake in

135. Wood Lake.

136. Kalamalka Lake.

137. See "Photographs," 6 July 1877, GSC176–C1 (PA 51065).

138. One of the most prosperous ranches in the Okanagan Valley, the Coldstream Ranch was established by Charles Frederick Houghton in the early 1860's but passed to Forbes and Charles Vernon in 1869. For Forbes Vernon, see below (G. M. Dawson to Margaret

trail, & got into a poor camping place, brushy & full of mosquitoes through ignorence of locality. Day part of time very warm, & ride seemed tedius. The ease which great distances are *seen* in this country, & the long time it takes to overtake them is discouraging.

The Railway so called, is a low spit forming the separation between Primeewash & Long Lakes, which are otherwise really one. It quite resembles the spits of Osoyoos Lake, but includes in it two little rocky patches, elevated a few feet above the lake, which would be otherwise islands. Both lakes, though shallow in places at the edges, & ends, are from the colour of the water seen from the hills above, very deep elsewhere. No brooks enter which will account for *the railway* It is evidently shaped (on the S. side) & maintained by the wash of the waves of the lake, & may have been formed by the same action, accumulating additional materiel when already the rocky islands, & perhaps from some cause shoaler water.

The country opens out very widely, the valleys becoming large, & with sides much more gently sloping, on leaving the north end of Long Lake (well so named)

Lakes. Johnny, who knows this part of the country, tells me that *Sxoocum L* of the map, receives a large stream from the Mountains, & discharges into Primeewash L, which again runs through "the Railway" to Long Lake, the latter flowing out into the head of Okanagan Lake.[139] [*Illus.*]

July 7. Moved camp this morning to a more eligible locality on the other side of the spring stream, near Mr V's house. A little delay caused in getting in horses, which had strayed far. After seeing the packs deposited, started out with Douglas* & rode five miles up the valley to "Nelson's"[140] where lime at one time burnt. large exposures of limestone, but could find no good distinctive fossils. followed base of hills & examined rocks on way back, then ascended the eastern flank of the high mountain[141] ⟨behind⟩ N of Vernons* farm. Examined rocks, & got a sketch of country, with bearings. Got back about 3 P.m. About 4 P.m. Johnny, whom I had sent to the head of Okanagan Lake for mail &c. returned, bringing a great stak of letters & papers. Got camera Carried out to the

Dawson, 22 July 1877). The ranch grew substantially in size until it covered over thirteen thousand acres when it was sold to Lord Aberdeen in 1891.

139. Vernon Creek flows into "Sxoocum" or Ellison Lake, then drains Wood and Kalamalka lakes, before flowing into Okanagan Lake.

140. The reference is to Nelson Duteau, who with his brother Vincent established a ranch in what is now Lavington.

141. Vernon Hill.

remarkable perched block,[142] & took photo. of it, & one looking Eastward, up the valley.[143] Evening dined with Mr Vernon*, & a Mr Johnson.[144] Got information statistics &c. & agreed to meet at Cherry Creek on Thursday evg. next.

This valley, great & wide, has never been formed by the present trifling brooks. A large flow of water must have passed through it. The divide is now at "Nelson's"* before referred to, & is so insignificant, that he has turned the brook there entering to the north, so as to cause part of it to flow East & part west. It all went west originally.[145] The bottom of the valley is chiefly formed by the coalescense of broad flat fans, with a little flat bottom land between them.

A very warm & fine day.

G. M. Dawson to Margaret Dawson, 7 July 1877, Coldstream*

I arrived here yesterday from the Southward, & am sending 10 m. to the post office at the head of the Lake for my mail, which I directed to be sent there. I do not know exactly when the mail goes out, but post this on chance of its reaching sometime. I have not received any letters now for more than a month, & so expect to have quite a budget of news when my messenger returns.

To begin with I am quite well, the weather so far has not been at all excessively warm, on the Contrary rather exceptionally cool & showery. I am Camped here near Mr Vernons* place. He is an English gentleman who does some farming here, besides attending to various public duties, as that of J.P. &c. This is Saturday. I propose staying here over Sunday, & perhaps Monday, as the rocks are interesting & the country all open. Then I start for Cherry Creek. It will take about 3 days going in (distance about 40 miles) a like time returning, so that I can hardly hope to get back here under eight days. Four day's more should then take me to Kamloops, where I will refit & prepare for another tour, though which of the many I

---

142. In his report, Dawson further noted of this prominent erratic boulder that it was "twenty-two feet long, sixteen and a half wide, and eighteen feet high. It is yellowish, highly calcareous and interstratified with layers of felspathic and quartzose materials, all the beds being much contorted. The rock on which the erratic stands is quite different in appearance from it" (Dawson, "Report on the Southern Portion," 150).

143. See "Photographs," 7 July 1877, GSC177–C1 (PA 801502), for the view eastward. The view of the "remarkable perched block" no longer exists, but was photo-lithographed and included in Dawson's, "Report on the Southern Portion," pl. V, opp. 160.

144. Unidentifiable.

145. Coldstream Creek, which now runs west (mostly in water system pipes) to the Okanagan drainage, though there is a dry creek bed east to the Shuswap drainage.

have planned I cannot yet say.

I want to get my Indian off, & so cannot take time to write much, nor have I much to narrate had I plenty time. When Kamloops is again reached I will be able to answer all letters &c.

This I suppose will reach you at Metis.

I think I have killed a dozen mosquitoes while writing these few lines. They have not been very abundant or troublesome yet however.

The Indian troubles we hear of to the South do not effect this part of the world at all, where all is peace.

July 8. Sunday. Got plant papers changed & other camp duties performed. Devoted most of time to reading the newspapers &c. Made a slight examination of rocks on S. side of valley. Had a bath in a little brook. Got latitude & time observation at noon, though half-baked in the operation. Altogether made a lazy day of it. Weather very warm Several large springs of deliceous cold water rise here near Mr V's house. The form a good sized brook as they issue. Temperature today 48.5°

[verso]

Observations July. 8. 1877. Vernon's* Coldstream.

Readjusted horizon glass, not being satisfied with it, & redetermined index error.

    Index error 4' 38" to subtract.

Alt of sun at noon 124° 57' 10"

    Latitude by obsn. = 50° 15' 29"

Sun at 7h 45m. P.m. 〈Solar〉 apparent time bears N78.5°W by compass.

[end verso]

July 9.

Sketch of possible position of rocks from boulder hill to beyond Nelsons Creek. [*Illus.*]

Delayed as usual by the straying of the horses, but managed to get off pretty early. Travelled till about 1 45 camping S of the Camel's Hump Mountain. Trail so far nothing to complain of.

Day very warm, & calm. Thermometer reading at 4 Pm a little above 90 in good shade. Stones literally too hot to handle on the hillsides. Camp at a pretty little meadow about 3 m. beyond the Bull meadow, which is a very extensive flat with fine grass, but swampy On leaving the big meadow plunge at once into woods, which continue, though generally open & often burnt, to here.

Nelson's brook, part of which he has turned toward Coldstream & part eastward, really divides its waters between the Fraser & Columbia. The watershed a feature of no importence in the wide continous valley.

Had a bath on getting to camp, but found the water very cold. This morning as I stood on a hillside, making a sketch of the country. Intensely warm & perfectly calm. Douglas* at some distance getting a specimen of a rock & the two horses browsing near, I heard suddenly in the valley below where all had been previously perfectly still — a Crack — *Crack* krrr *whish Smash.* A great rotten old tree falling without any provocative cause whatever, unless indeed one of the wood ants happened at the moment to gnaw through the last fibre that made the difference between standing & falling.

Continued signs of greater rainfall. P. ponderosa still however on Sunny Slopes, but Douglas fir most common. Larch[146] & cedar — a few — go west as far as Vernon's* thus overlapping P. ponderosa considerably Saw this p.m. a tall mallow with pale ⟨purple⟩ purple flower, same as formerly collected near waterton Lake,[147] but not seen since.

July 10. Horses off as usual, but not very far this time. Travelled on over a very bad trail, till 3.40, & then camped in the woods with little feed for the horses. Trail abominably crooked, & has never been cut out at all. Two or three little showers of rain in the afteroon with a few claps of thunder. Fine views in places of then snowy peaks of the Selkirk Range[148] between here & the Columbia, a specially extensive one where sketch of track survey made. Shot a grouse with revolver *en route*. Day being partly clouded, pleasantly cool.

P. monticola abundant about Camp. larch & cedar quite common, Some specimens of abies lesiocarpa seen on the higher ground passed over.

July 11. Up at 3.30 & off early, the horses having been tied up during the night to prevent their straying. Train for some distance Continues very bad, with abominable mud holes. Get to camp on level of flat above the deep Cherry Creek Valley about 9.30 a.m. Rigged shade for thermometers, & prepared to take sun at noon, but clouds prevent. P.m. visited & made preliminary examination of the lower diggings[149] on Cherry

---

146. Western larch, *L. occidentalis.*

147. Mountain hollyhock, *Iliamna rivularis* (Dougl.) Greene. Dawson is referring to his work as geologist/botanist to the Boundary Commission.

148. The Monashee Mountains, not the Selkirk Range.

149. As recently as the 1950's, the deposits mentioned by Dawson were still being actively worked. According to a Geological Survey of Canada report, "the deposits have been worked by hand, by an elaborate system of flumes, and by hydraulicking since the early 1870's and in the past two decades with the use of gasoline shovels. The gold is fairly coarse and nuggets up to 6 ½ ounces have been recovered. The Cherry Creek placers as a whole have yielded . . . 5,210 ounces for all creeks with a value of $80,332. Most of the placer mining was done between the years 1874 and 1895, but hydraulicking operations are reported to have yielded gold to the value of $20,000 in more recent years" (A. G. Jones, *Vernon Map-Area British Columbia*, Geological Survey of Canada Memoir

Creek,[150] & the silver lode. Got a fine specimen of the ore. Evening tried for gold in boulder clay gravel about camp but without getting a colour. Wrote up notes. The wide flat, on a part of which we now are, is most remarkable, so far in toward the mountains. The soil chiefly clayey probably of the nature of little modified boulder clay. Fine grass where burnt over, & a large swampy meadow.

Johnny communicates the following a propos of matches. Long ago the Indians did not know about matches, used flint & steel, but before that made fire by friction. The root of the poplar the wood chosen, & into a well dried stick of this a wooden drill turned between the palms of the hands, was fixed, till fire came. Pieces of dry cedar bark rolled up, were used to carry fire. Described as four or five feet long, which smouldering away, allowed the Aukutty Siwash to carry fire several miles or many when necessary. Cedar does not grow at Lytton, but the Indians obtained it from the mountains.

[verso]

July 11. Obsn. of polaris for lat. Camp above Cherry Cr.

9.37 P.m.	99° 6' 0"
9.43 P.m.	99° 10' 50"
9.48 P.m.	99° 13' 50"

watch set at apparent noon July 8. probably now a few minutes slow. See next obsn. for rate.

[end verso]

July 12   Start immediately after breakfast, & occupied all day examining the upper part of the creek, & making paced survey of it. Interview the various miners &c., amongst others Thorpe[151] & [blank] who have have lately been over to the head waters of the Kettle River from here, & have struck what they consider a good prospect there, worth following up sometime. They supply, from description, the map opposite, topographical & geological. [*Illus.*]

July 13. Mr Vernon* not having arrived last night according to agreement, waited in this morning, writing up notes & examining rocks about camp. hoped to get latitude & time, but sun clouded at noon. After dinner went down to lower part of creek, where occupied till past five finishing survey & examination of the gold mines & silver lead. Mr Vernon* arrived just about dark, with an Indian.

no. 296 [Ottawa: Queen's Printer, 1959], 138).

150. Actually Monashee Creek, which joins Cherry Creek.

151. Unidentifiable.

Morning cloudy, afternoon fine, evening showery & overcast, again preventing observations.

[verso]

Interesting for Geol. Rep. in connection with description of gold localities[152] to give something on gold its distrib. in B.C. & conditions of search. Old Channels — Possible Tertiary, undoubted pre glacial, & post glacial of different ages. Effect of glacial period in search for gold not seen to South. Old river channels generally then native &c. Spread of gold by glaciating agencies &c.

[end verso]

July 14. Start on foot as soon as the grass & bushes moderately dry for Vernon's* Silver lead on the North Fork of Cherry Creek.[153] Reach it after a fatiguing scramble up & down hill & over logs. Examine it, & after lunch set out on return. on getting to camp got horse saddled & rode over to the upper mining Camp, having been told that Christian's hydraulic apparatus[154] would be working. Found the ditch broken, however, & no work going on. Got a specimen of gold & some black sand, & returned. Rigged camera, & before sun too low got view from hill behind Camp looking up the Main Valley of the Creek.[155]

[verso]

Venus? on Meridian 9h 43m 30s July 14

Alt as by sextant. uncorrected 33° 33′ 10″

[end verso]

July 15. Sunday. Had intended starting this morning, but vernon* promising that the new trail would be finished by Monday to a brook about 8 miles from here, decided if possible to return by it, both to avoid the very bad old trail, & to see a new Section of country. Sent Jacinto & Johnny out with V's Indian to hunt for a route to the creek in question. Tried to get sun at noon, but watch being too slow, put off obsn. till too late. Took time in P.m. & worked it out. Packed specimens &c.

[verso]

Obsn. for time &c. July 15.

152. Dawson, "Note on Mines and Minerals," 134–44.

153. The main stream of Cherry Creek.

154. Dawson further commented in his Field Notebook that "the Christian & Schneider Claim, most paying now on the Creek, yielding as much as $10.00 as average earnings for all working days, per hand employed. Has been sluiced, but now prepared to go to work with hydraulic, & expect good pay. Working on a bench about 30′ above the Creek" (G. M. Dawson, Field Notebooks, RG 45, vol. 134, no. 2797, 23v, PAC).

155. Dawson actually took two views at this locality. See "Photographs," 14 July 1877, GSC178–C1 (PA 152385), and GSC179–C1 (PA 51064).

Time by watch 5h 27m.   Suns uncorrected alt 34° 40′ 10″
  ″ ″   ″ 5 31   40s   ″   ″   ″ 33° 24′ 40″
Add the Semidiameter.

Last obsn. worked out gives time 6h 2m 30s, making watch slow by mean time 30m. 50s. It has lost since Noon of last Sunday 26m. 4s. (apply this proportionally to get time for obsn of Polaris July 11. & having thus found the correct Lat, recalculate time for mag. variation.) At 7h 9m. 30s by Calculated true mean time. Sun bears N82W by Compass.

[end verso]

July 16. Off, but not very early. Pushin through wood & windfall by trail roughly pioneered yesterday, & when it ran out, got on as best we could, country nowhere *extremely* thick. Mr V, who had gone down in the morning to the mining camp overtook us about noon. Camped at 1.30 on a flat beside the 8 m. creek.[156] Day very warm. Prospected the brook in a very good place, but without getting a colour of gold. Got several trees of P. contorta, on a dry uniform bench, uniformly grown & situated cut, & proceeded to measure map of growth along 4 radii. Supper after dark, Mr V, returning late from a reconnaissance ahead, without having found the trailmakers, who were supposed to reach this brook tonight.

July 17. Off moderately early, & travel on as best we can through a good deal of windfall & brulé & some nice open woods. At 11.15 met the trailmakers, & got onto good trail, travelling fast. Staid behind the packs at a cool little brook to get lunch. Camped about 3 P.m. Day after noon remarkably close & warm, rendering exertion of any kind very difficult. Got a photograph of the Camel's Hump,[157] wrote up notes &c.

The *country* travelled over from Camp above Cherry Creek to camp on Ferry Creek, might, much of it, be brought under cultivation if cleared, & would not require irrigation. At some future day this may be a very pretty looking country. Even now in the open woods much feed for Cattle & horses, pine grass, lupin, & wild vetch chiefly, the two last attaining a great growth where partial clearing by fire has occurred. About the mouth of Cherry Creek are very extensive flats, & some fair sized flats, (occasionally showing good meadows where fire has cleared them) occur along the winding course of the Shuswap. The flat valley is bounded to the north, however, by steep rocky hills, & to the south by the same towards the afternoon, but in the morning by benches, which though well grassed in places are too steep {& narrow} in most cases for agriculture. Here at evening camp a pretty extensive & beautiful little prairie, with some fertile land & a large hay meadow. Woods partly open all around & with plenty

156. Probably Durand Creek.

157. See "Photographs," 17 July 1877, GSC180–C1 (PA 801503).

feed.

July 18. Started about 7 A.m. & rode on with Mr V, getting to trail already examined at Big Bull Meadows. Thence took various Cross trails to Coldstream, where we arrived before 1 P.m. having travelled pretty fast though the morning very warm, with the air almost motionless & when it moved a little feeling like the breath of a furnace. A few showers with a little distant thunder, & in the afternoon fine cool breeze from the ⟨west⟩ East. Found late papers with war[158] & other news of interest to which devoted most of afternoon. In the valley, east of Vernon's*, still room for several good farms, some of which would not need irrigation. Grazing on the hills generally good & abundance of timber for fuel, fencing, & building. "Nelson" [blank] has a farm of three hundred acres (precipitation limit E. of Cascades) a good part under cultivation & nearly all good land with plenty of water, & a few log buildings, Much fencing. Mr V, on being asked says if desiring to sell might probably expect 2500 for the place (This presumably a maximum price)

Much will be added to the grazing grounds of all this region when the thickly timbered upper hills & plateaux have been cleared by fire. The timber of these from its quality & position will probably be no loss, while that of better quality in the valleys should be scrupulously preserved & encouraged.

Had lunch & dinner with Mr V, & sat up late talking. Fine livid Sunset sky. Tent nearly blown down in night by thunder storm.

[verso]

Terraces of drift material, Seem, where they form isolated hills, or points of larger hills, within which no stream rises, the drainage-area not being sufficiently large — seem to be affected by a general *spread* in all directions under the influence of the weather. There being no water behind, or for any through the terraces {& form fans} their identity is destroyed & their material formed into a long gentle slope into the valley.

[end verso]

July 19. Off pretty early & travelled till 3.30 Camping a little beyond Round Lake of the map. Day very warm for a time, but a good breeze Somewhat moderated the heat. Pm. Clouded over & still remains sultry & perfectly calm. Camped beside a queer little pot-hole, which now nearly dry, though receiving a little stream which sinks away Got mail at head of Okanagan Lake post office. Mosquitoes now without limit & very fierce.

All the hills along route today are open or partly open with good feed everywhere. The flat land in valleys on which water may be brought, is

---

158. The Russo-Turkish war which lasted until March 1878, when the Russians convincingly defeated the Turkish forces.

however quite limited

The pot-hole pond at which camped separated by only a narrow ridge perhaps 30 feet high from a lake about half a mile long, also without outlet, & similarly Surrounded by drift material. Found a *spongilla* on the Shore, with specimens of *Planorbis trivolvis* &c. the latter not kept.

Called a couple of loons from the far end of the lake, to near where I was concealed in the bushes. Even after I showed myself they did not appear frightened thinking me a sort of human loon, — which I suppose I was!

The valley in which Round lake, & the others of the chain lie, runs from near the head of Okanagan Lake, westward (?) & continues that occupied by the E.W. portion of the Salmon River. The length between Salmon R. & Okanagan, another instance of the old drift-blocked channels holding lakes, so common in the country. It may have lain transverse to the direction of Current, or some other local reason may account for its being so much more heaped with drift than some of the others.[159]

July 20. Off early, hoping to travel most of way during ⟨....⟩ cool of day, but the distance — called 22 miles — Carried us well into the Afternoon, when the weather became excessively warm, standing persistently above 90° till nearly dark. Camped at Ingram's[160] Grand Prairie. The valley of Salmon River, where seen is not very wide, & with little flat bottom land, but there are still considerable areas, now more or less thickly timbered, which when cleared, — which they will eventually no doubt be — may be successfully Cropped. The lower end of Grand Prairie is swampy, with good Swamp hay. Further up, toward Ingram's* it becomes dry & opens out to wide dimensions, being evidently the filled up or drained bed of an old lake, into which broad sloping "fans" project in various places. Ingram* & Kirkpatrick[161] are established here each with a considerable area of land fenced in, while there still remains about 1000 acres (roughly estimated) of arable land unsurveyed & not claimed.

Ingram*, years ago, during the Cariboo excitement was enterprising enough to buy some 80 Camels,[162] which were shipped from the Amoor

159. The deposits were kettle terrace deposits, probably valley bottom terraces containing kettle holes, formed where a stream floodplain was constructed over stagnant ice blocks that left kettle holes upon melting. See Fulton, *Quaternary Geology*, 24.

160. Henry Ingram (d. 1879) was an American miner and packer who worked in the Cariboo then bought land at Grand Prairie (now Westwold) in the early 1860's.

161. Andrew J. Kirkpatrick (d. 1891), along with his wife Agnes, not only ran a farm but also operated a renowned stopping place for travellers.

162. For a further discussion of these camels and their arrival in British Columbia in 1862, see W. T. Hayhurst, "The Camels in British Columbia," in Okanagan Historical Society, *Sixth Annual Report* (1935), 244-51. The last of the six camels Ingram brought

River in Siberia. One vessel carrying them was ice-bound & the animals starved, the other landed 24 at San Francisco, which from there were brought up here, & used for packing on the Wagon Road. They were voted a nuisance, however, & prohibited on account of the fear which horses & mules entertained of them, rendering it impossible to pass them. Three of the Camels are still at Grand Prairie, the others having been killed or lost. The three are all females, unfortunately, & all born in B.C. They work well as draught Animals, stand the winter admirably, being even more hardy than the Cattle with which they run. Their hair, or wool, is said by Ingram* to be worth $1.00 a pound in New York, & should be a profitable culture at that.

[verso]

Rocks. It would appear probable, at present, on the whole, — that the Gneissic Series of Okanagan, the rocks of Cherry Creek &c. are the lowest, the limestone (or limestones & other associated beds?) next, & the green rocks like those of the Nicola Lake &c. overlying. The whole of these *may* be conformable & form one great series, though this cannot yet be proved clearly. The typical L.C.C. would represent the Limestones & some way below them. Do the Green rocks = the problematical *upper Cache Creek*. It will probably be necessary to visit Richardson's* typical locality.[163]

[end verso]

July 21. Horses away & start not quite so early as usual. Travelled across to *Duck's*[164] on the Thompson River, Called 20 miles — Day again very warm & sultry, & mosquitoes exceedingly troublesome at Camp.

Pass through another of these peculiar watershed valleys with a chain of small lakes & ponds, so common in this country.

July 22. Horses off again, & from their tracks have apparently taken the

to his farm died around 1896.

163. The gneissic rocks of the north Okanagan east of Lumby are now identified as Monashee Group of the Shuswap Complex, or as Okanagan Plutonic and Metamorphic Complex and undifferentiated phyllites (Cherry Creek locality) of Mesozoic or earlier age. The limestones are nearly all late Paleozoic in age. The "green rocks" now called greenstones or metavolcanics are in part of Triassic age (the Nicola Group rocks of the Nicola Lake area), but other greenstones are now recognized as belonging to earlier stratigraphic units. Dawson and his successors, until about a decade ago, thought in terms of the rocks accumulating relatively close to their present sites; they set these in a logical order from most to least metamorphosed and from older to younger as indicated by their fossil content. The interpretations are now no longer so simple.

164. Jacob Duck was an Englishman who came to British Columbia in 1863 to participate in the Cariboo gold rush but instead headed south to what is now Monte Creek, on the South Thompson River. Duck pre-empted land bordering the river and, with Alex Pringle, operated a well-known roadhouse.

straight road to their old Kamloops range. The stage from Okanagan appearing about 9.30 & the animals not yet back, decided to get on board, & reached the metropolis in time for lunch, meeting Jacinto & the animals on way back to Camp, when a few miles out from Duck's*.

Read up news, wrote home for morning mail. Ross* in here, but leaves this evening for below. Perry* expected down here with his trial line tomorrow.

The Indian commissioners[165] now here, though going down to Savona's ferry this evening on a short visit. Some difficulty found in arranging with them their reserve &c. the war now in progress in Idaho between their relations & the U.S. no doubt serving to make them extra troublesome. Find also that some anxiety here among the whites, & also among settlers in the Spellcumuchen valley[166] as to the attitude of the Indians, Various disquieting rumours being afloat.[167]

G. M. Dawson to Margaret Dawson*, 22 July 1877, Kamloops

Here I am back in Kamloops after having completed my first round. I arrived here this Morning, from Duck's* 18 miles up the South Thompson. The horses last night, finding themselves so near their old well known Kamloops 'range' took the liberty of striking for home, & after waiting for them a long time, I finally decided to get on the weekly stage from Okanagan which happened to pass, & leave the Camp to come in at leisure. We met the packer with the captured horses on the way here, but the Camp has not yet arrived.

We have been having very warm weather the last ten days or so, the thermometer ranging above 90 every day in the afternoon, & probably even higher during the middle of the day when we are generally travelling & have no time to observe. They say that here at Kamloops it has been above 100° on several occasions. The nights are generally cool, however, &

---

165. The three commissioners, Archibald McKinlay, Alexander Caulfield Anderson, and Gilbert Malcolm Sproat were members of the Joint Commission on Indian Land established by the Canadian and British Columbia governments to investigate Indian land grievances in the province. The commissioners spent most of the 1877 season in the Kamloops-Okanagan region. See Robin Fisher, "An Exercise in Futility: The Joint Commission on Indian Land in British Columbia, 1875–1880," *Canadian Historical Association Historical Papers* (1975): 79–94.

166. Probably the Spallumcheen Valley.

167. The reserve commissioners were so disturbed by the depth of Indian disaffection they found in Kamloops that they wired Ottawa claiming "Indian situation very grave from Kamloops to American border —- general dissatisfaction —- outbreak possible" (G. M. Sproat and A. C. Anderson to minister of interior, 13 July 1877, Canada, Indian Reserve Commission, Correspondence, quoted in Fisher, *Contact and Conflict*, 192).

this evening it is pleasant with a fine breeze blowing. I do not find the heat at all trying or oppressive, & am besides assured that we are not likely to have any more weather so warm this Summer. My plans are not yet quite settled for the next move, but it will probably be towards Shushwap Lake, which I hope to circumnavigate I think it will be pleasanter to do this while the weather is warm & fine & keep the autumn for additional land travel, However, when plans are fixed I will let you know. The mail closes this evening & I write now, without looking over a budget of letters lately received, some of which may require answers, & all acknowledgement, merely to catch it; Confessing at the same time, that instead of devoting myself to correspondence on first arrival, I took the opportunity of perusing the late papers — Sunday always has a more or less demoralizing effect, anyway; & I have always noticed that we "lay over" a Sunday we get thus demoralized & make a later start on Monday than any morning of the week.

Speaking of Sunday, I have on the table at which I now write a number of Copies of a form of service for travellers &c. specially intended for the use of C.P.RS. parties. It is issued I believe under Mrs Sandford Fleming's auspices, & printed "for private use" by Dawson Brothers. Neatly got up & approved by Anglican, Presbetyrean & Catholic Clergymen.

At Cherry Creek I delayed a little longer than I had intended, several causes cooperating to that end. First the trail in was uncommonly bad, one of the worst I have ever seen to be called a trail at all. Then Mr Vernon* promised to come in to show me a silver lead in which he is interested, & was a day behind. Then one of the above mentioned Sundays Came round, & finally it was proposed that we should go out by a new trail, which was in process & supposed to be nearly finished. My Packer & Indian, with another Indian Mr V. had with him went off on the aforesaid Sunday to blaze a way through to the new trail, but got only about seven miles. On Monday we started, & the animals being light, jumped logs & scrambled through bogs without much difficulty to a Creek about 8 miles off. From there Mr V. set off in the evening to find the Trail makers, who were working under his directions, but returned about dark unsuccessfully. Tuseday we struck off into the woods again, & at about 11 o'clock came on the trail Party, & from there had a good road. From our camp that evening Mr V. who is a great hunter strolled out & found a grizzly bear, but did not succeed in getting a shot at him, while I got a photograph of a mountain near at hand, & then {after} searching round some distance found a Part of the little stream we were camped at large enough & not too boggy to get a sponge bath, after having made a good sized "Smudge" which is now absolutely necessary when thus engaged. Wednesday we travelled on to Mr V's place Coldstream, from which I wrote a line before. This was a "tremenjus" hot day, perfectly Calm, & with the sun blazing steadily down in a way that would almost convince Anyone that it was a period of maximum not minimum *Sun spot*. The thermom. was 99 ½ in the shade when we got in, & we were glad to get a drink at the spring giving a name to the place, which rises at once out of the ground, cool & clear, & large enough to turn a mill. Mr V. has a fine large farm herc, very prettily situated, with a little flour mill & other improvements. He & his brother[168] have been here about 12 years, & his brother now being Minister of Public Works in Victoria he lives here quite alone in a cottage something after the style of a Cacouna house,[169] half the time cooking & doing all other necessary duties for himself, acting as J.P. & Gold Commissioner for the district, receiving his weekly budget of papers & periodicals from all parts of the world. He is an Englishman & an ex-officer in some regiment, & his father owns a fine Mansion Somewhere in Ireland I think, & ships him out a miscellaneous assortment of things supposed to be suitable for life in the Colonies, from time to time. He says he is as a cook good at "fancy fixings" but "somehow does not take an interest in ordinary cooking" such as boiling potatoes &c. As to the "fancy fixings' I can speak as he had made a very excellent Cake at the time of my visit.

The mail is closing!

July 23. Morning got specimen's packed, Some writing done, &c. & took the sun at noon for latitude. Afternoon writing & reading, not feeling very well. Evening went up to See Perry* who moved camp across the South River[170] & to within less than a mile of here today. Got specimens of the Coal from North River from him. It appears necessary to visit this locality from its proximity to the Railway line.

[verso]

Kamloops July 23. 1877. Obsn. for latitude

168. Forbes George Vernon (1843–1911) was chief commissioner of lands and works in the British Columbia government from 1876 to 1878. Vernon spent most of his early years in the province acquiring land and building up the Coldstream Ranch, but after the ranch was sold in 1891 he became agent-general for British Columbia in London and remained there until his death.

169. Cacouna (now St-Georges-de-Cacouna) was a resort community on the south shore of the St. Lawrence River, just east of Rivière-du-Loup, in Quebec. Throughout the 1860's, the Dawson family vacationed in Cacouna. For a detail and description of a Cacouna house, see G. M. Dawson to Anna Lois Dawson, 21 June 1867, Dawson Family Papers, MUA.

170. South Thompson River.

Sun on Meridian		119°	6′	30″
Index error			4	38

	2	119	1	52

	2	59	30	56
[Sun?] diameter		–	15	47

	59	15	9
refraction	–		35

	59	14	34
Par–	+		4

true alt.	59	14	38	
[Zen.?] distance	30	45	22	N.
Reduced declination	19	57	11	N.

Lat. by obsn.	50°	42′	33″	N.

[end verso]

July 24. Making various arrangements & purchases during the morning. Afternoon rode up to a prominent hill about 3 m. off to get bearings & examine the rocks. Found a volcanic breccia with bombs.[171] Wrote letters till late in the evening.

[verso]

Obsn. for Lat. July 24.

Sun on meridian 118° 41′ 20″

Giving with corrections as above

Lat 50° 41′ 59″

Mean of Obsns of Jy 23–24 = Lat 50° 42′ 16″

[end verso]

July 25. Got remaining paking & overhauling of equipment through & in the afternoon rode up to the camp to see that all ready there. The mail arrived at about 10 P.m. this evening bringing up a whole budget of letters & papers for me. A fortnights lot. Read recent papers, & letters & changed photo. plates & boxes ready for the new Campaign.

July 26. Get the pack train off pretty early, & started after it myself with Douglas* about 10 A.m. Track surveyed the route & examined rocks in the few places they appear, Camping at Ducks* (Duck & Pringles) got a

---

171. Large discrete masses of molten lava ejected into the air from a volcano.

bath, wrote up notes, read & turned in. Day hot, but not excessively so.
[verso]
Lake formation & Classes of lakes.[172]
1. Rock basins. Are there any proved in B.C. Fraser or Francois Lakes?
2. Lakes caused by original subaqueous arrangement of drift by currents or otherwise. Lakes of Lac Ronde Series,[173] Pool between Osoyoos & Okanagan on trail &c.
3. Caused by interruption of draniage by washing down of terraces of drift deposits, with formation of fans, generally or often in large lake bottoms, which subsequently lowering are divided up into several small lakes Fans also may be quite independent of drift & originate in natural decay of rocks, but in consequence of great quantity of drift deposits this not usual
4. Lakes Caused by moraines, Na-tal-Kuz, Buckhorn Lakes[174] & &c. &c.

Others due to causes of mixed character embracing one or more of the above factors. But nearly all depend in one way or other on the glacial period, & thus bear out Ramsay's* views,[175] though in many or most cases may not be actual rock basins, generalization yet holds.

Summit lakes, & strings of lakes in old valleys, especially where crossing summit. Instance as far N. as Smoky R. (see acct. Jarvis' Expedition)[176]

Absences of lakes in Cal. Oregon & W.T.[177] Possible elevation of country so as to alter drainage slopes. Tertiary lakes of Lignite formation probably thus caused by Mt. elevation & not as lakes now are here, due to drift &c.

---

172. Dawson's is a perfectly valid classification of lakes. Many if not most of the interior British Columbia lakes are held up, though not necessarily completely created to their full depth, by alluvial fans.

173. Or Round Lake. See description on 19 July 1877.

174. "Na-tal-Kuz Lake" is on the upper Nechako River; the "Buckhorn Lakes" are just south of the Chilanko River.

175. Dawson was referring to the theory of Sir Andrew Ramsay that great moving ice sheets, in favourable rock situations, scooped out depressions which subsequently became lakes. See A. C. Ramsay, "On the Glacial Origin of Certain Lakes in Switzerland, the Black Forest, Great Britain, Sweden, North America, and Elsewhere," *Quarterly Journal of the Geological Society of London* 18 (1862): 185–204.

176. E. W. Jarvis, under the auspices of the CPRS, led a survey team through the Smoky River pass in the winter of 1874–75. In his account of the traverse, Jarvis says of the lakes around the summit that they "lie in a long deep gorge running due east and west through the mountains, about a mile wide, and perfectly straight for seven or eight miles" (E. W. Jarvis, "Appendix H. Report on Exploration Across the Rocky Mountains by Smoky River Pass," in Fleming, *Report on Surveys 1877*, 153).

177. The scarcity of lakes in California, Oregon, and southeastern Washington stems from the limited extent of glaciation within these states. However, other origins for lakes apply there, such as volcanic collapse to form Crater Lake and faulting to form Klamath Lake.

? Can the absence of Terraces W. of Cascades be attributed to the great
rainfall removing them as soon as exposed: Probably great destruction in
such a country, but dry climate of interior almost equally poor for preservation of terraces. Absence of protecting vegetation & sudden floods. In
north with moderately heavy rain & rank vegetation well preserved.
[end verso]

July 27. Off pretty early, & travel on to Chase's Farm[178] at the lower end
of Little Shuswap Lake, making track Survey & examination of the rocks.
See Chase*, an extraordinary looking character — & try to make arrangements about Canoe &c. Engage an Indian on Chase's* recommendation,
who appears smart, & has the appropriately nautical name of Noah. The
only large Canoe I can hear of is one belonging to Chase*, but ten miles
down the river. Send a couple of Indians to bring her up, which they do,
but she proves considerably cracked &c. & it is evident that if we are to
make the voyage in her, it will take a day to put her in order. This must be
done tomorrow, or I must endeavour to hear of some other more suitable
Craft.

Day quite warm but, now that the sun is down rapidly cooling.

There are several very pretty looking farms along the river in todays
journey, & other places which with water — which might be pumped from
the river by windmills — would make good fields, though not farms of
great size. The water reaching the Thompson on this side is very little. The
country above must either be excessively dry, or drain off to the South
almost entirely. *Shushwap prairie*, on which Chase*, McBryan,[179] & one
or two? others have farms is an extensive flat, standing perhaps 15 or 20
feet above the lake & river. Fine land, & plenty water from a large Creek
coming in at Chase's*.[180] The area of the prairie may be about 2 square
miles or more, of which part is under cultivation, but all might be.

This prairie forms the South Western shore of the Little Lake It is flat &
does not suggest the character of a "fan" but may be due to deposit from
the large brook at Chases*, shoaling the lake when at a higher level, &

178. Whitfield Chase (1820–96) was the first settler at the foot of Little Shuswap Lake. Born
in New York, he arrived in British Columbia in 1853, mining in the Cariboo and working at various jobs around Kamloops before settling at Shuswap Lake in 1865. Chase
not only operated a sizeable ranch but also ran a store and hotel. See Mary Balf, *Chase:
The Man and the Village* (Kamloops: Kamloops Museum, 1980).

179. Alexander McBryan (d. 1911) gold mined in the 1860's then worked for several years as
a packer for the Hudson's Bay Company before pre-empting land in the Shuswap Lake
area in 1873. McBryan also ran a small store and hotel. Construction of the Canadian
Pacific Railway destroyed McBryan's ranch by slicing through the property and ruining
his water supply.

180. Chase Creek.

now draining it. The river finds its way out near the foot of the higher benches on the N. side of the valley.

July 28. Undecided whether to take the large old Canoe offered by Chase*, or two smaller ones, from the Indians. Visited Chase*, & found out what assistance we could get in the way of tools &c., & eventually decided to take & repair the large Canoe. On getting her out of the water, however, found so much work necessary, that went over to Indian village[181] to see what could be done there. After much talk, found that though some canoes which would do well enough, the owners Cared so little about loaning them, & asked such ridiculously high prices, that we could come to no terms. The Chief, anxious to keep things smooth on the eve of the Commissioners visit, appeared to think I might be offended at the demands of his Indians, & volunteered the information that if *he had* a canoe, it would be at my service for nothing, but that the Canoes I wanted did not belong to him & he could not make the owners part with them. He appeared very anxious that I should walk round & see his garden, — a few patches of potatoes & vegetables, irregular & unfenced — & especially that I should see his "ians" (onions) I supposed that he wanted me to buy some, but went with him, & found that it was his intension to make me a present. With many well sounding words, — rendered for me into Chinook by an attendant satelite — as to the *Klooshness* of his *tum tum*[182] &c. he pulled up a handfull of the largest of his little onions, & with a majestic wave of the arm presented them to me. I could not do otherwise than accept, & complement him on the beauty & fertility of his gardens; & in the afternoon took the opportunity of reciprocating, by presenting him with some tobacco Another long negotiation was subsequently opened as to my getting another Indian, but eventually succeeded in Securing the services of a man Called *Norass*, after diplomatic troubles to which the "Eastern Question"[183] is not a circumstance, but which will never, fortunately, appear in history. Finding that nothing else could easily be done, we set to work in earnest on the big old Canoe, which I propose to call the *Pseudomorph* Collected gum, nailed strips of blanket & tin over the gummed & caulked cracks. Scraped & shaped her bottom, made oars & paddles, strengthened her with thwarts &c. &c. When first put in the water she leaked badly, & had to be again taken out, dried by fire & gummed inside & out, & it was not till nearly dark that she was

181. This village is probably the one occupied by Niscanilth's people and was probably named for him. See Gilbert Malcolm Sproat to superintendent general of Indian affairs, 27 August 1877, Department of Indian Affairs, RG 10, vol. 3611, file 3756–12, PAC.

182. A Chinook Jargon expression meaning "delight or happiness."

183. That is, the issues surrounding Russia and Turkey in the eastern Mediterranean.

reported sea worthy.
[verso]

These are the Indians who have lately come down from Adams L, & want a reserve here,[184] in a better country for agriculture & stock. The appear to be living now chiefly on a small species of white fish (?) which they Catch in abundance with hook & line in the lake; together with a few potatoes from their gardens. Two or three canoes are generally out fishing on the lake, & now & then from one of them their proceeds across the water a snatch of their peculiar grunting sort of song. There are a good many families camped, forming a little village. Some in tents, more or less decayed, & all badly pitched (as is invariably the case) most under lean-too's of poles & bark. I saw a pot full of the fish, cooking over the fire, which arrived at the proper stage, was removed & the fish taken out & spread on a piece of Cedar bark. The various members of the family group then squatting round the bark, proceeded, quite unabashed by the presence of strangers, to eat the fish This they did without condiment or accompanyment of any kind, lifting the food to their mouths in the most natural manner in their fingers, & using two hands when the extraction of the little bones, which are numerous, became difficult. They hope to see the salmon up here soon.
[end verso]

G. M. Dawson to J. W. Dawson*, 28 July 1877, Little Shuswap Lake

I suppose I must write another unsatisfactory little note, just to tell you of my arrival here, & intension of leaving tomorrow morning for the Great Shushwap Lake. We got here yesterday afternoon, & have been occupied all day today in putting a great dug-out Canoe, which I have loaned for the occasion, in order. She has not been used for some time & had to be scraped, caulked, pitched, & mended in all sorts of ways, besides fitting paddles &c. We have got her tight & seaworthy at last, I believe, & though not a graceful looking craft I hope she may prove useful. In some respects I would rather have had two smaller canoes, but the Indians here were so exhorbitant in their demands & had such poor canoes, withall, that I decided to take this, which was made by & is now owned by a white man, the last settler up in this direction.

I am taking Douglass*, with my Indian Johnny, & two other Indians from this place, who appear to be active & Good. It may be a fortnight or

---

184. A group of Adams Lake Indians, under Chief Andre, had moved to a small parcel of land on Little Shuswap Lake. They found the winter too severe to raise cattle but wanted to retain the land as summer pasture. See Gilbert Malcolm Sproat to superintendent general of Indian affairs, 27 August 1877, RG 10, vol. 3611, file 3756–12, PAC.

more before I get back here again, as so much depends on the continence of fine calm weather. We have got a good Stock of provisions, besides fishing apparatus & a gun & so ⟨stand⟩ {run} no risk of starving

July 29. Went up to Chase's* to pay him for materials supplied & return tools &c. also to make various little arrangements about things to be left &c. Got Jacinto off with the Animals towards Kamloops, with orders to leave there again for here on August 8th. Loaded up Canoe & put off. Examined S. shore of Little Lake & camped some miles along N shore of Great Lake. Stopping for lunch about half way up the river connecting the two.[185] Made rather slow progress, & stopped early to gum some additional Cracks, though on the whole the Canoe tolerably tight. Windy & rather rough part of the time, with frequent little showers, rendering traveling, & especially track surveying unpleasant. Wandered away in the evening over the partly open hills, which here border the lake & Still show abundant P ponderosa, in search of game, but Saw nothing. Read, write up notes &c. & turn in, with a dull overcast sky, which though lighting up during the latter part of the afternoon, now appears again to "threat our house."
[verso]
  Advanced Noah by payment to Chase* $1.00
  "   Norass   "   "   3.00
[end verso]
  Tent pitched within a few feet of the waters edge, & looking out on the lake, which continues to lap rather Sullenly on the gravelly shore.
July 30. Off pretty early & travel till 5.20 with exception of lunch stop, & other little delays. Camp near the great bend of the lake, on the north shore. Day fine, with little wind, but rather too warm in the afternoon. Try the spoon-bait between various points but with no success. Copper Island, the Indians tell me is the only one in the lake, It is remarkable in its abrupt southern front & northern Slope following the dip of the beds. The water around it is deep, & the cliffs of rocks & broken masses may be seen clearly running down till the green colour of the water becomes too dark. Feeling sure that the usual monsters would be credited with inhabiting this lake, & thinking likely that they would be associated with this Solitary island, I proceeded to enquire, & found that it was even so.[186] Told that a

185. South Thompson River.

186. Dawson later added: "I had previously (in 1877) heard from the Indians that a monster or monsters of some kind lived about Copper Island. Mr. J. McEvoy subsequently ascertained that here also habits similar to those attributed to the 'water people' of Adams Lake were given to those of Copper Island. It is stated that they were here killed by three wood-peckers" (Dawson, "Notes on the Shuswap," 36). In the same article,

creature "all same as bear" formerly lived under the water near the Island, used to eat the Indians &c. Further told, that in the little lake, during winter, many little animals like horses Came out one night from the water, & running about on the ice, were known by their tracks & dung in the morning. This is said to have happened only about six years ago.

[verso]

Sun at Lunch Point, Noon = 115° 25' 50"

[end verso]

July 31. Travelled on about 14 ½ miles, camping pretty early as Noah informs me there is no flat ground for camping for some distance ahead. Day fine with light variable breezes, & not oppressively hot. Lake now more fiord-like, with little flat land along shore & few spits stretching out into it. Rock seen everywhere

[verso]

Observed sun at noon — Lunch Point — but lost the exact moment when on meridian, the reading giving probably a *slightly* too small alt. 114° 39' 30"

[end verso]

A poor dog, nearly starved, was seen on the shore where we landed to camp, he has evidently been left, accidentally or otherwise by some Indian, & seems now half afraid to approach though weakly barking at us with a poor remnant of defience on our first landing — as though left in charge.

A wonderful profusion of berries on the little ⟨....⟩ point where we are. The black berried haw — some bunches now ripe — Service berry — rather over ripe, berry of the large white flowering raspberry in great profusion. Wild cherries coloured but not quite ripe (Choke cherries nearly ripe in some places) Mahonia. Red berried *Vaccinum* (see specimens) Black berried raspberry (not a blackberry). Pigeon berry — ripe. Also sarseparilla beries[187] ripe.

Cedar & P. monticola now abundant along shores of lake, but no trees of great size.

August 1. Raining when I awoke this morning, giving us an excuse for a longer lie than usual. Rain continuing & even increasing, did not start till after noon, when prospect of clearing. Travelled on to former site of

Dawson records various other "stories" of the Shuswap Indians (ibid., 28–38). For a more recent collection of Shuswap stories, see Randy Bouchard and Dorothy I. D. Kennedy, eds., *Shuswap Stories* (Vancouver: CommCept Publishing, 1979). They include "The Water Monster," 85–88.

187. The "black berried haw" was the black hawthorn, *C. douglasii*; "Red berried *Vaccinum*" probably the red huckleberry, *Vaccinium parvifolium* Smith; "Black berried raspberry" the blackcap or black raspberry, *Rubus leucodermis* Dougl.; and "sarseparilla" the sarsaparilla, *Aralia nudicaulis* L.

Seymour, where now only the ruined walls of one house standing. Several showers during the afternoon, with rumbling of distant thunder

This is a romantic & pretty little spot for a town, if the Big Bend excitement[188] had only continued.

Got the Indians to paddle me round the bay at the end of the lake in hopes of getting some ducks, but saw only two, getting a shot but too far off for the light charges I have loaded.

Any quantity of raspberries & service berries on the old town site.

Aug. 2. A shower about daylight in the morning made me fear another wet day, but on getting up about 5 a.m. (having now come to the conclusion that this is early enough for all purposes) found the weather fine & clearing, with masses of mist rolling about the Mountains, or clinging to their sides. Got Canoe packed, & took a couple of photographs,[189] one looking up to the head, the other looking down the lake. Stopped for lunch a little before noon, & got the sun Just in the nick of time. The weather at Seymour so bad that unable to determine its latitude directly. In the afternoon a heavy thunder storm coming on, forced us to land & covering the ictus in the Canoe, to shelter in the bushes for about three quarters of an hour. Set off again, & camped about half a mile from the Narrows[190] leading into the other lake. The last portion of our voyage being tempestuous with a heavy breaking sea which made us glad enough to round a rocky point & land. Evening Showery with heavy thunder clouds hanging about.

Observed glaciation[191] in one place today on a vertical rock face near the water. The grooves being horizontal & parallel to the lake. This is the first undoubted instance yet found, & very remarkable that no more. May be that lake in lowering to present, remained long enough at each level to

188. The "Big Bend excitement" was a gold rush to a stretch of creeks along the Columbia River. In late 1864, a party sent by Governor Seymour to find a wagon route to the Kootenays prospected along the Columbia and found gold in paying quantities. News of the find spread quickly and by 1866 thousands of miners flooded into the area. However, the shallow diggings were rapidly exhausted, and the rush soon collapsed as miners moved to better paying localities. The town of Seymour, the transfer point where goods were loaded off steamers on Shuswap Lake for the overland crossing to the gold fields, prospered for a few years during the rush. At its peak it had twenty buildings. When the rush ended in late 1866, the town quickly died.

189. See "Photographs," 2 August 1877, GSC186–C1 (PA 51058), and GSC187–C1 (PA 51057).

190. Cinnemousun Narrows.

191. Dawson seems to be looking to striated surfaces as the primary evidence of glaciation, perhaps because he was ascribing till and erratics to the action of floating ice. Many of these latter signs of glaciation, such as large areas of fluted or drumlinoid terrain and marks of glacier-diverted streams, are found at both Shuswap and François lakes. Well preserved striated surfaces, however, are uncommon.

efface glaciation. However it may be accounted for it shows that it is by no means peculiar to François L. (absence of striation) & considering how little suited most rocks there to preserve marks, not strange that none seen. To a certain extent there is a repetition in this lake also of the *local character of boulders & beach pebbles*, though not so striking. The two lakes similarly situated, one to the Coast range however, the other to the Gold.
[verso]
obsn of sun at noon for Lat. at Lunch stop. Aug 2. 1877.
Uncorrected Double alt 113° 30′ 50′
[end verso]
At the head of the lake, the snow covered mountains of the Centre of the Gold Range are not seen, being concealed by lower & [reared], from various points today mountains covered with immense fields of snow are seen, & probably hold glaciers. The same thing observed at Cherry Creek, where the Snow Mts seen from Coldstream are invisible.

Terraces well marked on some of the mountains across today at various levels to a height of 1000 to 1500 feet at least. All narrow, however, & tree clad, coming out strongly under certain effect of light

Aug 3. A dark lowering morning with great masses of cloud & mist covering all the mountains, & drooping down on the lake. Rain set in soon after we got up, & shortly followed by wind, which raised such a sea that we were obliged to put down skids & draw the canoe up. Remained packed up all the morning, but no chance of getting off till near noon. Got lunch & then left, Crossing the Sinnemousam Narrows,[192] & then taking the west shore towards Salmon River. Camped nearly opposite Shickmouse Narrows[193] of the map. Showers at frequent intervals during the afternoon, making everything very uncomfortable, & a squall rising just as we were making for a sandy point to camp, obliged us to make for shore, & camp on a sloping pebble beach a little short of the intended locality. Drew the Canoe up, got Camp in order, wrote up notes & to bed.
[verso]
Unexpected complication of rocks of Shuswap L. throws light on the arrangement of the auriferous regions in the Gold Range. Also affords an interesting study of the manner in which the depressions are dependent on the Geol. features.
[end verso]
Aug 4. A day of trouble & difficulty. During the night, the constant lashing of the waves on the gravel at the door of my tent, never ceased, & the

192. Cinnemousun Narrows.

193. Sicamous Narrows.

wind though mostly passing overhead, every now & then Came in a gust, making the dying embers of the fire crackle & glow. Fearing for the safety of our "Pseudomorph", went out once in the night to See about her, but the weather, playing round one shirt tails, soon sent me back to blankets again. Morning opened with wind & rain, these Continuing prevented our getting off. Sat in tent & read. About 10 A.m. Saw a canoe dancing over the waves towards us, which proved to contain three Indians from a camp near Shickmouse narrows, across the lake. Their Canoe[194] [illus.] one of the *P. Monticola* bark, of the peculiar shape I have no where else seen but in B.C.! [Illus.] Extremely fast, & sea worthy to an extraordinary degree. After lunch, the weather looking more favourable, we packed up & embarked but were forced to take shelter behind a point only one third of a mile from Camp, by a squall of wind & rain. Lost much time here, & seriously thought of camping again, but eventually got off, & made a couple of miles or so further. In bucking out a specimen at one of the points, several splinters of hornblende schist[195] flew up into my right eye, & stuck there, being very painful & rendering me nearly blind for the time being. Weather again looking bad decided to camp & get mirror unpacked, did so & succeeded in extracting the splinters.

Camp in a pretty retired little cove, with sandy beach, & rocky points on each side, a charming place, but the dull stormy weather placing it at a disadvantage. Rigged up a fishing rod & succeeded in catching several good sized fish of the pseudo-white fish kind, of which a couple came in well for supper.

Aug 5. Off in good season, & with fair weather made easy progress Southward & South-westward. From the Indians account of the lake I had supposed that the map is quite wrong in regard to form & length of Salmon R. arm. This proves correct, the arm forming an extensive addition to the lake as hithertoo Known. Camped rather early, being Sunday, on a Sandy point on the West shore of the enlargement at the South end of the Salmon R. arm, which I propose to call Mallard Pt; as here, during the evening I shot eight fine mallard Ducks,[196] Which will constitute a pleasant relief from the monotony of bacon. Sat up late, getting an obsn. of Polaris, & another for time, my watch now being too far out to correct the lat. obsn.

194. Dawson later added: "the inner side of the bark, stripped from the tree in one piece, becomes the outer side of the canoe, which is fashioned with two sharp projecting spur-like ends, strengthened by wooden ribs and thwarts internally; the whole is lashed and sewn with roots, and knot-holes and fissures are stopped with resin" (Dawson, "Notes on the Shuswap," 14–15).

195. A rock consisting essentially of oriented crystals of the mineral hornblende.

196. Mallard, *Anas platyrhynchos* L.

Water of lake 70° when well aggitated by the wind.
[verso]

	(	Aug 5. Mallard Pt. Shuswap L. 8h 59m 30s
	(	by watch. Polaris (uncorrected) 100° 37′ 40″
double	(	
angles	(	Obsn. of —— for time. Watch 9h 27 ¼ m
	(	Star (uncorrected) 62° 14′ 10″

[end verso]

Aug 6. Off early, being a beautiful morning. Skirted round the great bay into which Salmon R. flows,[197] & which is low & swampy along shore, everywhere, but may, with the lower part of the Salmon R. valley, which seems quite flat, contain a Considerable area of land eventually arable, — now thickly timbered. If cleared would need no irrigation. Some of the benches would probably answer for agriculture, & the low undulating country about White Lake Creek.[198] Examined & sounded the entrance of Salmon River, & find it too shallow even at this stage of the water, for anything large to go up, being about 4′ on the bar, but deeper within. The river itself is also narrow & tortuous & does not look as if it could be navigated under any circumstances, though the Indians say Slack water extends to within a few miles of the waggon road. The do not go up it in canoes, because of the great quantity of lodged timber &c. Skirted & examined the whole South Eastern shore of the Salmon Arm, Camping about half a mile beyond an Indian Camp; just in the narrows leading to the Spillamachine L.[199] There are about 6 or 8 families in the camp, all apparently wretchedly poor, & ⟨the men⟩ some of the men as low & villainous looking as any Indians I have seen in this country. They are now spearing by torchlight, in the mouth of Eagle Cr,[200] a species of small salmon, which the Indians assure me does not go to or come from the Sea, but is now ascending from the lake to spawn. — Perhaps a landlocked variety of one of the smaller species of Salmon of this Coast.[201]

Day oppressively warm in the afternoon, but calm & otherwise perfect. *Aug. 7.* Off early, & travelled steadily on, from point to point up the lake, stopping for lunch at the Mouth of the Spellamsheen River.[202] Got obsn.

---

197. Salmon Arm.

198. White Creek.

199. Mara Lake.

200. Eagle River.

201. The kokanee, *O. nerka*, a permanently freshwater form of the sockeye salmon.

202. Shuswap River.

for lat. there, photograph[203] looking up lake, besides sketches & bearings. Sounded the bar at the mouth of the river, finding the deepest channel at this stage of the water from 6 ½ to 7 feet. Afternoon returning along E. shore of lake. Camped a few miles short of Eagle Creek a little after 5 P.m. Wrote up notes, packed specimens, changed plant papers & photo. plates &c.

Day warm & nearly calm, though with occasional light drafts of air going up or down the valley.

In the bay on the South side of the peninsula, a remarkable spring, bubbling up at this season through the water of the lake from a depth of 4 feet or so. (Described in field notebook)[204] The Indians call it *Pł-pł-poopł,* & say that if anyone goes near it, bad weather, wind or rain, is sure to follow.[205]

[verso]

Mouth of Spellamsheen R. B.C.

Aug 7. Obn of sun at noon for lat.

Uncorrected double alt. 111° 37′ 30″

= Lat 50° 44′ 54″

[end verso]

Aug. 8. A warm & very fine & calm day, though now showery with thunder. Travelled on up E. shore of lake, passing the mouth of Eagle Creek, & our former friends the Indians still Camped there. Bartered with one of them for some of the little Salmon, & examined a mineral which was carefully wrapped up in an old handkerchief, but proved to be a few grains of ordinary iron pyrites. Camped nearly abreast of Cinnemousum Narrows at 5 P.m.

Got a photo[206] today, looking up the lake, which should be a fine view, including as it ⟨too⟩ does, a fine pile of the Central snowy Mountains of the Gold range, very picturesque in shape.

Rocks, though for great areas not steeply inclined, undulate, & dip[207] at very various angles & directions, rendering the section comparatively complicated & [....], & very different from that of the opposite Shore.

---

203. See "Photographs," 7 August 1877, GSC188–C1 (PA 51056).

204. See G. M. Dawson, Field Notebooks, RG 45, vol. 134, no. 2797, 76v–77, PAC.

205. Dawson describes it more completely in "Report on the Southern Portion," 25.

206. See "Photographs," 8 August 1877, GSC189–C1 (PA 51055).

207. This area is now known to be underlain by complexly deformed metamorphic rocks of the Shuswap Complex, in which recumbent folds and folded folds are common. It is not surprising, therefore, that notwithstanding the relatively gentle dips, Dawson could not resolve the structure under the circumstances in which he was working.

Shot a white headed eagle[208] today with revolver, at a distance of fully 50 yards.

[verso]

Rocks similar, perhaps originally identical in composition may on subsequent metamorphism take very different characters. Conceive, that just as a dark cryst. limestone in one place, may represent a white marble with graphite specks in another — the gathering together of the colouring material greatly decreasing its effect on the general tint of the rock — So a dark trappean mass, or dark green dioritic & epidotic rock, may by more perfect Crystallization, possibly under different circumstance, be changed to a comparatively pale, whitish, or black & white spotted diorite &c. by the collection of the basic oxides in crystalline hornblende &c. Such considerations serve to explain the possible equivalency of pale C.C. diorities &c. with darker rocks elsewhere.[209]

[end verso]

Aug 9. A stormy night, but fine in the morning. Went northward up the North East arm[210] of the lake, getting a tossing in rounding some points & stopping for lunch on a sandy beach at the head of the arm. The scenery wild, & the sides rising steeply from the water for several miles toward the head with scarcely a vestage of beach anywhere, only a talus of great broken stones plunging down into dark indigo water, with here & there a great tree trunk, blown over by the wind, & pointing to the depths below. one might well imagine ones self in one of the fiords of the Coast, & indeed these lakes are nothing more. The Seymour & Shuswap lake constitute one, the North East arm & Salmon Arm another, & the valley of Eagle Creek & Spellamsheen Arm[211] other. The connections are accidental as compared with the main features of the Inlets. Adam's Lake is doubtless another of the Same series

Got a good latitude at the head of the arm, where a small stream[212] empties in flat ground by several mouths.

Indians occasionally go up this in Small Canoes to the little lake[213] shown on the map.

---

208. Bald eagle, *Haliaeetus leucocephalus* (L.).

209. A well-recognized phenomenon: a little colouring matter finely divided is more effective than the same amount distributed as a few large discrete grains.

210. Anstey Arm.

211. Mara Lake.

212. Anstey River.

213. Actually up Hunakwa Creek to Hunakwa Lake.

Weather very unsettled in the afternoon, with squalls of wind & rain. After waiting some time for cessation of the wind, as a long stretch of Shore with no haven or place to haul up the canoe had to be passed — at last get out, & with some difficulty & not without a little risk made a good long trip in the afternoon, Camping about 2 miles North of Cinnemousun. [verso]

Obsn. for Lat. Head of N.E. arm Shushwap L.

Uncorrected double alt. Sun at noon 107° 40' 00"

Indian Names of Some places on & near the Shuswap L. B.C.

Cīn-i-mousun "The bend"

Shi-hōw-ya. "Sudden melting away of snow". Head of N.E. Arm.

Hun-a-kwa-a-at-kwa. "one lake only" Little lake between last & seymour.

She-whun-i-mēn "They go away" = Seymour.

Kwieship (said quickly) "Buffalo Cr" Quiiest Cr.[214] of map.

Too-woot = Eagle Cr.

Skout-nun-hoo-*looh* {soft.} head of Spellumsheen Arm
        "far off"

Shi-whoots-i-mātl "many soap berries" head of Salmon Arm. {& Salmon River.}

Hoom-a-tāt-kwa. "Sits down in the middle of the lake (= Copper Island.

Hoop-a-kākt-Kwa. White Lake.

whispered.

Kwhe-koit "Slick sawing too & fro with {wind"} Scotch Cr.

Hus-tā-lin.

whispered.

Sik-ka-āx

whispered.

Kwa-ow-oot Little Shushwap L.

Spil-a-mi-chine = "Flat mouth"

Skick-a-mouus "In the middle". (said of men when side by side.

Shtle-al-lum. "many skin canoes in the water" head of Adam's L.

[end verso]

Aug 10. Another night of storm & tempest, but a calm & cloudless morning with just a few mist wreathes on the mountains. Off at 6.15 & made a good day, camping on a point[215] not quite abreast of Copper I. Shot two ducks today with a great expenditure of amunition, one having to be

214. Queest Creek.

215. Reedman Point.

chased all round a bay before captured, & a small teal[216] at that. Sounded Cinnemousun Narrows taking the centre in two places, & getting 10 & 12 fathoms respectively bottom of fine & coarse Sand. Temperature of water of lake this Pm. 68.5°.

Met two Canoes with Klootchmen going up the lake, both of which fought a little shy of our Pseudomorph — with becoming modesty (?) but entered into conversation readily enough when spoken to. The great news that *Hi you* Salmon[217] have come up to the little lake,[218] also that Louis* the Kamloops Chief had fallen from his horse & been nearly or quite Killed.

Aug. 11. Away unusually early, & reached old camp near Chase's at lower end Little Shuswap L. about 4 P.m. Stopped for lunch at the outlet of the great lake, & fixed that point by latitude. See several Indians, who all have one story to tell — *viz* that a great many salmon[219] are coming up. On getting into the river between the two lakes, we find this to be the case, a steady stream sculling up the Current, passing over the shallows under & around the Canoe quicker than we Can count them. hundreds must pass in an hour. They are jumping now in the river opposite our Camp, one plosh succeeding another constantly. The Indians are preparing with pitch-sticks & spears, for their fishery, which the continue all night.

Fine weather today, but very warm in the afternoon

Paid off Noah & Norass, & told them I would say tomorrow whether I will go to Adam's L. &c. Mail brought up by Jacinto, who was here in time & waiting for us

[verso]

Obsn. for Lat. at eflux Gt. Shushwap L.

Aug 11. Sun at Noon 108° 58' 30''
   (uncorrected double Alt.)

[end verso]

Aug 12. Sunday. Did not move Camp. Got specimens packed & other arrangements made. Afternoon rode three miles down the river, & got ferried across to the Indian Commissioners Camp. Staid there for dinner & returned to camp after dark.

Aug. 13. Got all packed up with intension of going across to N. Thompson by Adam's L. trail, but Noah, who was supposed to be

---

216. Probably blue-winged teal, *Anas discors* L., or green-winged teal, *Anas crecca* L.

217. Chinook Jargon for "many salmon."

218. Little Shuswap Lake.

219. Sockeye salmon, *O. nerka*, which spawn in vast numbers in the Adam's Lake/Shuswap Lake system.

engaged for the trip backed out, saying he would only go for $2.00 a day
&c. Made more careful enquiries from the other Indians & found that at
this season some 12 miles of the trail, which passes round the end of
Adam's L. would be more or less under water, with bluffs almost impossible to get horses round, also that even when past this many sticks in the
remainder of the trail. We could no doubt get through, but under the
Circumstances, not knowing of anything of particular interest there, do
not feel justified in sacrificing the time necessary. Swim animals across the
river, get packed, & make a late start, Camping about 3 m. higher up than
Duck* & Pringles. Found a covy of Prairie Chickens waiting for us at
Camp, one of which came in well for supper.

Day exceedingly & breathlessly warm.

[verso]

Adams L. The Indians tell me that Adam's L is about 2 ½ days Canoe
journey long — probably 50 miles. It runs north-Eastward for a few miles,
& then turns north, or a little west of north, & runs quite straight in that
direction. Its head bearing, — according to Norass — About N 40 W mag.
from foot of little Shuswap L. A river emptying in at its head, flows out of
another lake Some distance further on,[220] which is not however described
as being of great size. The valley connecting them is Said to be low & to
hold very fine timber, especially *P. Monticola*. This under present circumstances could not be run down to Kamloops &c. The Adam's L. Creek[221]
being almost completely blocked by drift piles, between Adam's &
Shuswap Lakes. No low land suited to agriculture is reported to exist, &
the Indians say high ⟨land⟩ {mountain} follows along the E. shore of the
lake, the W shore being lower, but still rough & rocky. The lake must be
very deep as it is said never to freeze across, while the Shuswap lakes are
frozen Completely over. Very large Salmon trout in Adams L. A lake
about as large as Little Shuswap L. discharges into Adams L. by a Creek
some miles in length reaching it near the bend, as I understand, on the E.
side.[222] The lake lies between Adams L. & Seymour & is Called White fish
lake,[223] that fish being very abundant there.

A trail goes from the Thompson near Clearwater to the head of Adams
L.

---

220. The Adams River which flows through Tumtum Lake.

221. Adams River.

222. Momich River.

223. The only lake of such considerable size on the east side of Adams Lake is Momich
     Lake, which drains into Adams Lake by the Momich River. The river, however, enters
     Adams Lake almost at the head of the lake.

Gold localities &c. *Eagle R Shuswap L* Mr Mowen[224] tells me some of his men got a good prospect on the N. branch of this river.

Columbia R below the great bend. Pay has been got on benches 40' or so above the river.

[end verso]

Aug 14. Off early & travel on toward Kamloops. Stay behind to examine limestone exposures of great interest, which connect the problematical green or Nicola series with fossiliferous beds. On reaching the ferry near Kamloops, find that Jacinto has stupidly crossed over with everything. Can do nothing but follow him, though had intended camping on the N. bank. Got specimens packed &c.

An extremely warm day, being 94 in the shade late in the afternoon.

Aug 15. Writing up notes, & overhauling *ictus*. Took Sun at noon to correct latitudes recently observed. Shopping, fitting puggary to hat &c.[225]

Got train down & party Camped across the river ready for start tomorrow. Wrote a few letters. A very warm & close day. Mail arrived late, near 10 p.m.

[verso]

Kamloops. Aug 15. 1877. Obsn. for Lat.

Sun at Noon = 106° 55' 10"

(uncorrected double Alt.)

[end verso]

G. M. Dawson to Margaret Dawson, 15 August 1877, Kamloops*

You will see I am now again at Kamloops, having returned from my Shushwap L. trip, which I propose to call the "Cruise of the Pseudomorph" after my good vessel (Canoe) of that name. I have been here all day writing up notes &c. &c. & start tomorrow morning early on a short trip up the N. Thompson to See a coal deposit there. The distance is about 45 miles, & it may be five or Six days ere I return. I had fully intended writing at considerable length to several at home, but the day has been uncommonly hot, & I have been pretty busy, & I have been almost tempted to go off on the present little trip without writing at all, & do so more fully on my return. However, thinking this not quite fair, — here is another of the short & unsatisfactory Kind.

The Shushwap L. trip occupied just fourteen days, all of which were spent in travelling with the exception of three half days, & a few odd hours

---

224. Unidentifiable.

225. Puggree (variously spelled) is a thin scarf wound round the crown of a hat and falling down behind as a shade.

lost from wind & stormy weather. The lake is a large one & very Crooked, & I suppose the Coast line is not much Short of 200 miles, all of which I have now Surveyed topographically & geologically, fixing important points by latitudes. The scenery is very fine. I often wish I Could now & then for a little while change personalities with some of you for half an hour, that it might be properly enjoyed. For myself I seem to have got *saturated* with Mountains &c. to such an extent that they hardly look picturesque to me. The weather is exceedingly warm again now, the thermometer Soaring up among the ninety's almost every day. On the lake we had some warm weather, but as soon as the sun went down the cool air off the lake made it pleasant as we were generally Camped on the very beach, my tent often opening not ten or fifteen feet from the water's edge.

I feel sure there are many things in letters now lying beside me requiring reply or notice, but must defer looking through for them till next time. I remember however, your questions about Eva*. My opinion, founded on little, is that the expense & trouble of sending her to france for a winter would not be warranted by the probable result, & I think you will find William* of the same opinion. She might make a sight seeing trip afterwards at some time with one or other of us if that is considered desirable or necessary. However you must not let my opinion influence you, not much at any rate, as I dont very well know what the educational privileges might be.

William* Is now I suppose home, I must write to him soon in answer to some questions of his. By the way, no one has ever yet told me what he is coming home for. I thought his "Mission" was to occupy the whole summer.

I have been thinking about clothes, & I believe I must have a new black cloth vest & trousers. The vest might open about an inch or an inch & a half lower than the last & both should if possible match my dress coat, a small piece of which might perhaps be obtained for a sample. A Suit of dark tweed for winter, with double breasted vest, Coat, & one pair of trousers would also be desirable. Will it be troubling you too much to ask you to order these from Cathie some time Soon?

In about a week I hope to write again, & meanwhile will look over old letters for points omitted. I have begun to use the travelling cup Father* gave me some time ago, finding a travelling cup very necessary in this peculiarly dry country.

The Salmon are running up here now very numerously. At the outlet of the Great Shushwap L. we could see them as we came down in the canoe, going up over the bars faster than we could count them — thousands in an hour — & this hundreds of miles from the sea after they have come up through all the bad water of the lower Fraser, & run the Gauntlet of the

Canneries below, where they are now being "Canned" at the rate of over 70,000 lbs. A day — Still fat & in good condition. The Indians are making a great harvest.

Aug 16. Breakfast at McPhadens[226] shortly after 6 a.m. & then went down & got put over to camp at the Ferry. Started between 7 & 8 & made fourteen miles to Perry's* Camp. Camping there pretty early. Day excessively warm. Thermometer 94 late in the afternoon, & not a breath of wind. Had a most refreshing bath in the N. Thompson which is much cooler than the South River, & illustrates remarkably well the difference between a stream coming direct from the mountains, & one passing through large lakes. The South River is warm & beautifully transparent with blue colour. The North, turbid & milky but cold. The sand carried by the latter (silt) is mostly pretty [warre?], the individual grains being visible & soon Settling. It has the colour & general appearance of the "White Silt" deposit, but is Coarser. It is peculiarly full of mica also, & quite glistens as it moves in the water. White silvery mica flakes line the sandy beaches in many places.

Johnny having sprained his hand badly the other day, I have a new Indian replacing him for this trip. Today at dinner he innocently put on the table among other condiments my bottle of Insects in Sawdust & alcohol!

Cool & very pleasant now that the sun is down.

Aug 17. Had intended getting out of camp very early this morning to avoid as much as possible the heat of the day, but the horses, who always seem to divine our thoughts in this respect, were nowhere to be found, & before they were hunted up — some miles away, & ready to start, it was very late. Travelled on all day, camping at 4.30, at Perry's* old "Location Camp 20" The weather excessively warm after noon, a little breath of wind which was stirring, following & keeping pace with us. Now, about dark, some clouds gathering with gusts of wind as if for thunder. Some fine & extensive flats along the river, which not having any irrigation priviledges are unoccupied. These, & many of smaller size on the South Thompson, & others elsewhere might easily be brought under cultivation by lifting water from the main river by wind mills — a process no more troublesome than the raising of irrigation water from Artesian wells in the Sacramento &c. Valley, by the same means.

---

226. Donald McPhadden (1847-1918) came to Victoria in 1865, moved to Kamloops in 1870, left for the Omineca country in 1871, and then returned to Kamloops where he operated a store and hotel.

[verso]

The rocks seen yesterday & today evidently represent those of Shuswap &c. but in a less altered state.[227] The green schistose &c. belt of the lake here represented by green rocks seldom schistose, but often evidently volcanic in origin. The schistose appearance may easily be due in part to compression during alteration producing a species of foliation,[228] but is probably in the main to be explained by the presence in particular cases of more fine water bedded volcanic sediments. The black shaly limestone of today almost certainly represents that of S. Shore of Shuswap L. The great mass of the green rocks at Nicola, & on S Thompson, evidently overlie one of the important limestones, & adhere to it. Whether the great mass of the more purely water formed sediments, quartzites argillites[229] &c. with some volcanic matter — occur below the same horizon it is difficult to say; also whether on working the sections out the gneissic, micaceous, & quartzite ⟨band⟩ zone of Shuswap can be shown to result from an aqueo-igneous alteration of this part of the series.

[end verso]

Aug 18. Left Camp about 7 a.m. being again delayed a little by the wandering of the horses — though hobbled. Hoped to reach the Indian Reserve[230] & Coal brook, Soon but the distance turning out much greater than anticipated, did not do so till late in the afternoon. Weather again oppressively hot. Waited about an hour befor the packs arrived, & after getting a cup of tea, set out to look for the Coal, up the little brook on which it is reported. Found some thin coal crops & beds of the Tertiary pretty well exposed. Made a preliminary examination of them, but find I have half a day's work here at least, & must wait tomorrow to do it.

The Indian Reserve flat is an extensive one, & spots are under cultivation. Above it is another long flat, with good grass &c. On the whole much more flat land at a low level on the N. than on the S. Thompson.

Saw many Salmon in the shallow water of Louis, & Barrière Creeks.[231] They appeared to be going up, on the whole, but not very eagerly. With the exception of the heads, ⟨fins, &⟩ tails they look bright red, having lost

227. Modern research does not support Dawson's assumptions, although the correlations are by no means settled. Dawson was looking along the North Thompson River at rocks now mapped as Permo-Carboniferous, not equivalent to the Triassic of Nicola Lake. The limestones and others of Shuswap Lake could also be Triassic although metamorphism has made this correlation very difficult.

228. Parallel orientation of platy minerals or mineral banding in rocks.

229. Hardened rocks composed of clay minerals.

230. The North Thompson Reserve along the east bank of the river.

231. Barrière River.

all their silvery gloss!!

Aug ⟨*20*⟩ {*19*}   Spent the morning examining the sections of Tertiary, including coal, in the brook. The valley very rough & much encumbered with driftwood when followed up. Afternoon rode about 3 miles up the valley to & beyond another brook, but without finding any Sign of coal in it.

Aug ⟨*21*⟩ {*20*}. off before 7 a.m. & travelled steadily till 5 P.m. making about half the distance, which must be good 25 miles, toward Kamloops. Day fine & not too warm.

[verso]

The White Silts[232] extend up at least as far as the Barriere R. forming near it banks 100′ high. They may probably go much further, & be the Cause (secondary) of much of the silty deposit now rendering the river turbid, & being deposited everywhere along the shores as the water falls. Primary cause with little doubt ice action in the mountains. The silts in both branches of Thompson probably laid down when steady but not rapid current flowing down broad arms from which no rapid fall (perhaps near sea level) The apparent absence of silts from Shuswap L would seem to show that at time of deposit ice must have filled its basin. otherwise the silts would as now have been deposited in it, & the *lower part* of valley be free from them. It may be said that the Current carried them out of the upper part of the valley, but the valley does not grow suddenly wide, or show any reason why current in such supposition should not have carried the silts away from its whole length.

The white silts like the river sediment hold much white mica in a finely divided state. When water flowing down over the banks evaporates, or sinks in, it leaves the mica scales arranged parallel to the surface, & gives the exposures a peculiar burnished & glossy Appearance.

232. In a later discussion of white silts, Dawson added: "It is believed that the general correspondence on elevation of the various and more or less separated bodies of water in which this white silt formation was formed, in itself constitutes a strong argument in favour of the hypothesis that these bodies of water were in direct communication with the sea and were governed in their level by that which it held at the time" (George M. Dawson, "On the Later Physiographical Geology of the Rocky Mountain Region in Canada, with Special Reference to Changes in Elevation and to the History of the Glacial Period," *Proceedings and Transactions of the Royal Society of Canada* 8 [1890], sec. IV, 44–45). Later research, though agreeing with Dawson's glacial origin for the silts, has proven him wrong in his idea of a marine influence upon the silts. Current indications are that "downwasting freed the uplands while stagnant ice tongues remained in the valleys, obstructing the flow of melt-water and producing glacial lakes in which extensive silt deposits were laid down. Sedimentation in the lakes was affected by stage of deglaciation at the time of lake formation, proximity to the receding ice-margin, and the influx of meltwater" (Fulton, "Silt Deposition," 553–54). These silts in turn are being eroded by the North Thompson River and contribute to some of its turbidity.

[end verso]

Aug 21. Reached Kamloops this afternoon, Left train & party Camped on N bank of river as wished to ascend Mt St Paul[233] tomorrow, & require horses over there for that purpose.

Aug. 22. Breakfasted pretty early this Morning, with Mr Blair,[234] & then together crossed the river, got horses, & proceeded to ascend Mt St Paul. Three hours climbing brought us to the top, with Scarcely any necessity of dismounting. The slope at the back being comparatively easy, & grassed. A fine view, but today somewhat obscured by mist in the distance. Got a number of bearings & good general idea of the country impossible otherwise to obtain. The extent of open grassed country in this vicinity is very great. The general plateau like appearance of the country, when viewed from a height, contrasts remarkably ⟨for⟩ with its mountainous aspect when Seen from the valleys below only. On this summit — about 3600 feet, the impression is that the general level of the higher hills in every direction is about equal to it, & the Summits in some directions — especially North Westward, appear from a distance to coalesce into almost continuous straight edged plateau. The same sort of thing appears in the region of Shuswap Lake, though the Mountains there are higher, the same at Cariboo, & elsewhere, in fact it seems here as though Mountains when broadly viewed are in reality remnants more or less well defined of plateaux — in this region at least.[235]

The wide valley occupied by the Thompson merges insensibly into that of Kamloops Lake, without any ⟨great⟩ {marked} increase in its width. It is from here easily seen that the lake even with a very slight rise in level must have stretched much further up the valley The lake in fact is a minor incident in the topography of the great valley in which it & the river are.

Returned to Kamloops by 1 P.m. & spent afternoon Packing specimens & making other necessary arrangements. Mail arrived in the evening with a budget which took me some time to glance through before going to sleep.

Aug 23. Packing & rearranging outfit. Getting supplies served out for long trip to the south. Writing letters. A cold Stormy & wet day, So much so, that though I had promised to take dinner at Perry's* camp I made up my mind not to go down. All prepared to start tomorrow morning to Sound the lake, but Ross* coming back this evening had changed arrangements,

233. Mount Paul.

234. Unidentifiable.

235. Dawson was stating a relationship later described as "accordance of summit elevations." Where such summits are represented by more or less gently rolling surfaces, the concept of these being relics of a formerly continuous upland dissected by major stream valleys can be supported. Where the summits are sharp, as in the higher part of the Cariboo Mountains, the case can no longer be made.

— steamer not to be up till 9 or 10 o'clock tomorrow morning &c.

G. M. Dawson to J. W. Dawson, 23 August 1877, Kamloops*

I write again from Kamloops, being here for a day at the Cose of one little trip & the beginning of Another. I think I wrote of my intention of going up the N Thompson about 50 miles, & it is from there that I have just returned. Tomorrow {friday} I hope to go down to the lower end of Kamloops L & return the same evening, Sounding the lake on the way. On Saturday if all goes well I will start for a two or three days expedition to examine the shores of the lake Carefully, & then early next week will get Pack train in order & off again for a long tour, during which the endeavour will be to cover as well as possible the yet unexamined Portion of the block of Country to the South, finishing about Clinton & Marble Cañon by tying in on Mr Richardson's* work of 1871. I am Particularly anxious to see some of his rocks now, especially his Upper Cache Creek group, which may now I think be more definitely placed.[236] I may not get back again to this place till the Close of the working season, when it will take a couple of days to pack up & leave.

Enclosed in this you will find a Note from Mr Dyer[237] of Kew, which though forwarded to me, concerns you more, & has evidently been addressed under the mistake that we were one & the same. There is also an account from Dawson Bros, which might be paid if you have any of my signed cheques left, but if not may lie till my return in the Autumn. You will also find a note from Mr. Craven, Announcing the degree of Princeton[238] about which you wrote, & an acknowledgement of the same, which I do not mail direct not Knowing whether these may be some [....]

236. "It was on the latter road, between Clinton and Lillooet, that Mr. Richardson first observed this group. . . . The base of this group Mr. Richardson supposes to be here, about two miles west of Clinton. The beds have generally a high westerly dip. They consist of a great volume of bluish, dove-colored, and white limestones often a good marble, interstratified with brown dolomitic limestone, red and green shale, and epidotic and chloritic rocks with others which closely resemble rocks of the Quebec group in the Eastern Townships of Canada" (Selwyn, "Journal and Report," 60).

237. William Turner Thiselton-Dyer (1843–1928) played a central role in the botanical life of late Victorian England by helping extend T. H. Huxley's emphasis on evolutionary principles and efforts in laboratory teaching. As assistant director (1875–85) and director (1885–1905) of the Royal Botanic Gardens, he oversaw the expansion of economic botany throughout the British Empire. See also *Dictionary of Scientific Biography*, s.v. "Thiselton-Dyer, William Turner."

238. Elijah Richardson Craven (1824–1908), a Presbyterian minister, was secretary of the trustees at Princeton College for almost fifty years. The correspondence related to Dawson's nomination for an honorary Doctor of Science at the New Jersey college. See Craven to G. M. Dawson, 30 June 1877, Dawson Family Papers MUA.

which should be attended to. If there is I would be much obliged if you could see to it for the present. I am very much obliged to the Princeton people I am sure, though I doubt whether I should not thank you in the first place. I have addressed Mr Craven* as *Rev* as he dates from A Manse & I know no other title for him. One more thing I have to trouble you about. — In writing to Mr Alexander* of Fraser Lake last winter, at the time I sent several books he wanted, I could not get a copy of "Lords Naturalist in B.C." I now have two Somewhere at home, one having been got through Dawson's, the other by some second hand dealer in London. Mr A.* writes that he would like a copy, & I have replied that I will send one of mine. He has remitted the price to the HB Co. at Victoria. If the two copies can be found (*two vols*) please get Rankine* to do up *strongly* the older looking one & address it as per slip enclosed.

J.M.L. Alexander* Esq
H.B. Co. Fort Fraser B.C.
C/o H.B. Company
Quesnelle
B.C.

The abstract of my drift paper Came from the Geol. Society yesterday. It has been in time for the Session, but was apparently read by title with a lot of other papers at the last meeting. I hope they may Publish it in full which will be more important.[239]

This is a sort of business letter, but I have not much at present to tell about myself, & no new discoveries of of interest to report. Yesterday I rode up to the summit of Mt St Paul, so Called, near here. It is 3600 feet in height & there is a very extensive view from it. The day was a little hazy, however; but notwithstanding, clear enough to get a number of bearing on distant points, & a general idea of the country, which were my objects in ascending.

Mr Selwyn* writes that it has been decided to exhibit minerals at Paris,[240] & I suppose it may be necessary to get some from here, Coal specimens at any rate.

---

239. Dawson's "On the Superficial Geology."

240. A reference to the Paris Exposition of 1878, held on a site covering some sixty-six acres in the centre of the city. According to Selwyn, "a very fine and varied collection of the economic minerals of Canada, and a stratigraphical collection of rocks and fossils was secured. . . . This collection was the largest and most complete representation of the geological formations and the mineral resources of British North America ever seen in Europe" (Alfred R. C. Selwyn, "Summary Report of the Operations of the Geological Corps to 31st December 1878," in Geological Survey of Canada, *Report of Progress for 1877–78* [1879], 2).

Aug 24. Went down to Perrys* Camp about 9 a.m. with Douglas* to wait then so stormy & wet that impossible to go out on the lake. Took lunch with Mr Perry* & then returned to town. Hope to get off tomorrow morning, early.

Dined by invitation with Mr Mara[241] the members of the two survey parties invited, but only Perry's* came owing to the very wet & stormy weather. Dinner on board the steamer "Martin".

[verso]

Superstition of the Spellamachine Indians. Told by Bennett.[242] that while a number of Indians engaged making irrigation ditch, noted that on coming into camp they would jump several times over the fire, & also tie up the legs of their trousers before going to bed. Found that this arose from the idea that a little lizzard — which very abundant — if once sighting a man, would follow him seadily by his tracks, till Catching up when asleep, it would enter by a certain aperture & kill him. By crossing the fire they intended to cause the lizzard to do so also & to be destroyed. When they saw the lizzards during the day's work they would take a twig forked at the end, & impaling the lizard on it tie the two ends of the fork together with a piece of grass, & stick the thing upright in the ground by its but end. The lizzard shortly dried into a mummy in this position. If anyone carelessly tossed away one of these lizzards, the Indians would quit work & search dilligently for it till found & secured as above —[243]

[end verso]

Aug 25 up at 6 A.m. & heard the "Pup" whistling when at my break-

241. John Andrew Mara (1840-1920) was a member of the Overlander Party that arrived in Kamloops in late 1862. Mara subsequently became a prominent local businessman and political figure who operated a variety of enterprises including stores at Seymour and Kamloops, lumber and flour mills, and steamers. Mara also served in the British Columbia legislature from 1871 to 1886 and in the House of Commons from 1887 to 1896. See also Thomas McMicking, *Overland from Canada to British Columbia*, ed. Joanne Leduc (Vancouver: University of British Columbia Press, 1981), 81.

242. Dawson could have been referring to either of the Bennett brothers, Preston or Frederick, who operated a ranch in partnership with Moses Lumby. Preston (1840–82), the more prominent of the two, came to the Cariboo in 1862, worked one season in the gold fields, then became a clerk in the Victoria Police Court. He later joined the Hudson's Bay Company in 1864 and worked as a clerk at Kamloops until 1867 when he took up land east of Kamloops on the South Thompson River. After being joined by his brother in 1868, Preston & Moses Lumby pre-empted land in 1870 in the Spallumcheen Valley. Preston was elected to the British Columbia legislature in 1878 and 1882, but died shortly after his re-election. Frederick continued in partnership with Lumby, but sometime before 1892 he left the district.

243. Such superstitions were widespread. This one is retold in Dawson's, "Notes on the Shuswap," 38.

fast. Got everything carried down & set off. Picked up Mr Brunell's[244] party & carried they a few miles down to their work, & then steamed on down to lake where Brunell's canoes left. Intended to spend the day sounding down the lake, but weather quite too rough. Steamer tied up in lee of a point. Got camp arranged, & wind moderating somewhat after lunch set off, & managed to get a few casts of the lead, nearly half way down the lake.

Aug 26 Up early & off. Examining S shore of lake in the larger of Brunell's canoes, a fine craft. Crew consists of self, Douglas*, Johnny, & an Indian Called *Bill* who is minus his nose, & has in consequence a most comical, not to say repulsive appearance. He has been lately paid off from one of the parties, however, & in the matter of clothes cuts me out altogether. Got on well today, with calm water & not too warm. Got photo.[245] of pillars of white silt & gravel near Cherry Cr.

Tried blasting for fish this evening, but killed a lot of very small whitefish only.

Aug 27. Down at Savona's Ferry about 10 a.m. & after a short stay proceeded to examination of N. shore, which turned out a long job from complexity of structure. Camped at mouth of Copper Creek, — proceeded to examine remarkable section of coloured rocks. Supper, & then hard at work till after dark writing notes & packing specimens. Got two photos.[246] today, one of the lower end of the lake, to show nature of barrier, the other from Lunch Pt. of mts on N. shore looking east, Their outlines & detail very picturesque.

More than enough distracted & perplexed by the rocks today. Nature seems to have been preparing geological puzzles hereabout. Cannot get the various volcanic series Satisfactorelly straightened out. It would of course be easy to say volcanic, volcanic, do — do —. & splash a big wash of colour over the whole, but satisfied that in this region two if not more distinct Series, between which in some places all criteria fail.[247] Litho.

244. Unidentifiable.

245. See "Photographs," 26 August 1877, GSC192–C1 (PA 51054).

246. See "Photographs," 27 August 1877, GSC193–C1 (PA 51068), and GSC194–C1 (PA 51067).

247. Dawson's frustration here is understandable. The rocks along the north shore of Kamloops Lake are well exposed but complex. On his map of 1877 (George M. Dawson, *Geological Map of a Portion of the Southern Interior of British Columbia* [Ottawa: Geological Survey of Canada, 1877]), Dawson did indeed "splash a big wash of colour over the whole." On his later map (George M. Dawson, *Kamloops Sheet, British Columbia, Geologically Coloured* [Ottawa: Geological Survey of Canada, 1895]), Dawson subdivided the rocks. For an up-to-date analysis of these rocks, see Thomas E. Ewing, "Regional Stratigraphy and Structural Setting of the Kamloops

criteria because regions near foci *must* have been extremely metamorp ⟨near⟩ even in newest series. Disturbance (amount of) for same reason. Inclusion of fragments to great extent for volcanic products hardening at once may form part of a superposed bed a [day?] or two younger. Stratigraphical evidence of all kinds from the fearfully distorted & jointed character of much of the region. No fossils of course —.

Lignite. Told that abundant in large loose peices from the mouth of Dead Man's Cr down for some distance. Most abundant & largest fragments near mouth of Creek.

Aug 28. Rather overslept myself this morning, & did not get off till nearer 8 than 7. Travelled from Copper Creek to Tranquille Camping on the beach not far from the Mill.[248] Got several soundings today, & a photo.[249] of Cherry Creek Bluff for Brunell, from nearly opposite. Day fine, with light winds & calm, though a little too warm during part of the afternoon.

On the very front of Battle Bluff, a little above high water mark, a fragment a few feet square remains of the original glaciated surface, polished & grooved. The remainder of the cliff is extremely rough faced owing to jointage. The flat spaces is coloured red, & has at one time evidently borne some design of which faint traces yet remain.

Found a broken & worn (beach worn) arrow head near Copper Cr.

[verso]

Told that the Kamloops & some other Indians had at one time a big fight on the lake near battle bluff, & that those of Kamloops coming off best, smeared the face of the bluff with the blood of their enemies. That since that time some of the old Indians, from time to time, renew the mark with red paint.

Told by Wheeler, of Tranquille[250] that he mined 10 or 12 miles up Scotch Creek Shuswap Lake, & that *just above* the gold bearing bar a very wide ledge of quartz *full* of galena[251] crossed the creek, which is here so narrow that one may step over it. He described the ore as lying in large lumps which a man could scarcely lift. They ran some of it into lead.

[end verso]

Group, South-central British Columbia,'' *Canadian Journal of Earth Sciences* 18 (1981): 1464–77.

248. A flour mill and sawmill owned by William Fortune that was originally built in partnership with James McIntosh.

249. See "Photographs," 28 August 1877, GSC195–C1 (PA 51072).

250. John Wheeler.

251. A mineral that is the principal ore of lead.

Aug. 29. Went about 3 miles up Tranquille Cr,[252] by the trail, examining the rocks &c. Looked at some curios, Mr Fortune,[253] at the mill was anxious to show me, & at her garden, & eventually got off again in Canoe. Spent some time at the bottom of the bay E. of Tranquille, looking for the plant locality, but unsuccessfully. Lunched at the mouth of the river, & then had a long & warm pull up stream, getting to Kamloops at 4.30. Got things repacked, & nearly everything ready for start tomorrow morning.

Evening changed & arranged photo. plates. Mail arrived, bringing me some letters, but no papers.

Aug 30. Expected pack animals down at 6 A.m, & up & ready for them. They did not arrive, however, till nearly ten, owing to difficulty in catching them. Spent the time in various additional preparations, writing letters, & getting four boxes of specimens packed & addressed for Victoria. Find my horse needs shoeing all round, & so after getting packs off stay to lunch at Kamloops, & afterwards with Douglas* set off after the train. Get into Camp, 12 miles from K. on the Mountain trail, at 5.30. At work writing up notes, & getting ictus in trim till late.

G. M. Dawson to J. W. Dawson, 30 August 1877, Kamloops*

Yours about Nova Scotia &c. arrived last night, but as I have just written at some length to William*, & My time is limited I cannot do more than acknowledge.

I had a letter from Mr Selwyn* the other day in which he speaks of the Polson Lake Copper,[254] & says he believes many of the rocks of that district are in origin, & *probably also in age* like the Volcanic (altered) lower Silurian of Wales. Felstones &c. I fear he is inclined to go on the lithological resemblances as a test of age, while really, I suppose, there is no interval probably in the simultaneous exhibition of volcanic energy in Wales & Nova Scotia.

I saw lately — in Nature I think — that one of the grants in aid of research — a small one — was given to Rowney & King to aid investigation of *Ophites*; so that we may expect something more of Counterblast to

---

252. Tranquille River.

253. William Fortune (1835-1914) was an Overlander who settled in Tranquille after marrying Jane McWha in 1866. Along with the flour mill opened in 1868, Fortune also ran a sawmill and owned a prosperous ranch. Later in 1878, he built the small sidewheeler, *The Lady Dufferin*, to work on the South Thompson River. See also McMicking, *Overland from Canada*, 81-82.

254. Polson Lake, Nova Scotia.

Eozoön Soon as the result.[255] In this Country much of the probable Carboniferous is altered to about the stage of Laurentians elsewhere, & the other overlying series pro rata, till we get true Coals &c. in Cretaceous & Tertiary. This being so I fear older rocks are fixed past recognition

Aug 31. Had a rather severe touch of diarrhea last night & this morning — an unpleasant visitant in camp. Off pretty early & travelled southward to the junction of the mountain & valley trails. Thence by route formerly examined to foot of Stump Lake, & then across another "mountain" & or plateau ⟨lake⟩ trail, toward Douglas Lake. Camp at a little duck pond, where try to shoot some birds, with poor success the only one killed being lost in the rushes.

This plateau, like that passed over yesterday, undulating, with bunch grass & groves of Douglas firs & poplar, little ragged rocky projections & swamps & pools, generally arranged ⟨line⟩ in linear depressions, but at times apparently current scooped in drift.[256] All more or less "Alkaline" as we learn here to our cost. Splendid feed everywhere, & scarcely any cattle to be seen.

These plateau pools alive with ducks, but without a dog can do little with them. Just about dark flock after flock, from 3 to 20 in a band arrive at the pond. Hurrying along through the air at a tremendous pace, & pitching down at last into the water with a *whir* like a glanced bullet. Putting on the brakes by backing their wings, the flock loosing its regularity as each bird disposes of its extra momentum as best it can.

Sept. 1. Off pretty early, & travel till nearly four P.m. For some time continue over the beautiful rolling plateau, which in part pretty thickly timbered with Douglas fir &c. Then descending a little pass into great open high level valley, with splendid feed, & crossing this, in a few miles reach the edge of the Douglas lake — Grande Prairie valley, at the middle of Chapperon Lake. The valley here looked into open & very pretty, a very large hay swamp, with rows of cocks in process — in the foreground.

255. See "The Endowment of Research," *Nature* 16 (May-October 1877): 117, where William King and Thomas H. Rowney were to be paid by the British government, on the recommendation of the Royal Society, for "Researches to Determine the Structural, Chemical, and Mineralogical Characters of a Certain Group of Crystalline Rocks represented by Ophite." King and Rowney, Irish mineralogists, challenged J. W. Dawson's assertions about the organic origin of the fossil *Eozoön canadense*. The elder Dawson carried on a bitter conflict with the two men for many years. For a summary of J. W. Dawson and the "Eozoön" controversy, see O'Brien, *William Dawson*, 145-50.

256. Dawson was observing drumlinoid topography shaped into streamlined forms by over-riding glacial ice.

Stopped here to get photo.[257] Descend into valley & then continue northward in the depression, which is open, & not well defined like most of
these great hollows. The west side is especially•indistinct. Pass two lakes
after leaving Chapperon, & at Camp find a small brook going out of the
lower,[258] & running toward Salmon R. Find here at Camp, a few stalks of
barley, wheat of two varieties, & oats, grown from seed accidentally scattered from Indian camp. All fine looking, the barley especially. The oats
ripe, the wheat & barley just beginning to turn yellow. Grown on the surface, on a dry hill-side under shelter — in part — of pines. This must be
very nearly 3000' & shows what may be expected of these higher valleys &
even of parts of the plateau, with care, cultivation & irrigation where necessary.

The vegetation of the plateau, where groves of Douglas fir begin to pre-
ponderate, almost in every particular resembles that of the Chilcotin plateau, noted in addition today, abundance of the little astragalus, & some
Geum triflorum, Castilleja, hieracium[259] &c.

[verso]

The peculiar great old valleys of B.C. — of which this one however not
a good type, not only not due to present causes, but not even those, in
many cases now occupied by the main streams. The rivers not infrequently
flow in from more gorge-like valleys, transverse or more or less so — in
direction, & then adopt for a part or the rest of their course the great old
valley. How were these *through* & inosculating valleys formed in the
General plateau of the country.[260]

Would be interesting to Compare denudation of homogenous, uniform
plateau by rivers.

257. The photo is listed in neither Dawson's Field Notebook nor the National Photography
     Collection, PAC.

258. The first lake was Rush Lake, and the second Salmon Lake, drained by McInnis Creek.

259. The "little astragalus" was milk vetch, *Astragalus* spp.; and "hieracium" hawkweed,
     Hieracium spp.

260. Dawson was impressed by his entry into a narrow valley transgressing a higher part of
     the plateau. The Salmon River passes easterly through this narrow section instead of
     turning westerly into the much more open extension of the valley across a relatively low
     plateau: an obvious anomaly whose explanation is not immediately obvious. Stream
     diversion as a result of an early glaciation could have established the valley, and diver-
     sion at the end of the last glaciation might account for the present course of the Salmon
     River into it. Dawson's speculation of a major marine submergence and planation is no
     longer accepted. Instead, it is believed that the land was worn down to a relatively low
     elevation of about fifteen hundred feet relief in mid-Tertiary time, then uplifted and dis-
     sected by streams. The stream-cut valleys were further enlarged and deepened during
     Pleistocene glaciation.

Denudation of plateau slightly heterogenous in comp, as in nature, formation of stream dissected plateau as that of Lig. Tert. at Woody Mt.[261] Possible eventual production of through valleys. Possibility of through valleys having been formed by general tilling of the country from north or south &c.

Then how plateau itself produced. The Tertiary ig. rocks in places give definitiveness, but other & older rocks also conform in general way. It is a plane of marine denudation of Ramsey*, or like such, but what the actual machinery forming these planes? Ramseys* explanation not quite complete or satisfactory.[262]

[end verso]

Sept 2. Though Sunday, as we had got on rather slowly the last few days, determined to do half a day's work. Got off rather late, & travelled till 1 Pm making 8 miles & stopping where some tertiary cliffs to examine. Day fine, though warm after noon, & with passing thunder storms. Shot one good dusky grouse[263] Soon after leaving morning camp leave the open & enter a timbered country. Douglas fir with some P. contorta & ponderosa in open groves, with pine grass, pea vine &c. & bunch grass where little open meadows. Country rather broken & trail, though lately cut out by government, very hilly & rather crooked. The river rapidly cuts down into the country & soon flows in a deep cañon-like valley, which is flat-b ottomed, though narrow. The general surface of the country seems at the same time rather to rise, & is now here rather mountainous.

Sept 3. Make a good early start, & travel till 3.20, Camping about 1 ½ mile beyond the first crossing of Salmon R; on the waggon Road. Eleven miles of travel brought us out this morning on Grande Prairie whence we have repassed on our former route. The valley followed to grande Prairie, by the trail, gradually widens on approaching it, & at its mouth holds a fine strip of land, flat, & with good soil now covered with open growth of *P. ponderosa*. This must average a mile wide, & is several miles long, &

261. At Wood Mountain (lat. 49°22′N and long. 106°23′W), the watershed "is a narrow flat-topped plateau composed of Lignite Tertiary strata, irregular in outline, but with a general east and west course, and furrowed on either side by the vallies of streams which ramify in it, and which, were denudation advanced a little further, might inosculate" (Dawson, *Geology and Resources*, 8).

262. Dawson is referring to Sir Andrew C. Ramsay's work on marine planation, first reported in "The Denudation of South Wales," *Memoirs of the Geological Survey of Great Britain* (London: HMSO, 1846), 297–335, elucidated and modified by publications in the 1870's. See Richard J. Chorley, Antony J. Dunn, and Robert P. Beckinsale, *The History of the Study of Landforms or the Development of Geomorphology*. 1.: *Geomorphology Before Davis* (London: Methuen, 1964), 304–13, 450–51.

263. Blue grouse, *D. obscurus*.

might all by irrigated by diverting the stream we have followed. It will some day make fine farms, & with the yet unoccupied stretch of the main prairie will make a perfect "happy valley" Kirkpatrick* has already about 60 acres of fine grain, of which the harvesting is now nearly complete.

Ingram* tells me that what he calls the main Source of Salmon R, is a great spring which boils up at once from the ground, larger than the stream we have followed. It comes out N of the stream referred to, a little east of the Waggon Road in Grand Prairie, & is probably the subterranean drainage of the valley leading to Duck's*.

Saw a fine half grown bear shortly before camping, but he scampered off before I could get a shot at him. Had he followed his first intention & gone up a tree, I had a good dose of buck shot ready for him. Shot one dusky grouse today.

[verso]

Sept 3.

Obsn. for time on & Libra (!)

(Most conspicuous star in S.W. & same formerly observed at Salmon R. Arm)

(

(Alt of star (uncorrected double 6.0° 0' 30"

(

(Time by watch 7h 33m

Obsn. of Polaris for Lat.

(Time by watch 7h 45m.

1. (

(Uncorrected double alt. Polaris 100° 42' 0"

(Time by watch 7h 50m

2. (

(Uncorrected double alt. Polaris 100° 45' 50"

[end verso]

Sept 4. Not quite so early as usual in leaving camp. Travelled on till after 3 Pm camping at Mr. Steels,[264] near Spellamsheen. Followed waggon Rd. previously traversed to Salmon R bridge (second crossing) thence struck off through a wide flat bottomed valley, with no watercourse, but a number of little pools. This runs a little N of East toward Spellamsheen. From "the Bridge" four valleys diverge. First the one mentioned, second that of the lower part of the Salmon R with the bold granitic mountain

264. There were three men in the area named Steele, probably related. All were farmers or stockraisers. James J. Steele of Grafton farm is probably the one to whom Dawson is referring.

seen at the S. end of Salmon Arm,[265] closing it in the distance. Third the valley of the upper part of Salmon R, down which we have come, & fourth the wide valley leading S. to the head of Okanagan Lake. It is a question which were originally the main drainage valleys of the region.

Had some difficulty & lost time trying to find the right trail through the first named valley innumerable cattle tracks tending to mislead. Steel considers the mt just N.W. of here to resemble Montreal Mt,[266] & it really does look much like it in general outline though Somewhat higher. He has taken up this place, a beautiful little prairie, only this spring, but has a little area under crop, mostly sown in June, but looking well. Wheat, oats, potatoes, turnips, Carrots, millet & Chinese millet, Indian corn, Hungarian grass, tares, & a few tomatoes. All without irrigation & probably with time yet to ripen.

Saw a large wild cat[267] on the trail today, but it knew too much to allow me to get within shot.

[verso]

Faults, dislocations &c.

Very commonly maintained that faults & dislocations are not marked, or but seldom marked by valleys or hollows, & frequently are not to be traced at all in surface features (Geikie Ramsey* &c.)[268] This however depends much on circumstances, & the class of rocks with which we are dealing & relative date of disturbance. It may be, is probably (no doubt) is true in many cases with formations, massive, & but moderately & regularly flexed, especially if the folding has taken place before the consolidation, or during the consolidation & metamorphism of the Sediment. Cracks may then be definite & close, even if accompanied by great faulting, & such a crack, unless bringing together very dissimilar materials, will not give any great hold to denuding agencies. When however, as in B.C. formations previously fully hardened & often crystallized, have been subjected to intense movement & sharply disturbed & folded, what elsewhere ⟨seem⟩ Are definite Cracks, seem to become shattered zones, & systems of parallel

---

265. Mount Ida.

266. The "mt just N.W." was probably Mount Connaught. "Montreal Mt" is undoubtedly a reference to Mount Royal in Montreal.

267. The bobcat, *Lynx rufus pallescens* Merriam, or perhaps the Canada lynx, *Lynx canadensis canadensis* Kerr.

268. See Ramsay, "Glacial Origin of Lakes," 189–90; and James Geikie, *The Great Ice Age and Its Relation to the Antiquity of Man*, 2d ed. (London: Daldy, Isbister & Co., 1877), 272, where he comments: "do the lakes lie in gaping fissures, or in chasms produced by dislocations of the solid rocks, or, as they are technically termed, *faults*? As a matter of fact, no single instance has yet been adduced, either at home or abroad, where a *fault* could be said to be the proximate cause of a lake-hollow."

Cracks, which seem both on the large & small scale to be very potent in shaping the present surface features. There is evidence that the L.C.C. quartzites, for instance were fully as hard & cherty[269] in pre Cretaceous times as now, but since then extensive mesozoic disturbance has occurred, & beds even of the Tertiary are to be found nearly on edge. Thus the older rocks of whole regions have become so Jointed & crushed that it is with difficulty that even a small hand specimen can be broken out with clean faces. This it is that renders the satisfactory investigation of these rocks of B.C. so difficult. In the east, we find in the typical localities even the oldest Silurians in attitudes not far from horizontal, & the sequence easily ascertained, while here the folding of the later rocks has in some cases so complete, that it would appear probable that horizontality would be even a *proof* of great age.[270]

[end verso]

Sept 5. Heavy rain in the night & continuation of same in morning, with little prospect of clearing. Remained in camp, & read some "globes"[271] of late date Mr S. happened to have. About 11 began to look fairer. Get off at 11.30 under a lowering sky, but travelled on to O'Keefs[272] at the head of Okanagan Lake, without getting much rain. Some fine farms hereabout & a good many Settlers beginning or preparing to begin.

Saw Mr Jane[273] of Local Survey camped near O'Keefs*, also Mr C Vernon* who had been down seeing the Indian Commissioners, now within a [mile?] & a half of here.

Saw three deer run across the road today, also several grouse, but did not get a shot at anything, & found very few rocks to examine.

Sept. 6. Lowering, chilly & damp, but with prospect of clearing. Got off, & travelled down W. side of Okanagan to what on the map Called Biche

---

269. A silica rock which occurs as bands or layers of nodules in sedimentary rocks.

270. Dawson here expresses frustration with the much more broken and complex geology of central British Columbia when compared with that of "the East" (St. Lawrence lowland or southwestern Ontario).

271. Presumably Dawson means *The Globe* newspaper of Toronto.

272. Cornelius O'Keefe (1847–1919), in partnership with Thomas Greenhow, operated one of the largest ranches in British Columbia. O'Keefe had arrived at the head of Okanagan Lake in 1867 after a short stay in the Cariboo. His land holdings eventually totalled over fifteen thousand acres.

273. John Jane (1833–1907) came to British Columbia with the Royal Engineers in 1858 and stayed on when the force was recalled in 1863. Jane spent many years as a surveyor, including a period with Walter Moberly of the CPRS. In 1874, he took part in the first survey of the Nicola Valley and in 1877 surveyed the Savona district. Later in 1881, he built and operated a successful general store in Savona. See Mary Balf, *Savona's Ferry* (Kamloops: Kamloops Museum, 1980), 16–17.

River.[274] Gave a call in passing to the Indian Commissioners, finding them at breakfast. Afternoon clearing, though with heavy wind up the lake, raising quite a sea on the beach, along which we travel for a short way to avoid a steep side hill.

On ascending the slope in one place today to examine a rock, heard just as I opened my compass, a movement among the stones, & looking down saw a large snake, fully four feet long, moving slowly. As his head, though threatening, was turned away from me, I finished reading the compass, took a look at him, & then left. He precisely resembled a rattle snake, but *had no rattle.*[275] On asking "Johnny" about it in the evening find that these snakes like the rattle snake otherwise, are not uncommon in the rattle snake districts, but while the true rattle's bite is almost always fatal unless immediate measures are taken, that of this snake is said to be frequently not fatal. The beast looks so much like a rattle snake that I think it must be a variety of the same.

The first large stream[276] crossed this morning, & that at which we are now camped, are full of *little salmon*, like those before found at Eagle Creek, but now spent, turning red like the larger variety & dying with head up stream to the last. In the brook in all stages from fairly good lively fish, to dead. The red colour of the flesh however lost, & the muscle flabby. These little Salmon the Indians say come from the lakes only, & run up the Streams. It is singular, that while they are found at the very mouths of the Creeks they show no disposition to return to the lakes, but prefer to die struggling up stream till the last.

Sept. 7. A very fine day. Continue down border of lake, by a rather rough & bluffy trail, fitted in along the faces of the hills & cliffs as found possible without work. An Indian or "natural" trail. Got well ahead of the packs, & saw no more of them till we waited for them to come up at Camping time. Camped at the bottom of a romantic-looking little rocky bay. Got the Camera out & took a very pretty view lookind down the lake.[277] Prowled round a while with the gun, but saw not a feather. After supper took to fishing, & caught three fine trout, missing about as many more through blunt hooks & bad gear generally. Wrote up notes, & turned in quite tired.

---

274. Shorts Creek.

275. There are no rattlesnakes in British Columbia without rattles, but sections of the rattle from the northern Pacific rattlesnake, *C. viridis oreganus*, can and do fall off. Perhaps the entire rattle apparatus of this snake had fallen off since it is unlikely Dawson would mistake the rattlesnake for another species.

276. Probably Equesis Creek.

277. The "very pretty view," if successfully exposed, has not survived.

[verso]

Formation of Terraces &c.[278] In Okanagan Lake, the lakes lying parallel East of it, & in lakes generally where the water is clear & allows the
Shoaler parts to be seen through, when looked down into from a height —
also in Kamloops Lake, as shown by soundings — the shore is found to
dip at a moderate angle below the water, & the bottom to shoal gradually
for a variable distance, & then to plunge suddenly down into blue depths
unfathomable by the eye. This first carelessly accounted for on the supposition that one or more lakes may have, from some change about outlet,
or change in slope of country generally, increased in depth & flowed over a
former bench. The phenomenon, however, one of much more general
bearing, & to be accounted for as follows. —

Debris & wash of the heavier kind, falling & being carried from the
sides into the lake, would in water naturally form a steeper sloping talus
(?) than on the land, but owing to the movement of the water of the lake,
in waves, it is spread out into a gently sloping, or nearly flat foot, as, to as
great a depth as the movement of the water usually or ever extends. New
material, from time to time piled on this is spread about in the same way,
till eventually any excess falls over the steep front, which in this way gradually extends the subaquatic *bench*, for such it is. Where a brook is continually bringing in material, the comparatively steep *fan* formed above
water, where it enters the lake becomes spread out to a nearly horizontal
form, & it is by the subsequent drainage of such *subaqueous fans* that
much of the arable land of the valleys of B.C. has been formed. Where the
lakes are widest, & most apt to be aggitated by wind, the spreading action
will of course be greatest, both as to depth, & efficiency in destroying &
carrying away the foot of a subaërial talus, or *scree*. If now the lake is
gradually being lowered, by natural cutting down of the bed of its affluent

278. At this point in his journal Dawson seems less concerned with new discoveries than
taking time to philosophize. Here he sets forth an idealized model to which he can compare his real-life examples. The model is handicapped to some extent by Dawson's concept of floating ice, his reluctance to accept significant glacial scour of basins into bedrock, and his use of such obscure terms as "lake alluvium" (deltaic deposits?). It
ignores some of the secondary effects of glaciation such as glacio-isostatic tilting, which
is a flood of sediment in earliest postglacial time followed by a later drop in sediment
load. The model also does not consider the interruption of the processes by climatic
change, associated changes in hydrology, vegetation, and sedimentation, or by renewed
glaciation. The nearest analogue could be Kamloops Lake (see Pharo and Carmack,
Sedimentation in Kamloops Lake) which was, at the end of the last glaciation, raised if
not created by an alluvial and glacio-lacustrine plug that is being gradually cut down by
the Thompson River. Simultaneously, the lake is being infilled at its eastern end by sediment brought principally by the North Thompson River (and to a much less extent by
the Tranquille River) such that in a few thousand years, at present rates of sediment
transport, Kamloops Lake will be filled. In most lakes, however, local circumstances
dominate and time is as yet insufficient for Dawson's model to be really applicable.

river or otherwise, the broadest benches will remain to mark the stages at which it stood longest — other circumstances being equal — & the ultimate result will be a wide gently sloping flat or plain with a river meandering through it, a chain of little lakes connected by a river, or, where the water supply is deficient — as in the upper arms & reaches of a lake into which no streams of consequence flow — a series of little lakes or pools, pitted in a flat bottom, the water from which is Carried away by evaporation, or underground percolation. This sequence, of course, presupposes the formation of a lake of some depth in a previously existing valley, as so often has occurred by blocking by moraines &c. during glacial period. If, the above meandering river having been formed, the lower part of the valley still continues to be cut down, or any general change causing greater slope seaward happens, the river in the old lake bottom is again brought into the state in which its predecessor may be supposed to have been, in most cases, during the original *formation of the valley*. It begins cutting down in the lake alluvium, forming a valley of greater or less width, generally more or less regularly terraced at the Sides. These terraces may be overspread by a layer of river wash, silty or gravelly, but are in the main Cut out of the old lowest lake bench, which will probably be finest at the bottom, & gradually coarser upwards. Putting aside cataclysms, & the possible change of slope in the country generally, the production of this lake, in a pre formed valley, May have occurred during the glacial period, by moraine blocking, greater iceberg deposit on certain region &c., or, in the case of a river with very gentle current, & sides heavily encumbered with drift material, may have arisen from the inwash of this loose material, at a particular point more rapidly than the river can remove it. In either Case it will be seen, that while the river below is cutting through the obstruction, & forming a series of benches ⟨— of which the highest will be the oldest⟩ — the lake will be also producing *by building up* a second series of benches, of what it may be possible to trace some, almost or quite continuously into those of the river. In both these cases the highest bench — considered as a feature — will be the oldest, but the *material* of the highest river bench will be among the latest of the drift — supposing the lake to be drift-blocked — deposits, while that of the highest lake bench, will be of the oldest deposits of the lake. When, however, the lake is once drained, & the river begins to Cut down & form benches along its whole length, the highest of this ⟨most⟩ more recent series, will be formed in the lake basin of the last of the lake deposits, — & probably for the centre of the lake basin the coarsest — while that at a corresponding height on the lower part of the river, will be in very old, — perhaps the oldest — of the glacial drift deposits. The drift deposits may, however, to Some extent cover the bottom of the lake basin, & when the river has cut down, in the course of time, through all the lake deposits, it will again begin forming terraces of which the higher are cut in the newer deposits, & the action of the river in this respect becomes similar through its entire length. Each of the original lake benches will be oldest — in itself — from its base up, while the age of the series will count from the highest bench in the valley down, & only in the centre of the lake will we find a continuous series of deposits from the formation of the lake to its final drainage, counting from the bottom up. Pre-glacial river deposits may of course also occur to a greater or less extent below all, but the cases where these will play a material part, or add to the complication will be few. Supposing then a lake & river valley, the lake blocked by moraine material, of which only the ⟨lower⟩ latest layer, however, spreads over its ⟨base⟩ {former bed}; in which it is wished to trace up a chronological sequence of deposits, we may have to proceed as follows. 1. lowest layer of drift in lowest river bench. 2 higher layers of drift, in next succeeding river benches & lowest lake bench. 3. oldest post-glacial deposit, in next, (upward) suceeding lake benches, also in highest lake bench, (from the bottom of its deposit up) & an alluvial capping of highest river bench (also from the bottom of alluvial deposit up. 4. next post glacial, in lower benches of old lake area upwards, as before. In higher lake benches in order downwards but in each case proceeding from the bottom of the bench to the top, & then to the bottom, or nearly to the bottom of the next lowest, on the lower benches of the lake area still upward, in the old bottom deposit. In the alluvial cappings of the river benches in order downward, but in each alluvium proceeding upward. 5. Latest deposits, present river flats of the river & lake areas alike.

With regard to the formation of present lake basins, the bearing of the formation of these lake terraces obvious, though at first sign it seems equally necessary to assume glacial ploughing for basins in soft material, as for rock basins (as in attached slip)[279] will also account for many of the pot holes, & some at least of the collateral lakes in the great old valleys.

The same reasoning will extend to, & explain the shallow water at the mouths of rivers, & streams at the heads of the coast fiords, which so rapidly deepens after a certain depth reached. Taking into account the greater oceanic disturbances of Storms & currents &c. the same sort of thing will

279. "Lakes cannot here have been filled from river to river though river valleys may & probably have. If filled lake were caused unless by blocking by fan (shallow lake) or by relative changes of level. No one or one Series of relative displacements will account for B.C. lakes (?) Must then assume general buckling of country. This we have no reason to believe. — improbable. Must then account for deep lakes. Deeper than outflow valleys much, whether dammed by rocks or soft material all same. Something either prevented the deposit of material where they are while active elsewhere, or has since scooped it out. Does not require to be *rock basin* to require this Solution. Equally impossible to explain basin in soft materials without lakes now all filling up Something different."

explain the submarine extension of the continental plateaux, without any necessity of Considering submerged continents. [*Illus.*]

[end verso]

Sept 8. Morning very threatening, & rain began dropping just as we got away from Camp. Continued on, however, & rewarded by clearing weather, & a very fine afternoon & evening. Got to Mr Allison's* about Noon, & had a short talk with him, getting full directions as to trail &c. He calls it about 60 miles over to Hay's*, on the Similkameen, giving something for crooks of the trail. Camped about three miles up the [blank] River of the map,[280] in a pretty enough little place, with good grass among scattered firs & pines.

A very fine view of the lake just in coming round the front of the hill into this valley. It here makes a knee, & bends Southward, round a rugged, but partly grassed & timbered mountainous point, looking almost amber yellow in the light of the afternoon Sun. The distant mountains in shadow, on the contrary, a deep purple-blue, while the lake itself roughened with white-caps an intense blue. Foreground of red pines,[281] & shores fringed with fir & aspen.

Products of the chase today — one badger.[282] He looked round in a most enquiring way, when I pointed the gun at him, & even before I had pulled the trigger I had relented — but still pulled it. Saw only three birds today, & they got up & gat too fast for me.

The W. shore of Okanagan Lake — generally — is rough, rocky, & more or less thickly wooded, rising from the water to high mountains. There are some benches, with prairies of limited size, but no extent of arable land except near the head, where a good many little Indian farms are, with room for more. At Allison's* also a considerable extent of bench, but mostly only fit for grazing. On the whole, however, much good feed for Cattle & horses through this country, & as far as appearances showing yet very little fed over.

Sept. 9.

Obsn. for time on & of Libra (?) same as formerly observed.

Time by watch ⟨37⟩ 7h 37m 30S

Alt. (double uncorrected of star 64° 24′ (probably good to within a few seconds)

Alt. of Polaris (double uncorrected) 99° 35′ 30″

Time by watch 7h 51m 30S

---

280. Probably Peachland Creek.

281. Ponderosa pine, *P. ponderosa*.

282. Yellow badger, *Taxidea taxus taxus* (Schreber).

Sunday, did not move camp, feeling entitled to a day of rest, & with plenty little camp duties to attend to. Day showery throughout, though this evening quite clear & fine looking. Reading, writing, & overhauling. Just before supper went out with gun, thinking that providence might have some breakfast in store for us; & returned after an hours walk with one grouse. Another was shot, but pitching among trees & bushes Could not be found. Oh! for a dog.

Got an observation on polaris, & for time, with some difficulty as I had to go to a distance from the tent to see through the trees, & the candle blown out by the wind.

Sept. 10. Up early, & off under rather threatening sky, which soon produced showers & squalls of cold wind, which alternated with glimpses of watery sunshine all day. Trail rough, crooked, & often obscure, giving much trouble. Rock exposures fortunately few, & uninteresting. Camp at 3.45 in a little pocket like valley, at an elevation by barometer of a little over 4000 feet. Shoot a solitary ruffed grouse,[283] which found sheltering from the elements in the ravine near camp, through which a small brook flows, but whether to the Similkameen or to Okanagan L. I do not Know.

Saturday, yesterday & today have presented similar meteorological features. Mornings overcast, with clouds flying up rapidly from S & SW. Clouds breaking up a little during day, but wind coming down to surface, & squalls of wind & rain passing. Evening nearly calm & clear, though tonight it has not yet (7.15) quite cleared off. Sky becoming perturbed & overcast again before morning.

Sept. 11. Travelled on over very rough trail, often hard to follow, till reach the edge of another great, & to me, nameless valley.[284] Here, as I was taking bearings, one of the mules appeared at full trot, dragging the pack ropes behind her, & covered with sweat. She had got into trouble with her pack, thrown it off, & started off on the trail. Douglas* led her back till he met Johnny coming on for her, but the incident caused some delay. Travelled on up the valley, the trail eventually following over one of the tributary valleys, through a divide valley, in which lie Osprey, Link, & Chain Lakes. Camped at the upper end of the latter, on a pretty little spot of prairie.

Shot three 'spruce partridges' near Camp, on the trail, & tried fishing in the lake, though without much success as no means of getting out to deep water. Got a series of observations on Polaris &c. for lat. & time, warmed up at a good fire & turned in.

---

283. Ruffed grouse, *B. onasa umbellus (L.).*

284. Probably the valley of Trout Creek.

General character of country travelled over today wooded, though seldom densely. No bunch grass country, but good pine grass & here & there meadows of swamp grass.[285]

Obsns. on Polaris for lat.

Time by watch 7h 34m 30S uncorrected double Alt 99° 14' 40"

| " | " | " | 7 | 41 | 30 | " | " | " 99° 19' 50" |
| " | " | " | 7 | 48 | 40 | " | " | " 99° 24' 40" |

Obn. for time on last star in tail of Ursa Major

Time by watch 8h 3m 50S. uncorrected double alt 75° 25' 10"

| " | " | " | 8 | 9 | 40 | " | " | " 73° 55' 10" |
| " | " | " | 8 | 19 | 0 | " | " | " 71° 26' 0 |

Sept. 12. Before observations completed last night, thermometer had fallen, under calm & clear sky, to within a degree of the freezing point. During the night it continued falling, & reached 25° at which it still stood in the morning. Nearly half an inch of ice on basin, sponge frozen, & ground crisp when we got up, with a dense fog hanging over the little lake.

Bundled up & started, expecting to follow the valley, but the trail ascended at once to the level of the plateau above, & crossing over a point of it, again descended to the valley. The plateau undulating & hilly with knobs of decomposing granite projecting from a sandy & bouldery Surface, now a mass of windfall, or brulé in the act of turning into windfall, with thickets of little Scrub-pines & altogether, even under the sunlight, an abomination of desolation. All the stream valleys & lakes, with their little meadows & grassy borders hidden, & the view of interminable dreary undulating hills only broken to the S.E. by the snowy peaks of the Cascades, which at this distance scarcely seem to rise much above the plateau.

The observations of glaciation from N to S at this elevation, however, very interesting.

Travelled on down the valley, for much of its length from half to three quarters of a mile wide, but much encumbered with brule & windfall, not a stroke of work having been done on the trail for a long time. Without Mr Allison's* recent tracks we would have found it difficult in places to keep the way. As it was the journey one of continued log-jumping.

Eventualy left the valley where open bunch Grass country reached, & struck across it, taking as it seems, the wron trail, among all the innumerable Cattle tracks, & going somewhat out of our road. At 5 P.m. finding a

---

285. Dawson's "swamp grass" is very difficult to identify precisely. Often the term is used for species of sedges, *Carex* spp., which are not true grasses. It seems likely, however, that Dawson would recognize a true grass and use the term "sedge" instead. There are many true grasses that grow in swampy ground but none that are specifically named "swamp grass."

little good water in a ravine, & not knowing exactly how far it might be to Hay's*, Camped on the plateau.

Sept 14.[286] Found the distance to Princeton about 4 miles. Took the summit of a prominent round grassy hill *en route*, & got a good view, & sketch of the country with bearings. Got down early, & dumped packs, intending to wait over noon to get latitude. Day became quite overcast however, & a heavy shower came on Just about noon. Had lunch, & on point of leaving when found on bars in the river some loose stones with Linnæ & other fresh water shells in them. Thinking it important to trace these up, & the day looking very threatening; decided to Camp here. Set off with Douglas* & an Indian to visit a remarkable paint locality of the Indians about 3 miles up the North Fork, which, from Indian information, I thought was likely the origin of the fossils. It proved to be so, & a very interesting section, with seams of lignite &c. Wishing to Cross the river to see the rocks on the other side, & there being some difficulty, from the nature of the ground in bringing the horses down to the river level, the Indian volunteered to Carry me over. Stripping off his boots & britches, he seized a stick & presented his back to me to mount. We crossed Successfully, though owing to the depth of the water my feet got wet, — & going up the shore a short distance I found a very interesting exposure with plant & insect remains. The day throughout threatening, & spitting rain, now fairly turned wet, the rain coming down in good style, with gusts of cold wind. I fagged away at the rocks, however knowing time was precious, though standing out in the rain in wet linen Coat, with straw hat & puggery dripping down back not pleasant. Mr Indian, crouched under a log, still grasping his stick, & endeavoured as far as possible to preserve those parts of his person left uncovered by the absence of his nether garment, from the elements. He seemed to think my operations rather long, & gently hinted that it was very Cold, also that *wake Si-a copete Sun.*[287] I did not want to give up, however, sooner than necessary as I knew I would probably not have another chance of visiting the section, & was rewarded by the discovery ⟨of a⟩ among other things, of some fish scales, the first vertebrate remains yet found in the Tertiary here. Finally, wrapping up my treasures in my handkerchief, I crossed the river as before, & bundling up our *ictus*, we set out for camp, reaching it just before dark, Cold, wet, tired, & hungry.

[verso]

It is almost startling to find as we gradually unearth the records of the Tertiary, that the face of Nature at a date so remote, that nearly all the

286. Dawson has the date wrong; it should be 13 September.

287. Or "wake siah kopet sun," Chinook Jargon for "nearly finished sun."

species have perished, & the nature of whole continents has been changed by physical causes, that taken as a whole all things were so much as now, yet without the presence of Man. That an observer, conveyed backward to a scene of those days, would have had to examine closely many of the plants & animals to make out the difference from those with which he was familiar; & that similar forms would be found subserving the same ends as now, & inter-related in a manner similar, & as complex as at present.

This is a propos of the various insect forms, especially of the little water skippers found today, & looking as though they might have skipped yesterday instead of countless years ago.

Hay's* tells me the second & third streams Crossed on the Okanagan-Princeton Trail, unite shortly below the trail, flow to Okanagan L, & is there called trout Creek. The next large stream also reaches the lake, about four or five miles above Penticten.[288]

Hay's* a quaint enough character, & has mellowed into oddity by long Keeping alone in this country. Tall & lanky, with a stoop, & general appearance of typical Yankee. On my asking about what could be grown at Princeton, he told me that he had grown almost all sorts of vegetables & garden stuff, including potatoes, Cabbage, cauliflower, cucumbers, squashes, beans, &c. but that his garden now appeared run out. The potatoes when he planted any "seemed to grow all to tops & not to bottoms" That cutting the tops off & manuring did no good, & that he had given it up as a bad job. There were he said still some gooseberries & asparagus in the garden, "but" taking his pipe out of his mouth "they seen all the time petering, & petering, & going back instead of ahead." In selling me a sample of gold containing grains of platinum, he Showed me his magnet, a large one, he said admiringly "She's strong, she draws, she draws powerful I tell ya, but she wont *touch* that platinum!" As if this proved the platinum to posess some extra-ordinary property of inertness, or rather resistance to ordinary forces.

[end verso]

Sept 14. Delayed a little by the Straying of the horses, which seem to find this part of the country too big for them. Got off at 8 a.m. & travelled northward toward Nicola, Camping at the fourth lake of the chain[289] which runs along the valley. Day cold windy & overcast, threatening, but without rain. Started on a wild goose chase (literally) round one of the little lakes, with no other result than getting well warmed up.

The lakes so far seen in this valley, are very evidently due to the obstruction of the Channel in the valley at various places by the debris

288. Probably Eneas Creek.

289. Allison Lake. The others are McCaffrey, McKenzie, Dry, and Round lakes.

from the sides, which here, the hills at the sides being in places high & steep & the valley narrow, take the form of actual rock Slides; rendering the cause of the lakes very apparent.

Tried fishing in the lake, but without success, & having had no luck with the gun, confined to our regular diet of bacon.

Sept 15. A miserable day. Morning opened with most profound atmospheric gloom, but soon brightened, giving great hope of a fine day. Travelled on, but clouds soon recollected & continued to obscure the sun most of the time, & bring squalls of cold wind with rain & sleet during the remainder of the day. The country after leaving the little gorge like valley, is but lightly timbered with Douglas fir & aspen, with here & there groves of *P. contorta*; & often large completely open areas. Broad bottoms border the little streams with some fine hay swamps, & the whole region forms a fine & very extensive Cattle range. In a fine day it would be beautiful, but today bleak in the extreme. Shot one partridge[290] by good luck.

Got out instruments in evening, the sky partly clearing, but just as all ready to begin Some clouds dodged up, & not Passing away again while I had patience to wait, I lost my observation.

[verso]

Sept 15. Obsn for time on last star in tail of bear

Time by watch 7h 51m 40s

Uncorrected double alt 74° 49′ 50″

(Instrument Slightly out of adjustment.)

[end verso]

Sept 16. Sunday. Up in the grey dawn, with a grey mist around & over us, & the thermometer down to 26°. Grass crisp with hoar-frost. Breakfasted & got off before 7 a.m., reaching Camp on "Hamilton's Creek Nicola at 2.20. The country passed over almost completely open & with fine bunch grass Showing yet very little sign of wear. A very extensive range.

Found a mail awaiting me here as per agreement but containing few letters. After reading these, devoted the afternoon to examination of the limestone exposure, & prove conclusively, I believe, its adhesion to the green series. Also got a few fossils, but I fear nothing very characteristic.

No frost in the Nicola Valley last night.

Sept 17. Moved down the valley to mouth of Coldwater, taking the south side, not previously seen, from the foot of the lake. A fine day. Had just sat down to dinner, near the road, when a herder & number of Indians with a great band of wild Cattle Came along, forcing us to skedadale & stand to one side till they passed.

---

290. Ruffed grouse, *B. umbellus*.

Many Indians now collected here, from different parts of the country, & more expected. The exact nature of the "play" I cannot understand, when all arrive there is to be a sort of cultus potlatch, & some Ceremonial burying of the dead, or rather reburying;[291] the bones being done up in white cloths. Met one man with his brother's bones (said brother having died last year over at Princeton — done up in cloth behind his saddle. The bones are being brought back in this instance to the native place of the former posessor. At present there are two camps of Indians, separated by a few miles, the ceremonies going on separately in each, & consisting so far as I can make out of klootchmen dressing up in their best & dancing while the men sing. Men dancing to imitate different animals, as rabbit, Coyote &c. all to drumming & Singing.

[verso]

Sept 17. Readjusted sextant this P.m. the horizon glass being a little out. Sun went down before new index error correctly determined (will get this again)

observed & acquil̶l, at first reading probably exactly on meridian (plot curve)

Time by watch 7h 58m.   & Aq. 96° 56' 30"
     "   8h 6m 30S. & Aq. 96 51 10
     "   8   11   20   &   "   96 45 50
     "   8   15   30   "   96 35 30

Observed Polaris
Time by watch 8h 22m 25S   100° 53' 20"
     "   8   33   101° 1' 0"
     "   8   49   101° 11' 50"

All uncorrected double alts.

Get true time by transit & Aquil̶, or obsn for time last made

[end verso]

Sept 18. Moved camp a few miles only, camping about half a mile below

---

291. This was a Thompson Indian practice. "Until a few years ago wealthy Indians opened the grave of a relative a year or two after death and occasionally in succeeding years. The bones were gathered up each time, and put in a new skin robe or blanket, after being carefully wiped clean. The people called to witness the gathering-up of the bones of a dead person were feasted by the latter's relatives" (James Alexander Teit, *The Thompson Indians of British Columbia*, Jesup North Pacific Expedition vol. 1, pt. 4; American Museum of Natural History Memoir vol. 2 [New York, 1900], 330). For further comments by Dawson, see his "Notes on the Shuswap," 12–13.

Coutlees.[292] Spend the day up 10 Mile Creek or Kozoom Kanix,[293] very uselessly as it turns out, for few exposures & nothing of interest. Could not find lignite locality. Shot one grouse.

Arranged for an Indian boy to put us on the right trail for Boston Bar tomorrow.

Sept 19. Horses at some distance this morning, delaying our start till 9 a.m. Got an Indian who knows the country to go with us as far as any danger of loosing the trail, & set out for Boston Bar, by the trans-mountain trail, going first Southward till we struck the Coldwater. Indian having brought us to that Part of trail, beyond which "no more forks" gratefully received his pay & returned, telling us we had five or six miles still to go to get water & grass for camp. This proved correct, & we did not stop till nearly six.

Day rather gloomy, but clearing in the afternoon & now fine.

Indian guide showed us an unfinished house, on the Coldwater, which he had built, but abandoned, fearing some white man would come along & pre empt the claim. He says he formerly had a house & little farm, or patch in which he grew potatoes, wheat &c., near the Mouth of the Coldwater, but a white man (Chapman)[294] came & preempted the land, against which there is of course no redress. There has been too much of this sort of thing in the Nicola Valley.[295]

Soon after leaving the Coldwater, bunch grass almost disappears, & pine grass in the open woods, or on bare slopes, replaces it. Much of the region just about camp pretty thickly timbered, with spruce &c.

Sept 20. A miserable day. Gloomy & raining in the early morning, looked like set in wet. Waited some time, & at length the sun getting out, & every appearance of clearing, we set out. Soon wind squalls, with dashes of cold rain, & one prolonged flurry of actual snow. The bushes thoroughly wet, & soon drenched feet & legs. When the Snow storm came on, some distance ahead of packs on a high hill, turned back about a mile to look for Camp, but could find no water. Packs coming up, we set out again, & after 5 P.m reached a place where the Indians had told Johnny a good camp. Very little feed for animals however. Got instrument out after dark,

292. Alexander Coutlie (1826–1901) had been a miner in California and British Columbia before settling in the Nicola Valley in 1873. Along with a ranch, Coutlie also built and ran a store and hotel. See also Pat Lean, "Alexander Coutlie (1826–1901)," *Nicola Valley Historical Quarterly* 6, nos. 2 and 3 (October 1983): 3.

293. Guichon Creek.

294. James Chapman (b. 1836) pre-empted land on the Coldwater River in 1871.

295. For discussions of land policy and the Indians, see Fisher, *Contact and Conflict*, 175–205; and Cail, *Land, Man, and the Law*, 180, 185–208.

much against my will, as it was cold & disagreeable. Found myself a little too late for meridian of Altair. Turned the horizon to Polaris, & it immediately clouded over, same thing occurring afterwards with two other stars. Finally took Mars for time, & hope to be able to work out lat. by some process from obsns.

[verso]

Sept 20.

    Obsn. of & Aquil‡ (The first very near the meridian if not on it)
        (?) 44m.

Time by watch 7h 16m 30″ Uncorrected double alts 97° 26′ 50″
    ″   7 50 30   ″   97° 24′ 50″
    ″   7 56 50   ″   97° 18′ 0″

Obsn. of Mars, (rising in S.E. near Moon) for time &c.

Time by watch 8h 30m 55s

Uncorrected double alts of Mars ⟨40° 3′ 20″⟩ {40° 3′ 20″}

[end verso]

Sept 21. Horses had strayed far during the night, much delaying start, though morning fine. Got off by 9 a.m. & travelled on by a very crooked trail, nearly all either up hill or down, rocky, & Constantly crossing the stream[296] in the valley. Coming to a little open & bushy patch, with traces of feed & some water, Camped about 5 P.m.

    Trees. Noted first specimens of *P. monticola* just after leaving Spi-oos Crossing yesterday, since abundant everywhere. *Abies lesiocarpa* & *Menziesii* appear soon after. Just after leaving camp this morning find *Th. gigantea, A mertensiana*[297] the Devil's Club & other coast vine species.

    Found several sandy narrow benches in the valley travelled down today, but general character, a narrow deep ravine like valley, not actually a Cañon, but with granitic Cliffs above & often great slides of immense angular masses reaching down to the water. Narrow bottoms densely wooded with large firs, spruces, & Cedars. Hillsides also wooded, but often rising above to partly bare rugged or rounded rocky summits, looking white at a distance. This stream bears about same relative position to ⟨of⟩ range as upper part of Coquihalla & has similar characters though not quite so boldly developed. Many small rills, streams & torrents fall in to main valley, but generally do not rise far back.

    Shot two grouse today.

Sept 22. Some of the horses having Cached themselves in the bushes, delayed start a little. Morning lowering & heavy, & before we got off turned into smart snow storm, big flakes falling abundantly, but melting

296. Spius Creek.

297. Mountain hemlock, *T. mertensiana.*

on touching the ground. On getting down to lower levels, the snow turned to rain, which continued from time to time during morning. Found ourselves not far from Boston Bar, arriving there about 1 P.m. Travelled on up the road to Jamesons,[298] 9 miles further. Stopped myself at Keefers[299] Camp about 2 miles lower down, & rode ⟨back⟩ on up to Jamison's after dark. Decided not to move camp tomorrow, but make a Sunday overhauling, now much needed.

Sept 23. Morning writing, reading, & examining rocks of neighbourhood. afternoon got horse & rode back on trail to see rocks passed after dark yesterday. Stopped for dinner at Keefer's* Camp, & rode back to my camp at the 34 m. house after nightfall. Day showery & windy throughout, with heavy rain in the afternoon.

G. M. Dawson to J. W. Dawson*, 23 September 1877, Lytton

I suppose by the time this gets home, you will be wondering why I have not written for so long, the truth being that no good chances have offered for some time back, a longer time than I had supposed I would be away from Postal chances, on leaving Kamloops. I am Camped today on the Waggon Road about 20 miles below Lytton, where I hope to be tomorrow evening. We got out on the waggon rd. yesterday evening, having Crossed by an Indian Trail from the Nicola Valley near the mouth of the Coldwater. Today being Sunday, & moreover a not very fine day, I decided not to move, but have a general overhauling of things, write letters &c. From Lytton I am not yet quite decided as to route, but shall probably go up the Fraser to Lillooet, spend a little time between there & Clinton &c., & then strike back for Kamloops, perhaps by a Circuitous route. Kamloops may be reached by about the 15th of next month, & before the end of the month, I hope to be in Victoria. If I then have to go up to Comox, this may take about two weeks, from which you will see that I can scarcely count on being home before the end of November. The railway parties are now on the way to Victoria, or soon will be, with the exception of two far up the N. Thompson, which will not be down till late, & are having, what with scarcity of Grass & abundance of rain, — a hard time of it. Marcus Smith* passed down day before yesterday, having come

---

298. A. W. Jamieson is listed at 34 Mile Post in *Guide to B. C. 1877–78*, 360.

299. George Alexander Keefer (1836–1912) was a surveyor and engineer in the employ of the CPRS. Keefer began his career in eastern British North America as engineer for various railway lines before joining the surveys in 1872. He remained with the Canadian Pacific Railway until 1886, supervising construction of the difficult Fraser Canyon section of the line. Later he was consultant on the construction of the Vancouver waterworks system and resident engineer for the Canadian Department of Public Works.

through from Manitoba *via* Yellow Head Pass. I did not see him Cambie*, who has been exploring up on the Skeena Came down via Quesnel some weeks ago, & is now up again at Kamloops. I hope ⟨perhaps⟩ to meet him on the way down tomorrow or next day.

On the way over from Nicola, we Crossed Several high divides, in a very much "Jumped up" Country. The weather was extremely broken, & scarcely any feed for the animals. We had two flurries of snow at elevations near 4000', & altogether it was fortunate that there was nothing much but *granite* to observe. I had intended making a paced section through, but soon gave up the idea, as the trail was extremely Crooked & with scarcely 100 yards level on the route.

Up towards Clinton I hope to see with some localities not yet examined, the rocks originally described by Richardson*, about some of which I have never been quite clear, especially on the Upper Cache Cr. Group. I will visit Marble Cañon the locality of the celebrated foram.[300] It is quite surprising to me how many questions are yet unsettled about the rocks of this part of the country, or rather how few I have been able to settle this summer, especially with regard to the relations & owing to absence of fossils, the ages of the beds. Plenty specimens have been collected, however, & when these are all brought together & work plotted, I hope for additional light. I dont of course know whether you have had any proof of my Geol. Soc. Paper, but have been thinking I would ask you to modify one thing in correcting it, if not too late. I believe I have said in one place that all the valleys must have been filled from rim to rim & afterwards gradually re-excavated & terraced. This statement may be a little too broad, as it is probable that in some instances, at least, the terraces & lateral accumulations of the valleys have been *formed* along the shores of retreating lakes, or arms of the sea. As given I dont think the Statement however is likely to do much harm & so do not attach much importance to its correction if it Should happen in any way to be inconvenient or too late.[301]

There are letters of Mother's & Rankines* which should be answered, but as there is really nothing to write about just now I must put off doing so. At Lytton I hope to find a mail, & may then be inspired with something of more general interest.

Today I feel lazy, & have not, besides, got through the last *Natures* which arrived Some time since.

---

300. Or foraminifera fossils. See 21 March 1876.

301. The changes Dawson requested were indeed incorporated into the published article, where he says of terraces that "many of the higher are accumulations along the shore of a great sheet of water, most of the lower have been carved out of deposits which at one time filled the valleys from rim to rim" (Dawson, "On the Superficial Geology," 112).

You will observe that I have Allowed myself to begin Calculating when I may get home again, as the time begins to look short, & half an hours talk is worth a hundred letters.

Sept. 24. After paying the somewhat exhorbitant bills for horse-feed, got away, but stopping to look at rocks the packs soon got ahead. Spent the day making a somewhat Careful examination of the Boston Bar, & Jackass Mt. rocks. Got quite benighted before reaching Lytton, & enveloped in a storm of wind & cold rain, which has been raging at Yale, all day, but only towards night got this far. There being no time for getting camp in order, went myself to Otiers (?) hotel,[302] found a mail at the post office, had a good Supper & turned in.

The day by no means wasted. The entire unconformity of the B. bar & Jackass Mt. series having been satisfactorally ascertained.[303] The rocks differ also generally in degree of metamorphism. The actual Junction not seen, but the two series found within {less than} 200 yards of each other in several places. Two explanations not requiring unconformity shown on opposite page, [*illus.*] but neither, I believe tenable. Fossils also found in three different places in the J.M.[304] rocks, & a Careful examination of the pebbles of the conglomerate made.

The apparent transition between the two series east of Boston Bar, is now anomalous, but as section imperfect, may easily be delusive. The last dip, for instance, got in rocks which in all probability J.M. may, as it was obscure, be really Cracking or cleavage. or it may be that the folds here pressed so tight that apparent conformity between series Caused.

Sept 25. Got specimens packed, addressed, & ready for shipment to Victoria, wrote letters, telegraphed to Robson* on disposition of mails (next to go to Clinton, others till Oct 12 to Kamloops) went across to point between Fraser & Thompson to see reported Indian burial place,[305] which

---

302. Or the Globe Hotel which was built in 1860 by the Belgian pioneer, Louis Vincent Hautier. One of the best stopping places on the Cariboo Road, the Globe was the first stop north of Yale on the Fraser River. See Lorraine Harris, *Halfway to the Goldfields: A History of Lillooet* (Vancouver: J. J. Douglas, 1977), 78–82.

303. No final answer has been found to Dawson's dilemma. A recent study of the area concludes: "discordant bedding attitudes on each side of the contact suggest that there is either an unconformity or a fault between the two" (J. W. H. Monger, *Hope Map-area, West Half (92H W½), British Columbia*, Geological Survey of Canada Paper no. 69–47 [Ottawa: Queen's Printer, 1970], 15).

304. Jackass Mountain series.

305. This site (EbRj 1) is well known but has received little attention from archaeologists. The site was briefly examined by Harlan I. Smith in the 1890's and reported in his *Archaeology of Lytton, British Columbia*, Jesup North Pacific Expedition vol. 1, pt. 3; American Museum of Natural History Memoir vol. 2 (New York, 1899). From

told by Mr Good* & the Indians so ancient that those now living know nothing about it, & do not even appear to Count the dead there as their friends. Find a wonderful display of bones & implements. Gather a large number of the latter, & return to Lytton. After getting packs off, go quietly over with Douglas* & appropriate seven skulls, the best we could find without excavation. Carry them back in a gunny sack & pack the whole collection in a couple of boxes for Victoria.[306] Set out after packs, which were to stop ⟨just after⟩ about 3 m. off, & reach camp, at a "ranch" just at dark. Afternoon cold & windy, but not wet.

[verso]

Indian ossuary at Junction of Fraser & Thompson Rivers B. C.

The point between the two rivers is somewhat less than a right Angle, & there is a delta shaped area, elevated probably on the average about 100′ above the rivers, with higher hills bounding it along the base of the triangle. The foundation of the point is rock, but the surface shows only sand & gravel. On it are various irregularities, of which one, the most striking, occupies the Centre, is roughly oval, pointing to the junction of the two Streams, & is about 150 yards long by 50 or 60 wide. The down stream end of the Mount is lowest & most sloping, so that it would look somewhat thus in Section. [*Illus.*] It is evidently natural in its chief features at least, & has only been appropriated as affording a Suitable site for burial. It is composed of sand, with little admixture of gravel, covered here & there with tufts of bushes, & maintains yet one large tree on the lower end. The prevailing & strong winds, owing to the dry loose character of the soil, have ripped the mound up in many places — probably owing to the destruction of vegetation naturally holding the soil, of late years — forming trough-like hollows, basins &c. & heaping new hillocks of blown

Dawson's description, the site seems typical of burial sites from the late prehistoric Kamloops Phase and the proto-historic period prior to the introduction of Christian burial practices. The Kamloops Phase represents the later prehistory of the Upper Thompson and Southern Shuswap Indians, dating from about one hundred fifty to seven hundred years ago. Archaeologically, the Kamloops Phase includes small side notched arrow points, pentagonal knives, tubular pipes, and an emphasis on stone grinding and polishing, primary flexed burials in pits, and cist burials with rock cairns. The artifacts associated with the burials as described by Dawson are also to be expected. Dawson's reference to flint flakes should probably be basalt, since worked flint is very rare while black basalt tools and waste flakes are common in local burial sites. For a full description of the Kamloops Phase, see David Sanger, "The Chase Burial Site (EeQw: 1), British Columbia," in *Contributions to Anthropology VI: Archaeology and Physical Anthropology*, National Museums of Canada Bulletin no. 224, Anthropological Series no. 82 (Ottawa: Queen's Printer, 1968), 86–185.

306. Two of Dawson's skulls lacked their lower jaw. Their measurements may be found in Franz Boas, "First General Report on the Indians of British Columbia," *Report of the British Association for the Advancement of Science, 1889* (London: John Murray, 1890), 814.

Sand on other spots. This natural action has bared the remains, & is further evidenced, — as more or less to be seen in all the country hereabouts, — by the polish imparted to the stones, & the dull surfaces of a few chance fragments of broken glass. Interments along summit & on both slopes, & even with partial exhibition, must be several hundred in number. Not contemporanious, but evidently covering considerable time & general appearance strongly suggests that oldest at lower point of ridge, & that even in times when used the sand under influence of wind gradually moving, & that that upper end ⟨part⟩ of mound not formed at time of first burials, but afterwards taken posession of. Fragments of bark &c. are to be seen in these last interments while nothing of the sort in lower, bones at upper end also fresher. Bodies have been crouched up, & in some instances almost seems as though bones had been laid together after death. Body Sometimes, or even generally in upright sitting posture, though Some seem certainly to have been crouched up & then laid on side. No trace of compression on skulls. Implements &c. — see specimens — evidently put immediately about particular bodies at time of burial, & in some cases a little mass of flint flakes scrapers &c. lying quite together as though in bags originally. Paint, yellow & red ochre, in many places near bodies, & in one case the head had been thickly covered with red ochre — see red skull — The more important people seem to have been buried about crest of ridge, as there best shaped &c. implements, also very noticeable that in the newer burials less care to properly supply the dead, indicating either a decrease or increase (?) of faith! Many of skulls, notwithstanding the very dry climate, crumble to pieces on handling & only some of the older ones bear removal. General appearance that even in older burials the things given to the dead more *intended to represent* certain forms of property than actually to be valuable. Thus many chest clips with Some & only a few with any shape, also arrow heads &c. Crooked, & evidently useless from slenderness of form or size for active use. Many pretty little pebbles, fragments of crystals & mica, also medicine pipes! rod like pieces of slate — very generally distributed — &c. No iron implements or traces of such found, the only metals being Copper, of which a few flattened pieces — possibly native — occur; & lead, of which a drop shaped piece seen, which may however have been thrown there subsequently, as with most of the things, quite on the Surface. A small blue glass head seen near one of the latest interments, but may not belong to it. Would thus seem that this must have been abandoned as burial place about the time of first advent of whites to the Coast, or before. Traffic with Coast shown by sea shells. Various small animals buried with the human remains, of which beaver, & the jaw of some small fur bearing carnivor like the martin distinguishable. These, with the bears teeth necklaces & assemblage of tools would seem to indicate rather a hunting people, though adzes apparently for Canoe manufacture. Some of bone, numerous; the bone so large that hard to tell whence derived. Only near one of the latest graves are some Salmon vertebræ to be seen.

[end verso]

Sept 26. Paced on up the valley about ten miles, where found Casinto Camped, having found some feed. Rather early, but rocks of neighbourhood interesting, & a good deal of writing &c. to do.

Day chilly & windy, with clouds hanging about the mountains, the tops of which on both sides of the river are covered with new snow.

The whole country along the river eaten perfectly bare, though in many places with good bunch grass in early days. More or less sloping benches & truncated fans, fronting bluffly on the river trench, & backed by gigantic & rugged mountains, which look greater the higher one Climbs about their feet.

The wind blows nearly always here, up the river, & it is seldom Calm, often a fresh Gale! In stormy weather, while the mountains up as far as Boston Bar are shrouded in dense clouds, coming in from the sea, & bathing Yale & all the Lower Fraser in rain. Large ragged cirro-Cumulus masses keep sailing up here at Lytton, clinging more or less tenaceously to the mountain summits, massing together sometimes & dropping unwillingly a little rain, but generally appearing to be, already squeezed dry & to be dissipating & growing less. This not only in hot, but in cold weather, when it cannot be the mere dryness of the interior air which causes it. At Seatoller, in the lee of Scawfell,[307] in Cumberland the greatest amount of rain falls of any place in England. Here, in the Lee of the Coast range, is a country with almost no rain, — why this difference? —

Sept 27. Got away about 7 A.m. & with the exception of about half an hour at lunch, on foot, pacing & examining rocks till 4 P.m. Camped about a mile up from the Fraser, in a little gorge-like valley which the trail going to the fountain[308] follows. Heavy rain last night, giving the mountains above an extra coating of snow, which now comes down to lower than before. Every available spot for cultivation appears occupied along this part of the river.

Got photo.[309] looking down the gorge & including some fine mountains of the style here forming the boundaries of the Fraser. Repaired Camera,

307. Scafell.

308. The Fountain is a flat at a sharp turn in the Fraser River some twelve miles below Pavilion that derives its name from a small natural fountain spouting out in the middle of it.

309. See "Photographs," 27 September 1877, GSC196–C1 (PA 51071).

changed plates, & turned in.

Most of rocks seen today might very well represent the green series in a more altered state. Perhaps certainty about these rocks may some time ⟨by⟩ be arrived at.

Sept 28. Heavy rain in early part of night, turning to snow, & when dawn broke the ground completely whitened & trees loaded. As signs of clearing, however, started, & paced slowly up the long hill to the summit. Trudged on till 2 P.m. through Slush, mud & water, with a continual shower coming down from the trees above. Then decided it was about time to stop, & finding a good camp waited till packs came up, when got changed & warmed. On the summit over four inches of snow in places, & many large limbs of trees, especially aspens, broken down by the weight. Little of interest geologically, or rather there may be much of interest, but little rock shows.

After camping took three photos,[310] & then rode off a short distance to examine rock of Mountain to right.

Some one has tried to make a little farm where we now are, doing a little fencing & putting up a log Cabin, but has evidently abandoned the endeavour.

This evening the hills on the N.E side of the valley are nearly bare, while those on the opposite are still almost completely snow Clad.

Sept 29. Surprised & disgusted to find the ground again white with snow, & a snow-storm raging, on looking out this morning. Nothing to do but to get off however, as the little short feed previously to be had here now covered. Carried on paced line, & after a few miles got below the level of the present snow line, though flakes still filled the air, melting as they fell. Came down to "The Fountain" before noon, & decided to Camp at once on Fountain Cr, the one we have been following down after lunch, paced a few miles out along the road towards Clinton, & rode back.

A bad headache in the evening, caused, I believe by handling dynamite, in endeavouring to split up a great log for fire-wood; that article being scarce.

Nothing but sage & lynosiris on the hills about here, so obliged to put the animals into a field of the Fountain Farm, Lawrence L'Artoise.[311]

Everything grows here in profusion, & to great perfection, & no frost has yet been experienced, though all agree in stating that this is the most inclement September on record. Lartoise (?spelling Italian) has two or three grape vines, from which he presented me with a fine ripe bunch of

---

310. Only one of the three photographs mentioned by Dawson remains. See "Photographs," 28 September 1877, GSC197–C1 (PA 51070).

311. Lorenzo Lotolo operated a ranch at Fountain. He is presumably the person meant.

grapes. Cabbages, cauliflowers, tomatoes &c. in great abundance but no market. Fine fields of grain, now harvested; but no market remunerative at present prices. Crop averages about 1000 lbs of wheat per acre, & sometimes reaches 3000 lbs under very favourable circumstances. Fields have now been Cropped for 16 (?) years without manure. Stated that after growing pease on the ground for one year, a splendid crop of wheat always harvested the next.

Sept 30. Sunday. Got off from Camp about 9 A.m. & paced down to Lytton Ferry[312] riding back, & arriving again at camp about 5 P.m.

Interesting exposures of the JM. rocks &c. & many boulders of limestone about the fountain, full of the peculiar large foraminifer already obtained from Marble Cañon. Packed specimens, wrote up notes, reading a little & to bed.

The trail from the Fountain to Lillooet, makes a semicircle or more, round the base of a great mass of mountains, of which the peaked Mt, — formerly photographed — is one. Great mountains are also piled together on the other side of the river, which following the line geologically indicated winds through them. Bridge River at its junction with the Fraser, strictly follows the strike of the rocks, & as seen from above looks white & angry, as its roar, mingled with that of the great river, ascends to the ear. A little triangular bench, at a high level, at the junction of the two streams is occupied by a number of Indian Cabins,[313] huddled together, & looking remarkably insignificant among the roots of the mountains. Today, with the mists rolling about them & frequently hiding the summits, I have seldom been so much impressed by the Solemn magnificence of the scenery. Behind Lillooet, can be seen the remarkable gap, leading like a portal to the Chain of lakes by which access was in early days obtained to the whole country.[314] Then Lillooet was indeed a busy place, full of packers & pack trains, bustle & business. Now a quiet enough little collection of houses, with fields, — many of them worked by Chinamen — wherever the benches are flat enough & water can be got on them.

Monday Oct. 1. Morning dull, overcast & drizzling rain, which continued at intervals all day, with a blustring bitter northwind, which seemed heavy & clinging to the ground So that it blew equally up hill & down. Paced on under considerable disadvantage to the mouth of Marble Cañon, where Camped on border of stream

---

312. Dawson means the Lillooet ferry.

313. Nxwistn, or "place of foam," now deserted.

314. Dawson's reference is to the Harrison-Lillooet Road from Harrison Lake through Lillooet, Anderson, and Seton lakes into Lillooet.

All the ground suitable for farming on both sides of the river here, is taken up, though the usual & not unreasonable complaint of want of market is made.

Nearly smoked to suffocation in my tent tonight, the wind persistently coming the wrong way.

Oct. 2. A fine morning & day, with some bright sunshine for a change. Carried paced line through Marble Cañon to Hat Creek, examining the rocks. Got one photo,[315] but by no means the best that might have been had, had one been able to choose place before hand.

The scenery very fine, & quite the style for a tourist resort if only less out of the world. A wonderful transverse fracture & natural pass, with splendid cliffs of white limestone & marble rising in places at least 2000 feet above the bottom of the valley, & often wonderfully jagged & rough. One detached column rises at least 400′ on the brow of an abrupt mountain, the Summit is sloping & occupied by a few small trees, the sides quite perpendicular, rendering it unapproachable except by the birds of the air. Two beautiful blue lakes in the cañon, formed by interruption of the natural drainage, into one, on the opposite side, a pretty little thread-like waterfall,[316] comes from a great height. Today the summits of the Mountains still frosted from the late snowstorms, the dark colour of the foliage concealed, & the whole so Silvery that it appears often almost to blend with the sky itself

Oct. 3. Took two photos.[317] one looking down Hat Cr. The other into the Marble Cañon. Then rode off up Hat Cr, in search of the Coal, which with aid of directions left written on a scrap of paper by the trail yesterday, by young Mr Martly[318] — was easily found. It proved to be the most gigantic lignite seam yet, 42 feet thick in one place & bottom not seen.[319] Rode a few miles further up the valley, sketched the Mountains, & returned to Camp about 2 A.m. Devoted P.m. to examination of limestones in vicinity & search for fossils, the latter rather unsuccessful. The peculiar forams Seem restricted to certain belts of the limestones which they then almost constitute. They are more abundant toward this end of

---

315. See "Photographs," 2 October 1877, GSC198–C1 (PA 51069).

316. Crown and Pavilion lakes. The waterfall drains into Crown Lake.

317. See "Photographs," 3 October 1877, GSC199–C1 (PA 51078), and GSC200–C1 (PA 152380).

318. Arthur Hugh John Martley (1855?–1942) was the only son of Captain John Martley who founded the well-known ranch, "The Grange." The younger Martley, along with managing the ranch, was an accomplished hunter and trapper and prospected throughout the area. See his obituary in the *Bridge River-Lillooet News*, 15 May 1942.

319. The Hat Creek lignite is described in Dawson, "Report on the Southern Portion," 120.

the Cañon, but just about here rare.

Wrote up notes turned in & after reading a while went to Sleep. A heavy freeze on.

Oct. 4. A fine clear cold morning, with the ground slightly frozen. The higher hills, & on going up Hat Creek a few miles, nearly all the hills, are yet covered more or less thickly with snow from the late falls, which seems so lothe to melt, that an early winter may be expected — our friends the horses, having got filled up in the spare day, yesterday, spent last night in travel, & to my great annoyance did not put in an appearance till 10 A.m. Took a photo.[320] of limestone cliff in the interim. Off a last, & travelled on examining rocks & pacing till about 5.30 Pm. when came up with camp about 2 miles from the Bonaparte R. Clear & cold tonight, with every probability of another heavy frost.

Oct 5. Off in good time. Completed pacing a few miles down Hat Creek, to the Waggon Road, & connected with Mr Richardson's* work at Hat Cr. bridge.[321] Rode along waggon road, & found camp at third of string of little lakes,[322] a few miles from Clinton. Examined the rocks pretty carefully in the most interesting places, & collected specimens. A very cold raw & unpleasant day, but without rain or snow. Douglas* shot a Coyote[323] this morning as we came along, & I afterwards a grouse, which make up our day's game bag.

A very curious erie & uncanny-looking bird is common in this country, especially among the mountains. It is of a general drab grey colour, back & belly, but with black tail, & outer part of wings [black?] with the exception of some white spots which show most prominently when in flight. It has a very large pointed bill-like beak, & large feet & strong legs, with a harsh Croak or half *caw* or Creak. It flies about among the pines, grating out its horrid monotone. It seems to frequent lonely places because of their solitude, which its presence for some reason only renders deeper. Now & then it may be seen to jump to the ground, seize one of the great cones of P. ponderosa & flying to a limb, hold the cone steady in its Claws, & proceed to extract the seeds by repeated blows with its pick-axe bill. Having finished it throws down the cone & — Croaks! (Clarks

320. See "Photographs," 4 October 1877, GSC201–C1 (PA 152381).

321. James Richardson accompanied Selwyn to British Columbia in the summer of 1871, then separated from the director at Kamloops to survey along the Cariboo wagon road and, later, Vancouver Island coal deposits. His published report deals only with the latter. See Richardson, "Report on the Coal Fields," 176.

322. Probably one of the Alkali Lakes.

323. Coyote, *Canis latrans lestes* Merriam.

Crow?)[324]

The great Blue Jay also very common, & Sets up the most tremendous screaming on ones approach, especially if some neighbours are within hearing. Now & then one may be caught at work on the ground, & when thus taken by surprise it is most vociferous in its scolding. By its plumage, however, it is a perfect dandy among birds.

[verso]

Sections examined today full of interest. — *First* as good & typical L.C.C. cherty quartzites as can be found, proved to be conformable & a part of a serpentinous formation, part or the whole of which separated by Richardson* into the Upper Cache Cr. for no reason that I can see. The interleaving of typical cherts & the Serpentines &c. most convincing & complete.[325]

Second. The origin of some of the serpentinous rocks as volcanic breccias, or in some cases of aggregations of volcanic material too fine to be called breccia (tuff[326] or ash) is conclusively Shown in several places. In some cases rather ordinary greenish volcanic breccias, graduate into more compact greenish rocks like those from which the fragments may be supposed to have been derived. In others the become serpentinous, often very markedly so, & all these are associated with other pure serpentines of which the origen, from analogy with the portions of the mixed rocks which have been serpentinized, — is easily guessed. Calc. matter associated with Some of the rocks in the manner indicated in the notes.[327] The serpentine no doubt product of decomp of some igneous mineral, very probably olivine[328] (vide — ? on Cornish Serpentines) & whether formed soon after ejection, or subsequently during the process which led to the silification of the associated quartzites &c. matter of speculation. These sections, with those of the Tertiary rocks, apparently becoming

---

324. Clark's nutcracker, *N. columbiana*.

325. Dawson means recrystallized chert. For a discussion of the relationships between Cache Creek and Nicola beds, see William B. Travers, "Overturned Nicola and Ashcroft Strata and Their Relation to the Cache Creek Group, Southwestern Intermontane Belt, British Columbia," *Canadian Journal of Earth Sciences* 15 (1978): 99–116, who observes that middle or late Triassic radiolaria are found in the matrix of the Cache Creek rocks, implying that these accumulated, with large and small blocks of older debris from a submarine slope to the east, at the same time as rocks mapped as Nicola Group farther east. In Jurassic time these two units were telescoped into juxtaposition with rocks of the early to mid-Jurassic Ashcroft groups. This involves plate tectonics, a process that was not recognized until more that fifty years after Dawson died.

326. A rock formed of compacted volcanic fragments, including ash, generally smaller than four millimetres in diameter.

327. See G. M. Dawson, Field Notebooks, RG 45, vol. 134, no. 2799, 25, PAC.

328. Or chrysolite, an abundant, olive-green, ferromagnesian silicate mineral.

serpentinous, on Kamloops Lake, of great importance.

Third. In the volcanic breccias & green, & serpentinous rocks of this part of the Cache Cr. series, I believe I have at last my "green series" of Nicola L &c. &c., with probably also the green rocks of the Shushwap Series. How this green, volcanic portion of the Cache Cr, is related to the Carboniferous fossil limestones, whether of ⟨of⟩ about the same age, or younger or older, remains to be Seen, & may perhaps be proven by fossils accompanying the limestones of the green series.[329]

[end verso]

Oct 6. Rode on to Clinton, examining rocks by the way, Secured mail, & bought a number of little things now needed; drove on the Lillooet Road & Camped at Kelly's Lake, about ten miles from Clinton. Examined rocks with view to making ⟨chain⟩ paced section of most characteristic part on return.

Day bleak overcast & chilly, & plenty snow yet lying not far above the level at which we now are. Everyone says the weather most unprecedented, & unite in prophesying a spell of very fine weather, which however seems to put off Coming.

Oct. 7. Rode off immediately after breakfast to get some idea of the country between here & the Fraser. Followed a Waggon Rd, made this summer for some distance, & then struck into a trail, making altogether about 8 ½ miles of track-Survey Cross section. Rode back as fast as possible to save some time in afternoon, & also in prospect of a promised visit from Clinton of the Fosters.[330] On getting back to Camp found they had been & had just left, Mrs F, having brought out an apple pie as an offering.

Wrote up notes, reading, wrote letters &c.

Oct. 8. Horses delayed us a little this morning. Got off about 8.30. Rode about a mile & a half down the trail, & then took to the side hill, on which proposed to measure section of rocks. Pacing & scrambling along the slopes till 3.30, when, though would have liked well enough to Continue section a little further, obliged to knock off & start for Clinton. Rode down the road as fast as possible, & on arriving at Clinton, posted letters, Called on Mrs Foster*, & left box of specimens in express office, addressed to Victoria. Then rode on about five miles further, finding the Camp

---

329. This problem of relationships and Dawson's tentative construction of a Nicola Series as well as his assignment of it to the Triassic is dealt with in his "Report on the Southern Portion," 171.

330. Frederick William Foster (1831–1915) came to British Columbia around 1860 to participate in the gold rush. Reaching Lillooet, Foster opened a store. When the Yale wagon road was constructed, Foster moved his business to Clinton then opened a branch at Ashcroft. Along with his mercantile activities, Foster was also a participant in mining ventures in the Clinton area.

where I had wished it, near the Bonaparte. Arrived just before dark, as hungry as a wolf.

A very fine Indian Summer like day, the first good weather for a long time. The aspens in many groves are now nearly bare. The leaves have not turned bright yellow this year in most places, owing to the bad weather. They are freckled & blackish, & require a very bright Sun to prevent them having a funereal aspect.

Oct. 9. Crossed the Bonaparte, & make track survey & examination of rocks of E. Side, down to two miles past the 124 m. House. Camped on a small stream,[331] not marked on map. The trail followed rather rough, being up & down hill nearly all the way. Morning lowering & gloomy, finer during P.m. but still cold & windy. No houses between Saul's,[332] where we first crossed the river — & the 124 m. house. The valley narrow, with little land suited for agriculture or hay. Slopes bare with bunch grass & sage. Stream now not large, easily fordable where bottom hard, tortuous, & Sometimes running beneath pretty high banks, with Canon-like aspect.
[verso]

Lakes &c. The lakes on the Waggon Rd South of Clinton (For number see Mr Richardson's* plan)[333] are some of them, especially those southward & lowest in the series, very evidently dammed by fans & wash from the sides of the narrow valley. The upper ones are not so Clearly formed in this way, & probably Some at least are holes left in terraces when the water stood at a higher level, as before explained.

Kelly's Lake, is deep, with a shallow bordering the shore, very well marked owing to the clearness of the water. The valley is narrow, with high sides, quite mountainous, & it appears — though not examined very closely — to be held in by a rather steep fan.

The sketch made in field note book[334] today, shows pools apparently held in by very distinct though rather small, moraine ridges, These would appear to have been formed as lateral moraines, by a gradually decreasing glacier, coming into the main valley at an angle by the valley leading S.E. Such at least the only way I can account for their formation, unless on supposition of retreating glacier from the north, which would probably have left more decided marks.
[end verso]

---

331. Scottie Creek.

332. Isaac and William Saul were pioneer farmers in the region. William sat in the Legislative Assembly as member for Lillooet.

333. Richardson's survey of the lakes was part of his 1871 season. The plan was not published.

334. See G. M. Dawson, Field Notebooks, RG 45, vol. 134, no. 2799, 35v, PAC.

Oct 10. Travelled on down valley, arriving at Cache Cr about 1 P.m. Turned immediately & proceeded up the valley toward Savona's Ferry, Camping at 8 m. Creek.[335] Morning cold & lowering, afternoon fine, evening clear but cold & windy. An Indian passing tells us wind always comes thus out of the valley of the 8 m. Creek. — Certain it is that it makes Camp very uncomfortable. Wood extremely scarce, but even the small fire I have scraped together makes me suffer martyrdom from the smoke, which it is impossible to dodge.

Found this afternoon a man hauling wood, from whom asked way, & where would find good camping place. Said he thought the next house was the best place for wood & water, but if we went on to the next beyond, he "guessed we would be able to scrape together enough chips for the night" "Oh but" said I "we can buy some wood from the man anyhow" " *No* (emphatically) you can buy nothing from him" "You Cant hows that?" "Why the old man would *give* you d—m near half the ranche if you only asked for it."

Oct. 11. Off in good time, travelled on to Savona's Ferry, Crossed the animals &c. & got well started on the Mountain trail toward the lower Thompson &c. A fine day, & good Camping place tonight, for wood water & feed. Found at mouth of Deadman's Creek a sandy hill which had been used as a burial place,[336] & partly excavated by the wind like that at Lytton, but both size of burying ground & excavation on a much smaller scale. Found however a few tools &c., amongst others a good chisel, & the Crutch like top of a Klootchmans stick for digging roots.[337] Generally made of wood, but this neatly of bone. See the women now occasionally in the fields digging potatoes with a stick of the same shape. Several skulls lying about, but all more or less battered, though fresher looking than those of Lytton. Evidently newer altogether, as found two pieces of iron, one of which must have been a Knife.

The Thompson Valley, is the continuation of the same wide trough in which Kamloops L. lies, but below the lake filled with benches & fans.[338]

---

335. Probably Battle Creek.

336. The two known archaeological sites at the mouth of Deadman Creek (EeRf 7 and EeRf 19) were locations of pit houses that do not contain burials.

337. "Roots were dug with an ingenious tool known as a patsa ('pacha') in Lillooet and Shuswap or pitsa ('peecha') in Okanagan. Ranging in length from about 0.3 to 1.2 metres (1 to 4 feet) it had a curved pointed tip and a short crosspiece at the top for a handle. Digging-sticks were formerly made of hard wood, such as oceanspray (*Holodiscus discolor*) or Saskatoon, or deer antler" (Turner, *Food Plants of Interior Peoples*, 28).

338. Dawson is describing the deltaic infill of a former glacial lake subsequently cut by the Thompson River. See Ryder, *Inventory and Geology, Ashcroft*, 16.

The river follows the southern side, though making wide benches, & sometimes almost touching the northern. Rock is seen frequently at the waters edge at the south side, Seldom or never at the north, — in the length examined today. Thus no proof that Kamloops L. a rock basin, rather indeed evidence to the contrary in continued width of valley, floored for the most part with detritus, which extends to an unknown depth.

Several hollows in the detritus, lying N of N edge of valley (immediate) of river. These do not open out to river, but appear to be pot-holes, left during the gradual filling up of the formerly more extended lake, by benches &c. The same sort of depressions that elsewhere often become lakes.

Now (8 Pm) An Aurora, the best I have seen for a long time. General brightness or irregular arch reaching at times to Ang. height of 40°. Some coruscation about western end. (Afterwards rose to 50°, forming pretty symmetrical arches, & with considerable Motion.

Oct. 12. A fine morning, with hoar frost on the grass & a skim of ice on pools. Travelled on, at first not very far from the Thompson, of which we occasionally caught glimpses. The trail passes over a sort of irregular plateau, sloping in the main towards the river, or rather to the edge of the great trough in which it flows. The "plateau" if worthy of the name — is seamed with small streams running to the Thompson, while to the south, it is bounder by higher hills, generally pretty thickly wooded, & which probably soon unite to form the main high-level plateau of the Country, the height of which here probably averages about 4500'. The lower plateau, or sloping region averages about 3000'. The trail then leaves the vicinity of the Thompson, cutting across the corner toward Cornwall's*; & passes at about the same level, by wide valleys or depressions, among small rocky hills. Pools & lakes like those of yesterday abound, & are now *full* of ducks of all species & geese, the former very tame. Though without a dog, managed to Kill four, a mallard, two shoveller's,[339] & a green-winged teal. Bunch grass & P. ponderosa, characterize the greatest elevations reached today, & the whole country passed over from Savonas Ferry, splendidly adopted for stock. The grass in many places, however, already pretty well eaten down.

Had some trouble & riding in the morning trying to ascertain which the right trail, Cattle tracks being so Numerous, & running in all directions. Can only arrive at approximate certainty by exhausting possibilities of all trails but one, & then following that. Much practical experience needed to choose by instinct the leading trail from cultus tracks, but can generally be done by attention to main direction, & accounting for tracks by the known

339. Northern shoveler, *Anus clypeata* (L.).

habits of Cattle.

[verso]

In viewing the country across the Thompson, from the heights today, find a very general grand uniform dip, at low angles, of the Tertiary Igneous rocks — which are in great thickness — away from the valleys. Thus in the Angle between Thompson & Deadmans Cr, dip North westward. At the Angle between Thompson & Bonaparte — North Eastward, & in the intervening region, — if at all noticeably — northward. In the centre of this block the higher regions of the plateau; around its edges the sloping & broken country, generally pretty open & forming stock ranges. May it thus be that the present main drainage features of the country — or many of them — were produced by a folding or buckling up of the surface of post Miocene date, & that we must look elsewhere for the Pre Miocene & Miocene rivers. Gentle dips like these would as a rule be hard to detect, especially when superposed on more marked inclinations of the older beds. Only by such broad views of the less disturbed regions, like that of today, would they become apparent, yet may by [potent] physically, especially if — as probably — the country bent *in the Cold*, with consequent extensive Cracking. This probably the last bending of the country, & if the former foldings caused volcanic action, this may not have been sufficient for that purpose.[340] (*vide* other valleys in this regard) [*Illus.*]

[end verso]

Oct. 13. A long & hard day. Up before the sun, & got into camp at night just before dark. On leaving camp struck the Thompson in about 3 miles, & then continued down it, though much bothered for a time by blind & cattle-trails. Found Brunel's Camp *en route* but saw none of the staff, who were out somewhere on line. He is working back over difficult points in his location. Found some very interesting sections of rocks, but the train far ahead & obliged to hurry on to overtake before night. A beautifull Indian Summer day, with magnificent views of mountain & river, if one had time enough to take them in & enjoy them, but nothing today but — S30W 1.5 m. D N20E⟨60 then climb onto ones horse again nudge him with the spur

---

340. Dawson was very up-to-date in his thinking about the time of origin of the main drainage features. The rocks he was referring to as Miocene are, however, now known to be Eocene, but the relationships he described are still correct. The "cracking" of the ground associated with bending of the cold rocks might be a little overdrawn, and it is not at all certain that such occurred in British Columbia to the extent of controlling river courses. The erosion of hard and soft rocks whose distribution was modified by the folding Dawson describes, as well as their tilting and local rupturing, have definitely led to marked modification of the drainage pattern. Dawson was concerned with the fossil river channels as sites for placer gold and was correct in predicting that auriferous gravels under the nearly flat-lying Tertiary volcanic rocks would show little or no relationship to the present river systems.

& hurry on. Camped on a bouldery flat where nature seems to have been manufacturing Cobble stones of varied size & material. The boulders are brought here by a little stream, which must be a "terror" when in the berserker Mood & rolling them about.

Oct. 14. Off pretty easy, track-surveyed down to the mouth of the Nicola, & then commenced paced line up the Nicola Road. Got a photo.[341] of remarkable bluff of Tuff & dykes, & then told Casinto to go on & camp about 4 P.m. Got into Camp just as getting too dark to see to work longer. Douglas*, unfortunate as usual, pitched the tent in his hurry on a bed of cactus, & gave us twenty minutes work clearing the hateful prickly pears out with the shovel, while they stuck to everything like burs.

Another magnificent day, & a really splendid view of the towering mountain below Spences bridge & across the Thompson.[342] The great rifts about its summit full full of dark shadow, a transparent blue haze Surrounding it, & the bridge & houses looking like very pigmies below.

Solaced this evening by an excellent duck stew, which Johnny had got up before our arrival.

While getting photo. of bluff today, sent Douglas* back on the road to act as a figure to give dimensions. When I gave him the signal that all was over, he began to run back, but was suddenly seen to jump sideways, & it appears that he had almost stepped on a large rattle-snake, which had been near him as he stood, but began to rattle when he moved. Rattlesns are said to be very abundant on the lower part of the Nicola.

[verso]

Where we are Camped the Nicola appears to turn abruptly, & at the same time looses much of the rugged character of valley heretofore shown, the hills sloping more gently & the bottom land being wider. So far the road has almost exactly followed the river, Crook for Crook.

[end verso]

Oct. 15. Another very long day, pacing from morning to night with the exception of about half an hour while taking a photo.[343] of Tufaceous Sandstones &c. To dark to read the compass for the last stretch into camp. Day chilly, with dropping rain during the forenoon, & a coating of stratus all day, though promising well at dawn.

Oct. 16. Had thought today's would be a short day's work, but before all the turns were made & my paced line Joined up with work formerly done on the coal exposures, found it about 4 P.m. Road back to camp on the Indian Reserve, getting in about 5. A fine day but partly overcast. Heartily

341. See "Photographs," 14 October 1877, GSC202–C1 (PA 51080).

342. Probably Arthur Seat.

343. See "Photographs," 15 October 1877, GSC203–C1 (PA 51079).

glad to get to the end of this pacing.

Oct. 17. Set out for Kamloops *via* the Ten Mile Creek, Kozoom Kanix of the local map, by which name the Indians, however, do not Know it. The upper part about the lake Called by them *Ma-mt* from the white fish in the lake, the lower part *Na-a-ik* from the abundance of Kinnikinnick berries.[344] As Gischon[345] (? spelling) is the only settler on the creek, it may well be called Gischon's Cr. Camped at a small stream a few miles above the head of the lake.[346] Fine bunch grass & open slopes everywhere. Gischon has a nice place, & though (by bar. (revise) about 3000′ high grows grain of all Sorts & potatoes with success. Found yesterday that the Nicola people are beginning to appreciate the advantages of fall wheat, & many of them find they can grow it without irrigation. This important in view of the large tracts of land in some parts of the province, on which water cannot easily ⟨by⟩ be brought.

A fine typical Indian Summer day, with a morning mist, but calm, & warm like summer about noon. Tonight clear & calm

Oct. 18. Another very fine day. Got a fairly early start, & travelled steadily on till 4.30, but made little greater distance than yesterday because of the crooked character of the trail. Crossed the watershed between the Nicola & Kamloops streams, a broad gently undulated or flat plateau, with innumerable pools, lakelets & marshes. Many with ducks, & one full of wild geese which flew away on the approach of the bells, with great clamour. If this plateau country & the slopes about the sources of the streams on either side were but a little lower, it would form a fine farming country with a very fertile soil. Even as it is it is probable that at least the hardier cereals could be grown. They should be tried. Partly covered with open woods of Douglas fir & P. contorta, partly open & producing fine bunch grass, & partly swampy with good grass for hay, it constitutes at present a very fine stock range. The whole country, indeed, between here & Nicola is admirably adapted for stock.

Met today a little Cavalcade of Indians, returning from a hunting camp up on the plateau, towards Nicola Lake. Three men, with several women, young & old, & a bevy of children, all mounted, the women & children sitting on the summits of packs tied up in fresh deer skins & packed with spruce boughs, containing the deer meat, the product of the hunt, Colts

344. Kinnikinnick or bearberry, *A. uva-ursi.*

345. Joseph Guichon (1844?–1921) and his brother Pierre came to British Columbia in 1864 and worked as packers in the Cariboo before taking up land at Mamit Lake in 1873. Soon thereafter Pierre died. Joseph later bought the Mickle Ranch on Nicola Lake in 1882; in 1907 he built the Quilchena Hotel, which still stands today. He retired to Vancouver in 1918 and left the ranch to his three sons.

346. The whole stream, now called Guichon Creek, flows through Mamit Lake.

running too & fro among the horses, & the men mounted with more dignity, each Carrying his long-barreled musket ornamented with brass headed nails & nearly covered with a buck-skin case, across his knees. No useless finery displayed, though the youngest & best looking of the women had a little of the usual red paint rubbed into the skin of her face. All looking dirty enough, but fat & happy, clad in such rags as no dealer in second hand clothes would care to put a price to, but which while in organic connection with the Siwash not looking so bad after all. On meeting the first man, who was riding ahead, & who carried his gun, I said in a tone intended to express surprise — "What! have you killed no deer!" Oh said he *Hi-you Mowich Chaco*,[347] waving his hand in a triumphant manner toward the hill; & sure enough in a few minutes the party in the order above described, & with the *Mowich*, appeared. They lead on the whole truly careless shiftless (in more senses than one) but happy lives; travelling, — those of them who do not work for the whites, or pack on the road — from place to place in a comparatively Circumscribed area of country, according to the season. At one time hunting deer, at another trapping marten, taking Salmon or whitefish, or digging up their little patch of potatoes, — for they nearly all have "gardens" Somewhere — but their glory has departed.

Their physiognomy is very varied, & though occasionally a really fine, & often a pleasant enough face, is to be met with, many are baboonish & repulsive.

Oct. 19. Up with first dawn, knowing that long drive into Kamloops had to be made. Sun rose clear & fine, but the valley of the lake below filled with great rolling masses of drifting mist, from which the mountains rose like those pictures one sometimes sees of the world floating in a mass of clouds. In descending soon became involved in the mist, but steered on North eastward by the dim image of the sun, & compass till the waggon Rd struck about 6 m. west of Cherry Creek. Travelled on along the road to Kamloops, making track survey & examining the rocks. The numerous little lakes & pools full of ducks which, however, rather shy. Took a few random shots at them, exhausting my supply of loaded Cartridges. Got to Kamloops just at sunset, getting a fine aspect of the magnificent view from the hills behind the town up the N. Thompson. The poplars fringing the river now brightly golden contrasting finely with the dark green of the pines, the grey of the bunch-grass & sage bush slopes, & the purple Shadows filling the valleys. A magnificent Indian Summer day. Got mail & took up old quarters at McPhaden's*.

Oct. 20. Busy all morning with Douglas* packing & overhauling *ictas*.

347. A Chinook Jargon phrase meaning "plenty of deer approaching."

Afternoon got a "buggy" & took Camera up the hill & to two or three places of which wished views.[348] Evening reading writing &c. Another Splendid day.

Oct 21. Sunday. Completed packing, took another, & probably better view of Kamloops.[349] Afternoon rode up on the hill to visit a reported Copper lead, found quartz but no copper. The rocks exposed well for a short distance in small ravine a little below & west of the "C.P.R. Camp" appear to belong to the L.C.C. Volcanic. The consist of greenish & greyish, sometimes almost nacreous[350] schists, & green compact rock. Str. N. 80W. vert. or high dip southward.

Oct. 22. Drove out to Cache Cr in a light trap with Mr Barnard*, getting there nearly an hour in advance of the stage. The usual fog hanging over Kamloop's Lake, & clinging about the adjoining hills till nearly noon.

Deadman's Cr appears to run up with a wide valley about 10 miles at least, from road, with general bearing of N.25.W.

Oct. 23. Finding an extra with McMillan* & part of party ready to start out this morning, decided to go on in advance of the ordinary stage. Drove on to Lytton, after stopping for dinner at Spences Bridge, where compared barometer with Mr Murry's[351] Mercurial, & got from him specimens of fossils found on Jackass Mtn.

[verso]

My small aneroid used during summer read — 28.865
Mercurial Corrected 28.779

$$28.862$$
$$28.779$$
$$\overline{}$$
$$.086$$

[end verso]

Looked at rocks behind the 89. m. stable while changing horses, they appear fully to justify conclusion formed from their inspection from other side of river, that the limestone is underlaid by a mass of igneous rock, of the same age as the breccia on the E. side.[352] The rock is greenish &

---

348. See "Photographs," 20 October 1877, GSC205–C1 (PA 51082); GSC206–C1 (PA 51083); and GSC207–C1 (PA 51085).

349. See "Photographs," 21 October 1877, GSC208–C1 (PA 51086).

350. Having the lustre of mother-of-pearl.

351. John Murray (d. 1896) was a Spences Bridge general store owner and fruit farmer.

352. Later geological work illustrates a still more complicated (faulted) structure behind the 89 mile stable, north of Venables Creek, than that shown by Dawson. Also, the rocks opposite and below Spences Bridge as far as the Nicoamen River are volcanic, not

compact, & in some places clearly bedded conformably with the limestone. [*Illus.*] In fragments of a dark limestone evidently from the hill immediately behind the stable, fossils are abundant, the locality would probably well repay a few hours, or a day's collecting.

Granites & gneisses appear to form the prominent Mountain just across from, & below, Spences Bridge; & probably continue nearly to follow the W. side of the Thompson from that down, crossing finally a short distance below Nicommen. The volcanic rocks, however, appear in patches, forming the lower hills near the river on the W. side in several places. The gneisses &c. resemble those seen on the Lytton-Lillooet trail.

Oct. 23.[353] Travelled only from Lytton to Boston Bar today. Wet in the Afternoon.

The B. Bar rocks at Mouth of Anderson River on upper side are blackish, often striped with grey, shales, with broad bands of greyish fine-flaky shale.[354] Quite like the rocks seen in descending over the Mountain to Boston Bar. D. N30 E average angle 30°, but apparently nearly vertical in the bed of the river.

Oct. 24. from Boston Bar to Yale. A showery day. Looked after baggage & made enquiries about boxes previously sent out. Got bed on board Steamer Royal City, which leaves at 4 a.m.

Oct 25. Yale to New Westminster. Stopped at Colonial Hotel, but found great difficulty in getting anything as a great ball given by the fisheries in progress & waiters & many had partaken too freely. Looked into drill shed where ball going on. The hall very prettily decorated with flags nets &c.

Oct 26. N. Westminster to Victoria, making an easy & quick passage. Got luggage stowed in CPR. office, & took up quarters in Driard House.

[The period from 27 October until Dawson's departure from British Columbia is documented in a small pocket journal, loose in the main personal journal for 1877.]

Oct 27. 1877. Left New Westminster 8 a.m. had a fine run over to Victoria in the "Enterprise" arriving there between 3 & 4 P.m. Looked after luggage & took up quarters in Driard House.

---

granitic and gneissic. Granites and gneisses appear along the Thompson River only below the Nicoamen River.

353. Dawson has the date wrong as it should be 24 October. The dates for the next three entries are also incorrect. Dawson has duplicate entries in his two different diaries for 27 October.

354. Steep dips are normal for the Boston Bar rocks. The flatter dip reported by Dawson could have been a result of down-slope creep.

Oct. 28. Sunday Not quite decided whether possible to get off by the Dakota on Tuesday, all depending on what may have to be done in Baynes Sound matter. Go over & roughly pack valises &c. in hotel. Afternoon for a walk. Sharp frost last night.

Oct. 29. Get carpenter to work packing & overhauling specimens & make all preparations possible. See Roscoe[355] & discuss proposed visit to Baynes Sound, find, however, that the steamer does not go up till Tuesday week, & that then necessary to stay a fortnight till next trip to get time to examine the rocks & return. Decided eventually to go if special arrangements could be made to enable me to get ⟨off⟩ up to Baynes Sd & back by the steamer's first regular trip in time to leave Victoria by the steamer of Novr 10. The company,[356] however, found that the steamer demanded to much & so eventually decided to get what information possible by discussion of latest plans with Mr Richardson* & transmit to them by return; & to visit the locality next spring if possible. The great object to know where best place for boring, preliminary to sinking shaft.

This once decided proceeded to make every effort to get off tomorrow, & succeeded in getting my 21 packages in order before going to bed.

Oct 30 Paid bills, got drafts on San Francisco at bank. Telegraphed to Mr Selwyn* & made final arrangements for leaving. Drove down to Esquimalt with Dr Tolmie*. The harbour gay with war vessels, the Shah, Opal, Albatros, & Rocket being anchored there. Got off from the wharf after some difficulty, & about 10 Pm rounding the light on Cape Flattery.

[Dawson arrived in San Francisco on the morning of 3 November, and stayed there until 5 November, visiting acquaintances, shopping, and attending the theatre. He caught the train east and, travelling via Omaha and Chicago, reached Toronto on 12 November 1877.]

355. Probably Francis James Roscoe (1831–78), who came to British Columbia in 1862 and settled in Victoria, where he operated a successful iron and hardware business. In 1873 he was elected to the House of Commons but declined re-nomination for the 1878 election. See his obituary in the *Victoria Daily British Colonist*, 21 December 1878.

356. Probably the Baynes Sound Coal Company which was trying to operate a coal mine. See October 1878.

Dawson's 1878 Route

28 MAY-12 JUNE: Travelled from Victoria along the Inside Passage to Cape St. James on southern tip of Queen Charlotte Islands.

12-15 JUNE: Explored Houston Stewart Channel.

16-18 JUNE: Sailed northward into Carpenter Bay and on to South Cove and then into Harriet Harbour in Skincuttle Inlet.

20-21 JUNE: Explored Inlet, into Huston Inlet and back out to the mouth of Skincuttle Inlet around the Copper Islands and Burnaby Island.

23-30 JUNE: Exploration around Burnaby Island, Burnaby Strait. and Juan Perez Sound, finally berthing at Skaat Harbour (Wanderer Bight).[1]

1-4 JULY: Explored Juan Perez Sound, De la Beche Inlet, and Hotspring Island.

5-9 JULY: Finished exploration of Juan Perez Sound and Darwin Sound, then sailed westward from Echo Harbour around Bent Tree Point to Klunkwoi Bay and on to Crescent Inlet. Up to Richardson Island and then north along the west shore of the channel to the open sea at

---

1. Current topographical names are given, with Dawson's most frequent usage in parentheses.

Laskeek Bay to Clue Village.

10 JULY: Visited Dana Inlet, Rockfish Harbour and Skedans Village.

11-22 JULY: Exploration of inlets between Laskeek Bay and Cumshewa Inlet and around Cumshewa Inlet itself.

23-24 JULY: North around Spit Point and along south shore of Skidegate Inlet, then across inlet to Skidegate Village.

25-30 JULY: Explored Skidegate Inlet and visited Cowgitz coal mine.

31 JULY-2 AUGUST: Exploration of Skidegate Channel through to western shore and return.

3-4 AUGUST: Camped at Skidegate Harbour.

5-10 AUGUST: Sailed northward from Skidegate Inlet along east coast, around Rose Point, then to Masset Village.

11 AUGUST: At Masset Village.

12-17 AUGUST: Southward down Masset Sound to Juskatla Inlet with a short trip up the Mamin River, then around Juskatla Inlet and back to Masset via the north shore of Masset Inlet.

18 AUGUST: At Masset Village.

19-22 AUGUST: Sailed from Masset along north coast of Graham Island to Virago Sound and Naden Harbour.

23-24 AUGUST: West along coast to North Island and Parry Passage.

26 AUGUST: Overland trip across Cape Knox to Lepas Bay on the west coast of Graham Island.

27-29 AUGUST: Sailed around Lucy Island and then east to Port Simpson.

30-31 AUGUST: At Port Simpson.

1-12 SEPTEMBER: Sailed to Metlakatla, then southward to Bella Bella.

13-17 SEPTEMBER: Sailed from Bella Bella to northern Vancouver Island, then around to west coast of the island and into Quatsino Sound.

18-26 SEPTEMBER: Explored Quatsino Sound.

27-28 SEPTEMBER: Sailed from North Harbour around Cape Scott to Bull Harbour on Hope Island.

29-30 SEPTEMBER: At Bull Harbour.

1-6 OCTOBER: To Fort Rupert and Alert Bay.

7-11 OCTOBER: Sailed south from Alert Bay through Discovery Passage to Cape Mudge.

12-17 OCTOBER: Sailed to Denman Island, Fanny Bay, Nanaimo, and Victoria.

18-30 OCTOBER: At Victoria.

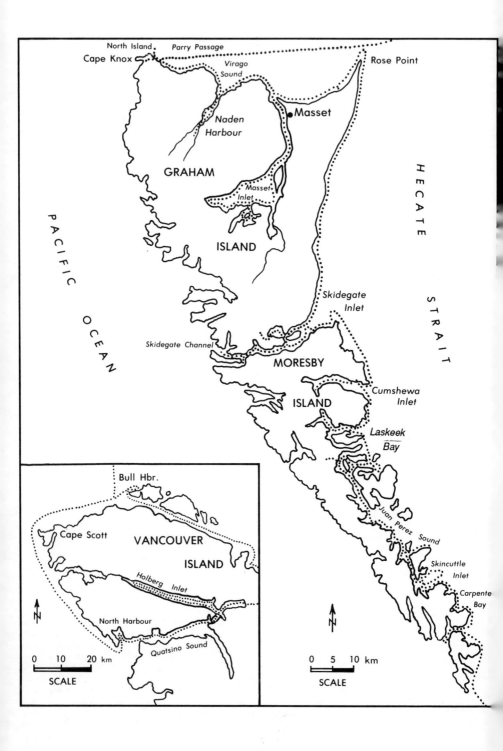

III

1878

[Dawson left Montreal on 30 April by rail via Toronto and Port Huron to Chicago. He travelled with his youngest brother, Rankine. The reason for Rankine's presence is unclear, though the Dawson family probably hoped that a summer season with George would benefit the youth, whose unsteady character was already a problem. They arrived in San Francisco on 8 May and at noon on 10 May left for Victoria on the steamer *Dakota*. Dawson used a smaller pocket journal until his departure from Victoria on 27 May 1878, when he began his main 1878 journal. In the current edition, entries for Dawson's voyage to Victoria have not been included.]

May 13. Entered Esquimalt harbour at 6.30 A.m. after a remarkably quick & pleasant passage. Got Carriage over to Victoria & put up at Driard House. Find Torrence[1] still here. Get luggage up Go about various matters of business. Enquire about Craft. Find Douglas[2] not yet here but had given him time to the 15th. Enquire about other Craft in case he does not turn up.

---

1. J. Fraser Torrance, a Montrealer who was then a British Columbia gold commissioner and who later worked for the survey.

2. Probably the veteran west coast mariner Abel Douglas (1841?–1908) who had captained the vessel used by James Richardson in his geological explorations. Douglas lived for many years in Victoria until 1906, when he moved to Seattle.

G. M. Dawson to Margaret Dawson*, 13 May 1878, Victoria

Here we are in Victoria at last, after a remarkably fast & pleasant passage from San Francisco, & an uneventful railway journey over the west. The steamer brought us in here early this morning, So early that we had to content ourselves with a cup of coffee on board & come on to Victoria for breakfast. Fraser Torrance* is still here, leaves for the interior next friday to visit first — I believe — Cherry Creek.

Today I have not been able to more than go round making enquiries. Capt. Douglas* with his schooner is not yet here. He has still a day to the date at which I appointed to meet him, however, & if he does not turn up in time I think I shall have little difficulty in procuring a suitable Craft here from someone else. Meanwhile it will take a day or two to get other preparations made & plans more definitely laid.

Capt. Lewis[3] of the HB Co who has Sailed much on the Northern Coast Says the natives of the Queen Charlotte Islands are not to be feared & also advises me to go up there at once as the weather in the spring & early Summer is best. He says that when once the wet rough weather begins in autumn it generally lasts on through the winter. Rankine* begins already to look sunburnt & well though still thin enough. He is a singularly reticent travelling Companion & when anything particularly pleases him only Chuckles internally or whistles. I hope to improve him during the summer.

When in San Francisco we went to the Chinese Theatre, where I had not been before. It was well worth seeing for once, though the music, composed of peculiarly reedy & squaky notes, mingled with tones of horns & gongs, was anything but Enjoyable. The first part of the performance was a comedy, which to those who did not understand what was being Said, seemed long drawn & stupid, especially as much of the conversation was Carried on in a sort of sing-song. After this Came to a happy end an exhibition of tumbling began, which was quite wonderful. The dresses throughout were wonderfully gay with silver gold & silk. The audience was almost altogether of Chinamen, who seemed to enjoy the display heartily. The atmosphere was rather dense with tobacco smoke before we left, which was at about 11 P.m. & how much longer the fun lasted I do not Know. In a day or two I will be able to write giving Plans more in detail,

---

3. Captain Herbert George Lewis (1828–1905) was an early citizen of Victoria who came to the northwest coast in 1847 with the Hudson's Bay Company. Lewis worked on various vessels, including the *Beaver* and *Otter*, before giving up his command in 1886. Later, Lewis was agent for the federal Department of Marine and Fisheries, then shipping master for the port of Victoria until his death. See his obituary in *Victoria Daily Colonist*, 31 March 1905.

till which time excuse this little scrawl & Believe me.

G. M. Dawson to Bernard James Harrington*, 13 May 1878, Victoria

The quartz excitement[4] still Continues here, though the present aspect of affairs is that all the available Capital of the place having been absorbed in various more or less precarious speculations. Stock jobbing is at a standstill. From various sources I hear of assays Made in San Francisco & elsewhere, for private parties, the result of which was more favourable than Any tried at the survey. If you can find time to make trial of the samples lately forwarded, before long, I feel Sure it would be appreciated here by the Govt. people.

The proof of my map,[5] corrected as well as I can do it, was sent back from Toronto. I hope you have received it safely. There were errors both in the black & in the colours.

In the copy of the report I brought with me, the memorandum, — which was to be printed on a separate slip and inserted — relating to the two maps of which the publication is postponed, were omitted. This was probably accidental.

In leaving I forgot to say that I should like to have the box of rock specimens which Mr. Weston[6] prepared shipped as ordinary freight during the summer. July would be soon enough, as I may not find time to do anything with it till my return here in the Autumn. The Casella thermometer[7] if another comes out, should be forwarded, by post if possible, to

---

4. Dawson is referring to hopes in the Cariboo region around Barkerville that "notwithstanding the remoteness of this district, the existence of settlement and of a considerable mining population in it, justified the attempt to develop 'quartz-mining'. This feeling brought about the premature quartz excitement of 1877 and 1878, which was based on exaggerated ideas of the richness of certain known lodes, and on erroneous views as to the facility with which gold might be extracted from the pyritous ores which these afforded. From the collapse of this excitement, vein-mining received a severe check" (Dawson, "Mineral Wealth of B.C.," 56–57).

5. Presumably "Map of part of British Columbia between the Fraser River and the Coast Range," prepared to illustrate Dawson's 1876 report and published in 1878 in the survey's, *Report of Progress for 1876-77.*

6. Thomas Chesmer Weston (1832–1911) had come to Canada in 1859 at the request of Sir William Logan to join the Geological Survey of Canada. Weston not only became an expert in fossil collecting but was also the survey's first librarian. He spent some thirty years with the survey. For a colourful narrative of Weston's years with the survey see his *Reminiscences Among the Rocks: In Connection with the Geological Survey of Canada* (Toronto: Warwick Bro's & Rutter, 1899).

7. Casella's was a London instrument firm under the direction of father Louis P. and son Louis M. Casella. Dawson's is probably a maximum or minimum thermometer (or both) to measure temperature extremes.

save expense, to my address Care C.P. Ry. office Victoria. I will try to Keep the people there posted as to our whereabouts.

Enclosed is a slip with a few addresses to which Mr. White[8] might forward Copies of the Rep. of Progress[9] when published in complete form.

Please excuse me for troubling you with these little things. Love to Anna*, to whom I must Soon write — & to Eric[10]

May 12-17   Victoria looking after equipment & making preparations. Douglas* not arriving on 15th make arrangements on following day with Capt. Sabotson[11] for schooner Wanderer. Evg. of May 17. dine at Mr McDonalds.[12]

Sunday May 19. Writing & Pm for a walk by Beacon Hill & Ogden Pt.

G. M. Dawson to Anna Lois Harrington*, 19 May 1878, Victoria

I still date, worse luck, from this place, but hope to get away this week, though the precise day is yet uncertain. When we got here, after a remarkably quick & pleasant passage from San Francisco, Capt Douglas* & his Craft were not to be heard of, but as I had given him till the 15th I was obliged to wait till that date, making enquiries in the meantime as to other available Chances. On the 16th I made an arrangement for the schooner *Wanderer* of about 20 tons & as soon as she is ready for sea will be off. She belongs to a man Called Sabotson* who is getting new sails for her ⟨....⟩ & as Soon as these are ready all will be complete. Since engaging the Wanderer I have heard that Douglas'* schooner which Mr Richardson* formerly had was blown ashore in a squall somewhere near Comox & so much damaged that she Cannot be put in repair for some time. The *Wanderer* is I think a good Craft, with plenty beam, & built originally for a Pilot boat. If the Captain & Crew, the latter Yet to be selected, turn out

8.   Probably James White, draftsman with the Geological Survey Canada.

9.   The Geological Survey of Canada's *Report of Progress for 1876–77*.

10.   John Eric Harrington (1877–95) was the oldest of Bernard and Anna's children. Chronically ill, Eric never survived beyond young adulthood.

11.   John Sabiston (1853?–98) was the son of John Sabiston, a prominent Nanaimo pilot from 1867 until 1896. The younger Sabiston later died of brain disease in New Westminster.

12.   Senator William John Macdonald (1829–1916), as noted below, had been on the same railway train across the continent as Dawson. He had come to British Columbia from Scotland in 1851 and after working for the Hudson's Bay Company went into business for himself. He was a member of the Vancouver Island Legislative Assembly from 1860–1863, of the Legislative Council of the United Colonies from 1867 to 1868, and one of the three British Columbia senators from 1871 until 1915.

well all will be right.

There are as you may suppose innumerable little things to look after here & it would seem that we Cannot even get a clear half day for any work about this place. Tomorrow I shall make a vigorous effort to clear off the remainder of my list, so that any days remaining may be free from little engagements Rankine* Comments on the fewness of good looking girls in this part of the world, especially in contrast with their abundance in San Francisco. The best looking & therefore most highly esteemed he has yet encountered is a Miss McDonald,[13] daughter of the senator of the same name who travelled over the ry. with us & asked us to his home the other night to dinner.

The weather is fine & settled looking now, though there have been a few windy Cold days since we landed. I long to be off taking advantage of the fine time. When all is ready, following advice, I shall strike straight away for the Queen Charlottes & after spending as much of the summer there as the Country seems to warrent & weather permits, shall begin to work back toward Vancouver. I enclose a little memo. for Mamma.[14]

May 20   Business of various Kinds in connection with outfit
May 21. Morning about town on business. P.m. walk to Limestone exposure at Indian reserve Esquimalt & hunt for fossils. Evg. walk out to McDonalds*.
May 22. Morning as usual going about numerous little affairs. P.m. go by invitation to Croquet at Gov. Richards* stay for dinner at which Capt & Mrs Robinson[15] & Miss Dupont.[16]
May. 23. Enquired about Sails which it now appears Cannot be finished before Saturday. Had hoped to go off on Friday. Visit schooner which now nearly ready. Tell Mr Charles[17] he may have the use of the boat on

---

13. Most likely Flora Alexandrina (1867–1924), the eldest of Senator W. J. Macdonald's three daughters. She would have been nineteen or twenty at the time. (Edythe Mary and Lilias Christiana were four and six years younger.) She married Gavin Hamilton Burns in 1890. The senator's home was Armadal, a gracious house built on twenty-eight acres at Ogden Point in the James Bay district.

14. Not in the Dawson Family Papers.

15. Captain James Robinson and Mrs. Ada C. Robinson. Robinson was one of the early navigators of the Fraser River, employed first as master of passenger ships and later with survey ships of the Department of Public Works. He was a member of the first Legislative Assembly after the union of British Columbia and Vancouver Island.

16. Probably Miss Clara Elizabeth Dupont (1843–1923), principal of Angela College, a Victoria girls' school endowed by Baroness Burdett-Coutts.

17. Probably William Charles (1831–1903), head of the Hudson's Bay Company's British Columbia operations. Born in Scotland, Charles joined the company in 1854 and came to British Columbia in 1858 where he was in charge of a number of posts. In 1874 he

the Queens Birthday.

P.m. for a drive & scramble to top of Cedar Hill with Mr McDonald*.
Evg. row on the harbour.

May 24   Queens birthday holiday making everywhere interfering with
work on Sails &c. Morning walked to Beacon Hill & Clover Pt to see Base
Ball match & rifle firing. P.m. up "the arm" with a party of Mrs
Robertsons[18] including Duponts*, Powells*, Poolies* &c. to see the races
& regatta. The Indian Canoe races specially interesting from the excitement & vim with which the competitors went to work. Got back about
dark. Evg. Called on Mrs Bowman*.

May 25   Find it will be impossible to get away on Sunday morning as
had hoped owing to non completion of sails & Carpenter's work. Make
arrangements which I think will secure completion of work & enable us to
get away on Monday morning. Get supplies Shipped down to wharf &
preparations as far as possible completed. Evg. dine with Keith* & a party
of friends.[19]

G. M. Dawson to Bernard James Harrington*, 26 May 1878, Victoria

Your note of May 7th enclosing copy of petition as to Surveys of
Mineral lands *etc* of B. Columbia, arrived yesterday.[20] If the govt. think
of doing anything in the matter the coming autumn would probably be a
good time to concert measures. So much unfounded speculation has been
going on in "quartz" that even should the mines prove rich there will be
much disappointment in regard to dividends, while in the event of the
practical working tests which will have been made during the summer
turning out unfavourable there must be a collapse. At Cariboo at present
one would have the ungrateful task of endeavouring to bring down the
expectations of the people to the level of common Sense, while definite
statements of the value of leads could only be given on the result of assays
not Satisfactorally made on the spot. By the Autumn whatever the issue I
think they will be ready to be grateful for any assistance.

was appointed chief factor and moved to Victoria where he resided until retirement in
1885.

18.   Margaret Bruce (Eberts) Robertson was the wife of Alexander Rocke Robertson, a
      prominent lawyer and man of affairs. He came to Victoria in 1864 and she came after
      their 1868 marriage, both from Chatham, Ontario. They were cousins and she the sister
      of D. M. Eberts, variously attorney-general, speaker, and justice in British Columbia.
      See "Robertson, Alexander Rocke," *Dictionary of Canadian Biography*, 11: 756–57.

19.   Dawson has apparently missed an entry for 26 May 1878.

20.   The reference is untraceable.

I am sorry to date still from Victoria, but have been delayed here by circumstances beyond control. Capt Douglas* was not here on my arrival. After waiting till the date fixed I engaged another schooner, "the Wanderer" & have since heard from Douglas* that his Craft has been ashore up near Comox & has been considerably damaged. The Wanderer was the only suitable Craft here, & will I think do very well. I have had to wait however til a new suit of Sails could be got ready, besides having to make various little alterations & arrangements on board. We are about ready at last, & tomorrow Morning I hope we shall get away

P.S. Mr A. C. Anderson* of this place would be glad to have one or two additional copies of his notes on N.W. America, reprinted from the Naturalist.[21] I do not know whether there are yet any spare copies. If there are plenty one might also be sent San Francisco

[Dawson's voyage to the Queen Charlotte Islands is documented in his journal, "Queen Charlotte Islands Cruise George M. Dawson 1878," which spans the period 27 May to 17 October 1878. A list of expenditures, several sketches, a letter to Dawson, and some rough notes are excluded.]

May 27. 1878. After two weeks of preparation & vexatious delays, get off at 7 P.m. this evening on our Northern cruise. Morning spent in packing up & stowing away things not again required till return to civilization & getting stuff put on board schooner. The sails, which have been the chief part of the delay, ready at last, — the mainsail & jib bent on in the Morning, the foresail after receiving its last stitch brought down & bent in the afternoon. Paid bills & said goodbye for the second or third time to acquaintances in the streets, & now almost myself surprised to find that we are really off

Beat out of Victoria harbour as the light fades from the hills touching with a rosy tint the Summits of the Olympian mountains long after the last glow has gone from the hills about Victoria itself. Pass outside Ogden Pt with a freshening south easterly breeze, & round Trial Island with the last of daylight. Pile away the miscellaneous mass of luggage with which our little Cabin is filled & turn in, tired enough & ready for a good sleep.

May 28. Wind through the night unsteady & light So that ⟨when⟩ on coming on deck about 7 a.m. find we were not much beyond Sydney Island. About 9.15 while engaged stowing away *ictus* a shock, followed by a grating sound brought us to the deck, to find that by trying to shove too

---

21. Perhaps the most scholarly of Hudson's Bay Company employees, Anderson wrote several accounts and descriptions, including *Notes on Northwestern America*, which the twenty-two page reprint from the *Canadian Naturalist* is referred to here.

close to Portland Island we have got on the reefs running off it. The tide
fortunately making, so that we get off again at 11 A.m. uninjured & only
sorry for the delay. Collected a few star fish & Shells while ashore, the
former with many rays like the *Solaster*[22] of the British Coast but larger.
The "tangle" now begining to reach a considerable length, & floating out
with the tide in dense masses from all the reefs & shoal patches. Each stalk
tapering downward to its attachment, ending on the surface of the water
in a buoy from which a tuft of brown Streamers depend.[23] Wind light,
with showers of rain till evening, when a fresh breeze, with occasional spitting rain carried us against the tide through the False Narrows & into
Nanaimo Harbour, where, though without any important business of my
own I had promised to call to convenience Sabeson*.

The vessels lying at the wharves, with the occasional rattle of a truck of
coal descending into their holds as they are loaded makes us realize that
we are in a Coal-bearing region, where one of natures old store houses is
being ransacked for the benefit of the present generation.

The beautiful little islands among which we have been sailing all day,
are peculiar in the wall like (mural) cliffs which the outcropping Edges of
the Coal bearing Sandstones present on one Side, while the other slopes
more gradually down to the water & is generally covered with an open
growth of pine ⟨small⟩ trees with occasional little patches of prairie &
grass-grown points. There is, however, with all very little soil on these
islands & few of them are suited for anything but the maintenance of a
few sheep or Cattle. Here & there a settlers house may be seen on some
spot of good land, also an occasional little establishment for the trying of
Dog-fish & many a little Shanty & potato patch of the Indians, whose
canoe may be Seen with a little bag like sail shooting before the wind from
one island to another.

The general outlines of these islands show singularly well the dependence of physical features on geology or rather on those arrangements of
the rocks which it is the province of geology to study. The sandstones &
conglomerates may be traced in long chains of islands following the stricke
while from the Shales & softer beds the channels have been hollowed, as
has been worked out in detail by Mr Richardson*.[24] To what extent the
Strait of Georgia glacier may have assisted in the shaping of the Surface &
how far the action of the other denuding agents may have been active it is

22. Could have been one of three species, all of which are quite similar: smooth sun star,
    Solaster endeca (L.); Dawson's sun star, *Solaster dawsoni* Verrill; and Stimpson's sea
    star, *Solaster stimpsoni* Verrill.

23. Giant kelp, *Macrocystis integrifolia* Bory.

24. See Richardson, "Report on the Coal Fields," 176.

impossible now to say.[25]

May 29. Obliged much against my wish to remain at Nanaimo till Sabiston* had got through business &c. &c. this being his home.[26] Got away at 12.30 P.m. Crept round with a very gentle air by the Channel to Departure bay, & getting outside ran more briskly up the open gulf going east of the Ballinacs. Sky overcast at sunset but a clear spot & bright glow in the North-west.

G. M. Dawson to J. W. Dawson*, 29 May 1878, Nanaimo

We have got so far on our way northward & hope within a few days to begin work on the Queen Charlotte Islands. The Schooner *Wanderer* seems Suitable for our purpose, with plenty beam & built originally for a pilot-boat. Exactly when it may be possible to write again it is impossible to say but no opportunity wil be neglected of letting you Know at home how we are Please, however, do not let long want of letters Cause any anxiety, as this is only what may be expected. The only vessel Calling regularly at the Northern Ports is the *Otter* & she makes but three trips in the summer, at uncertain dates. Letters addressed to Victoria will be forwarded to Port Simpson near the Mouth of the Skeena River by the otter & if I am lucky I may get one or two mails during the summer. It seems so short a time since we wrote last in Victoria that there is nothing to fill up a longer letter with, so please excuse the present unsatisfactory scrawl & believe me your affectionate son

May 30. Fair wind having died away during the night, find ourselves at 7 a.m. off Cape Lazo nearly becalmed. Get the tow net rigged & Catch a number of little crustaceans &c. Fair wind gradually springing up Carried us in good style past Mittlenatch Island & to Cape Mudge, but left us off the latter place again nearly becalmed. Favoured by a light air & the tidal current drift past the village of the formerly piratical Ucultas[27] — There appear now to be about 16 houses in all & a large number of Canoes — &

25. Dawson had already concluded, in a June 1877 paper, that a great glacier had filled the entire Strait of Georgia. By 1881, largely on the basis of this 1878 trip, he believed that some of these islands were examples of moraine deposits of clay and sands from the Strait glacier. See Dawson, "On the Superficial Geology," 95; and Dawson, "Additional Observations on Geology," 279.

26. Rankine put it differently: "As Sabiston, our bold captain, lives here, & has very recently married, I am afraid that we shall be here all morning" (R. Dawson to J. W. Dawson, 29 May 1878, Dawson Family Papers, MUA).

27. The Euclataw or Lekwitoq (also Lekwiltok) were a Kwakiutl group who controlled the narrow waters of Discovery Passage at Cape Mudge and raided travellers using the inside waterway.

on into Seymour narrows. Get through safely with the latter part of the ebb but there being no wind find it difficult to get the vessel out of the stream into Plumper Bay where it was wished to anchor to wait for the next ebb. Try to bring the schooner Along with sweeps & then more successfully by the boat towing ahead. Get at last into a fair eddy & drift into the bay, anchoring at 9.30 P.m. Went ashore in the boat to a spring the sound of which could be heard from the schooner as it trickled out from the roots of the Cedar trees on the beach. Water beautifully phosphorescent when touched by the oars.

⟨June 1.⟩ {*May 31*} Having rather overslept ourselves did not get anchor up till 7 a.m. Weather quite Calm & in endeavouring to get out of Plumper Bay into the force of the ebb stream got involved in eddys & whorls which Carried us back into the bay. Finally by aid of sweeps got out & continued slowly moving along main channel with the stream, being caught every now & then by an eddy & turned round & round several times. Go off in boat to shore nearly opposite deep Water Bay, for fresh water, having heard a stream running in there. Get at length a little wind & Creep on with freshening breeze first with the tide & then against it. Finally, finding that no progress could be made against the current anchored in the lee of an island[28] beyond the mouth of Nodales Channel, for an hour. Went ashore to examine rocks & collected a few plants. Off again but soon in a perfect calm & moving only with the tide

Scenery very fine in all directions, the mountains rocky & generally with scarcely any Soil yet supporting Great trees, & in some instances thickly wooded from base to summit. Mountains of Vancouver Shore highest & increasing in height, the Prince of Wales & Newcastle ranges[29] with much snow. Other & still higher mountains of the mainland seen from time to time over those of the islands & bear great fields of virgin snow, which in some cases is seen to form immense drifts behinds crags & summits. Passed a couple of Indian Canoes today, the first containing besides a number of Indians, women & men, a white man. The Indians from Some one of the northern inlets & would not even now dare to pass the robbers of Cape Mudge but for the presence of a white. One man ⟨paddling⟩ {rowing} with a short pair of oars, the others, men & women, paddling in the old style. Ictus in heaps in bottom of Canoe & faces daubed with ochre & other pigments giving them a peculiarly repulsive appearance. One woman with a broad mark in red ochre on her upper lip, in the place where a mustache ought to be, looked very comical & defiant.

28.   East Thurlow Island.

29.   Newcastle Ridge.

As I write a breeze Sprung up ahead giving us at least a chance to tack, which with the ebb tide will push us along — slowly.

At about 10 P.m a steamer going north passed us — probably the Otter.

June 1. Anchored early this morning in a cove N. of Helmkin Island[30] to wait for the ebb tide, the wind having died away. off again at 5 a.m. & beating all day to windward, part of the time against the flood tide which scarcely allowed us to make anything. wind strong westerly & Cold, though cloudy no rain & high barometer. Little to do but read, eat, & walk the deck wishing we could get along a little faster. Remarkable absence of life, scarcely a gull or other water bird, no seals, porpoises or whales. The great depth of the water may in part account for this. The Vancouver shore Still steep — too & very mountainous tree-clad mountains rising in Many places at once from the water's edge to a great elevation, & still bearing some snow. Extensive valleys, or rather deep persistent valleys, but narrow, run in from Salmon River, Adam's River, & Robson Bight of the Chart. These appear to take a general South Easterly direction, which is also that in all probability of the axes of the mountain Ranges.

June 2. Falling calm early this morning & the tide turning against ⟨up⟩ us, anchored in a little rocky bight just east of Beaver Cove. Get off again after a few hours, about 6 a.m. Almost a dead calm but floated on past Alert Bay, where ⟨West Euson, one⟩ West Huson[31] one of the well known traders &c. of this coast lives. He has a few houses, & a wharf, & near him is a rancherie[32] with a number of Indian houses of the usual build. Most of the Natives are now up Knights Inlet Eulachon fishing[33] & potlatching. The Nimpkish Indians[34] have moved over to Huson's* place on Cormorant Island, from their old ground near the mouth of the Nimpkish River.

---

30. Helmcken Island.

31. Alden Westley Huson (1832?–1913) was born in New York and came from California to the Cariboo in 1858. In the early 1860's, he settled on the British Columbia coast where he operated a trading schooner along the east side of Vancouver Island, opened a store at Suquash, and then in 1881 went into the cannery business with S. A. Spencer and Thomas Earle at Alert Bay. Huson later sold his share of the cannery and worked a stone quarry. See his obituary in the *Victoria Daily Colonist*, 7 January 1913.

32. A common name for an Indian village.

33. Eulachon, *Thaleichthys pacificus* (Richardson). For a brief account of northwest coast Indian eulachon fishing, see H. A. Collison, "The Oolachan Fishery," *British Columbia Historical Quarterly* 5 (1941): 25–31.

34. A division of the Southern Kwakiutl.

Becalmed & tide setting against us just west of Cormorant Island. Followed out by a canoe from Alert bay, which proves to contain a white man & an Indian, the former has just arrived at the bay from his place of abode some fifteen miles further Eastward.[35] Brings a letter left for me by the Otter at Alert Bay, one from G. Hamilton* of Stuart Lake which has been to Montreal & back again. Two fine deer in the canoe, one of which I purchased at the moderate price of $1.50. They are hunted by dogs on the small islands, being run off into the water & shot Swimming.

Anchor for some hours in the afternoon off point west of Nimpkish, waiting for the tide. Land & take a couple of photographs[36] & spend the rest of the time fretting at our slow progress. Off again at 4 30 beating up against a strong head wind which has blown up since noon.

The Islands now generally low & the land along shores of Vancouver also much lower than before though not so regularly flat & even as that about Comox for instance. High Mountain Ranges Seen up the Nimpkish Valley beyond the large lake[37] still bearing Much snow & probably always carrying some.

Some fine Douglas firs on Cormorant Island & elsewhere about here but prevalent trees the Menzies Spruce[38] & Hemlock, with some Cedars &c. These attain a fine growth but their dimensions are by no means appreciated till they can be compared with some object of human construction, such as a house or vessel.

June 3. Off Early & floated westward with the tide; there being no wind — beyond the end of Malcolm Island. Entirely becalmed at about 5 miles from the Vancouver shore till nearly 1 P.m. when a light air began to spring up. Had the large dredge over & brought up some sticky green sand & two or three little brittle stars.[39] Tried the small dredge, but did not get bottom owing to the Current. The light wind coming up, stopped dredging & tried to get on our way. Wind freshened in the afternoon, but as always, dead ahead & beating against it past Fort Rupert, & into Goletas Channel. When off Fort Rupert the wind was quite strong. Passed an indian Canoe scudding before it with a little sail & though pitching her ends clear of the water, apparently making good weather. The occupants in high spirits, bore down on us & took in their sail apparently just to have a look at the

---

35. Unidentifiable; his "place of abode" would have been near today's Suquash, between Port Hardy and Port McNeill.

36. See "Photographs," 2 June 1878, GSC221–C1 (PA 152382), GSC222–C1 (PA 152384).

37. Nimpkish Lake.

38. Sitka spruce, *P. sitchensis*.

39. An echinoderm of the Class Stelleroidea, which is impossible to identify precisely.

Craft, then hoisted & flew away again.

The country from Nimpkish up to North End of Island is all moderately low along shore & for a considerable way back. The hills nowhere of great height. Coal rocks may not improbably occupy a considerable area. Feel almost tempted to stay our Slow progress here & get to work studying them out. After the interruption of the masses of Crystalline rocks about Johnstone Straits &c., the channel between Vancouver & the main appears to open out just as southward in the Gulf of Georgia. The islands are low & the whole appearance like a repetition of the Coal basin to the south-East.

Calms & head winds are our luck it would appear & the barometer gives no promise of a change.

June 4. Beating up Goletas Channel all night with very light head winds. Stopped soon after daylight about 5 miles east of Shushartie Bay to get water. R. went ashore & got specimen of the rock. A fair wind of short duration Carried us to Mouth of Bate Passage. Boarded by a Canoe with a couple of Indians & a boy, which Came off from a little cove, where an Indian House. One of the Indians a chief & calls himself Chip he is said to have saved the lives of several white men in a little vessel near Fitzhugh Sound.[40] The Indians were about to Massacre the crew when he warned them. A number of indians were Killed in the fray which followed. Appear to have no other object in visiting us than to talk & beg a little tobacco.

The tide carrying us through Bate Passage, we Get a flow of wind which after taking us a couple of miles off shore leaves us becalmed till after 2 P.m. rolling gently in the long ground swell of the Pacific agains which there is now no barrier. Porpoises, sea birds, & a sea-lion[41] sporting about in the calm water with patches of Kelp & tangle & floating frayed logs & stumps dipping about in the swell or appearing & disappearing alternately among the long rollers. Drizzling rain for some hours & then a westerly breeze which gradually turned to north, heading us off & died nearly away about dark, while we were yet many miles from Cape Calvert & directly off Cape Caution. At sunset dark neutral clouds in the west & north west Cape Calvert swathed in wisps of fog blue & dark, while southward &

---

40. Actually "Cheap," a version of "chief." Cheap or Kuē'quhila, was a chief at Nuwitty and, when described by Franz Boas from his 1886 visit, then over sixty. See Boas, "The Houses of the Kwakiutl Indians, British Columbia," *Proceedings of the United States National Museum* 11 (1888): 206–7; "The Indians of British Columbia," *Popular Science Monthly* 32 (1888): 632–33. He enters Dawson's narrative again below, 14 and 15 September.

41. The "Porpoises" could have been either the Dall porpoise, *Phocnoides dalli* (True), or the harbour porpoise, *Phocna vomerina* Gill; the "sea birds" are impossible to identify; and the "sea-lion" was a northern sea-lion, *Eumetopias jubata* (Schreber).

eastward the serried peaks of the Coast Range & summits of Vancouver Island, Snow covered, grow with a magnificent rosy hue

Land along shore all round the point of the promontory of Cape Caution, quite low.

June 5. Light breezes all night & fog from about 1 a.m. On coming on deck this morning nearly calm with dense fog & position uncertain. Sight Egg Island during a break in the fog after a time, & also when the mist began finally to clear away about noon saw some of the dangerous rocks of the Sea Otter Group breaking heavily. A long even swell Setting in from the Open Pacific causes a perpetual roar along the exposed shore to leward, & from the outlying rocks great sheets of foam may from time to time be seen to rise. Getting at last a good side wind, run into entrance of Fitzhugh Sound, where then utterly becalmed & remain so till about dark when a light head wind coming down the sound enables us to get under way again. The heavy swell setting in rendered our position most uncomfortable during the delay. The little Craft rolling & tossing too & fro with all her sails booms &c. rattling & flopping in a most irritating manner. The weather has been throughout most adverse to our progress.

Saw a fur seal[42] today. R. had the line out at 60 fathoms for Halibut[43] but unsuccessfully.

The land near the shore about Cape Caution is low as also is that of the island between the two Entrances to River's Inlet,[44] & the southern end & most of western margin of Calvert I. The south end however pretty evidently cryst. & all the rest may not improbably be the same.

A Sea lion is said to have come up quite Close to the vessel last night, & "bellowed".

June 6. Nearly becalmed all night, but early in the morning get a light breeze in the right direction. This soon dying away left us again becalmed & drifting out of Fitzhugh Sound with the tide, which at present Seems to have a permanent Set outward. Got the boat ahead towing toward Safety Cove, when a good breeze from the North coming on, ceased towing & began beating in. Breeze died away about sundown to a light air, leaving us again drifting outward with the tide. Run back with the last of the breeze, there being no anchorage along the shore, to Safety Cove & anchored at ten P.m., thus loozing again nearly all our day's work — a couple of miles or so.

A very fine day, warm & bright.

---

42. Northern fur-seal, *Callorhinus ursinus cynocephalus* (Walbaum).

43. Halibut, *Hippoglossoides* spp.

44. Probably Walbran Island.

Two canoes full of Indians from Kitimat[45] *en route* to Victoria passed us while the northerly breeze was blowing strong. Each Canoe with one of the peculiar Sails, careering along before the wind in good style.

Saw a number of whales in the distance this evening breaching repeatedly.

June 7. Morning Calm & cloudy. While waiting for wind got a supply of fresh water & had a glance at the Crystalline rocks of Safety Cove. The tide nearly low & the most beautiful natural acquaria formed by the sides of the cove, which dip steeply down in the clear water. Sea Anemonies of remarkable size & beauty. One variety bright green, a second, with plumose tentacles milk white.[46] Star fishes barnacles & shells of different kinds coating the rocks. A light South Easterly wind springing up got anchor up & beat out of cove. Run for a while with light fair wind, & then met a strong head breeze, against which beating for some time, till it veered westward & made a good side wind for running up the passage kept on all the afternoon making excellent time, & to some extent making up for the terrible delays of the early part of the week.

Fitzhugh Sound & its continuation northward in Fishers Channel, constitute a magnificent water way; wide & free from dangers & straight as an arrow. The land immediately bordering it though hilly, or even in places mountainous is low compared with that at the sides of the higher parts of the inlets penetrating the Coast Range. No high snowy mountains are in sight ⟨at⟩ except at a great distance. Hill & valley alike are densely tree-clad, with Cedar, hemlock, & spruce, spruce hemlock & Cedar in one monotonous spread. The trees do not attain a very great size, & there are many dead trees in the woods, even where no fire has passed. No appearance of any land fit for agriculture, nor of any rocks softer than the old crystalline series.

June 8. Worked up a few miles during the night & this morning in entrance of Lama Passage drifting in with the tide. Air very light all morning but continued to progress slowly, aided by the tide. At noon got a South Easterly breeze with rain which Carried us into Bella Bella (McLochlin Bay of Charts) Found Mr Mckay[47] had gone to Fort Simpson,

45. A Northern Kwakiutl, Haisla-speaking group, living on Douglas Channel.

46. The "bright green" anemone was probably the giant green anemone, *Anthopleura xanthogrammica* (Brandt); and the other with "plumose tentacles milk white," possibly the frilled anemone, *Metridium senile* (L.).

47. Probably Joseph William McKay (1829–1900) who was a long time Hudson's Bay Company employee in British Columbia. In the early 1850's, McKay led explorations which established the coal reserves at Nanaimo. Later appointed a chief factor, McKay spent time at Kamloops and Victoria before retiring in 1879. Upon retirement McKay took the position of Indian agent at Kamloops, then Indian superintendent for B.C.

so unable to present my letters of introduction or see the lode Col
Houghton[48] was anxious I should visit. Schooner did not anchor but after
I had completed a short visit to the H.B. Post, & given the gentleman in
charge a couple of letters for the *Otter* on her down trip, filled & stood on
with a light but fair breeze, anchoring in Kynumpt Harbour Millbank
Sound.

The H.B. post at Bella Bella[49] prettily situated on a sloping hillside. A
small stream coming from a lake behind the Post, falls into the bay near
it. A little sloping patch of garden for which most of the soil was, I am
told, Carried from some distance. A number of Indian houses & shanties,
& a little flotilla of Canoes anchored off. A remarkable target-like white
erection on one side of the harbour stated ⟨to be⟩ (on a painted board
below it) to be in memory of "Boston a Bella Bella Chief".[50] Part of the
design on the target a couple of the curious *Coppers*[51] of the Fort Rupert
&c. indians.

48. See below, 30 August 1878, for McKay's "Chimseyan Lode." Lieutenant Colonel
    Charles Frederick Houghton (1839–98), was a prominent pioneer settler and politician.
    Houghton came to British Columbia in 1863 and obtained his military land grant in the
    north Okanagan Lake region. After building up considerable land holdings, Houghton
    was elected to the House of Commons in 1871. Appointed deputy adjutant-general of
    militia for British Columbia in 1873, Houghton later served in the Riel Rebellion and
    was deputy adjutant-general in Montreal. He retired in 1896. See Ormsby, "Some Irish
    Figures," 76.

49. Fort McLoughlin at Bella Bella was established in 1833 by John McLoughlin, superin-
    tendent of the Columbia Department, Hudson's Bay Company.

50. Boston was one of several Heiltsuk or Bella Bella chiefs of the 1830's. Walbran
    describes him as "sharper and shrewder" than the others. His village was at the head of
    Lizzie Cove, Lama Pass. See John T. Walbran, *British Columbia Coast Names,
    1592–1906: Their Origin and History* (reprint; Vancouver: J. J. Douglas, 1971). O. C.
    Hastings photographed the memorial a year later; his photograph is in the British
    Columbia Provincial Museum, no. PN2404.

51. Dawson made the following observation on coppers: "another article of purely conven-
    tional value, and serving as money, is the 'copper'. This is piece of native metal beaten
    out into a flat sheet, and made to take the form illustrated in the margin. [*Illus.*] These
    are not made by the Haidas,—nor indeed is the native metal known to exist in the
    islands,—but are imported as articles of great worth from the *Chil-kat* country, north
    of Sitka. Much attention is paid to the size and make of the copper, which should be of
    uniform but not too great thickness, and give forth a good sound when struck with the
    hand. At the present time spurious coppers have come into circulation, and though
    these are easily detected by an expert, the value of the copper has become somewhat
    reduced, and is often more nominal than real. Formerly ten slaves were paid for a good
    copper, as a usual price, now they are valued at from forty to eighty blankets"
    (Dawson, "On the Haida," 135). He is probably in error by asserting that the coppers
    were of native metal, all extant specimens being European copper.

A very large Canoe here, now lately finished. Said to be 60 feet long & much better finished than that sent to the Centennial.[52] Valued at from $150 to 200 & the Indian who made it expects to be able to sell it to the Fort Rupert Indians for that sum. Of little real use but imposing on State occasions.

Bought a basket of Clams[53] from one of the Bella Bella Indians. Cleaned out some for specimens & had part of the rest in chowder for supper. Visited by a Canoe full of Haida Indians on their way to Bella Bella, & three days from Skidegate. They have besides dried fish & fish oil for trade with these tillicums when they get to Victoria, Some gulls eggs from rocks outside & a young deer. Bought from one of them some fossils which he had been taking to Victoria on Chance of seeing Mr Richardson* there. He had worked for Mr R. when he was on the island. Three more Canoe loads of Haidas are they say also on their way to Victoria not far behind.

Had the line over tonight in about 6 fms where anchored. on hauling up found a huge many rayed star fish which dropped off at Surface disclosing the head & shoulders of a Silver dog fish — a parrot beaked little elasmobranch[54] of remarkable appearance. This fellow had taken the hook & then been Snapped off behind by some larger fish, probably a shark. The star fish promptly appropriated what was left. There would seem to be much activity in the struggle for existence down below.

G. M. Dawson to Margaret Dawson, 8 June 1878, near Bella Bella*

Bella Bella is near the Entrance to Millbank Sound, & if we get there this afternoon, as we hope to do, we shall have been nearly twelve days en route from Victoria. I do not know what chance there may be of Sending letters south from here, but as the Otter has probably not yet got so far on her return trip from Wrangel, there may be a pretty early opportunity. We have had a most provoking series of head winds & Calms ever since embarking, & the delay occasioned has been most annoying. This

---

52. The Bella Bella had a reputation for canoe building. The one for the 1876 United States Centennial Exposition in Philadelphia was purchased at Alert Bay in June 1875 by James G. Swan, acting for the United States Centennial Commission, after which it became property of the United States National Museum. The canoe which Dawson saw may well be that later collected by Indian Superintendent Israel W. Powell, on commission for Heber R. Bishop and New York's American Museum of Natural History and now a feature of that museum's South Entrance.

53. Probably butter clams, *Saxidomus giganteus* (Deshayes).

54. Ratfish, *Hydrolagu colliei* (Lay and Bennett). An "elasmobranch" is a fish belonging to the Elasmobranchii, the group of cartilaginous fishes comprising the sharks and rays.

especially as I have been unable to see much of the coast which we have ⟨traversed⟩ passed so slowly, as we have been comparatively seldom at anchor, & then only overnight. We have been drifting about in the passages becalmed, carried by the tides now one way now another.

I do not know that I shall make any stay at Bella Bella, at any rate it will not be for long. A Certain Mr McKay* of the Hudson Bay Co. has some lode here which he is prospecting & which I may try to take time to visit.[55] On leaving Bella Bella we shall I think strike across from the mouth of Millbank Sound to the Queen Charlotte Islands & it will not I hope be many days now before we are actually at work. Had I known so much time was to be wasted on the passage I think I should have contented myself with coming to the North End of Vancouver Id. where there appears to be an interesting field. How long we may stay at the Queen Charlottes must depend on the interest of the country there. I think it will be best not to devote much time to the examination of the Crystalline rocks, except in such Cases as something of peculiar interest occurs. To make the main object the definition of the area of Coal measures, & if this proves not very great to leave some time in the Autumn for the north end of Vancouver.

The schooner which I have is Called as I daresay you have been informed before both by myself & Rankine*, the "Wanderer." She appears well suited for the work, though much time might be saved by having steam power. The "Captain" is a young ⟨may⟩ man Called Sabiston*, the son of a pilot at Nanaimo. He is efficient enough though perhaps a little opinionative. I have besides a man Called Williams,[56] who has sailed often about this part of the Coast, & also about the Queen Charlotte Islands. He is a good worker & will I think do well. Lastly there is the Cook & general utility Man — though also a sailor — A german or something of that sort who goes by the name of "Dutch Charley".[57] As a Cook he does well & is obliging & civil enough. We have had an abominably lazy time of it so far with seemingly nothing to do but wait for next meal time to come round. The little cabin is littered with books

55. McKay's Hebrew Mine was at Neekas Inlet on the north side of Spiller Channel. "Some work was done several years ago on a vein containing pyrrhotite or magnetic iron-pyrites and copper pyrites. This deposit is known as the 'Hebrew Mine,' and appears to deserve further examination as a copper-ore" (Dawson, "Mineral Wealth of B.C.," 153).

56. Possibly John Williams, listed in the 1881 census as a "mariner." Born in Wales and residing in Victoria, he was, at the time of enumeration, thirty-six years old.

57. Unidentifiable. Rankine added that "our cook is going to be quite a success I think. He cooks very well & keeps things beautifully clean, besides wasting very little" (Rankine Dawson to Margaret Dawson, 8 June 1878, Dawson Family Papers, MUA.)

&c. &c. & if only on a pleasure cruise one would be able to get on well enough. The annoyance of loosing time however constantly presses on one, & renders it even difficult to apply oneself to reading.

When off Alert Bay, not far South of the north end of Vancouver, a man came off in a boat with a letter for me, which had arrived the day before by the *Otter*, which left Victoria for the north a couple of days after us. This proved to be a note from Mr Hamilton* of Stuart Lake — in the interior — It had been to Montreal & was directed back to Victoria & so up here. We had a few letters & papers before leaving Victoria, but it is now ⟨scarcely⟩ {hardly} likely that we shall hear again for a long time, perhaps a couple of months. The same applies to letters written home, of which this may be the last for some time. I hope you will not allow yourself to feel anxious as it may be quite impossible to let you hear till we return from the Islands. I fear also that there may be some difficulty in getting Rankine* back in good time, but I will of course do the best I Can in the matter. This Northern Coast is so much further off in reality, when one comes to travel to it by the slow means which exist, than it appears on the Map. We are drifting down Lama Passage as I write, with the tide but without a breath of wind & when the flood comes in if still Calm there is nothing for it but to anchor somewhere & wait till wind or tide favours us again.

I believe I sent a little memorandum about clothes to be ordered from Edinburgh. These may of course come out any time, with Father's* if he orders any.

I cannot think of anything else worth writing about, but if occasion offers will add a postscript at Bella Bella. William* will now be with you I suppose. Please give him my love, as also to Anna* & all at home. I forgot to take any of William's* printed Certificates with me but so far have had no use for them.[58] You might mail one or two to Victoria in case anything should turn up when I get back.

Please tell Father I got a copy of *Nature* before leaving Victoria, also an *Illustrated News*

June 9. off from Kynumpt Harbour early, first with a very light breeze, which freshening Carried us at last round the rocky islands off Cape Day,[59] & out into the wide Pacific. The long swell breaking furiously on the rocks as we pass them. Six or eight miles off the land the wind going down left us rolling & making a little progress at intervals, westward during the night.

58. Presumably William was seeking employment as an engineer.

59. Day Point.

When inside Cape Day Saw something waving on the surface of the water which at first taken for a Shark's fin but proved to be a deer swimming from the South to the north shore of the sound. Williams* & R. jumping into the boat dashed after it & succeeding in turning it before it reached the south shore — to which it endeavoured to return — drove it off till bearing down on it with the schooner, I shot it from the deck. A young doe not fully grown but in fair Condition.

June 10   rolling miserably in the swell without wind for some time. Wind then Rising got off westward & ⟨made⟩ {saw} the land near Cape St James before night. Wind freshening went on the other tack to get to windward of the Cape. Blew hard all night rising to a gale with a very heavy sea before morning. Found us about thirty miles northward. Up during much of the night scanning the Channel & trying to preserve things in cabin from coming to grief as the flew from side to side.

June 11. Went round on the other tack ⟨about⟩ & early this morning expecting to make Cape St James. Weather very heavy, but wind gradually failed till land well in sight ahead it left us. Rolling & tossing with out Any wind All the afternoon, in a heavy pitching Sea. Had the Holibut line over but could get no bottom with 90 fms. Breeze from westward springing up about 8 P.m. got under way toward the land.

June 12. Up early this morning to see Cape St James & the southern end of the Queen Charlotte Islands. Took a sketch with bearings. Wind fell very light before we made the point at the southern side of the bay leading in to Houston Stuart Channel. Beating slowly in all morning. Afternoon about 3 P.m. Anchored in snug bight behind Ellen I.[60] of the plan. Took a couple of photographs[61] & made cursory examination of rocks of vicinity.

Weather remarkably fine, warm & summer-like but provokingly little wind for sailing.

Where we are anchored in a snug little bay, rocky islets thickly tree clad down to the shore, with the wooded mountains of the N side of the Channel make a picturesque scene. An Indian house on the shore but has evidently not been inhabited for some time. See no sign of Indians. Rowed round to bay in which *Village* marked on the plan, in the evening, but found only the marks of some old houses.[62]

---

60. Rose Harbour.

61. See "Photographs," 12 June 1878, GSC223–C1 (PA 51097), and GSC224–C1 (PA 152383).

62. "The villages marked as occuring in Houston Stewart Channel," Dawson noted, "do not exist; they have been little collections of rude houses for temporary use in summer, and have now disappeared" (Dawson, "On the Haida," 169–70).

The appearance of the land about Cape St James very remarkable. Mountains, falling southward toward the cape, & often fronting the sea in bold Cliffs. The little chain of islets[63] off the cape are vertical faced, with rounded tops, bare of trees & apparently the secure resorts of sea fowl. Even the smaller rocks of this group have the same remarkable post like form. Noted a natural archway in the rocks of a promontory a short distance South of Houston Stuart entrance.[64] Another small group of bare whitish sea washed rocks lie some miles offshore north of the Entrance — the Danger rocks[65] of the Chart.

June 13. Breakfast at 6 a.m. & off with Williams* Charley & R. in the boat. Explored the southern shore of the channel & Bay as far as Outer Pt.[66] Rain set in shortly after we got away & continued with little intermission throughout the day, Soaking us & making it disagreeable. Lunched at a cove a short distance inside outer Pt. & returned in heavy rain. Stopped at several gull populated rocks & deprived them of their eggs, which — those of them which were not half hatched — made an agreeable addition to our supper. Saw many Seals, a few porpoises, some eagles & innumerable little black & white Guillamettes (?) & a few pairs of a black bird with long bright red bill.[67] No Indians appear, nor have we met with any recent signs of their habitation, which is at least odd. The very abundance of gulls eggs on rocks easily accessible, would seem to urge their prolonged absence.

The rocks everywhere about this passage are crusted with Acorn shells & the large mussels, between tide marks, with occasional patches of Lepas (?) &c. Below high water mark in some places the large urchins are very thickly strewn over the bottom. Sea anemones, starfish[68] &c. &c. are everywhere abundant.

---

63. Kerouard Islands.

64. Presumably Moore Head is meant.

65. Renamed Garcin Rocks in 1948.

66. Most likely Hornby Point and Quadra Rocks.

67. The "Seals" were probably hair or harbour seals, *Phoca vitulina richardi* (Gray); the "eagles" bald eagles, *H. leucocephalus*; "black & white Guillamettes," pigeon guillemots, *Cepphus columba* Pallas; and the "black bird with long bright red bill," the black oystercatcher, *Haematopus bachmani* Audubon.

68. The "Acorn shells" were possibly shells of the giant acorn barnacle, *Balanus nubilis* Darwin; the "large mussels" California mussels, *Mytilus californianus* Conrad; and "Lepas" goose barnacles, *Lepas* spp. The "large urchins" were possibly the giant red sea urchin, *Strongylocentrotus franciscanus* (Agassiz); the "Sea anemones" are impossible to identify; and "starfish" one of several species such as the common starfish, *Pisaster ochraceus* (Brandt).

The Mountains & hills evenwhere rise steeply from the shore & the appears to be no arable land. Scarcely indeed any Soil properly so called anywhere. The trees, — among which there appears much dead wood — grasp the almost naked rocks.

June 14. Off early. Rowed westward up the channel against a strong tide. Examined the shores of Rose Harbour,[69] stopping for lunch on its western entrance pt. Continued out to Fanny Pt,[70] without seeing any Indians, but when sailing back, saw a smoke as if made to attract notice, on Anthony I.[71] Shortly after supper a canoe full of Indians Came along side, they having observed our sail, & as we had supposed ⟨seen⟩ made the smoke. All young men, several of them just returned from Victoria with their earnings, & as they informed us "lots of whiskey"   They are having a grand dance today over at the Ranch.[72] The Indian lads well dressed, mostly in civilized costume, & brought with them in their canoe a couple of telescopes! Inform us that they have plenty Holibut & plenty fur seal Skins, the latter they wish to trade. Tried to get all the information I could about the country from them but not very Successfully.

Found fossils in the limestone today. Day cool & showery throughout with South-westerly wind.

June 15. off dredging all morning in the strait opposite our harbour. Drift down with the tide which running strongly, with the dredge rope over the bow. Bottom chiefly shelly & very clean. Get a number of interesting things though much dead stuff. Many beautiful byezoons, some Corals, & one species of brachiopod. (Terebretella?)[73] After lunch set out to look for fossils about two miles westward, opposite the Mouth of Rose Harbour. Efforts Crowned with unexpected success, finding *belemnites ammonites*[74] &c. Sufficient at least to fix the age of the series of rocks which have been examining as Mesozoic & enable them to be correlates

---

69. The present Rose Inlet; Rose Harbour is now the name of Dawson's "Snug bight" of 12 June on the south shore of Houston Stewart Channel.

70. Cape Fanny, at the northwest entrance to the channel.

71. Anthony Island is the location of Ninstints or SgA′ngwā′-i village. See John R. Swanton, *Contributions to the Ethnology of the Haida*, Jesup North Pacific Expedition vol. 5, pt. 1, American Museum of Natural History Memoir vol. 8, pt. 1 (New York, 1905), 277. Dawson calls it Kun-xit village, which is actually a lineage name. The village was abandoned after 1884. See Dawson, "On the Haida," 169. As the best preserved Haida village, it is now a World Heritage Site.

72. Like rancherie, a common term for an Indian village.

73. The "byezoons" were moss animals of the phylum Bryzoa or Ectoprocta; the "Corals" one of several species such as the orange cup coral, *Balanophyllia elegans* Verrill; and the "brachiopod" the common Pacific brachiopod, *Terebratalia transversa* (Sowerby).

74. Coiled cephalopods, highly diverse in structure and prolific in species and genera.

with those of other localities.

Morning very fine, but becoming overcast & finally clouding over with occasional showers & becoming cold. Got sextant ready to take latitude at Noon but no chance, & must now leave without getting it. A canoe with two men, a woman & a boy came in tonight. They are I believe from Gold Harbour.[75] They offered to catch us some fish, but on returning the line which they had borrowed for the purpose brought only three sculpins,[76] & three other very small fish. They are going tonight to make a fire in some woods resorted to by sea-birds & club them as they fly past, disturbed in their slumbers.

June 16. Got anchor up & schooner under weigh & then followed the shore, examining it & making running Survey round into next inlet.[77] The schooner had come to an anchor in a snug cove on the south side[78] before we Caught up to her, shortly after noon. Being Sunday, decided not to do any more work today, this especially as I have a headache owing to loss of sleep from mosquitoes last night. Day fine & the swell on the outer shore not too much to prevent Easy landing.

June 17. Heavy rain in the night, & southerly wind. Morning still overcast & showery. Made a rather late start, & occupied till after 4 Pm in making a running survey & examination of the shores of this as yet to me nameless inlet. Rocks uninteresting, & the day on the whole not pleasant, a surf rolling in making landing on the outer points difficult. Saw great numbers of seals today playing in the water & even on the rocks. Some mothers carrying their young on their backs, the two heads coming up out of the water together in a most amusing way.

June 18. A dull threatening morning which soon fulfilled its promise by beginning to rain. Rain & wind in squalls, with low clouds & flying scud on the mountains all day, the monotonous patter still continuing as we swing too & fro with the wind uneasily at anchor. Worked round the coast from last anchorage to Harriet harbour of Pool,[79] in Skincuttle Inlet.

75. Haida from Chaatl and Kaisun, villages associated with "Gold Harbour," the waters adjacent to Kuper Island on the west coast, moved to Haina or New Gold Harbour on Maude Island near Skidegate between 1870 and 1875. The ground for the new village, Dawson noted, was "amicably purchased from the Skidegate Haidas" (Dawson, "On the Haidas," 168).

76. A sculpin of the family Cottidae.

77. Named by Dawson Carpenter Bay after the English naturalist, William Benjamin Carpenter.

78. Named South Cove by Dawson.

79. Francis Poole was a mining engineer who investigated copper reports in 1862 on behalf of the Queen Charlotte Mining Company of Victoria. He abandoned his mines in 1864 after shafts had been sunk on Burnaby and Skincuttle islands. Dawson thought his

Some difficulty in landing on the exposed outer points. The schooner sailing round in the meantime met us at 1 P.m. & after seeing her Safely into the harbour returned to finish work up to mouth of harbour & examine Iron ore deposit marked on Poole's Map.[80]

The general aspect of the Inlet south of this, which we have Just left, & the Country Surrounding it is much like that about Houston Stewart Channel. Thickly wooded mountains rise everywhere from the waters Edge to heights frequently exceeding 1000 feet but rarely if ever more than 2000 (eye est.) The shore is generally rocky & the water off it bold. Beaches are unfrequent & not extensive 〈"Sabiston" harbour〉 {South} Cove of the plan is a good anchorage for small schooners. Depth of a considerable part of the bight not over about 10 fath. & anchorage at 6 fathoms with good holding ground. The upper end of the inlet is well sheltered, & receives two large streams, but is encumbered with rocky islands & many rocks, rendering access difficult. The timber in this region being of small stature is not of any great prospective value, & 〈the〉 agricultural land does not exist.

As we felt our way from point to point round the coast today, in the rain & drizzling mist we continually looked awkwardly for the view round the "next point". When the promontory was rounded which gave us a view of the magnificent sheet of water at the entrance to this inlet, its dimensions magnified by the mist appeared grand. We knew not where to look for a harbour but by good luck got into this one

June 19. Heavy rain during the night, & morning opened with a steady downpour & light southerly wind. Delayed starting out for work, for some time, but at last tempted to go by an appearance of clearing up. Worked along a few miles of coast under great difficulties, the rain recommencing almost immediately after our departure & continuing very heavy, with masses of mist which prevented anything but the land in the immediate vicinity from being seen. Decided to give up survey for today, & got back to Schooner chilled & wet through, for very little. Wind which began to rise about noon soon increased to a gale, which has since continued coming in very heavy squalls over the mountains which hem in our little harbour. Rain leaking through the Cabin roof renders our abode far from comfortable. Reading & attending to other "home" work during afternoon.

book, *Queen Charlotte Islands: A Narrative of Adventure in the North Pacific*, ed. John W. Lyndon (London: Hurst and Blackett, 1872), "chiefly remarkable for the exaggerated character of the account it contains" (George M. Dawson, "Report on the Queen Charlotte Islands 1878," in Geological Survey of Canada, *Report of Progress for 1878-79* [1880], Report B, 17).

80. Poole, *Queen Charlotte Islands*, 162, notes a deposit of "magnetic iron ore" east of

The Schooner has gradually dragged from her first position, under the influence of the gale, to a place nearly in the throat of the harbour, & though both anchors are now out, with plenty cable, she swings uneasily as the squalls strike her, & leave us not without fear that ⟨....⟩ she may drag outside altogether & force us to take to the open. Some of the squalls actually carry the Crests from the little waves in this harbour & scatter them before in a cloud of spray. The holding ground cannot be good, & is probably a fine sandy gravel of granitic fragments, like that composing the little beach near us.

June 20. Continued examination & running survey of coast westward up the Inlet. Finding the entrance of a large bay,[81] — as it proved — though it looked at first a possible passage — obliged to go far enough to prove its character, which took up much time. Came upon a rock around which the tide was rising, quite covered with seals. These on our approach, to the number of 20 or 30 Shuffled off rapidly into the water. Soon they appeared again, heads bobbing up in all directions to get a look at us & then sinking again.

A showery disagreeable day.

June 21. Ran with the wind to the outer Islands at the Mouth of the inlet,[82] & examined the group inwards. Then sailed across to point at N entrance of bay[83] & continued examination of coast westward. Found the abandoned copper mine[84] which Poole* Superintended years ago. Little sign now that human beings ever inhabited the spot

Visited a couple of rocks *en route* today from which a few gulls eggs — very acceptable at supper — were obtained. Williams* Caught on a rock a young seal just born, with the placenta still lying near it. The little fellow is quite active & seems well able to take care of himself though I fear we have no food suitable for him.

Got back to Schooner after a long run against a head wind across the bay, at 6.15 P.m. A day of rain & cold wind, heavy heavier heaviest being the three categories of the former. The climate indeed seems to be a wet one. This evening as I write it still rains, the drops flying in columns before a strong Southerly wind.

June 22. Heavy rain & wind during the night, & when called at 6 a.m. for breakfast rain descending in sheets. This continued without intermission

Harriet Harbour.

81. Huston Inlet.

82. Copper Islands.

83. Poole Point, Burnaby Island.

84. On the southeast tip of Burnaby Island between Bluejay and Pelican coves.

till 3.30 in the afternoon. No prospect of being able to do any out door work so plotted yesterday's survey & attended to other little matters. About 3.30 the weather suddenly cleared, blue sky appearing. Set to work to make a plan of the harbour, which before 7.30 Pm almost completed. Intended to get a photograph, but clouds & mist hanging about the mountains prevented. Showers are again falling this evening, but not without lucid intervals.

The seal brought in yesterday has been sprawling about the deck all day, uttering from time to time its pecular Cry of *wah* or *mwah* (a sort of gurgling watery *ma*) in a plaintive tone. At times it becomes quite vociferous for a moment or two & then relapses into silence. At first it shrunk from being handled, but is now becoming quite used to it & even seems to enjoy being Caressed. It already has its likes & dislikes, knowing where to find a warm sheltered corner & how to crawl to it. Williams* tied a halibut line to it this morning & threw it over for a swim. It did not like the operation, & when it was about to be repeated in the afternoon, & the rope was brought out it immediately seemed to realize the position & set up a great noise. Thrown into the water it swam well but tried always to regain the deck by attempting to climb the side & continued ⟨uttering⟩ bellowing & mwawing till again hauled in, when it was quite Content. For an animal but one day old it certainly shows great intelligence. It sprawls up to ones legs & pressing its nose about on ones boots or trousers seems to smell them Carefully. It even appears to follow one when one goes away. Its cry reminds one of that which a half drowned baby of goodly size might utter. *Charley* is trying to feed it on oatmeal & water rice & water &c. We have no means of weighing it, but it must be over 30 pounds, or at least up to that figure.

The red billed ⟨plover (?)⟩ {oyster Catcher} haunts the coast here everywhere & one seldom approaches a rocky point without hearing their Cries of alarm as they ⟨hear⟩ see one approaching their nests. They are most grotesque birds with their black plumage, heavy bills & clumsy feet, & withal silly, for the anxious noise they make is a certain means of attracting one to their nests. These are built on bare rocks or rocky points, or gravelly spots of islands &c. They are sometimes on the edge of grassy patches, but never among the grass & no attempt at concealment is made. The eggs two in number are deposited either on some Crumbled portion of the rock where they Cannot roll off, or in a shallow nest, if such it may be called, formed of some small rocky fragments collected together, or of broken & rounded pieces of shell from the beach. In some Cases the nest is conspicuous from being entirely composed of shelly fragments. The birds themselves, though evidently paired generally go in little flocks, feeding together on the shore at low tide. When disturbed they set up a sharp cherraping which they continue not only when on the ground, but when on the wing. Even at night when near their citadels one can now & then hear several of them in conversation, as though they had been awakened by Some disturbance. Their flight is rapid & undulating & when at rest on a rock they frequently sit closely down on the tangle, doubling their legs under them.

June 23. Up at usual time & after breakfast got Anchor up & schooner away for a little bight.[85] about 6 miles off near the entrance to Burnaby Strait. Set to work in boat finishing plan of Harriet Harbour. Next went across to point of Bolkus Is. & made examination & route survey of these. Showers beginning in the morning continued to occur with greater frequency & the day soon became an inquestionably wet one drenching showers with squalls following each other up out of the south-west with scarcely any intermission. Soon thoroughly soaked, chilled, & disgusted & glad to reach the schooner, which we did about 1.30 P.m. Afternoon terribly wet & showers still frequent & very heavy. Mountains all swathed in mist & the wind every now & then rising in force, begins to howl in the rigging. A good fire makes the cabin endurable, but even now difficult to get clothes dry or keep up a sufficient sequence of dry boots & socks. The continuance of this wet weather now begins to become very irksome, interfering as it does so much with our work.

July 24.[86] Morning cloudy as usual, but with high barometer & appearance of clearing, & promise of a better day. Set off notwithstanding light showers to explore Burnaby Strait, & found it opening through into a wide expanse with many deep bays & islands. Got out far enough before turning to satisfy ourselves that an opening probably exists through to the west, & another round to the east, & that it will be safe & desirable to bring the schooner through tomorrow to same anchorage as a base for the exploration of the new region. About 1 P.M. the showers which for some time had been increasing in frequency & duration coalesced into steady rain, which continued, growing heavier all the time, with strong south westerly wind during the rest of the day. About ten miles from the schooner when we turned & had a hard tussle against the wind & driving rain all the way back, getting in after 7 P.m. cold & wet to the skin. Scarcely possible often to see one point from another in taking bearings, & almost impossible to form any correct estimate of distance, or to examine the rocks properly   note book sopping all day.

July 25. Heavy rain Continues nearly all night, & on awakening this morning hear the patter still continuous on the deck. Rain continues descending

85. Probably Swan Bay.

86. Dawson mistakenly wrote "July" rather than "June."

in an uninterrupted deluge all day with heavy squalls of wind, rendering outdoor work impossible & rendering it advisable not to move the schooner from her present shelter in "Tangle cove"

Tried fishing, but with poor Success, getting only a couple of Sculpins & two Crabs, the latter however of an edible size.

Tangle cove. Is a good anchorage for a small schooner, well sheltered from winds & not too deep. The centre of the entrance between the islands is however occupied by a rock which dries at low water, & must be carefully avoided.

Harriet Harbour is good, even for large vessels, which should enter at the West entrance, keeping nearer to the west shore than to that of Harriet Island, from which shoal water & rocks run out some distance.

The Narrows of Burnaby Strait of Poole may be called *Dolomite Narrows*. They are partly blocked by rocks but may probably be passed with safety by small schooners. The openings running westward to the South & North sides of the Narrows are probably both good harbours,[87] though no soundings were made. The latter especially is very roomy & well sheltered, & might accomodate a large fleet.

[verso]

In passing through Dolomite narrows afterwards find the channel both narrow & crooked with only six to eight feet of water at low tide, probably less at springs. Tidal Current not very strong.

[end verso]

All the waters about this end of Burnaby I. should however be navigated with great caution as there are many rocks scattered about, a large proportion of them covered at H.W.

High land & steep slopes of mountains here as elsewhere rise almost always from the shores. The surface is generally covered with trees, a considerable proportion of which are dead at the tops & many scrubby & ill grown. Where a little flat land exists, as at the heads of some of the bays, along the E. side of Burnaby Strait north of the narrows &c. timber of good growth occurs, & does not appear to hold much dead wood. The trees are chiefly spruce (*a. menziesii*)[88] & hemlock, with some cedar, & alder in groves, especially in the immediate vicinity of the shores. If the climate admits of agriculture these strips of flat land (including probably also some flat islands like Bolkus I) are only suitable & these could only be cleared at great expense of labour. In the narrow passages the trees seem almost rooted in the beach & their branches hang down thickly nearly to

---

87. Bag Harbour and Island Bay, both named by Dawson.

88. Possibly the Douglas-fir, *P. menziesii*, but Dawson also could have been referring to the Sitka spruce, *P. sitchensis*.

the high-water line. Verdant green grass also spreads down literally in some places to meet the tangle growing on the sea washed part of the shore, & indeed judging from our experience so far there is really no reason why the tangle if it can grow without salt should not grow in the woods & on the mountains. Ferns, — the common polypodium — grow abundantly on the trunks & even on the boughs of trees both living & dead, & green moss forms great club-like Masses here & there. Some large trunks overthrown & dead, though scarcely sheltered by other trees bear a perfect garden of moss young trees & bushes though far above the ground

The Mountains near the head of Tangle Cove, & running northward & north westward from it are the highest we have yet seen. Some probably reaching 3000'. Parts of their slopes are bare of trees, & apparently mossy.

June 26. Morning threatening with heavy showers & violent squalls. Got away with schooner after breakfast & sailed down to narrows, hoping to pass without any difficulty. Anchored just before the narrowest part & went ahead in the boat to examine it. Found water very shoal & many rocks & as tide falling & current against ⟨the⟩ us judged prudent to wait till the water deeper & on the rise. Afternoon did some dredging but did not find any very productive bottom. Caught a great number of Crabs, with a hoop rigged with netting baited & put overboard. Got a photo.[89] of the narrows between showers at about 5 P.m. Tried to take latitude at noon, but clouds interfered. Many & heavy showers with squalls all day but some patches of blue sky now & then & better appearance of Clearing than for some time back.

June 27. Heavy rains in the night & early morning, rendering the character of the day so doubtful that breakfast was not ready till 7 O'C. Showers still continue, but barometer rising, & appearance of clearing. Take provisions for two days & blankets, thinking it probable we may get so far from the schooner that it may be best not to return. Measure a base with M.T. & Carry running survey & triangulation down the passage. Day broken with occasional heavy showers, but on the whole a great improvement on any for a long time. Camp at 6 Pm on a contracted little gravelly beach between rocks. Boat anchored out in front.

Try to get obsn. on polaris, but though seen at first, by time instrument ready concealed. Turn in at 11 Pm. a fair night but cloudy & with plenty Mosquitoes about.

Passages & channels seem to open out in all directions with innumerable islands, forming a puzzling maze, espcially when only half-seen through misty clouds & rain.

---

89. See "Photographs," 26 June 1873, GSC226–C (PA 51091).

June 28. Up early & off after breakfast. Spend much of morning coasting a great bay which unexpectedly opened out.[90] Stopped at 11.30 & made arrangements to get obsn. on Sun, which fortunately successful. Got also two photographs[91] looking up the Channel. Came back to schooner in the afternoon most of the way under sail making good time. Looked out a place for the schooner to go to at next move, with work for the boat along the north side of the inlet.

Day almost altogether fine, only a few stray drops falling on us at one time. Sun out for considerable intervals. The higher Mountains to the westward still however continue more or less shrouded, & showers of rain are evidently falling among them from time to time. Looking out on the open sea to the east, the day is evidently quite fine, with scattered Cirro stratus clouds & not a drop of rain falling. The area of great precipitation appears to be pretty local & to centre in the western range of hills of the islands.

June 29. Examined & paced a section formerly seen on the N.W. part of Burnaby I,[92] occupying till noon. Lunch, & took a couple of photographs,[93] & then examined North shore of the island, finishing at the outer North East point,[94] from which the Skincuttle Islands[95] visable to the south. A desolate "World's End" looking spot. Low land spreading out from the bases of the hills covered with open growth of large, but gnarled trees, the trunks of which fork upwards. Gravel beaches, clean washed & with evidence of heavy surf filling the Crevices between the rough rocky substratum of the shore. The rocks low, but much broken & forming a wide zone between the border of the woods & low tide mark. Shoal & rocky still further out as evidenced by the wide *laminarian zone*.[96] A strong south-easterly wind blowing & over half the horizon a limitless view across the ocean. In a cove just behind the point an old Indian house.[97]

90. Island Bay.

91. See "Photographs," 28 June 1878, GSC227–C2 (PA 152372) and GSC228–C2 (PA 152370).

92. This became Section Cove. The exposed rocks are discussed in Dawson, "Queen Charlotte Islands," 55, fig. 2, and 56.

93. See "Photographs," 29 June 1878, GSC229–C2 (PA 152371) and GSC230–C2 (PA 152362).

94. Scudder Point, named by Dawson.

95. Meaning the islands, his Copper Islands, off Skincuttle Inlet, of which Skincuttle Island is one.

96. A seaweed, *Laminaria* spp.

97. The reference is to Scudder Point. In his "Queen Charlotte Islands," 21, Dawson terms the house "strongly built." The site is Skwa-ikun on the C. F. Newcombe map in

The beach not good & Cannot imagine what a house Should be built in Such a place for unless as a stopping place when in rounding the cape winds found adverse.

June 30. Got large dredge put in order this morning, & after getting supply of water, — a somewhat difficult matter as the stream flowing into the bight we are anchored in empties into a lagoon & flows out salt upon the shore at low tide — got off for the north side of the great inlet into which Burnaby Strait opens.[98] Met an Indian canoe with three men, two women, & three dogs, the first we have seen since leaving Houston Stewart. They are going to gather eggs on some of the outlying rocks & have come from *Clue's*[99] to the north. They had a dead seal on board, which was apparently supplying food for *the Crowd.*

Got a Cast of the dredge in 70 fathoms, bringing up a few good shells. Intended getting more dredging on the way across, but sounding in the middle got 94 fathoms, no bottom. Having a bad headache & day not being specially Suitable postponed further dredging. Spent some time looking for an anchorage but finally found a good one between some islands, though reaching it with some difficulty with the sweeps owing to adverse tide & wind.

A beautiful little *cottus*[100] of a new Kind brought up on the hook here, but minus its body, a voracious dog fish having bitten it off as it was drawn up through the water.

No heavy rain today, though several showers, & weather on the whole cloudy.

Wanderer Bight[101] Anchorage for small Craft in 8 fathoms pretty well sheltered. Wide tide flats which drop off Suddenly at Edge of low water mark into deep water. Either of the Coves inside wander bight would probably be better anchorages for schooners though the nearer one much less easily accessible.

July. 1. A fine day with much clear sky & scarcely a drop of rain. Off at usual hour & occupied till near 7 p.m. in examining the shores & islands of the opening next north of that to which the name of Juan Perez

Swanton, *Haida Ethnology*, opp. 277.

98. Juan Perez Sound, so named by Dawson.

99. The village of T!anū' or Tanu, but often called Clue's or Klue's village after the hereditary name of the chief Xe-ū'. See below, 7 July 1878.

100. A sculpin of the family Cottidae.

101. Skaat Harbour.

applied.[102] Got two photos.[103] at noon stop. At work till midnight on plotting & notes.

[verso]

Microm. Telescope. July. 1. reads by observations on sun. 18″ too little. This probably approximately Correct.

[end verso]

July 2. Off at usual time, taking blankets, & food for two days. Worked along coast of inlet to opposite "Observation point" when Crossed over & continued on west side of inlet. Turned off into a deep inlet[104] which presented some appearance of running through to the west, but find it to terminate. Could find no place to Camp but a little rough beach in this inlet, a triangular patch of depression in a shore-line generally of solid rock plunging into deep water. Mountains rising wall-like above it to a height of some 3000′ as steep as trees can grow on, but well covered with vegetation. Looking across the inlet scarce half a mile wide bare granite mountains rise to a height of probably between 4000 & 5000 feet, with their upper gorges & shady hollows full of drifted snow fields. Found scarcely room to spread our blankets down among the great boulders of the shore, & stones from above.

The main inlet which we have been following (Juan Perez) with a remarkably direct general course gives off a number of great bays & long arms to the west.[105] These run up among the mountains of a range which follows nearly Parallel to the west. Low at first gradually increases in height & appears to Culminate near the head of the inlet of tonights camp in great massive mountains, bare & rocky, or even with snow on their summits. — by far the highest we have yet seen. This range is no doubt the axial one of this part of the Q.C. Islands. A fine day.

July 3. Much pestered by the Mosquitoes in the night & breakfasted & got off this morning in a perfect storm of black flies. Coasted out of the inlet on the north side & then continued northward to Island No 19,[106] where lunched & got obsn. for lat. A long row home, Part of way against a

---

102. This is difficult to follow; the best construction seems to be that Dawson did not realize that this should really be considered a part of Juan Perez Sound and not another opening.

103. See "Photographs," 1 July 1878, GSC231–C2 (PA 51089) and GSC232–C2 (PA 152363).

104. De la Beche Inlet, named by Dawson after the geologist Sir Henry De la Beche.

105. Dawson mentions only Werner Bay and Hutton Inlet in his "Queen Charlotte Islands," 21. These, he wrote, "owing to the short time at my disposal, and comparatively uninteresting character of the rock sections, were not examined to their heads."

106. Most likely Murchison Island.

strong wind. Got back to schooner at 6.30 & found a canoe alongside with the indians we had seen a day or two since on their way to collect eggs. They tell us that the hot spring of which we have heard so Much is on the island near which we are anchored. Visit the locality, & find a number of Sources all perhaps rising from one place, but flowing out among broken rocks at some distance probably from point of issue. Temperature very various according probably to distance from source &c., but warmest too hot to bear comfortably with the hand. Altogether a considerable body of water.[107] Slight smell of S.H.2 & a barely perceptible saline taste. Full of green confervoid growth. large patches of mossy surface near Sources, not overgrown with sal-lal or bushes like rest of I. Heat prevents their growth. On stripping off the moss the ground warm everywhere. Very slight whitish incrustation on stones. Indians bathe in a natural, muddy reservoir.

[verso]

The rock of vicinity of hot spring shows no more sign of recent volcanic origen than that of other neighbouring islands. All these in great part of bedded igneous rocks, but old & dipping at high angles, associated with argillites.[108] Near the intrusive hot spring the predominant material is a whitish rock (see specimen) in ⟨which⟩ association with which & Caught up in it blackish hard argillites. In some places argillites intersected by dykes of the material. Many other places among islands where similar circumstances occur. No reason to argue recent volcanic action.

[end verso]

July 4. Went round to the hot spring & took photo. of the mossy patch beneath which it rises. Could not get view embracing the pools & this also. Got second photo looking up the inlet.[109] Returned to schooner & set sail, proceeding up the inlet with a fair wind. Corrected some of sketches by bearings as went along. Took several soundings & had the dredge over in 43 fathoms but nearly lost it on a rough rocky bottom in a tideway. Got plotting brought up to date. The inlet seems to open out in various directions as we advance, there being now four openings to large bays or

---

107. Hotspring Island, named by Dawson. The site on the southwest side of the island was "easily recognized by a patch of mossy green sward which can be seen from a considerable distance. Steam also generally hovers over it. The actual source of the water is not seen, but is probably not far from the inner edge of the mossy patch" (Dawson, "Queen Charlotte Islands," 22). He had no thermometer to measure the heat of the warmest streams.

108. Hardened rocks composed of clay minerals.

109. See "Photographs," 4 July 1878, GSC235–C2 (PA 51103) and GSC236–C2 (PA 51099).

branch inlets or Channels in sight from near here.[110] Anchored in a snug little harbour (Echo Hr) on the SW shore. Entrance narrow & bold, within expands. Grassy beach at head, & little passage running off to north which opens into a wonderfully secluded inner basin, which however for the most Part shallow. This receives a large stream[111] from the rocky & in part snow clad mountains which are piled at the head of the harbour.

Took photo of harbour after anchoring.[112]

July 5. Off in good time, & worked eastward down one side of the inlet to connect with former furthest pt, then westward back on the other. Turned into opening nearly opposite Echo harbour, which at first supposed to be a large bay, but proved to open out in two directions, the main passage trending north & then eastward,[113] & all clear to the open sea! A strong breeze drawing in, & head tide made it difficult to get far. Turned & after opening the inlet well out & ran back under sail.

Saw two indians fishing at a distance today, & continue to observe many signs of recent chopping, & habitation. We must now be near the Clue village.

Echo harbour. Least depth near mouth about 11 fathoms at H.W. within everywhere about 15 fathoms, shoaling gradually near the head at first, & then running steeply up to a flat nearly dry at low water. Well sheltered from all winds & good soft holding ground.

The main passage,[114] outside Echo Harbour continues to carry the flood from the S.E., the Ebb from the N.W. The tides thus draw through & do not run out from both ends to the open. The current must be over 2 knots at times.

A little fine timber on flats here & there, but very little flat ground. Spruce, hemlock, & Cedar. Yellow Cedar[115] fairly abundant in small trees.

July 6. Took blankets this morning, intending to stay out two days. Rounded the point beyond Echo Harbour to the westward[116] & found a large bay,[117] the inlets at the upper end of which run up among the roots of a mass of high jagged & heavily Snow clad Mountains, probably the

---

110. Dawson is now in Darwin Sound.

111. Longfellow Creek.

112. See "Photographs," 4 July 1878, GSC237–C2 (PA 51100).

113. Through Richardson Passage into Richardson Inlet.

114. Darwin Sound.

115. Yellow cedar, *C. nootkatensis*.

116. Bent Tree Point.

117. Klunkwoi Bay, so named by Dawson.

highest yet seen.[118] The next opening beyond this large bay is that called Crescent Inlet as a provisional name.[119] It is a fiord, some miles in length, but quite narrow & hemmed in by steep wall sided mountains something like those of the Inlet of July 2.[120] At its head this turns round toward the mountains of the bay first referred to, but without reaching them. The mountains on the north side are the highest. One of conical form when viewed from the entrance proves to be a somewhat prolonged ridge running parallel to the inlet, with several peaks. A second, & considerably higher has a triple summit, & slopes very steeply down to the waters edge This by reason of a coloured patch on it was called provisionally Red Top.[121] Notwithstanding the steep sided character of this inlet there is a good deal of beach around its sides.

Got observation for lat. at noon, & a photo of the Red top Mountain.[122]

On wishing to camp, after having worked some miles north of mouth of last inlet, could find no water. Ran across the channel, about 2 m. to A bay in a large island,[123] where found a little Spring, plenty wood, a good beach, no flies, & altogether a charming camping place. Put tents up under some fallen & half fallen trees of gigantic size, which form a complete screen seaward.

July 7. Worked along the West shore of the Channel to the open sea, which when opened out displayed a perplexing lot of little islands, some lying very far off the coast. Set [Rip.?] marks & ran across a large bay eastward,[124] but the sun being behind the marks could not seem them distinctly enough to read on them. Could therefore not fix positions of outlying islands. At point where marks to be read from, came on rounding it, Suddenly on the Indian village, Called Clue's village.[125] Went ashore &

118. Part of the San Cristoval Range. The two highest peaks west of the inlet are Apex Mountain and Mount Laysen.

119. It has been retained.

120. De la Beche Inlet.

121. Redtop Mountain.

122. See "Photographs," 6 July 1878, GSC240-C2 (PA 152367).

123. Richardson Island.

124. Laskeek Bay.

125. Clue village, sometimes called Laskeek, but more properly Tanu. It is described, with Dawson's photographs, in George F. MacDonald, *Haida Monumental Art: Villages of the Queen Charlotte Islands* (Vancouver: University of British Columbia Press, 1983), 88-100. Dawson himself wrote: "the channel between the islands is so open as to afford little shelter, while the neighbourhood of the village is very rocky, and must be dangerous of approach in bad weather. There are about thirty carved posts here, of all heights

had a talk with the Indians obtaining some information from them. Asked for the chief Capt. Clue[126] So called & taken up to his house & introduced to him   The village consists of perhaps twelve or fourteen of the large houses usual on the coast, & bristles with totem poles carved into Grotesque figures. Some of the houses entered through holes in the bases of the poles, but Clue's* by an ordinary door. Descending some steps one is in a rectangular area depressed somewhat below the level of the ground outside, with several broad steps running round it, on which the family goods, bedding &c. placed. In the Centre a square area not boarded in which a bright fire of small logs burns, the smoke passing off through apertures in the roof above. Clue* with some of his friends occupied positions on the further side of the fire from the door. Squatting on Clean mats, several women, who however kept in the background.[127] A couple of boxes brought out on which a well educated Siwash asked Self & R in tolerable English, to sit down. These placed near Clue*, & the Indian having first asked who was tyie[128] accordes the nearest post to Clue* to me. Had a short conversation & then pleading the late hour got off again on our way to the schooner. Our reception by Clue* quite a Ceremonial one, for which occasion offered as he was evidently waiting in some state, & all in order to receive a large party of Skidegate Indians[129] who are expected, & are to join in a bee or potlatch the occasion of which the erection of a new house

[verso]

Position of Indian villages in Rocky wave lashed spots.

There are about 32 upright totem poles in the village of all ages, heights, & styles. Of houses about sixteen, including one unfinished,

---

and styles, with sixteen houses. The village, extending round a little rocky point, faces two ways, and cannot easily be wholy seen from any one point of view, which causes it to look less important than the last [Skedans], though really possessing a larger population than it, and being in a more flourishing state than any elsewhere seen in the islands" ("Queen Charlotte Islands," 169).

126. Variously Kloo, Klew, Klue, Clew, and Cloo from one of his highest names Xeū' (meaning "the southeast"). He often went by Kitkane or Kitkune (Gitku'n, according to Swanton, a Tsimshian word). See Swanton, *Haida Ethnology*, 96, 278. Both names were hereditary. He was a young man, having succeeded his uncle of the same name on the latter's death in 1876. See James G. Swan, typescript diary, 56–57, University of Washington Archives, Seattle.

127. For photographs and a description of Haida houses, see Margaret R. Blackman, *Window on the Past: The Photographic Ethnohistory of the Northern and Kaigani Haida*, National Museum of Man, Mercury Series, Canadian Ethnology Service Paper no. 74 (Ottawa: National Museums of Canada, 1981), especially 113–35.

128. Or "tyee," Chinook Jargon for "chief."

129. Haida from Skidegate village on Skidegate Inlet.

though evidently some time under way. Indians appear very comfortable, & moderately clean. The Skidegates down today & a great gambling game in progress, a number of little polished sticks being shuffled up in soft cedar bark.[130] A grand dance in prospect for the evening.

[end verso]

Met a canoe on the way with fresh halibut & got a fine large fish for a dollar. Got back to schooner after 8 P.m. having made a prodigiously long round today, but without doing a vast deal of solid work.

July 8. Got anchor up & schooner out of harbour, & then set out in boat with Williams* & R for the S. shore of the entrance to the channel. At work all day & back at night to the schooner at her new anchorage. Plotting work till late.

July 9. Cross the inlet & work outwards along the shore of the large island opposite.[131] Getting to the Indian village pay a rather lengthened call with the object of getting such facts as I can about possible coal &c. Hear confirmation of the story of a spot on one of the islands outside that of the hot spring, from which bitumen, or something like it oozes.[132] Present Chief Klue* with a pound of tobacco, & finding no objection made take a photo.[133] of the village. Would have taken several but the rain threatening all the morning now began. Lunched near the village & then ran across to the outer island[134] on the outer part of which a very good section of great thickness of the dark argillites & flaggy limestones[135] here & there a poorly preserved amonite. Came back amid rain & wind with a heavy breaking sea, round the east end of the island & got on board schooner at six p.m. Heavy rain still continues at 11 P.m. At work plotting ⟨work⟩ notes &c. till late.

130. "Gambling is as common with the Haidas as among most other tribes, which means it is the most popular and constantly practiced of all their amusements. The gambler frequently loses his entire property, continuing the play till he has nothing whatever to stake. The game generally played I have not been able to understand clearly. It is the same with that of most of the coast tribes, and not dissimilar from gambling games played by natives from the Pacific Coast to Lake Superior. Sitting on the ground in a circle, in the centre of which a clean cedar mat is spread, each man produces his bundle of neatly smoothed sticks, the values of which are known by the markings upon them. They are shuffled together in soft teased cedar bark, and drawn out by chance" (Dawson, "On the Haida," 129). For a fuller treatment of the game, see Swanton, *Haida Ethnology*, 58–59.

131. Lyell Island, named by Dawson after Sir Charles Lyell.

132. Tar Rock. See Kathleen E. Dalzell, *The Queen Charlotte Islands*, vol. 2, *Of Places and Names* (Prince Rupert, B.C.: Dalzell Books, 1973), 208.

133. See "Photographs," 9 July 1878, GSC242–C2 (PA 37753).

134. Kunga Island, named by Dawson.

135. Beds of limestone consisting of layers from one to ten centimetres in thickness.

July 10. A very wet night, & heavy rain early this morning, rendering one uncertain whether to start along the open coast for Cumshewas,[136] as had intended, or not. This especially as barometer very low & not showing any inclination to rise. All appearance of Clearing ⟨at⟩ after breakfast, got anchor up & away. Called at the Indian village to try to engage an indian known to Charly, one of the Skidegates who are visiting here. Find that all left early this Morning. Got some information from Indians who Came off in Canoe, by which it appeared that a large inlet between this & Cumshewas, with a large island in its entrance.[137] Wind light, did not get to end of former work till so near noon that thought it best to have lunch on board. Got off shortly after noon, instructing the schooner to go round to the other side of the island & find an anchorage. Rowed about 8 Miles up a long inlet,[138] which finally became very narrow, & though still running on, took such direction that seemed very improbable it would turn Seaward again. In much doubt what to do, as getting late, but finally decided to sail back down the inlet, & look for the schooner on the other side of the supposed island. Did so, but on rounding the point, find a second great inlet,[139] with the wind again blowing out. Caught sight of the sail far up the inlet, & rowed laboriously down to a fine harbour[140] in which schooner at anchor, a distance of probably eight miles arrived on board after 9 P.m. guided by fog horn & lantern. R. tired out with rowing & self cold & tired also.

Williams* rocked overboard by the boom near the point had a wet & cold row to the schooner. Fortunately in falling Caught side of boat, or might have been more serious.

Long heavy swell from seaward today & strong winds from the land. — westerly winds.

Passing the Indian vil. this morning in bright sunshine all alive like an anthill with Indians in blue, red Green & white blankets. Hard at work holding the "bee" for the erection of a new house for Chief Klue*. Cedar planks of great size hewn out long since in anticipation, towed ashore some days ago, now being dragged up the beach by the united efforts of the motly gathering, harnessing themselves in clusters to ropes as one sees in old Egyptian pictures of the movement of masses of stone, though numbers engaged here of course smaller. Heaving & howling or ye-hoving in

136. A major village to the north on Cumshewa Inlet.

137. Perhaps Selwyn Inlet and Talunkwan Island are meant.

138. Dana Inlet, named by Dawson after geologist James Dana.

139. Probably Logan Inlet, named after Sir William Logan.

140. Rockfish Harbour, so named by Dawson.

strange tones to encourage themselves as they strain at the drawing. The large Cedar beam lying on the beach is being elaborately carves as a door pillar for Klue's* new house[141]

July 11. Off as usual though morning threatening, to examine the maze of inlets &c. which has opened up between Laskeek & Cumshewas. Drizzling showers in the morning, followed in the afternoon by almost continuous rain with squalls of wind. These seem concentrating into a blow from the South East

On our return, after joining with yesterdays work at bottom of first inlet, find a heavy wind & sea rolling in which gave us a hard tussle to weather the shore, with its numerous points & get into our harbour. Crept slowly round among sharp chopping seas, & finally, having opened the sea, tilted into the mouth of the harbour on grand rollers too large to be dangerous to the boat, but which sweeping on the rocks at the entrance surrounded them with a seething mass of spray & foam.

Weather still wet, barometer going down & the sound of the breakers outside constant.

July 12. Raining nearly all night & this morning still raining with wind & heavy swell & low barometer. Judged it best not to attempt out door work & consequently devoted time to reading &c. Schooner beached at high tide & bottom scraped in afternoon. Pm only showery Took a short walk along the beach & went for an hour fishing, Catching a few rock Cod.[142] Evening barometer rising & some appearance of clearing though light Showers Still continue.

July 13. Every appearance of clearing this a.m. with high barometer but showers beginning soon became almost continuous & continued very wet till after Noon. Later cleared up partially & ceased raining. Got a rather late start, the boat having grounded owing to the extremely low state of the tide. Did a good day's work however, getting sight of the extremities of the three remaining branches of this great inlet. After completing work got a good breeze to carry us nearly all way back to schooner, & having arrived early at the Mouth of the harbour put a line over to try for a fish. Found the fishing very good & caught about 3 dozen good sized "rock cod" of at least four species. Very gaily coloured & spawning to a degree. First rate eating however. At work till late plotting & writing up notes. Got observation on polaris after 11 P.m.

July 14. A rather late start again owing to Charley who overslept himself. Worked round the shore in the boat nearly to the Indian village

---

141. It is Tanu House 5 of MacDonald, *Haida Monumental Art*, 93, which includes a history and description of the house, along with Dawson's photographs.

142. Or rockfish, *Sebastodes* spp.

(Skedan)[143] at the S entrance to Cumshewa's Harbour. Then boarded the schooner which not far behind & run on with very light wind anchoring on N side of bay at about 10 P.m. Morning very bright & fine but afternoon clouding & evening showery & calm. A couple of Canoes Came out from the Indian village to meet us, freighted with Indians who brought a quantity of wooden bowls &c. to trade as curiosities. The Chief Skedan[144] in the larger Canoe, dressed in a good suit of black, a middle aged man of less power than Klue* apparently & commonplace mind. Presented his "papers"[145] which simply said that he was a good sort of Indian &c. &c., with the exception of one which written by one of a number of people who were shipwrecked in 1852–53 on the coast, in the schooner ⟨name⟩ {Olympia}.[146] The writer said he had no doubt their lives due to this man & another who objected to the other Indians carrying out their intention of murdering them at once. Gave the Chief a small present of tobacco & proceeded to bargain for some of the Indian curiosities. Skedan* says very few indians here at present, nearly all in "Vic-toi"[147]   village occupies an exposed situation on a gravelly neck at the point South of Cumshewas Hr. It bristles with "posts" & must be more carefully examined.

July 15. Raining with thick mist & strong wind this morning, a state of affairs which continued with little abatement during day. A heavy sea running in the bay & breaking on the shore. Remained about schooner all day, making only a short extension to the shore to see the rocks, which diorites. The little cove on the North Side of Cumshewas Hr, in which we are anchored is that in which McCoy built a house some years since for trading purposes.[148] Hoped to induce the Indians to catch dog-fish & make

---

143. Skedans or Koona village (Swanton's Q!ō′na). Dawson described it as being more important than Cumshewa. "Many of the houses are still inhabited, but most look old and moss-grown, and the carved posts have the same aspect" ("On the Haida," 169). See below, 18 July 1878. It is fully described in John and Carolyn Smyly, *Those Born at Koona: The Totem Poles of the Haida Village Skedans Queen Charlotte Islands* (Saanichton, B.C.: Hancock House, 1973); and MacDonald, *Haida Monumental Art*, 78–86.

144. Chief Skedans or Skedance, chief of Koona. The name was hereditary.

145. Indians usually collected testimonials from Europeans and showed them to visitors, even though these sometimes contained unflattering remarks.

146. There is no record of an *Olympia* being wrecked on the Queen Charlotte Islands at such a time, but the incident sounds similar to that of the *Susan Sturgis* pillage, though it was Edenshaw of the Massets who was then the dubious hero. See below, 23 August 1878.

147. Like other Northwest Coast languages, Haida contains no sound equivalent to the English "r."

148. McCoy Cove. Dawson uses the name McCoy in his text, but corrects it to McKay in his "Queen Charlotte Islands," 28. Captain Hugh McKay established a base and trading post at this point in 1869, but it was abandoned about six years later. According to

oil but found it did not pay, the Indians constantly going to Victoria & being without habits of steady industry. House Sill Standing. The Cumshewa Indian Village about 1 ½ mile further up the bay on the same side. Clearly visable from here, with its row of "posts" & houses. Very few Indians said to be there at present.

Chief Skedan* finding it a profitable business yesterday came across today with a lot more masks, rattles &c. &c. to sell & succeeded in inducing me to take a good many at rather exhorbitant rates.

Told by the Indians that only three kinds of mammals in the *Haida illihie*,[149] viz: Black bears, now in the mountains but common along shore when the hook billed Salmon begin to run; Marten (as far as I can make out) & Otter. There is also a mouse, however, or Small mouse-like Animal two of which have been seen by us along the beach,[150] but of the existence of which my Indian informant did not seem to be aware. Says there are plenty frogs, but no snakes on the islands.[151]

July 16   Being unable to learn from the Indians exactly how far it was to the head of Cumshewa's Harbour, or rather inlet, took our blankets with us this morning. Took three photographs of the Indian village *en route*, with special reference to the Curious *totem poles*.[152]

In examining the shore found very interesting sections of the Coal bearing rocks, with abundant fossils. Did in consequence only a comparatively small stretch of Coast, camping in a little well sheltered cove[153] with good water & plenty dry wood. Altogether a charming camp. Up till late getting obsn. of Polaris for lat.

Fine & very warm day.

[verso]

General character about Cumshewas
separation between high & low country

Kathleen E. Dalzell, McKay's Cove was renamed McCoy Cove in 1921 after a fireman on board the *Lillooet*. See Dalzell, *Queen Charlotte Places*, 268.

149. Chinook Jargon, "illahee" meaning country, land, or earth.

150. The "Black bears" were American black bears, *Ursus americanus carlott* Osgood; "Marten" marten, *Martes americana nesophila* (Osgood); "Otter" the river otter, *Lutra canadensis periclyzomæ* Elliot; and the "mouse" probably a deer mouse, *Peromyscus maniculatus keeni* (Rhoads).

151. Dawson was correct in that no snakes were indigenous to the Queen Charlotte Islands, while the northwestern toad, *Bufo boreas boreas* Baird & Girard, was found there.

152. See "Photographs," 16 July 1878, GSC243–C2 (PA 37752); GSC244–C2 (PA 38151); and GSC245–C2 (PA 38150).

153. Doubtless his Boat Cove.

shoal character of harbour.

[end verso]

July 17. Boat aground this morning but got her off without much trouble & proceeded on our way, examining the head of the Inlet. Returned along south shore, getting back to schooner at 7.30 after a long pull. Took one photo of snowy mountains near head of inlet.[154] Tried to get Sun. lat. at noon but cloudy. — A fine day though more overcast, & not So warm as yesterday. On returning on board found three Indian women with little things for sale among which two large spoons made from horns of the Mountain Sheep[155] very ingeniously. Bought one for $1.00 though $2.00 at first asked for it.

July 18. Besieged by Indians with various things to sell this morning, curiosities new potatoes about the size of wallnuts[156] &c. Got away at last, & pulling across the harbour Carried work on to Skedan's village, arriving there about noon. Took five photographs of the village & totem posts,[157] which here appear very interesting. Had lunch, & then examined the large bay S. of the village,[158] Connecting Satisfactorelly with the other work. Had hoped to have a fair wind back but this dying away, a wind sprang up Out of the inlet, giving us a long pull back against wind & tide. Arrived on board at 8 P.m. Soon after dark Capt Klue* & three of his people arrived, disgusted that they had not been knowing enough to offer *ictus* for Sale when we were {in} their country, & having heard that Skedan was making a big thing out of us. Brought with them one remarkable mask with a nose about 6 feet long, a dancing pole highly prized & gaily painted & a head ornament composed of cedar bark into a ring of which a great number of imitation arrows, in wood & feathered, were stuck   All these they valued much & had evidently brought their best things to cut out Skedan & his friends, mistaking our taste for homely illustrative articles for those gaudy

---

154. See "Photographs," 17 July 1878, GSC247–C2 (PA 51105).

155. Probably from stone sheep, *Ovis dalli stonei* Allen, which are found only on the mainland north of the Skeena and Nass rivers. The horn was steamed into a spoon shape and the narrow handle usually carved.

156. The Haida had begun growing potatoes early in the nineteenth century. See J. H. Van Den Brink, *The Haida Indians: Cultural Change Mainly between 1876–1970* (Leiden: E. J. Brill, 1974), 34–35. In his "On the Haida," 113–14, Dawson wrote: "the potato, called *skow-shit* in Haida, introduced by some of the early voyagers, now forms an important part of the food supply. A Skidegate Indian told me that it was first grown in Skidegate, but I do not know how far this statement may be reliable."

157. Only four photographs remain. See "Photographs," 18 July 1878, GSC248–C2 (PA 37754); GSC249–C2 (PA 44329); GSC250–C2 (PA 38148); and GSC251–C2 (PA 38153).

158. Skedans Bay.

& good to the uninstructed Siwash. After a deal of talking felt almost obliged to buy one & got the mask for $2.00.[159] Had also to give them permission to sleep on deck as they showed signs of staying in the cabin all night if not.

Skedan's village shows signs of having passed its best days. Some time since though not quite so deserted as Cumshewa's   It has always been a larger village & many of the houses are still inhabited. Most, however, look old & moss grown & the totem poles have the same aspect. Of houses there are about sixteen, of totem poles about 44. These last seem to be put up not merely as hereditary family Crests, but in memory of the dead. An old woman is getting one put up now, at which most of the tribe is away at work, in memory of a daughter who died in Victoria lately. The flat topped, boarded totems are more frequent in this village than elsewhere seen.[160] One of these shows a curious figure leaning forward & holding in its paws a genuine *Copper*[161] like those described to me by Mr Moffat[162] as in great request & much worth among the Ft Rupert indians   At least one other *Copper* in view on the posts here, but the second observed not in Evident relation to any of the Carved figures

The village situated as usual in a wild rocky & sea-washed place, on a shingly neck of land connecting a broken little rocky peninsula with the shore. on the peninsula two remarkable, symmetrical, conical hillocks, which form a good landmark when coming from the South.

July 19. Examined rocks between anchorage & Indian village, including the metalliferous veinlets pointed out by the Indians. At the village found the old Chief himself, Cumshewa.[163] He had heard that I wanted to see

159. Some of Dawson's purchases are illustrated in his "On the Haida." Most of the artifacts he collected were placed on loan to McGill College and are now in the McCord Museum.

160. These are grave or mortuary posts, the boards holding the remains of the dead.

161. The pole is the "Bear and Copper Mortuary" (no. 17C) of John and Carolyn Smyly, *Those Born at Koona,* 89; and Memorial 10X1 of MacDonald, *Haida Monumental Art,* 82. The box front is now in the Prince Rupert Museum, without its copper.

162. Hamilton Moffatt (1832–94) joined the Hudson's Bay Company in London in 1849 and the following year was posted to Victoria. He later served at Fort Rupert and Fort Simpson before retiring in 1872. The following year he was appointed to the department of Indian affairs in Victoria. See Walbran, *Coast Names,* 340–41.

163. Swanton identifies the village as St!awā's and the chief as Gô'msiwa. See his *Haida Ethnology,* 273. Dawson commented: "the village generally known as Cumshewas, is situated in a small bay facing toward the open sea, but about two miles within the inlet to which the same name has been applied. The outer point of the bay is formed by a little rocky islet, which is connected with the main shore by a beach at low tide. The name Cumshewa or Kumshewa is that of the hereditary chief, the village being properly called *Tlkinool,* or by Tshimsians *Kit-ta-was.* There are now standing here twelve or fourteen houses, several of them quite ruinous, with over twenty-five carved posts. The

the reported coal & was ready to come with us & show it, on the understanding that he should be paid. This I promised provided he really
showed us some coal. A rather pleasant & quiet old Indian, speaking very
little Chinook but trying to make himself as agreeable & useful as possible.
Found the coal in small fragments in sandstone. Examined locality & collected specimens. After lunch paced several miles of beach for section, &
remained Collecting fossils, which occur in great abundance in Some
places — so long that did not get back on board Schooner again till 8 P.m.
At work till late on notes &c. Found a canoe alongside on return, with a
number of Holibut Indians appeared considerably disappointed that I
should buy only one, which I did for half a dollar.

July 20. Anchor up Early this morning, & spent greater part of bay dredging outside the harbour. Could find only shelly bottom, Which though
yielding no great variety, gave some things of interest. Evening visited the
Indian Village, plotting work & notes till late.

About sundown two large Canoes with two masts Each, & the forward
one with a large flat hoisted, hove in sight round the point. Turn out to be
Kit-Katla Chimseyan Indians with loads of oolachen grease for Sale.[164]
They have slept only two nights on the way from Kit-katla   They come
here on a regular trading expedition, & expect to carry back chiefly blankets in place of their oil. Only a few of the Haidas Seem to understand
Chimseyan so that have the curious spectacle of Indians communicating
with each other by this vehicle. Quite a picturesque scene when the Canoes
grounded & the Kit Katlans assisted by the Haidas carry up blankets used
as bedding, miscellains little things & the Cedar bark boxes which hold the
precious oil.[165]

Arrival of Chimseyans to sell oolachen grease to Haidas   Evening sky
just loosing glow of sunset. Two Canoes appear round point. Sails clued
up to masts, of which each Canoe has two. A bright red piece of bunting
flying from the Canoe ahead. Who are these. Haida looking attentively
pronounced Chinseyans & proved correct. Soon in good view. Greater
part of occupants women. All fairly well dressed & wearing Clean blankets
to make a good appearance on arrival. Faces of some painted black or dull
red giving a wild appearance, which rendered comical by the top pieces

population is quite small, this place having suffered much from the causes to which the
decrease in numbers of the natives have already been referred" (Dawson, "On the
Haida," 169). For a further description, see MacDonald, *Haida Monumental Art*,
67–74.

164. These would be Coast Tsimshian from Kitkatla village on the mainland. Eulachon were
abundant in Tsimshian territory but absent from the Queen Charlotte Islands.

165. For a similar description of the trade, see Dawson, "On the Haida," 136–37.

which civilized [*tilis/titis*?] of various patterns but all intended for the male sex. {Some children, several very patently half breeds.} Dip paddles with a slow monotonous persistency after a long day's work. Tell us that have only slept two nights since leaving Kit-Katla. Come in to beach at Haida Village & received by its inhabitants, who appear anxious to assist in every way. Bark boxes holding the greese set into the water beside the canoes. Other things carried carefully ashore. Canoes hauled up, & then the greese boxes carried carefully up beyond high-water mark, the villagers assisting. A large box an inconvenient load for one man. Regular system of merchandise. Expect to get blankets from the Haidas for the grease, each box being worth from 6 to 10 blankets or say from $12 to $20. The grease notwithstanding its offensive odour a very favourite article of diet with the Indians. Remember that also packed into the interior by the *grease trail*,[166] & in fact radiates in all directions from the great oolachen fisheries of the northern part of the Coast. Indians in Victoria value very much, but there very dear.

Cumshewa's Harbour of map really a long inlet & should be Called Cumshewa's Inlet. It differs in its somewhat greater width & the low character of the land on its Northern shore from the other inlets to the south, & in fact marks the junction of the Mountainous & flat countries on the East Coast of the island. There is more beach along its shores than in the southern inlets & wider tide flats. These only indication of shoaler water, which not only in the Inlet itself, but now extends far off the coast, probably marking the submarine extension of the soft Coal bearing formation in an uncrumpled state. The heads of Some parts of the Inlet, however, appear deep & have bold shores, this only on a smaller scale what found on grand Scale in Many of larger fjords. The Mountains to south bear snow in abundance which without doubt lasts all Summer. They are as high as any yet seen & the mountainous country does not therefore die away but suddenly breaks down in this direction.

The Southern head of the Inlet almost (quite?) meets ⟨that of⟩ an arm of that explored last.[167] From the southern or south Western extremity an Indian trail leads over to the head of Tasso or Tasoo Harbour,[168] which Can be traversed in half a day, & is not infrequently used by the Indians, who do not permanently reside in Tasoo. ⟨From the Mouth of the stream

---

166. Eulachon ran on many mainland rivers, but the most abundant catch was on the Nass River. The numerous trading trails across the mountains and into the interior were customarily called "grease trails," because of their frequent use as trading routes for the highly valued eulachon oil.

167. As Dawson later realized, Cumshewa Inlet does connect with Selwyn Inlet to the south, creating Louise Island.

168. From Sewell Inlet to Tasu Sound on the west coast of Moresby Island.

near McCoy's House, & opposite our anchorage, another trail starts for Gold Harbour.[169] This is further off, the journey occupying two ordinary days travel. Trail said to go through a comparatively low country & to pass by one or more lakes. Is probably pretty easily traversed or Indians would go round by Skidegate by water.⟩

[verso]

{"no such trail"}

[end verso]

The two symmetrical little knolls near Skedans Village form good landmark from south for southern entrance of harbour. ⟨Cumshewas⟩ {not Cumshewas} Island[170] on the north bristles like a porcupine with dead trees. Must be dangerous to run into harbour or Inlet in thick or dark weather for besides general shoalness of shores in this vicinity, An extensive rocky reef[171] lies a little to north of centre of opening well outside. Beyond this perhaps half a mile further East is a second reef bare only at low water. Others not seen may exist besides these, & the low Islands to the south[172] are probably well fenced with reefs also.

At southern side of mouth of harbour very regular depth averaging 20 fathoms with shelly bottom everywhere. The bar at the entrance to the harbour is not a spit as shown in Chart but a wide bank or flat stretching from the south shore. Comparatively little of it dries, but at this season all thickly covered with kelp, which buoys it well.[173]

Vessels should be very cautious in approaching the shore everywhere in this vicinity either outside or inside the inlet as it runs shoal a long way. The bay in which McCoy's house is built affords fair anchorage for small schooners off the edge of the tide flat which wide. The anchorage marked, with soundings, inside Island on North Shore[174] must be a mistake, for at high tide can see bottom nearly all way across the supposed anchorage & kelp abundant off its mouth. The best anchorage for large vessels probably on S shore opposite the long beach which fronts the low ground of estuary of a large stream.[175] This probably one of the places marked on the chart.

July 21. A fair day on the whole though generally overcast, & Showery in

---

169. Kuper Inlet.

170. Dawson here realized that Cumshewa Island, a small barren rock, was not what he meant. The island referred to is Kingui Island.

171. Cumshewa Rocks.

172. Skedans Islands.

173. Fairbairn Shoals.

174. McLellan Island.

175. Mathers Creek.

the evening, with mist. Got off in good time & Carefully examined & paced the section along part of N. shore of harbour. Chief object to get an approximate thickness for the Shaly argillites &c. In this probably fairly Successful. In returning called at Indian Village & engaged a young Indian to whom I had spoken before, to go with us to Skidegate & perhaps further. A rather heavy-looking fellow, whose chief peculiarities appear to be a long back & short legs. Speaks Chinook of Course, but also some English & is too proficient in swearing, a habit no doubt contracted on former cruises on schooners. Evening writing up notes, Sorting specimens &c. till late.

July 22. A dull morning with dropping rain & thick fog. Barometer high however, & as the Indian boy engaged yesterday has turned up, & otherwise all ready. Decide to set out for Skidegate, leaving the Schooner to follow as soon as she Can. The fog gradually Cleared up, but heavy rain soon began & continued without intermission almost all the morning, Soaking us Completely. After lunch became fair, though still clouded. Sea moderately Calm, & So made good progress along the Coast, Camping at about 5.30 Pm in a wide bay.[176] Hauled up boat on skids.

July 23. Off Early, with fair weather & Calm sea soon made Spit Point at entrance to Skidegate & then examined along south shore of inlet for some distance, stopping at the point East of Alliford Bay, in a pretty little cove with sandy beach. The Schooner not having yet appeared, decide to stay here where we have a good view of the entrance to the harbour in preference to going across to the rendevous near the Indian Village.[177] Got a good fire going & soon very comfortable

[verso]

From the mouth of Cumshewa's Inlet to Skidegate Inlet the coast is all low, rising in a few places at the shore to a height of 200′ to 300′ only, & generally very much less than this, though gaining some such elevation at no very great distance back.[178] A series of wide open bays, separated by low spit-like points is found. The points are generally elevated about 20 feet above high water & are composed of gravel &c., being evidently rough spits formed by wash in opposing directions when the sea stood somewhat higher than at present. In some places these now bear fine woods. With the low shore — so different to that we have been accustomed to further south — the beach becomes flat, & very shoal water extends a great way off shore. Near Cumshewa's the beaches are almost altogether formed of boulders, but toward Skidegate they become finer, though still plentifully

176. Probably Copper Bay.

177. Skidegate Mission on the Graham Island shore of Skidegate Inlet.

178. Part of the Skidegate Plateau.

Strewn with erratics, which occasionally become very thick About the projecting points. Large boulders appear far from Shore at low tide. The erratics probably derived from the mts. of the interior of the Island. Spit Point at South Entrance to Skidegate particularly flat, & runs off into the long bar which Stretches across mouth of Inlet. This very shoal seaward, but falls off suddenly inward, into deepwater. The land about the Entrance to the inlet on the North Side is also quite low & flat, & from a little height Can be seen stretching a great way, the horizon line being in the end broken only by Scattered clusters of trees projecting above it. Further on, the hills begin to rise on both sides of the Inlet, & towards its head ranges of snowy mountains appear, probably equaling in height any we have yet seen.

[end verso]

July 24. Raining in the Morning, but caught sight of schooner beating into the Inlet soon after daylight. Got breakfast, & then put things in boat & started across toward her. Got on board & soon anchored in bight opposite Woodcocks Fishery,[179] now run by a man Called Smith, & his partner Macfarlane?.[180] Found a small sloop belonging to Collins[181] lying at Anchor, but just waiting for a wind to set off, & going direct to Victoria. Wrote letters to forward by this Chance, & after Early lunch examined the coast westward for a considerable distance. Collecting fossils & marking down attitude of rocks. Went round in the evening to the village to see the Indians dance. Returned late & went to bed at once quite tired out.

[verso]

Indian Dance.[182] Landing from our boat after dark at the south end of the fine sandy beach opposite Skidegate Village, find this part of the town

179. Now Skidegate Landing in Sterling or Skidegate Harbour.

180. J. McB. Smith, together with William Sterling, had established an oilworks to extract oil from dogfish livers in 1876. His foreman and perhaps partner was Andy McGregor, presumably Dawson's "Macfarlane." See Dalzell, *Queen Charlotte Islands, 1774-1966,* (Terrace, B.C.: C. M. Adam, 1963), 107–8; Johan Adrian Jacobsen, *Alaska Voyage, 1881-1883: An Expedition to the Northwest Coast of America,* trans. Erna Gunther from the German of Adrian Woldt (Chicago: University of Chicago Press, 1977), 20; and Newton H. Chittenden, *Exploration of the Queen Charlotte Islands,* (reprint, Vancouver: Gordon Soules, 1984), 73–74.

181. Unidentifiable.

182. This account was published, almost verbatim, by Dawson in his "The Haidas," *Harper's New Monthly Magazine* 45 (1882): 405-6. The draft is in file 69 of the G. M. Dawson Papers, RBSC. In his published report, Dawson writes of six kinds of Haida dancing ceremonies and calls this one, in the Skidegate dialect, *Kwai-o-guns-o-lung.* See Dawson, "On the Haida," 127–28. The term may be the same as Swanton's Q!ā′igî′lgañ, which he labels as a song and part of the Wāgał potlatch, a Haida equivalent of the Cannibal Dance. See Swanton, *Haida Ethnology,* 162–70, especially 166.

apparently quite deserted, but see some dim light at a distance, & hear the monotonous Sound of the drum ⟨at some distance⟩. Scrambling as best we may along the path which winds along the front of the row of houses, & narrowly escaping falls on the various obstructions in it, we reach the front of the house in which the dance is going on. The door is to one side of the middle, & not through the bottom of the totem post as in the older fashioned buildings. Pushing it open a glare of light flashes out, & entering, we find ourselves behind & among the dancers, who stand inside the house with their backs to the front wall. Pushing through them we cross the open space in which the fire, — well supplied with resinous logs is burning, & seat ourselves on the floor among a crowd of onlookers at the further End, having first taken off our hats at the request of some Indians near us. The house oblong of the usual Shape, but not excavated in the Centre as is often the case. The floor boarded, with the exception of a square space of earth in the middle for the fire. The Chattels of the family piled here & there in heaps along the walls, leaving the greater part of the interior Clear. The dancers as already described occupy the front end, the audience the sides & further {in} end of the house. The smoke from the fire, — which the only light — escaping by wide openings in the roof. The Audience nearly fill the building, squatting in various attitudes on the floor, & Consisting of Men women & children of all ages. Their faces all turned forward & expressive of various emotions lit up by the fire. {Skidegate village about 25 houses & some 53 totem posts.} The performers in this instance about twenty in number, dressed according to no uniform plan but got up in their best clothes, or at least their most gaudy ones, with the addition of certain ornaments &c. appropriate to the occasion. All or nearly all wore head dresses, variously constructed of cedar bark rope ornamented with feathers &c. or as in one case with a bristling circle of the whiskers of the Sea-lion. Shoulder girdles made of Cedar-bark rope, variously ornamented & coloured, with tassels &c. very common. One man wore gaiters covered with fringes of strung puffin[183] bills which rattled as he moved. Nearly if not all held sprigs of fresh spruce, & were covered about the head with downy feathers which also filled the warm atmosphere of the house. Rattles were also in order. Different from the rest however, five women who stood in front, dressed with some uniformity, Several having the peculiarly beautiful mountain goat shawls which are purchased from the Mainland Indians[184]   The head-dresses of these

---

183. Could have been from either the horned puffin, *Fratercula corniculata* (Naumann), or the more common tufted puffin, *Lunda cirrhata* (Pallas).

184. Presumably the famous Chilkat blankets, made almost exclusively by the Chilkat Tlingit of Alaska.

women were also pretty nearly the same consisting of Small mask faces Carved in wood & inlaid with haliotis[185] shell, these Attached to Cedar bark & built round with gay feathers &c. stood above the forehead. The faces of the women — as if All engaged in the dance — gaily painted, vermillion being the favourite colour. Another important feature the master of the ceremonies, who stood in the middle of the back row, slightly higher than the rest, not particularly gaily dressed, but holding a long thin stick with which he kept time & lead off the singing. A second man in the dance also held a stick, somewhat different from the first, being white & with a split & trimmed feather in the top. Do not know whether this man any part of the Ceremony. He, however, had a pronounced place on one side in front of the row of dancers.

The performer on the drum — a flat tambourine-looking article formed of hide stretched on a hoop — Sat opposite the dancers & near the fire, So that they Could mutually see each others movements. The drum beaten very regularly in "double knocks", thus — tum tum — tum tum — tum tum — &c!

With this the dancers kept time in a sort of Chant or Song to which words appeared Set, & which rose to a loud pitch or fell lower according to the motions of the Master of the Ceremonies, who besides keeping up the time now & then slips in a few words of direction or exhortation. To the drumming the dancing also keeps time, following it closely. At every beat a spasmodic twitch passes through the crowd of dancers, who scarcely move their feet from the floor but move by {double} jerks, shuffling their feet a little at the same time. Those who dance best, especially the 5 women already alluded to turn about half round in three or four jerks, & then turn back again in the next three or four. The heads of these women also moved as though loose & set on pivots, jerking idiotically as they moved. When the chorus swells to *forte*, the rattles are plied with tenfold vigour & the noise becomes very great. After a performance of ten Minutes or so the Master of Ceremonies gives a sign & all stop, ending with a loud *Hugh*! After a few minutes repose the movement begins again, with the drum.

The crowd of gaily dressed, gaily painted savages by the kind light of the fire present a rather brave & imposing appearance, & when in the heat of the dance I suppose the Indians may yet almost imagine the old palmy days when hundreds Crowded the village & nothing had eclipsed the grandeur of their ceremonies & doings, to remain. The occasion of the dance as far as I could learn, was the passing of a young man one degree toward being a "Chief," or head of a family. They gradually take rank passing a

185. Northern abalone, *Haliotis kamtschatkana* Jonas.

stage when they get a house erected, and becoming of some importance when the totem post has been erected a Potlatch of blankets occurs on each occasion.
[end verso]

G. M. Dawson to J. W. Dawson*, 24 July 1878, Skidegate

Having arrived at a little trading post, or rather station for dog-fishing & the manufacture of oil, we find a small sloop on the point of Sailing for Victoria, & take the opportunity of writing a few lines to let you know that we are well & where we are.

No news from home has reached us since leaving Victoria & there is no chance of our hearing anything till we reach Fort Simpson, which may be some time next month.

We have now Completed a running Survey along the East Coast from near the South End of the Islands to this place. The shore has proved very complicated a maze of inlets & islands occupying much time in examining even imperfectly. The geology is interesting enough, though no points of special importance have occurred yet. All the fossils hithertoo obtained are Mesozoic, but appear to be of two horizons. The highest that of the Coal bearing rocks, the lower perhaps Triassic or somewhere in that vicinity. I must not, however, occupy all my time in giving geological notes. — The weather has proved not quite so bad as some accounts would lead one to suppose though quite wet enough at times, & Seldom too warm or dry. of late it has been considerably improved & I hope it may continue so as work goes on so much faster.

I will probably remain here a week, & may be in the vicinity for a longer time should I decide to visit a few places on the West Coast *via* the Skidegate Strait. 〈?Skidegate Channel?〉 If ten days or a fortnight brings all this to a conclusion, less than a week should see us round at Masset. Two weeks should see us through about the North End of the Island, & we may then probably make over to Fort Simpson, & set on our way Southward, with time to spend on the N. end of Vancouver should weather admit. One Cannot of course, however count on keeping fixed dates, nor Calculate the time necessary for the southward trip. Should this reach safely it will be by a lucky Chance & no opportunity may again occur of sending a mail till we are nearly back to Vancouver at least.

Rankine* is well, & now occupied in writing at some length to Mother, so that you may have more news than contained in this Short note.

July 25 Heavy rain this morning renders us rather late in starting. Crossed the inlet & worked slowly round Alliford Bay & E. end of Maude

Island. Collecting a number of fossils. One place where particularly good near the Indian village (Gold Harbour tribe)   stopped some time & soon surrounded by nearly all the inhabitants of the place, men women & children. The latter were specially troublesome as they set to work pounding out, or trying to pound out the fossils with stones &c. & no doubt ruined many. Told them on leaving that if they would collect a number & bring to schooner tomorrow, I would pay them. Back for supper a little befor 7 P.m.

A long visit from Smith* & his partner.

The climate is said to be exceedingly wet here in winter, — only three fair days last winter — For two last winters no snow, but sometimes a good depth. This summer Said to be more southerly, with clouds & rain than usual, indeed quite exceptionally so according to Smith*.

July 26. Off in good time. A remarkably fine bright morning. went round to Indian village & took three photos. of it.[186] Then examined rocks at next point outward, but finding beyond nothing but Sand & beach, returned, looking at Bare & Tree Islands[187] *en route* & rowed on to where left off work yesterday. Worked on round Maude & Lina Islands &c. getting back to Schooner with fair wind about 6.30 P.m. Showers during day notwithstanding the fine appearance of the morning. After supper went with Mr Smith* to see some fine spruce trees behind the fishery. These have been used to some extent for making barrels for oil, & a quantity of wood lies ready split up for that purpose. The timber very fine. Tall & straight, though not of such great diameter as occasionally obtained.

July 27. Away in good time, Crossing to the gold harbour indian village to find a Man acquainted with the locality of the Coal said to exist further up the inlet than the mine,[188] who would go with me to the place when I am ready. Found the last two or three canoes just leaving for Gold Harbour, whither the whole tribe is now *en route* to make a fishery of Mackerel[189] for oil, as I understand it. Find two old men who explained as well as they could to Johnny where the Coal was. Worked along Coast south of Maude Island, with fine weather but a strong head wind, which delayed us

---

186. See "Photographs," 26 July 1878, GSC253–C2 (PA 38152); GSC254–C2 (PA 37755); and GSC255–C2 (PA 37756).

187. Jewell and Torrens islands.

188. Dawson noted that it was "reported by the Indians that a well-marked coal seam occurs about fourteen miles from the original locality in a south-easterly direction on the south shore of Skidegate Channel [Inlet]" (Dawson, "Note on Mines and Minerals," 120).

189. Possibly the chub mackerel, *Scomber japonicus* Houttuyn.

much. Found one remarkably good locality for fossils on South Island[190] stayed a while to Collect. Got back to schooner, — now Moved up to anchor cove[191] — by 6.15 P.m.

A fine day & evening with rain on the western hills but none eastward.

July 28. Breakfast at 7 a.m. Then sailed to various islands noting the rocks, & returned along shore examining the section from Lina Island. Got back to schooner at 1.30. Dinner. Did not go out again in P.m. reading, going over notes &c. Morning fine, gradually clouding & persistent heavy rain in the afternoon.

Found an Indian grave. on Reef Island, which my Indian informs me is that of a doctor, who died about ten years ago. A square box like structure about 5 feet high, made of cedar boards split out, & roofed with the same, but with the addition of a pile of stones to keep the whole in place. A board having fallen out, looked in to the last home. The back of the house covered within by a neat Cedar bark mat. The body in a sitting posture, the Knees having originally been near the chin, but the whole now slipped down somewhat. A large red blanket wrapped round the shoulders. The hair, still in situ & black & glossy, done up in a knot on top of the head & secured by a couple of Carved bone pins. A carved dancing stick leaning up in one corner, in front of the Knees a square cedar box, no doubt containing other necessary properties for the next world. The tomb under some spreading spruce trees near the rocky edge of the island overlooking the water. Do not know why in this instance they have departed from the usual custom of putting the dead in similar little houses behind the houses of the living in the village.[192]

July 29. Examining the rocks along the shores of the *Long Arm*[193] all day today, getting back about 6.30 after finishing with a couple of hours fatiguing Scramble through the gigantic & dense woods of the country, in search of "No. 2. Coal Mine"[194] — a search which proved unsuccessful. Day windy & with shower Succeeding shower in almost uninterrupted succession, the Mountains being constantly veiled with mist

---

190. Sandilands Island.

191. Immediately northwest of Anthracite Point, Long Inlet.

192. As Dawson was correctly informed, this would be a doctor's or shaman's interment. The body of such personages was often placed in a grave house with their ritual accessories at such sites away from the villages. Dawson makes clear the distinctive burial of shamans and describes it in detail in "On the Haida," 123–24. For a recent examination of Haida mortuary practices, see George F. MacDonald, *Haida Burial Practices: Three Archaeological Examples*, National Museum of Man, Mercury Series, Archaeological Survey of Canada Paper no. 9 (Ottawa: National Museums of Canada, 1973), 1–5.

193. Long Inlet.

194. Located opposite the Cowgitz Coal Mine. See below, 30 July 1878.

Found the *Echinopanax*[195] abundant in the woods today for the first time.

July 30. Had boat put on beach, & Williams* set to work to make some repairs on her, Indian to Cut wood for fires, & then set out with R. & Charley for the Coal Mines.[196] Walked up the track, which broad & well laid, with two fine bridges, one of which has now fallen. Trees have also fallen across the track in Many places, & thickets of bushes & weeds grow upon it. The bunkers screens &c. & all the arrangements for shipment have been very complete. The broad gauge line leads from the screens to the wharf, about a mile. The screens at foot of an incline, which worked by fall against empty trucks, double track drum with friction brake at top. From this tramway leads up a pretty steep incline to the Hoopers Creek Tunnel, & into it. Some grading done on line toward Hutchins Tunnel, but rails probably never laid. A rank growth is rapidly covering everything, chiefly Salmon berry bushes, with fire-weed &c.[197] In ten years it will scarcely be possible to trace anything. Tunnels beginning to fall in, & some partly full of water from blocking at mouth   Had a fatiguing day of it, Scrambling through the woods & up the terribly tangled & encumbered stream beds. Rain falling steadily, bushes & trees completely saturated, ground generally almost spongy & full of water. Returned about 3 Pm wet to the skin, cold & tired. Plotted some of back work, wrote up notes &c.

Perhaps sufficient certainty may not very unreasonably have been supposed for the Coal seams, but by obtaining thorough Knowledge of their horizon & tracing by pits from surface might have fully proved the area at comparatively small cost, & before completing Such elaborate arrangements for mining & shipment.

July 31. Start for exploration of Skidegate Straits. Camp beyond the

---

195. Devil's-club, *O. horridum*.

196. Coal was first reported on Skidegate Channel by William Downie in 1859. The Queen Charlotte Coal Company was organized in 1865, by a group of Victoria merchants who obtained a crown lease. With evidence of good quality anthracite, the Cowgitz Coal Mine began with ample funding and optimistic prospects. Tunnels were driven and tramways constructed to tidewater, a wharf and housing for workers built, and screens and other equipment erected. Various problems, however, prevented any coal shipments until Christmas 1870 when the first 435 tons were shipped. Though mining continued, the seams proved very difficult and extraction of the coal tedious. The final blow came with the loss of a ship loaded with coal bound for San Francisco. See Dalzell, *Queen Charlotte Places*, 69, 105–7. For technical descriptions of the seams and mine, see James Richardson, "Report on Coal-Fields of Vancouver and Queen Charlotte Islands, with a Map of the Distribution of the Former," in Geological Survey of Canada, *Report of Progress 1872–73* (1873), 57–62; and Dawson, "Queen Charlotte Islands," 71–77.

197. Fireweed, *E. angustifolium*.

second narrows[198] in a very bad place for wood, which unfortunate as all very wet from almost Continuous rain. Few good Camping places about here the present spring tides rising quite to the Edge of the woods, in fact often covering the lower branches of the trees in sheltered situations. All the dead wood wet & much of it rotten, & owing to the heavy & continuous rains a gentle ooze of water trickling out all along the beaches just about high water mark.

Aug. 1. Continued exploration, turning southward by a channel[199] used by the Indians when *en route* for Gold Harbour, but soon stopped by a dry beach about ¼ m. across, which cannot have more than 4 feet on it at H.W. Turned back & continued out to West Coast by passage to north,[200] which wide & deep, with the swell of the open pacific heaving in at its mouth. Can this be Cartwright Sound of the map? Having estimated distance to outer point, & assured ourselves of the open character of the passage, returned, getting over the second narrows just in time, before the change of tide. Camped in a large bay on North Side of inlet.[201] Heavy & almost constant showers during day.

The trail marked on Chart as about 3 m. to the West Coast from the Long Arm, comes out to the head of this bay. The valley from this end looks quite low. Trail not much, perhaps never, now used.

Aug 2. Continued track Survey on opposite side of strait, getting to the E. end of the first or East Narrows about 11 A.m. Found here two Indians who had agreed to come to show us the Coal. This they did, but the deposit not a very promising one, & involved much scrambling about through the wet woods to get at & examine it. Having lunched & satisfied the Indians for their trouble continued survey, getting back by way of channel S. of South Island, to schooner at Fishery about 6.30 P.m. Got dry clothes & at work on notes &c.

Many showers today with strong S.E. winds but not Continuous rain.

Aug 3. Rowed round this A.m. to Indian village to find an Indian to accompany us to Masset. One named Mills recommended by Smith*. Found him at home, but the talking appearing interminable asked him to come round to Schooner *tenas polikely*[202] & talk it out. Bought some Indian *ictas* & then Setting sail Crossed the Inlet. Examined junction of

---

198. West Narrows.

199. Buck Channel.

200. A continuation of Skidegate Channel. Cartwright Sound is to the north.

201. Called North Arm by Dawson, later renamed Trounce Inlet.

202. Or "Tenas plaklie," Chinook Jargon for "evening."

aqueous & agglomerate &c. rocks[203] E. of Alliford Bay, & then sailed across to Maude I. Completed track survey of S. side of Maude I & returned on board about 7 P.m. Found Mills waiting, with a number of other Indians, Some wanting to sell Curiosities &c. & others only prompted by Curiosity to roost about the schooner. Had an almost interminable wa-wa with Mr Mills & finally consented to pay him one dollar & a half a day while on the trip, & give him a potlatch of Three dollars in consideration of his trouble in returning by the Shore on foot. Glad to get the decks cleared at last, the cabin fumigated, & quiet restored. One very friendly Siwash with a square peaked Cap, proud of a little English, marched down into the Cabin, lifted a Chart, unfolded it, & began turning his head to one side, pointing places with his finger, & pretending to look very knowing, but really appearing very Monkeyish.

Today almost quite fine, with occasional spells of actual Sunshine & spots of blue sky among the clouds, giving everything a more chereful appearance.

Aug 4. Remained on board nearly all day, writing up notes, plotting &c. Mr Woodcock[204] arrived from Gold Harbour this Am. having been delayed for nearly a week waiting for a fine time to make the outside stretch between the two inlets. Says he cannot remember a summer with so much broken weather, in this region.

Rocks about Gold Harbour & adjacent inlets according to him nearly all volcanic. Specimens show to be altered volcanic materials felspeltic & dioritic like those seen abundantly further south. In one place in Douglas harbour[205] "slaty" rocks. The quartz lead worked formerly[206] occurred on a little projecting point, was quite thin, & ran out in all directions to a feather edge. The whole of the visible lead blasted away. The gold obtained by the H B Co. & shipped to England, nearly free from quartz filled three shot kegs (each originally holding 112 lbs of shot) Mr W. did

---

203. The "aqueous" rocks are those produced by the action of water; and "agglomerate" rocks pyroclastic rocks consisting of coarse fragments and finer material.

204. William H. Woodcock, who established Woodcock's Landing on the Skeena. According to Walbran, he died in Victoria in 1877, but Newton Chittenden met him in 1882 at Fort Wrangel, where he had been for several years.

205. Douglas Inlet.

206. The reference here is to the Gold Harbour or Mitchell Inlet gold discoveries. Reportedly discovered by the Haida in about 1850, the deposits were explored by the Hudson's Bay Company in the spring of 1851 when John Work led an expedition to the area. Work found nothing, but a later party headed by Captain Mitchell on the *Una* discovered quartz veins with gold. The ore recovered by Mitchell was lost when the *Una* was wrecked off Neah Bay on the Washington coast. Another season's work almost exhausted the small vein, though mining has continued intermittently. See Bessie Doak Haynes, "Gold on Queen Charlotte's Island," *Beaver* 297 (1966): 4-11.

some prospecting on this old ledge, going down several feet till no trace of vein could be found. Formed favourable opinion of the deposit if large Company to take up & by driving transversely test the ⟨lead the⟩ ground thoroughly. Other veinlets holding gold elsewhere but all *very* small & not at all continuous.

Yellow Cedar   A magnificent grove with trees over four feet through & rising up 80 feet ⟨& start a⟩ clear, occurs at the head of a lake above Gold Harbour.[207] Might pretty easily be brought out.

Indian Name of Gold Hr. *Skai-to*[208]

Skatz-sai, or angry waters. Name of Gold Hr. tribe & of the chief also, as usual.[209]

[verso]

2 ½ point blankets[210] the recognised Currency among the Coast Indians, now equal to about $1.50   Everything is worth so many blankets, even a large blanket Such as a 4 point, is Said to be worth so many *blankets* par excellence. The H.B. Co. & traders even take blankets from the Indians as money, when in good condition, & sell them out again as required.

Near the Skidegate village on a piece of flat ground behind a gravelly beach are two flag poles, which were erected last summer. This was done to signify the ⟨function of⟩ conclusion of a perpetual peace between the Skidegates & Gold Harbour Indians, between whom, — owing to some complicated intermarriage — there had been a dispute as to the ownership of the land, & at various times much blood shed. Flags hoisted on the poles blew away last winter, but the poles themselves "are there till this day"

207. Moresby Lake.

208. The Newcombe map and Swanton list it as Sqai'tāo with the comment "sometimes spoken of as a town, was only a Haida camp formed during the rush for gold to Gold Harbor" (Swanton, *Haida Ethnology*, 280).

209. The village was Kaisan (Swanton refers to it as Qai'sun) on the west coast of Moresby Island. Skatz-sai gives the name Skotsai Bay, behind today's Saunders Island. The chief, according to Swanton, was Nāñ na'gage shilxa'ogas, the last name becoming Dawson's Skatz-sai and others' Skotsai. See Swanton, *Haida Ethnology*, 280; and MacDonald, *Haida Monumental Art*, 117.

210. Dawson commented in his published report that, "the *blanket* is now, however recognized currency, not only among the Haidas, but generally along the coast. It takes the place of the beaver-skin currency of the interior of British Columbia and the North-west Territory. The blankets used in trade are distinguished by points, or marks on the edge, woven into their texture, the best being four-point, the smallest and poorest one-point. The acknowledged unit of value is a single two-and-a-half-point blanket, now worth a little over $150" (Dawson, "On the Haida," 135).

Between this place & the village a log sct in the ground, about twelve feet high, & carved like the totem posts, marks the grave of a former Tyie Skidegate, who is said to have died very long ago — perhaps forty years — to have been a *delate hias man, Skookumtyie,*[211] & to have had curly hair.

On Bare Island.[212] of the Chart, opposite the Village, the Indians formerly had a fortified or palisaded Camp to which they might retire in time of danger. No trace appears now to remain.

Mr Smith* Says he believes now about 250 Indians in all centre at Skidegate Village, though the greater number generally in Victoria. About the same number probably live at the Gold Harbour Village on Maude Island, though this looks much smaller, being quite new, & all the houses occupied. The land on which it stands was purchased by the Gold Harbour Indians from the Skidegates as being in a better place than that formerly occupied on the West Coast. A great number of Indians must have lived about this inlet at one time. Smith* says 12,000?? Some estimate of their number at Certain dates Can be formed by ascertaining ⟨for certain do⟩ in how many Canoes the tribe travelled.[213]

Cod fish[214] *& Mackerell.* Saw both taken in cove where fishery established. Skidegate. The cod not very large, but apparently quite the same as in the east. The Mackerell about the same size but a rounder & stouter fish. The Caudal fin not so deeply notched. Colour paler & not so steely & the spotting not so distinct. Evidently a mackerell but a distinct species from the eastern. As far as I can ascertain these fish are now abundant on the West Coast at Gold Harbour, & from them the Indians make a grease which serves them instead of oolachen oil.

Indian villages. Beyond the third narrows, or place which is dry till high water, on the channel followed by the Indians when going to Gold Harbour, is a large village Called *Chaatl.*[215] Further on, at the mouth of the entrance to Gold Harbour &c., as shown on map, a smaller village Called *Kai-shun*[216] Both these villages are now practically abandoned, the

---

211. Chinook Jargon, "a very big man indeed, big chief."

212. Torrens Island.

213. In 1884, Newton H. Chittenden estimated a population of 100 at Skidegate and 108 at New Gold Harbour. See Chittenden, *Queen Charlotte Islands*, 36. New Gold Harbour was abandoned in 1893.

214. Probably the Pacific cod, *Gadus macrocephalus* Tilesius.

215. Swanton's Tc!ā′aɬ on the south side of Chaatl Island (Swanton, *Haida Ethnology*, 280). For a description, see MacDonald, *Haida Monumental Art*, 122–126.

216. Swanton's Qai′sun, east of Annesley Point at the entrance to Inskip Channel on the west coast of Moresby Island (Swanton, *Haida Ethnology*, 280). For a description, see MacDonald, *Haida Monumental Art*, 116–20.

Indians living on the E. end of Maude Island as before stated. They are, however, really the former chief places of the So-Called "Gold Harbour Indians" & are still resided in at certain seasons.

Sea Otters.[217] Are Said to have been abundant on both sides of the Islands, & almost everywhere. None are now got on the inside, the animal here having being completely exterminated. A few are still obtained on the West Coast, especially outside Houston Stewart Channel about the so called *Ninstance illaghie*. It seems however that the Haidas do not themselves often take them, but Chinseyan Canoes engaging in the hunt pay a tribute or toll to the Ninstance Indians for the privilege. So ⟨great⟩ {definite} is the idea of property of certain bands of Indians in certain parts of the country & their right to all the products thereoff.

Succession of Chiefs. A chief dying his next eldest brother succeeds to the rank, or should he have no brothers, his sisters eldest boy.[218] Should neither of these relations exist, the chieftancy drops, & either the consensus of opinion creates another chief, or the most opulent of the ambitious Indians attains the rank by making a bigger potlatch than any of the others. The chief takes a hereditary name on assuming office, becomes *Skidegate, Cumshewa, Skedans* &c. just as ruler of Egypt always Pharo

New potatoes. Well grown, mealy & nearly ripe on Aug. 2. Skidegate. The potatoes planted by the Indians are of late varieties or they might be ready even before this. They are also planted in little irregular patches, the stalks crowded much to thickly together.

Skidegate passage, or strait, all narrow beyond Maude Island, but two Especially narrow places which may be Called the first & second "narrows" The first of these about three miles long, & averaging not over quarter of a mile wide. In one place probably not over 200 feet. At high tide appears deep open channel with only a few rocky islets & rocks, but a low water Almost dry for long stretches, with a narrow & crooked channel winding between gravel banks. The second narrows much Shorter, & probably not less than 0.2 of a Mile where least, but very shoal, with several rocks near the channel in the middle. Through both these channels the tide runs with great violence, probably attaining 5 Knots. Tides from W & E meet about the first narrows. A small schooner might be brought through the strait by passing the narrows at slack water, high tide, but probably could not get through both narrows at one tide as the slack water lasts scarcely any time. Our small schooner has passed through, but unless for some particular purpose probably not advisable to use the passage. Another "Narrows", occurs on the channel turning S toward Gold

217. Sea otter, *Enhydra lutris lutris* (L.).

218. By principle of matrilineal descent, inheritance was by the sister's son.

Harbour[219] & the Indian towns Probably not over 4 feet of water on this at high tide, & dries for a width of at least quarter of a mile. Passage only for Canoes or boats at H.W.

A wide valley runs through to the Second narrows, the water only occupying a gutter in the bottom. Low land, densely wooded thus fringes the strait on each side, slopes gradually up to the foot of the Mountains, which then rise steeply. This is also the Case with the arm projecting to the north,[220] on which scarcely any rock exposures occur along the beach. From this a low valley leads through to the Long arm, which is followed by the trail. Beyond the second narrows the Passage takes on the Character of the West Coast Inlets generally, steep rocky sides with little or no beach & bold water. The timber at the Same time becomes extremely scrubby on the Mountains, with many dead trees in the woods. Scarcely any soil clothes some of the slopes, among the foliage on which much bare rock Can be seen. The summits are also frequently bare, or show the pale green tint characteristic of bushes &c. as distinguished from the more usual Conifers. These upper slopes look to be grassed from a distance — but are not really so. If originally as thickly covered with soil as the Mountains elsewher they would soon have lost their covering from the slides, which in this preeminently damp country Seem to occur constantly, from water trickling along the surface of the rock. The Yellow cedar begins to abound in small trees after entering the narrow part of the passage.

The axial mountains of the Island, bearing snow still in extensive patches, Cross the passage west of the Slate Chuck Creek & Coal Mine. The peaks of these are not here remarkably rugged. The mountains on the West Coast more rounded & lower, without ruling form. Those E. of the axis apparently composed of beds of the Coal-bearing Series in great part & show long slopes & abrupt escarpments, after the manner of mountains formed of tilted sedimentary rocks. No extensive granitic or gneissic area seen in crossing the islands by this channel.

[end verso]

Aug. 5. Weather threatening & showery with low barometer probably indicating wind. Almost decide not to leave, but appearance of Clearing, & light wind induce us to get off not-withstanding the low Barometer. Start about 9 A.m. Go round to the Indian Village & pick up Indian "Mills" who is to assist in the boat & act as guide. Find a head wind, pretty strong, but continue rowing on against it till after 4 P.m. Boat found to leak very badly, so Camp early, not far past Lawn Hill, to repair

---

219. Probably Armentières Channel on the east side of Chaatl Island.

220. Trounce Inlet.

her.

Aug. 6. Weather this morning still rough & stormy, an easterly wind Causing a heavy sea. Decide to get off, but on getting outside the little harbour in which we have been, find the water so rough, that with the shoal stony beach it is nearly impossible, or at least very risky to land at points, & bearing Cannot be got out of boat. Run on for a few miles under sail & then rounding a little point, land in the lee, & camp about 9 A.m. About Camp abundance of drift wood, So make large fires & sit down in shelter from wind & rain. In the afternoon, still no appearance of abatement, pitch tents. Sand in everything, eyes, blankets, food & boots.

Aug. 7. Similar S.E. wind with rain continues, heavy sea piling on the beach, & the water outside covered with white-Caps. Remain in Camp all day, for though might have probably run on safely under sail, could not land, or attend to survey. Got Mills at work giving words for vocabulary, & explaining various Manners & Customs of the Indians.

[verso]

All the Indians, or nearly all about here have a perforation through the septum of the nose.[221] When asking "Mills" what the use of it he explained by saying *spose hilo connoway Siwash hi-you hi-hi.*[222] This like other marked events in life marked by a potlatch. The nose is perforated at from two to five years old, according to my informant, the father on the occasion *Hi-you mache ictus.*,[223] — or gives away in a potlatch much property.

[end verso]

Aug. 8. A fine Morning at last. Off early, & almost immediately get good Sailing breeze, from S.E., without a too heavy sea. Keep on all day under sail, landing only at one place for lunch, bearings, & to examine Clay Cliffs. On landing obliged to haul the boat up & remove all the things from her, Launching her out afterwards through the ⟨small⟩ breakers not without some trouble. Stop at the mouth of a large lagoon, which must be near Cape Fife[224] of the map. Its entrance forms a good harbour for boats, & Can be Entered at high tide. A very strong current, like a rapid river, flows in & out, & at l.w. the channel is Crooked & shoal, to the sea,

---

221. "The septum of the nose is generally perforated in both males and females, and was formerly made to sustain a pendant of haliotis shell or a silver ring, though it is not now used in this way" (Dawson, "On the Haida," 109).

222. Or "spose hullel konaway siwash hi-yu he-he," Chinook Jargon for "when shaken, all Indians laugh a lot."

223. "*Mache*," is unlisted in Chinook Jargon dictionaries. Fortunately, Dawson provides his own translation.

224. Fife Point.

but good enough for Canoes.

Mills' three dogs, which have followed us till today along the beach — though faring rather scantily — have given up under the quick travelling & long distance of today. When last seen, about noon, were travelling on along the shore, the two larger ones apparently quite understanding the matter & taking the easiest way, the smaller keeping as near to the boat & edge of the sea as possible & looking wistfully toward us. They have probably gone back to Skidegate.

Mills tells me Some strange stories of the superstitious notions of the Indians with regard to Rose Spit, round the Camp fire this Evening. Though much above the average in intelligence he evidently quite believes them.

Aug. 9. Off Early, with very fine Calm weather, & little sea. Row round the much dreaded spit without any difficulty, & find the sea on the west side not heavy. Continued on to mouth of river at Tow Hill,[225] where lunched. Then went about a mile further to sheltered bay where Indians are living making dog-fish oil & drying halibut.[226] Mills says this is the only place to stop this side of Masset, or might have gone further. Got some photos. of the hills &c.[227] Examined rocks at next point,[228] where Tertiary Sandstones, with fragments of lignite occur.

Aug. 10. A Magnificent day, clear & warm, & almost perfectly calm. Continue on along shore for some miles, when land to examine rocks. Find fossils abundant   stop to Collect them & get observation for lat. Determine index error of instrument. Arrive at Masset about 4 P.m. finding a heavy tide running out of the inlet. Find schooner at anchor. Land & take photo. of Indian Vil.[229] to use up last plate of set. Interview gentleman in charge of H.B. Co post.[230] Pay off Mills & Billy. Engaged all

---

225. Hiellen River.

226. Dawson puts it a mile and a half west of the Hiellen River and writes of "several rude houses, inhabited by the Masset Indians during a portion of the summer while they are engaged in curing halibut and making dog-fish oil" (Dawson, "Queen Charlotte Islands," 34). It is at the site of the former Yagan village, Swanton's Ya′g$n, in *Haida Ethnology*, 281.

227. See "Photographs," 9 August 1878, GSC256–C2 (C 51370); GSC257–C2 (C 51371); GSC258–C2 (C 51369).

228. Yakan Point.

229. See "Photographs," 10 August 1878, GSC259–C2 (PA 38149).

230. Martin H. Offut had established the Masset post in 1870 and retired in December 1878, though a Mr. A. Cooper had replaced him from 1871 to the fall of 1874. Offut was not an old company man, apparently joining the service recently, perhaps only for the Masset posting. He had become known to the Masset Haida through his residency among the Tsimshian of Port Simpson. His wife was Tsimshian. See Dalzell, *Queen Charlotte Islands*, 76–77.

evening putting fossils &c. away, writing up notes &c. Take observation on Polaris for lat, & another for time. To bed at 12.30.

The "Otter" has been here. Left last Monday for Victoria. My mails are at Fort Simpson, as they did not know where I was, or what plans might be, did not like to bring them here.

[verso]

The Coast between Skidegate & Masset, in some respects resembles that between Cumshewa & Skidegate. A bare open stretch with no harbour & scarcely even a Creek or protected bay for Canoes or boats, for long distances. The beach is gravelly & sometimes coarsely stony to a point near windbound camp of track Survey.[231] Beyond this it becomes sandy, & though not without gravel continues generally of Sand, all the way to Masset.

Lawn Hill is evidently Caused by the outcrop of volcanic rock described in field book,[232] is probably Tertiary. Beyond this for some distance, & including the region about Cape Ball, cliffs, or low banks of drift-clay, & sands characterize. They are generally wearing away under the action of the waves, & trees & stumps may be seen in various stages of descent to the beach. In some places dense woods of fine upright clear trees, are thus exposed in section, & there must be much fine spruce lumber back from the sea everywhere. Very frequently the timber seen on the immediate verge of the cliffs, & shore is of an inferior quality, rather scrubby & full of knots. The soil is generally very Sandy where shown in the cliffs, or peaty in bottom places where water has Collected. Sand hills or sandy elevations resembling Such, are seen in some places on the cliffs, in section, & there is nothing to show that the Soil away from the Coast is universally sandy, but the fact that the upper deposits of the drift spread very uniformly & are of this character. Further north the shore is almost everywhere bordered by higher or lower sand hills, Covered with rank Coarse grass; beach peas[233] &c. &c. Behind these are woods, generally living though burnt in some places. The trees are of various degrees of excellince, but most generally rather under-sized & scrubby. This part of the coast is also characterized by lagoons, & is evidently making, under the ⟨Constant⟩ frequent action of the heavy South East sea.

231. His camp of 6–8 August, a few miles north of Lawn Hill.

232. See George Mercer Dawson, Field Notebooks, RG 45, vol. 292, no. 2803, 76v–77, PAC. The tertiary age of Lawn Hill is confirmed in A. Sutherland Brown, *Geology of the Queen Charlotte Islands*, British Columbia Department of Mines and Petroleum Resources Bulletin no. 54 (Victoria, B.C.: Department of Mines and Petroleum Resources, 1968), 115, and fig. 5, Sheet B.

233. The "grass" is impossible to identify; "beach peas" seashore peavine, *Lathyrus japonicus* Willd.

Rose point & spit is a most remarkable promontory, dependent apparently on no geological feature, but Caused merely by the meeting of the sea from the S & SE, with that from the West, which comes in from the open ocean round the North End of the Island. The ⟨lower on⟩ protunal part of Rose point, near Cape Fife of the Map does not differ in any respect from the low wooded coast to the south, but back from the Shore line are ⟨neither beaches⟩ both lagoons, & lakes, which appear from the Indian account to be very numerous, & neither more nor less than ancient lagoons now filled with fresh water. Further on, the point becoming more exposed & narrower is clothed with stunted small woods, which in turn give place to a bare expanse of rolling sand-hills, covered with rank thin growth of grass. Beyond these, the narrow gravelly point is covered on top with heaps of drifting sand, & great quantities of bleached timber, logs & stumps, piled promiscuously together. Where the point is covered at high tide, this ends, & it then runs on with a slightly flueuous course as a narrow steep sided gravelly ridge. This Slopes away under water, & at the time we passed (tide about ¾ in) there were two islands of gravel lying off on the same general Course. The sea from two directions rolling together on the shallow water of the spit, with a heavy tidal current running across it, must indeed when wind is added make a very unpleasant Surf for Canoes or boats. Two vessels have been lost on the spit, one a H.B. Vessel[234]

From Rose pt to Masset, the minor indentations of the Shore are so slight, that it may be described as forming one grand Crescentic bay of [blank] miles in diameter.[235] With the exception of one or two small rocky points the beach is smooth & regular, almost altogether sand in Some of the bays, coarse gravel, showing evidence in its steep slope above ordinary H.W. of very heavy sea at some times. Low sand-hills everywhere form a border to the woods, which densely cover the land, & grow thick & scrubby toward the shore, whatever they may do further in. The trees are chiefly *Abies Menziesii*. The water far off the shore is very shoal, especially on approaching Masset, where kelp is found forming great fields far out to sea.

[end verso]

Sunday Aug. 11. Writing up notes & attending to various home duties in morning. Went to Church at 11 A.m. summoned by the bell which has

---

234. The company lost two vessels named *Vancouver* on the spit: the first in 1834, the second in 1854.

235. "Twenty-one miles in width" (Dawson, "Queen Charlotte Islands," 34).

just arrived for the mission here, under Mr Collinson,[236] a fellow worker with Mr Duncan*. The congregation besides ourselves consisted of two Haidas Several Chimseyans, & Mr. Offutt* of the H.B. Company. Nearly all the Indians of the place are now away at at house raising & potlatch in Virago Sd.

Dined with Mr Collinson*. Got some newspapers in the Afternoon & gleaned many items of interest. Returned to Mr Collinsons* for tea, at his invitation, & spent a pleasant evening chatting about things in general. Made preparations for tomorrow, wrote up notes, & turned in.

[verso]

Potlatch.[237] Mr. Collinson* gives me some additional light on this custom.

When a man is about make a potlatch, for any reason, such as raising a house &c. &c. he first, some Months before hand, gives out property, money &c., So much to each man, in proportion to their various ranks & standing. Some time before the potlatch, this is all returned, with interest. Thus a man receiving four dollars, gives back six, & so on. All the property & funds thus collected are then given away at the potlatch. The more times a man potlatches, the more important he becomes in the eyes of his tribe, & the more is owing to him when next some one distributes property & potlatches.

The blankets, ictus &c. are not torn up & destroyed except on certain special occasions. If for instance a contest is to be carried on between two men or three as to who is to be chief, One may tear up ten blankets, scattering the fragments, the others must do the same, or retire, & so on till one has masttered the others. It really amounts to voting in most cases, for in such trial a mans personal property soon becomes exhausted, but there an under-current of supply from his friends who would wish him to be chief, & he in most popular favour is likely to be the chosen one.

At Masset last winter, a young ⟨man⟩ man made Some improper advances to a young woman, whose father hearing of the matter, was very

---

236. William Henry Collison (1847–1922), who was born in Ireland and attended the Church Missionary College at Islington, came to the northern British Columbia coast in 1873 to assist William Duncan. Arriving on the Queen Charlotte Islands at Masset in 1876, Collison later worked on the upper Skeena River with the Gitksan and was archdeacon of Metlakatla from 1891 until 1921 when he retired. See also W. H. Collison, *In the Wake of the War Canoe* (Toronto: Musson Book Co., 1916).

237. The celebrated Northwest Coast potlatch varied from group to group. For the Haida potlatch, see Dawson, "On the Haida," 125–27; Swanton, *Haida Ethnology*, 155–81; George Peter Murdock, *Rank and Potlatch among the Haida* (New Haven: Yale University Press, 1935); and Abraham Rosman and Paula G. Rubel, *Feasting with Mine Enemy: Rank and Exchange Among Northwest Coast Societies* (New York: Columbia University Press, 1971), 34–68.

angry, & immediately tore up twenty blankets. This was not merely to give vent to his feelings, for the young man had to follow suite, & in this Case not having the requisite amount of property, the others of his tribe had to subscribe & furnish it, or leave a lasting disgrace in the tribe. Their feelings toward the young man were not naturally, of the Kindest, though they did not turn him out of the tribe as they might have done *after* having atoned for his fault.

Totems[238] are found among the indians here as elsewhere. The chief ones about Masset are the Bear & the Eagle. Those of one totem[239] must marry in the other.

[end verso]

Aug 12. All prepared early this morning to set out for the exploration of the reported great sheets of water above here. Waited some time for the tide to slacken, as it was running out like a mill race. Got away at slack water, & soon had a good Current with us. Kept distance partly by time, & partly by eye estimate, though difficult to get it exactly owing to the unknown but varying strength of the Current, & numerous eddies. Stopped for lunch at the Mouth of a small river[240] where post pliocene shells were soon found, not far from the waters edge. Deposit in many respects comparable with the Saxicava Sand of the East.[241] Reached the head of the narrow Passage just as the tide began to run out. Kept on a couple of miles, camping in little bay where a nice stream, & remnants of former Indian Camps.[242] Night being Clear, got a good set of observations for latitude & time.

Saw great numbers of wild geese[243] today, on the tide flats, & strips of green grass & weeds which run along the shore just above high water.

Aug. 13. Travelled on, skirting the Eastern Shore of the first great

---

238. Actually crests, which are owned by families and include a large number of animals, fish, and other natural phenomena. See Swanton, *Haida Ethnology*, 107–18.

239. Or clan. The Haida are divided into two exogamous phratries or clans, the Raven and the Eagle.

240. Perhaps Watun River.

241. According to J. W. Dawson, who described these eastern Canadian deposits, "the Saxicava sand, in typical localities, consists of yellow or brownish quartzose sand, derived probably from the waste of the Potsdam sandstone and Laurentian gneiss, and stratified. It often contains layers of gravel, and sometimes is represented altogether by coarse gravels" (J. William Dawson, *The Canadian Ice Age: Being Notes on the Pleistocene Geology of Canada*. . . [Montreal: William V. Dawson, 1893], 60).

242. There were a number of such camps along Masset Sound. This may, however, be the site of the village of Gîtînq!a. See Swanton, *Haida Ethnology*, 281.

243. Canada geese, *Branta canadensis fulva* Delacour.

"lake"[244] Passing the mouth of a large river,[245] which opens in an extensive bay with very wide flats dry at low tide, find several canoes full of Indians looking out for salmon. One of these contained the old "Doctor" of the Masset Village,[246] with his assistant. The old man distinguished by an immense & dirty mass of grizzled hair rolled up behind his head. This is never Cut, & in it his medicine is supposed to lie. On our approach he shouted "good day" which soon proved, however, to be all the English he knew. Inquired whether all "King George men"[247] & on answer being given in affirmative said "very good" "Aukook Illaghie King George Illaghie, Aukutty Bostons tike Kapswallow fie mika Kloosh-naanich."[248] He then immediately wound up with the broad hint "Hilo tobacco?"[249] The old Man further informed us that there were no salmon today, but would be very many tomorrow. Just as he spoke the ripple of one going over the flat was seen, & he & his assistant were off like an arrow in the canoe, which was managed with great dexterity & turned about in an incredibly short space. On overtaking the fish, the assistant hurled a spear, which however missed its mark, falling harmlessly into the water.

Stopped for lunch at the mouth of the Second "lake"[250] a narrow Passage[251] blocked by a large island,[252] & through which the tide runs with great velocity, especially at ebb. Started round part of shore of upper lake, & camped near the Mouth of the Ma-min River, near an Indian Camp.[253] Went some distance up the river, on which Coal reported to occur, but could find nothing nearer to coal than a few pieces of obsidian. Got thoroughly wet struggling through the woods in heavy rain, & in coming back got involved among small creeks & lagoons of the delta.

244. Masset Inlet.

245. Yakoun River.

246. Perhaps Dr. Kwude, a lineage chief and well-known Masset shaman.

247. British or Canadian as opposed to "Boston men," Americans.

248. Or "Okuke illahee King George illahee ahnkuttie Bostons tiky kapswolla pe mika kloshe nanitch," Chinook Jargon for "this country is English; long ago Americans wanted to steal. Be careful."

249. "Hilo," Chinook Jargon for "no."

250. Juskatla Inlet.

251. Juskatla Narrows.

252. Fraser Island.

253. Mamin village occupied by the Mamun-Gituni of Masset. See Dalzell, *Queen Charlotte Places*, 409. It is not recorded in Swanton, *Haida Ethnology*.

[verso]

Tides at Masset. Aug 12. Day of full moon. H. water at 30 minutes past noon.

Aug 13. H. water at 1h 15m. P.m.

The current runs in up the channel 2 ½ hours after falling by the shore. Ebb runs about 3 hours after water begins rising on the beach.

Rise & fall about 14 feet springs. (Est. only)

Aug. 13. Passage to inner, or upper lake.[254] Tide turned to run in at 20 M. past noon.

The rise & fall of the tide in the first lake 8 to 10 feet in the second or upper, less, probably averaging about 6 feet.

[end verso]

Aug. 14. Had made arrangements last night with a brother of our Indian (Jim) to go up the river & show R. the coal, while I went on with running survey of upper lake. Very heavy rain in the early morning. No Indian appeared, & breakfast also late. After some time, the Indian arriving, & assuring me that still possible to go to coal & return before night, decided to carry out old plan. Day continued overcast, with heavy showers, rendering out-door work far from pleasant. Got back to camp about 7 P.m. & found R. & Indians back before me, warming themselves at a fine fire, where we were glad to join them. R. had ascended the river in Canoe some distance to a great log-jam, & then walked Some miles. The "coal" proves lignite.

Aug. 15. Off early. Crossed the upper "lake" making some soundings by the way, descended the rapid, — for such the outflow now is, with a strong ebb tide. The water breaks White in several places, & the speed must be nearly ten knots. Continued along S.W. Shore of Main lake, Camping at the head of a long Inlet with an unpronouncable Indian name.[255] Tent pitched on a rather quaking Sod of grass where intersected by numerous little creeks into which the tide flows Got observation for latitude, which much needed here, & then turned in. Day overcast with showers.

Came unexpectedly today on an old Indian & his wife Camped on a small Island on the lake, the old man engaged in Making a canoe, & a temporary bark house put up near a trickle of water. He actually presented me with a couple of small salmon, in exchange for which complement I gave him a small piece of tobacco all I had. He was very polite, & quite a good example of the better Class of old-time unimproved Indians, different as daylight from dark, from those who have been working on Schooners, or

---

254. Masset Inlet.

255. Probably McClinton Bay, called Tin-in-ow-a by Dawson on his map.

in Victoria, & have learnt various "white" ways, including the use of oaths & slang.

Aug. 16. Hurried in leaving this morning by the tide, which beginning to run out, threatened to leave our boat dry. Made the round of one more great inlet,[256] & then worked along the north shore till nearly 6 P.m. Camping a few miles west of the main outlet. Day fine on the whole though with occasional showers & S.W. wind. Sky, however, continually overcast, as usual! Our Camp a little north of the Mouth of the River Called *Ain*, on a fine regular beach, with abundance of drift-wood at hand. A trail leads over from the beach, about 300 yards to the river, passing through woods in which some fine spruce trees. The stream a large one, navigable by Canoes, though said to be impeded by sticks. Said to flow at no great distance, out of a great fresh water lake,[257] on which the Indians have a canoe, or Canoes.[258] The lake is described as very large, even comparable with this one in size but very full of islands. It is firmly frozen in winter, & is a hunting ground & berry-gathering region. Where the trail strikes the river, are two Indian houses, & a fence & Salmon trap arranged across the river.[259] A neat stage of logs for landing on, little steps Cut out in the bank to the door of the principal house, & other signs of care. No Indians here at present, the salmon fishing not having begun in Most of the rivers.

Aug. 17. Off early, Knowing that must catch as much as possible of the ebb in the long Channel leading down to Masset. Worked along shore to entrance & then down the West shore of Channel, reaching schooner just before 6 P.m., in heavy rain, which has continued most of afternoon, though fine in morning.

A bad headache today rendered work a drag. Evg. wrote up part of notes which have got sadly behind.

[verso]

Aug 17. The Indians have some stories of their simplicity when first brought in contact with the whites. "Jim" Says the first white men they

---

256. Dinan Bay.

257. Ain Lake or the larger, more distant Ian Lake.

258. Dalzell notes that "an old canoe is said to lie in the vicinity of this lake. Ranging in length from 50 to 90 feet, depending on the narrator, quite finished it was left covered with shakes awaiting help with launching. It is said that the builders succumbed to small-pox before this could be effected" (Dalzell, *Queen Charlotte Places*, 422).

259. Dalzell calls it Kogals-Kun village, (*Queen Charlotte Places*, 422) while the Newcombe-Swanton map renders it K′ogālskun (Swanton, *Haida Ethnology,* 279).

Ever saw Came to North Island,[260] Arriving at the season (Aug. or September.) when the Indians all away at their various rivers Catching Salmon. One Man (?) in the village at North Island saw them & their vessel.[261]

Childish Stories of surprise on seeing various unknown articles, or as one of my Indians put it "Aukutty Siwash dam-fools." Indian given a biscuit. thinks it wood. encouraged to eat it. no water, finds it very dry. Molasses, tastes with finger, pronounces very bad & tells friends so. Axe, strikes fancy as being So bright, "like a beautiful salmon skin." Use unknown. Takes handle out & hangs it round his neck. Gun, similarly misconstrued. Takes flint off & hangs it round his neck.

The north shore of Graham Island about Masset, generally low with shoal water extending far off. At Masset {instead of} the wide open bays generally met with find a funnel shaped entrancle, leading to a narrow Passage. Entrance holds some shoal water, & two bars, but navigable passage. Where passage begins to narrow, find three Indian villages, one on E. shore not far in from outer pt. Here principal village at present.[262] H.B. store & mission (the latter now established two years come next November). Anchorage opposite here, but strong tide. The second village,[263] about a mile South of this, on same Shore, the third, on the west Shore.[264] Land all low, no hills, lagoons in places along shore. Generally densely timbered, but reports of "prairies" here & there in the interior.

The timber does not attain a very great growth along the shore, but no doubt is of good growth where sheltered inland. In proceeding up the

260. Langara Island.

261. Probably a reference to Juan Pérez on the *Santiago* out of San Blas, Mexico, who arrived off Langara Island on 18 July 1774. On the following morning he was met by three Haida canoes followed by more later in the day. See Warren L. Cook, *Flood Tide of Empire: Spain and the Pacific Northwest, 1543–1819* (New Haven: Yale University Press, 1973), 54–65.

262. Ut-te-was, in Dawson's "On the Haida," 163, containing "about twenty houses, counting both large and small," with over forty carved posts. This was the village called Masset, now Haida. Swanton lists it as āatē'was, in *Haida Ethnology*, 281. In 1891, when Dawson visited the Queen Charlotte Islands on his return from the Bering Sea, he "found Masset considerably changed since I saw it 13 years ago. Still many totem poles standing and some of them in good preservation, but most of the old Native houses have either disappeared or have been abandoned. Commonplace frame houses of rather small size taking their places" (Journal, 2 October 1891, G. M. Dawson Papers, RBSC). For a description, see MacDonald, *Haida Monumental Art*, 131–70.

263. Ka-yang, in Dawson's "On the Haida," 164, where he mentions that it was not particularly examined. Listed as Q!ayā'ñ by Swanton, *Haida Ethnology*, 281.

264. Yan, in Dawson, "On the Haida," 163, where he describes it as showing "about twenty houses new and old, with thirty carved posts." It is Swanton's Yan, *Haida Ethnology*, 281.

Inlet, find, near the entrance to a lagoon which runs back on the E. side to nearly abreast the Indian villages, the land pretty Suddenly attains a greater elevation, forming a flat or gently undulating surface at a height of about 100 feet above the water. This formed of drift deposits, Clays & gravels below, hard bedded sands above. This in many extensive areas becomes broken down to lower country. Inlet slightly tortuous, with average width of 1 mile (?) (say 1 ½ to ¾ mile) Through the whole length (— miles)[265] the tide runs with a rapid current, especially at ebb, & there is no harbour Capable of sheltering vessels from the tide. Masset or *Maast* island[266] (which has given its name to the region) appears to offer protection, but the water behind it all very shoal (much of it not over 1 fm. at H.W.) & great area dry at l. water. At the point Just inside the island a fair anchorage might perhaps be found, sheltered completely from the sea, but exposed to most of force of current. The "Otter" said to have anchored here on one occasion.

At its south end, the passage expands suddenly, & a great sheet of inland water is Seen, bordered by continuous low wooded land northward & eastward, by hills, rising to mountains in the distance on the west & South, & studded with islands. The lake lies at the junction of the hilly with the low country. Where bordered by low land the shores are flat, with wide bouldery beaches, bare at low tide, or sandy flats, stretching far out. Where the outline becomes tortuous, & the fiord like projections run up among the mountains, the shores become much bolder, with deep water close to them, & narrow rocky or bouldery beaches dipping steeply away. At the head of the inlets & about the mouths of Some brooks, only are wide flats found. The water in these fiords does not appear, however, to be very deep, differing much in this respect from the inlets of the mainland. on the South side of this "lake" nearly opposite its entrance, is a narrow passage, with mouth partly blocked by islands, leading into the second or upper lake, the indian name of which means the "belly of the rapid".[267] The tide runs through here with great velocity, especially at ebb, when it forms a genuine rapid, with much white water.

Kelp grows abundantly nearly across the channels on both sides of the island, showing that they Cannot be very deep. The second lake is much smaller than the first, & separated from it probably by a rocky barrier. Its Eastern edge is formed as in the former case by low country, while its Southwestern is long & fiord-like, with steep banks. It lies in the same line

265. "The length of Masset Sound from its seaward entrance to the point at which it expands widely is nineteen miles" (Dawson, "Queen Charlotte Islands," 35).

266. Maast Island.

267. Called by the Indians Tsoo-skatli (Dawson, "Queen Charlotte Islands," 36).

of junction of hilly & low country as the first lake.

Many streams enter the lakes, as might have been anticipated from the wet character of the country. Of these the largest are probably as follows, & well deserve to be called rivers.

1. Stream flowing into the S.E. corner of the first lake, with large sandy flats about its mouth.[268] This was formerly passable for canoes a long way up, & is reported to head in a large lake,[269] which may lie along the line of junction already indicated. Up this stream the Indians formerly travelled by canoe till they reached the lake, or at least got so far on the river, that they walked across to Skidegate in half a day, reaching that inlet by the valley of the Slate Chuck Creek. A fire has now passed through the forest, & many trees have fallen, blockading the river, so that for a long time the Indians have only gone a short distance up it bear hunting. The same fire has also blocked & Caused to be disused, a trail formerly going from the mouth of the river to the E. Coast near the old indian village at Cape Ball.[270] The Indians say that the fire which Killed the trees at Dead-tree point near Skidegate,[271] arose somewhere on the Masset Lake,[272] & this fire it may probably have been which caused the windfall above aluded to.

2. River joining the upper lake at E. end, & coming apparently from the South.[273] On this the Coal is found. Navigable for Small canoes several miles, though much blocked by logs. It probably rises to the S.W., in some of the valleys like those which further north hold fiords.

3. A stream (Ain) joining the lower lake not many miles west of its outlet, on the North shore. This has its Mouth on an extensive gravelly flat, for the most part densely wooded, & fronted by a fine & very regular beach. Several Indian homes are at its mouth, & a couple at about half a mile up it.[274] It is Said to rise in a very large lake flowing out at perhaps three miles from the shore. This {fresh water} lake probably lies between the masset expansion, & Virago Sound & may occupy an analogous position to those just described.

These & many other streams are counted as "salmon rivers" the hook-bills in autumn running up them all as far as they can.

268. Yakoun River.

269. Yakoun Lake.

270. Either Gā̵li'nskun or Lā'nas. See Swanton, *Haida Ethnology,* 280.

271. About seven miles north of Skidegate village.

272. Masset Inlet.

273. Mamin River.

274. See 16 August 1878.

The exposures of rock on the borders of the lakes are strictly limited to the Western & South-western sides, the opposite shores being composed of drift material. The drift of the Eastern shores is much more mixed in origen than that of the narrower western waters, where the rock fragments are almost altogether local in origen. At Several places a terrace, pretty well marked, & apparently about the level of that formerly measured at Skidegate, seen.

Seems in some aspects not improbable that the "lakes" along the western borders of the hills mark the former spread of the glaciers from the mountains, at the time the drift deposits, clays, boulder-clays, sands &c. were being deposited. They may thus occupy original hollows, formed partly by Glacial Erosion no doubt but more from the absence of drift materials elsewhere thrown down. No very evident moraines, & must therefore suppose that force of waves sufficient to level any material of this kind as it was deposited.[275]

The rocks appear to be all Tertiary volcanic,[276] in many places & over great areas nearly flat, or gently undulating, & seen in Nearly horizontal beds far up in the mountain slopes at the heads of some of the fiords. In other places the beds are locally remarkably disturbed, as perhaps to be expected in a volcanic region. Much siliceous infiltration & many localities where chalcedony & agates[277] abundant. Considerable proportion of trachytic acidic rocks.[278] A remarkable absence of exposures of ordinary bedded Tertiary deposits, which may be supposed to underlie the igneous, but seen only in the one locality where "coal" reported, about six miles up the Ma-mit River.[279] Perhaps whenever exposed deeply hollowed away & inlets now occupy the valleys. The hills do not form the boundary Southwestward of the Tertiary area, but are also, as above described, formed of Tertiary volcanic rocks, which, for aught known may extend far in that direction. The centres of volcanic Activity would appear

---

275. The arms of Masset Inlet appear to be glacier-scoured channels formed by ice tongues moving northeasterly from the high country of southwestern Graham Island.

276. The volcanic rocks are indeed Tertiary, with a radiometric date indicating a Miocene age.

277. "Chalcedony" was a cryptocrystalline variety of silica, consisting essentially of fibrous or ultrafine quartz, some opal, together with water, which is either enclosed in the lattice or in the macrostructure of the mineral. "Agates" were banded chalcedonic silica.

278. "Trachytic" is a textual term applied to volcanic rocks in which feldspar microlites of the groundmass have a subparallel arrangement corresponding to the flow lines of the lava from which they were formed. "Acidic" is a term applied to any igneous rock composed predominantly of light-coloured mineral having a relatively low specific gravity.

279. Mamin River.

probably to have been amon these ranges.[280]

The drift deposits[281] on the whole resemble those of the Coast About Cape Ball &c., being Clayey below, with frequent gravel beds, Sandy above, & All very hard. No true boulder clay recognised unless that of Echinus point may represent. Many glaciated stones on beaches, especially towards heads of fiords. Glaciation found in a few places   The *Saxicavas* are probably true drift fossils, of those from the Ma-min R. Some drilling may obtain as to whether not later. Bedding well marked in both Clay & sand deposits, false-bedding common in latter. Differ from drift deposits near Victoria in greater regularity & promenence of bedding of Clays, & comparative absence of large stones & boulders in these.

The Smaller, greenish *Echinus*[282] very abundant in all parts of both lakes, & the inlet below. Salmon the only fish Caught in any numbers. Kelp in many places. The ordinary bladder weed very abundant along shores, also Eel Grass.[283] Probable that oysters would succeed well if introduced, as water probably warmer, & much fresh water, with wide flats.

[end verso]

Aug. 18. Sunday. At church, & spent most of day with Mr Collinson*. Also visited Mr Offutt* of the H.B. Co, obtaining Some facts about furs &c. Took photo of Mission premises, & another of Masset Inlet,[284] in the afternoon.[285]

Names of Indian towns.

Kung village at Virago Sd. (Rough K)[286]

---

280. The eruptive centres have not been established.

281. For the glacial record of this region see John J. Clague, Rolf W. Mathewes, and Barry G. Warner, "Late Quaternary Geology of Eastern Graham Island, Queen Charlotte Islands, British Columbia," *Canadian Journal of Earth Sciences* 19 (1982): 1786-95.

282. Probably the green sea urchin, *Strongylocentrotus droebachiensis* (Müller).

283. The "bladder weed" was bladder wrack or rockweed, *Fucus furcatus* C. Agardh.; and "Eel Grass" was eel-grass, *Zostera marina* L.

284. See "Photographs," 18 August 1878, GSC260–C2 (PA 44332) and GSC262–C2 (PA 44327).

285. The right page of the journal here covers elevations and plans of a Haida house, one that was almost literally reproduced in Dawson's report, "Queen Charlotte Islands," plate XIV. In the journal it is labelled: "diagram with measurements of Indian home at Virago Sound Q.C.I. Type of many but rather larger than now usual. The upright boarding of the ends & sides, with the roofing, is omitted for greater clearness."

286. Located at Mary Point on Alexandra Narrows between Virago Sound and Naden Harbour. Also known as Nightasis, Kung was settled by Albert Edward Edenshaw and his followers in 1853. Edenshaw moved to Yatza in 1875, but Kung was not completely abandoned until a few years later. It is Swanton's Qʌñ, *Haida Ethnology,* 281. Dawson elaborates that "it has been a substantial and well-constructed one [village] but is now

Yā-tzā. New village beyond Virago S. = knife.[287]
Ut-te-was. Village near H.B. Co &c. Masset
Ka-yung. Village above last on same side.
Yān. Village on W. side Masset harbour.

Coast between Masset & Virago Sd. Everywhere low, & differs from that east of Masset, in being rocky, or covered with boulders along the shore line. No wide sandy bays occur. The points are chiefly of low dark rocks, which probably all belong to the Tertiary igneous series.[288] The timber seen along the shore, not of great size, but pretty interspersed with open grassy spaces, which often border the sea, but do not run far inland. Water very shoal a long way off shore, & great fields of kelp filling the bays & extending far off the points.

Virago Sound or *Ne-din.*[289] Wide funnel shaped mouth, contracting soon to narrow passage — only ½ m wide in one place,[290] & then expanding again to large & magnificent land-locked harbour. Low land, densely wooded, borders the whole inlet, though hills & mountains are not far off to the South & west. Rocks Seen along shore, only near bottom of har-

rather decayed, though some of the houses are still inhabited. The houses arranged along the edge of low land, facing a fine sandy beach, are eight or ten in number, some of them quite large. The carved posts are not very numerous, though in a few instances elaborate" (Dawson, "On the Haida," 163). See also MacDonald, *Haida Monumental Art*, 177–83.

287. Swanton's Yats 1, *Haida Ethnology*, 281. Established by Albert Edward Edenshaw in 1875 on the northern coast east of Virago Sound to attract trade from Kaigani Haida of Prince of Wales Island. It is doubtful if it was meant to be an all-year village site, and it was abandoned in 1883. Dawson adds: "like many of the Haida villages, its position is much exposed, and it must be difficult to land at it with strong northerly and north-easterly winds. This village site is quite new, having been occupied only a few years. There are at present eight or ten roughly built houses, with few and poorly carved posts. The people who formerly lived at the entrance to Virago Sound are abandoning that place for this, because, as was explained to me by their chief, Edensaw, they can get more trade here, as many Indians come across from the north. The traverse from Cape Kygane or Muzon to Klas-kwun is about forty miles, and there is a rather prominent hill behind the point by which the canoemen doubtless direct their course. At the time of our visit, in August 1878, a great part of the population of the northern portion of the Queen Charlotte Islands was collected here preparatory to the erecton of carved posts and giving away of property, for which the arrival of the Kai-ga-ni Haidas was waited, these people being unable to cross owing to the prevalent fog and rough weather" (Dawson, "On the Haida," 162–63). See also MacDonald, *Haida Monumental Art*, 184.

288. The points along the north coast are confirmed as Tertiary rocks of Masset Formation in Sutherland Brown, *Geology of the QCI*, 115, and fig. 5, Sheet C.

289. The "wide funnel shaped mouth" is now called Virago Sound, while the "land-locked harbour" is Naden Harbour.

290. Alexandra Narrows.

bour, & at anchorage cove ⟨opposite⟩ {at} Indian village.[291]

E. Shore flat & long flats With boulders at l. water. W. shore comparatively bold. Many Small streams, & several of some size. The Ne-din River,[292] probably the largest in the islands enters at S.E. angle. Went up it about 2 m. in the boat, its course being moderately straight, & trending a little west of true south. It flows out of a large lake,[293] — probably ten miles or more on longer diameter — at a considerable distance. The lake Can be reached by canoe in about half a day from the mouth, but Indians say that many trees here ⟨filling⟩ fallen across the river last winter. The hollow occupied by the lake Can be clearly seen among the mountains, when the range viewed from a distance.

Aug 19. Did not get away very early, having to buy several little things at H.B. Company's store, & make other arrangements. Followed coast round from Masset to Virago Sound, camping in entrance of latter, opposite the Indian Village.[294] Day nearly Calm, warm, & with only occasional, but very heavy showers. A heavy sea setting in from the west, prevented landing on the part of the Coast setting in that direction. Saw a very large shark,[295] off the outer point. It followed the boat for a little while, & frightened Indian "Jim", who said that that sort of fish often broke Indian Canoes & ate the Indians.

Aug 20. Coasted round the greater part of Virago Sound, Camping near its SW extremity. Went about two miles up the Ne-din River, joining at the S.W. extremity.[296] This a large stream, filled with the usual brown water. The day windy, blowing almost a gale from the west outside, the harbour showing many white caps. Entered in the river no wind, warm Sun & apparently different climate altogether. Camped near Some Indians, who shot a bear while we were pitching the tents. Tried to ascertain from the Indians, particulars as to distance of lake &c., with probable wish to see it. Indians speak however of many fallen sticks across the upper part of the stream. Could scarcely get to lake in half a day from the ⟨mouth⟩ mouth of the river.

Aug 21. Coasted remainder of inlet, & getting round early to the Indian

---

291. Kung village.

292. Naden River.

293. Eden Lake.

294. Kung, putting the camp on the east shore.

295. Probably a basking shark, *Cetorhinurs maximus* (Gunnerus).

296. This would actually put him in Naden Harbour.

village — now quite deserted for the potlatch at the next (new) town.[297] Schooner appeared in the afternoon & anchored about 5 P.m. in cove opposite Indian Village. At work till late on notes &c.

[verso]

Tow & Tow's brother. A hill resembling that called Tow on the coast between Masset & Rose Spit, occurring on upper arm of upper lake Called Tow's brother.[298] Story that on some occasion Tow's brother devoured the whole of some dog-fish, which in dispute between them, & that Tow becoming Much angered went away to the open coast where plenty dog-fish, leaving his greedy brother.

Indian food. Indians eat the Cambium layer of *Abies Menziesii*, & the *hemlock* & not that of *pinus Contorta* which also occurs in Some places.[299] Many thickets of Crab apple fringing the shores on the Masset "lakes" much fruit on them but not yet ripe. Told that next month ripen. Then collected, boiled, allowed to remain covered with water till mid winter when gone over, stalks &c. removed & the whole mixed with oolachen grease *quantum suf.*[300] forming a delicious pabulum according to Indian notions.[301]

Canoes. The Haidas great Canoe-makers. At this season many occupied roughing them out in the woods on the Masset lakes & rivers here & there. Bring them down to villages later on & work away by little & little in winter. They frequently take canoes over from here to Ft Simpson for Sale, getting the coveted oolachen grease, & other things in exchange, together with an old Canoe to return in. Afraid to venture across the stretch ⟨from⟩ {to} Rose Spit, they coast round by S end of Alaska, & run across Southward when fine weather & a westerly wind. Old Edensaw[302] says that formerly when starting for Victoria he frequently

---

297. Ya-tza.

298. Towustasin Hill.

299. Dawson was probably referring to the Sitka spruce, *P. sitchensis*, rather than the Douglas-fir, *P. menziesii* ("*Abies Menziesii*"), since the latter's cambium was not used by the Haida. Also, in his published report Dawson refers to *A. Menziesii*," as "the spruce" (Dawson, "On the Haida," 114). According to Nancy Turner, Dawson was probably correct about Haida utilization of mountain hemlock, *T. mertensiana*; and the non-use of the shore pine, *P. contorta*. See Turner, *Food of Coastal Peoples*, 65.

300. I.e., sufficient quantity.

301. The wild crabapple, *Pyrus fusca* Raf., was widely used by all coastal Indians, including the Haida. Dawson's description of Haida methods of use corresponds closely to that of modern ethnobotanists. See Turner, *Food of Coastal Peoples*, 204.

302. Albert Edward Edenshaw (or Edensaw) (1810?-94) was one of the most prominant Haida of the nineteenth century. He was suspected of complicity in the 1852 plunder of the *Susan Sturgis* off Rose Point Spit. He established Kung in 1853 and Yats (Yatza) in

had 40 men in a canoe, besides various articles of property.

Number of Indians. Mr Collinson* estimates the population of the whole north Coast, Masset, Virago Sound &c. at about 700. No considerable percentage of these Indians Are at Victoria, a few go to Wrangel &c. Villages on outer west Coast, & near North Island now abandoned. *A considerable population of Haidas on S. islands of Alaska.*[303] Not the case however that these the original stock, from which islands peopled. Indians Say that no Haidas here till comparatively lately (Mr Collinson* thinks about 150 years ago)   Internescine wars then occurring drove Some of the northern bands from the islands to find a home across Dixons passage,[304] & these still entirely distinct in language from any indians of mainland, connected with those of this island, & speaking even the Same dialect. More difference between the Masset & the Skidegate Indians than between them & those still further north.

Fur seals begin to appear in some abundance about the first of April, & the season lasts for about six weeks   About 800 skins purchased here each year for the last two years, before that as many as 2600, 2300, 1800 purchased in a single Season. Some years many young fur seals shot in the inlet opposite the village.

Sea otters. Now very scarce. Greatest number purchased in any one season for last ten years about 24, some of these coming from the Alaska side. Shot at all seasons. Hunted as follows. A number of Indians in canoes scattered over the water. Otter seen, Shot at by one Canoe, but not with any intention of hitting, dives. All Canoes concentrate & wait. Otter keeps long under water, but at last comes up. Shot at again, & so on till at last weak & breathless Can keep down very Short time. All canoes now in narrow space, & at last, when the otter can scarcely keep down at all, Some man kills it. He & his fellows in the same Canoe get the whole of the money given for the skin. If any Indian shoots at & wounds the otter, & he is afterwards killed by another, the first has to pay to the Second the damage done to the skin by his Clumsy shot, thus very Careful when &

1875, before settling in Masset in 1883. In 1853 Commander James C. Prevost described him as "decidedly the most advanced Indian I have met with on the Coast: quick, ambitious, crafty and, above all, anxious to obtain the good opinion of the white man." See Barry M. Gough, "New Light on Haida Chiefship: The Case of Edenshaw, 1850–1853," *Ethnohistory* 29 (1982): 131–39; and Mary Lee Stearns, "Succession to Chiefship in Haida Society," in *The Tsimshian and Their Neighbors of the North Pacific Coast*, ed. Jay Miller and Carol M. Eastman (Seattle: University of Washington Press, 1984), 206–17.

303. These are the Kaigani Haida who migrated in the eighteenth century to the southern portion of Prince of Wales Island.

304. Dixon Entrance.

how they fire, & no general & dangerous fusilade as might be expected.

Bear Skins 50 to 100 purchased annually. The Haidas not very good hunters. do not kill the bear at the best Season, necessary to follow into woods to do so. In spring attracted to shores by the abundance of succulent young grass &c. Indians then kill many. In fall, when Salmon running, come down on shores to get fish. again many killed.

Forty to fifty Land Otter Skins purchased at Masset, & 100 to 150 *Marten* Skins Annually.

Elk (wapiti)[305] are Certainly known to exist about the north west point of the Island, but very seldom killed, as not followed inland.

Salmon, according to Mr Offutt* (squire) of H.B. Co. two runs of salmon. First a small fish with bright red flesh, very good. Begins to run about middle of July & lasts about a month. Not in very great numbers, & not much sought after by Indians as they are then occupied at other things. ⟨About the time⟩ These seem to answer to the "suckeyes" of the Fraser. About the Middle of August the run of larger "silver salmon" begins.[306] They are red fleshed & good while yet in salt water, caught about the mouth of inlet &c., but become hook billed, dog-toothed, lean, & pale-fleshed when up the rivers. They run into all the streams, even very small brooks, are large, & easily Caught, & constitute the great Indian Salmon harvest. The Indians follow them up the inlet. Run lasts till about January. These probably answer to the hook billed salmon of the Fraser, but seem from all accounts to be a much better fish.

Trout.[307] Speckled, good fish, to be found in some streams at all seasons.

Potatoes grow admirably about Masset in the sandy soil.

Barley has been tried experimentally, found to grow to great height & ripen well.

Trees. The *spruce* often attains a good size, & is at times very large. Common everywhere, & well grown away from coast. *Yellow Cedar* not, as far as I can learn, found anywhere in large groves of great trees. Scattered everywhere in hilly district in small numbers. Alder attains fine growth frequently, fringing the shore mixed with the more formal

305. The American elk or wapiti, *Cervus canadensis nelsoni* Bailey, was not native to the Queen Charlotte Islands but has been introduced to Graham Island. Another subspecies, *Cervus canadensis roosevelti* Merriam, is native to Vancouver Island.

306. The "small fish with bright red flesh" was the sockeye salmon, *O. nerka*; and "silver Salmon," probably the pink salmon, *Oncorhynchus grobuscha* (Walbaum), even though "silver salmon" is a variant vernacular for coho salmon, *Oncorhynchus kisutch* (Walbaum).

307. The "trout" were probably rainbow trout, *S. gairdneri*, or possibly coastal cutthroat trout, *Salmo clarki clarki* Richardson, or the Dolly Varden, *S. malma*.

evergreens in many places. Crab apples abundant. Hemlock abundant &
well grown. Cedar, fine trees on the flats in some places.
[end verso]
Aug 22. Devoted day to dredging in Virago Sound & harbour, at same
time ascertaining depth of the harbour in several places. No very striking
specimens procured, & general great paucity of life. Upper part of harbour
all mud, with many dead & broken shells, fragments of twigs &c. & but
few living specimens. On getting back to schooner found several Indian
Canoes about, with various things for sale. Bought some bone pins from
one man, also some salmon.

Southerly wind all day, falling to calm at times. Frequent showers of
rain, uniformly overcast.

Timber   fine spruce timber found a little way back from the Shore,
probably every where round this harbour. The Ne-din River probably
large enough to allow logs to be floated down from the lake above.
Aug 23. Leave Virago Sound in the boat, for North Island. A fine morning, though fog banks hanging about.

Sea not very heavy though sufficiently so to prevent landing except in
Sheltered situations. See a very large shark, which followed the boat for
some distance, occasionally Showing its back fin above water. Length estimated at over 20 feet. Get round to the new Indian Village,[308] shortly
after 10 A.m., land, & proceed to make arrangements about getting a new
Indian who knows the coast west of this, & dispensing with Jim.

There is quite a collection of Indians at the new town at present, on the
occasion of the erection of the first totem post, & potlatch consequent
thereon. The Kaigani indians from the S. end of Alaska are daily expected. It is intended to abandon the Village in Virago Sd.[309] as it is found
that this place is more in the way of traffic & better suited to the wants of
the Indians. Edensaw* says Indians from the north are constantly coming
over here, but not to Virago Sd. This may be, as this is the furthest northern pt. & is besides marked by a low but conspicuous hill,[310] which may
serve as a landmark to Canoes making the traverse.

Edensaw*, the Virago Sound Chief, & the Masset Chief[311] are both
here. The former a decent looking & well dressed old man — though sus-

308. Ya-tza or Yats 1. See 19 August 1878.

309. Kung. See 19 August 1878.

310. Klashwun or Little Mountain, about 340 feet on its west side and visible for a considera-
    ble distance. See Dalzell, *Queen Charlotte Places*, 447.

311. Chief Weah.

pected of complicity in the robbing of a Schooner in former years[312] —
the latter a stout indian, remarkable from his grey hair & beard. Took
photo. of the two chiefs, & of as many of the rest of the people as would
come. Most, however, disliked the idea, & especially the women, not one
of whom appeared.[313]

Edensaws* great village was formerly on the shore S. of North
Island.[314] It was abandoned finally about ten years ago for Virago Sd, &
now another move is to be made. Long ago Edensaw* says his country
was at Rose Point,[315] & here his people as he says landed originally when
the flood went down.

Got away from the Indian Village at last, & rowed round the long
point[316] against a heavy sea & westerly wind. Continued on for some miles
in heavy breaking sea, & then ran into the mouth of a small river,[317]
known to my new Indian pilot, & moored the boat in still water. Camped
on a snug point, with trees shielding from the wind & plenty drift-wood.
Night fine. Got good observations for lat & time, though had to readjust
my sextant, the horizon glass having by some means got a little out.
[verso]

First white men. Edensaw* Says the name of the first white man Known
to him, or handed down to the present time as having been communicated
with by the Indians is *Douglas* Captain of some vessel. This was at North
Island. Edensaw* thinks, however, that white men Seen before Douglas, &

---

312. The incident occurred on 25 September 1852. Edenshaw, acting as a guide, was aboard
the *Susan Sturgis* with his wife and child when it was attacked by a group of Masset
Indians just off Point Rose. According to the ship's captain, Matthew Rooney,
Edenshaw tried to dissuade the attackers but Chief Weah of the Massets refused to
listen. Edenshaw, seeing the futility of his attempts, then joined in the plunder. He did,
however, manage to bargain for the lives of the captain and his crew. Edenshaw was
suspected of arranging the entire affair, but his complicity was never proved. See
Gough, "New Light on Haida Chiefship," 131-39.

313. See "Photographs," 23 August 1878, GSC265–C2 (PA 38154) and GSC266–C2
(PA 38147). The latter print is reproduced and discussed in Margaret B. Blackman,
"'Copying People': Northwest Coast Native Response to Early Photography," *BC
Studies*, no. 52 (1981-82): 92, and pl. II.

314. Dadens.

315. Hiellen, Swanton's Ɬi'elAñ *(Haida Ethnology,* 280), on the east bank of the Hiellen
River near Rose Spit, was Edensaw's original home. In the early 1840's, he led his
StA'stas lineage to K!iū'stA and reasserted dominance over the K'awas lineage, who
had already settled there. For Edensaw's moves, see Mary Lee Stearns, "Succession to
Chiefship," 204-18.

316. Klashwun Point.

317. Jalun River, named by Dawson.

that to the very first, the story below relates.[318] It was near winter when a ship under Sail appeared near North Island. The Indians very much afraid. The chief also very much afraid, but thinking no doubt that the duty of finding out about the new apparition devolved on him, put on all his dancing clothes, & going out to sea in his canoe danced. The Indians say the men dressed in dark Clothes were supposed to be shags,[319] (which look somewhat human as they sit upon the rocks) & that the unintelligible character & general sound of their talk confirmed the idea. One man would say something & then all would go aloft. Say something else & all would come down. A feat the Indians thought almost like flying.

[end verso]

Aug 24. Tide far out this morning, but managed to get boat down the now shoal river, & out to sea. A fine morning but frequent fog banks drifting past Coast along, landing without difficulty where wish, as now sheltered from force of westerly swell by north Island. Stopped to take photo. of very remarkable pillar like rock, in a bay.[320] Rock quite isolated, over 80 feet high Sloping top covered with bushes. Formed of coarse conglomerate. The Indians have some story about the rock which I cannot exactly understand, but it would seem that according to them it was small formerly, & that some Chimseyan Indians wished to remove it, probably this accounting for the hollow eaten in the base on one side. Since then it has grown very much. The Indian name is Hlā-tad-zo-wōh

Make parry passage & stop at Indian Village on S. shore of North Island[321] for lunch. See on end of Lucy Island of Map the decayed remains of a shark which has been 25′ long. It came ashore dead, or nearly so, & much *grease* was tried out of it by the Indians.

Afternoon coasted up E. shore of North Island to Northern point.[322] A strong westerly or north westerly wind blowing but did not experience its force, or that of the waves till we reached the north point, when glad to turn back, & return under sail to the Indian Village, where camped.

Sky clouded during early part of evening, but got a couple of observations on the pole star later on.

---

318. William Douglas was commander of the British merchant ship the *Iphigenia Nubiana*. He was off Langara Island in August 1788 and returned for a week's stay in June 1789. The reference to an earlier visitor was perhaps to Pérez.

319. Or pelagic cormorants, *Phalacrocorax pelagicus pelagicus* Pallas.

320. Pillar Rock, so-named by Dawson, in Pillar Bay. See "Photographs," 24 August 1878, GSC267–C2 (PA 51118). The view was photo-lithographed and included in Dawson, "Queen Charlotte Islands," pl. II, opp. 40.

321. Dadens.

322. McPherson Point.

Aug. 25. Left tent & most of things at camp. Crossed the passage, examined rocks along the S. shore. Then rowed out to Lucy Island of the map, across a wide bay with a high cliffy Island in it.[323] The swell raised by the prevalent westerly winds & intensified by the Strong breezes of the past few days rolling in about a hundred feet from Crest to crest & breaking very heavily on the beach, where it would be impossible to land in a boat. Got back to Camp against heavy tide about 2 P.m. Spent part of afternoon getting Indian words from "Harry". Schooner in sight beating up toward passage. Thought her so close at about 6 P.m. that put things in boat & started out towards her. Got into a tide rip which threatened to carry us out to sea, & wind at same time dying away came to conclusion that Schooner would not get in this evening, & might be so far off as to interfere with tomorrows work if we were on board. Put back & slept at old Camp.

Rain in the night

[verso]

Seen from a distance, the hill *Tow* does not look so abrupt as when Seen from near the shore on either side. It appears to be separated by a small gap from a second low broad hill, which is probably that seen South of Rose Spit, on the E. shore, but here appears in line with Tow on the spit, or nearly so. This appearance has Caused these hills to be drawn as they are on the map.

Coast between Virago Sd & North Island. Generally low land, with occasional rocky cliffs of no great height along shore, but generally alternating low broken rocks & gravelly beaches. Few Sandy beaches occur. Some rocks seen at a little distance off shore, but no sign of wide shoal belt like that E. of Masset. Trees along Shore of the usual Character, generally scrubby, owing to their exposed situation. Green grassy patches along the edges of the forest, & on sandy & gravelly spits of old formation. The remarkable rock pillar occuring in one bay has been described elsewhere.[324]

North Island is all composed of low land, probably in no place rising over 300 feet. The country to the south Similar, though higher hills appear about abreast of Frederic Island on the West Coast.

[end verso]

Aug. 26. Found the schooner at anchor in Bruin Bay   Put things on board, & then set out for the abandoned Indian village[325] from which trail to the west coast starts. Took Harry as guide & Crossed by the trail, which

323. Cloak Bay and Cox Island.

324. Pillar Rock, at 24 August 1878.

325. K!iū′stᴀ. See Swanton, *Haida Ethnology,* 281.

little more than ¾ mile to bay S. of Cape Knox.[326] The trail a very devious one, over & under moss-grown logs & through thickets, all soaking wet from the frequent showers. Come out at the mouth of a little creek on a fine sandy beach on which the waves are breaking with a regular steady roll, from end to end. Went along shore to next point south,[327] from which got bearings & sketch of Coast as far as in sight. The Shore remarkably rugged, here & southward. Broken rocky cliffs & rocky pinnacled islands, with reefs still further out. On all these a great ocean swell forever breaking & the water yeasty with foam, & a mist hovering along the whole Coast-line from the spray of the breakers. Ate our lunch in a shower of rain at the mouth of the Creek, & then returned by the trail. Found no boat, & after waiting some time set out along the shore toward the bay in which schooner lies. Found the boat high & dry on the beach, having been Carelessly allowed to become so by the men cutting wood. Got put on board the schooner by an Indian Canoe which fortunately there. Boat brought back by men after 9 P.m. when the tide rose again.

An unpleasant anchorage as so open that the swell from the Eastward & Caused by the tide rip keeps the Schooner in a state of perpetual roll.

Aug. 27. By time water casks had been filled, no wind in harbour waited some time with sails up, then got off with light air, but carried away by the eddy. Had to get boat out to keep schooner off rocks. Getting out of eddy got into main tide, which breeze not sufficient to enable us to stem. Made the round of Lucy I. & after an ineffectual attempt to get out against the tide in the North Passage,[328] Came to anchor opposite old Camp, & new Indian Village. Got off at slack water, after a few hours, though again nearly carried down on rocks by tide. Proceeded Eastward with light wind & strong tidal current. Got a couple of soundings in the evening.

Aug 28. About opposite Virago Sd. this morning & continued on general north eastward course, with light easterly winds all day. Got two Casts of lead at 111 & 130 fathoms in places pretty well fixed by bearings, though weather thick. Also had the dredge down for about half an hour at the former locality, & brought it up full of sand & brittle stars, with a few shells. Attended to some duties about outfit. did a little plotting &c. one very beautiful spiny star fish. Carmine-coloured[329]

Evening nearly becalmed in gently rolling swell.

---

326. Lepas Bay, named by Dawson.

327. Probably Lauder Point.

328. Parry Passage.

329. Perhaps the spiny sun star, *Crossaster papposus* Linnaeus.

Thermometer thrust into mud of dredge went down to 47°
Aug 29. In sight of Zayas Island early this morning. Under Sail all day, getting inside Port Simpson about 8 P.m. Light westerly winds & fair weather with occasional glimpses of the sun. Views of the Southern promontory & islands of Alaska through mist & clouds which seem constantly to enwrap them. Passed pretty close to Zayas Island, to the north, also to N. Shore of Dundas Island. These outer Islands, as before remarked further south, generally low, & seem to show slope of surface of older cryst. rocks westward. Landed on an island of the "Gnarled group"[330] & got specimen of the rock, also little vein with some copper pyrites, & evidence of glaciation Seaward.

Rocks of all these islands appear to be granitic or at least wholley-crystalline.

A very fine view looking up Portland Inlet as we Came up this evening the mountains on its E. side Singularly bold & abrupt. A fine peaked Snow-Clad Mountain[331] seen behind Port Simpson, the same on which a bearing formerly obtained from near Rose Spit. Like the rest shrouded in grey clouds & seen only partially & occasionally.

The rock of which note made on the Chart this morning, off Zayas Island, is probably the "Devils ridge"[332] of which the position is doubtfully indicated on the chart. At the time Seen, breaking heavily occasionally, but not often. The sea moderate, & the tide nearly full. It would be a dangerous rock for vessels entering the channel for Port Simpson, from Dixon's Strait.[333] Nor is it alone, for with the generally low character of Zayas & other islands, the bottom does not appear to deepen ⟨good⟩ fast or regularly. Breakers observed far out from Zayas Island in several directions & little rocky islets near shore.

Got large mail here, the first we have reached since leaving Victoria. Up late enjoying letters & looking over papers.
Aug. 30. Spent most of day with Mr McKay* of the H.B Company looking at his specimens, & gathering items of interest about the Coast. Got a photo. of the village of Port Simpson, R. afterwards getting another of

---

330. Gnarled Islands.

331. Probably Mount Griffin.

332. West southwest of Jacinto Point, Zayas Island.

333. Caamaño Passage from Dixon Entrance.

the harbour from a hill.[334] Visited Mr McKay's* "Chimseyan Lode"[335] The H.B. post or fort[336] here much in the usual style, in good repair. Building painted white & red facing on a quadrangle, Surrounded by a pallisade which once had bastions. One of these still standing ⟨last⟩ used as a hay barn. A loft of Chilcat Indians from the Country bordering on the Esqumaux, in Alaska arrived to trade today & all day examining goods & haggling over them. Brought down a valuable lot of furs which they have themselves bought from the interior indians.

G. M. Dawson to Margaret Dawson*, 30 August 1878, Port Simpson

by the superscription you will see that we have left behind us the North American Hebrides, & have again got to a place with a name, the northern point of Brit. Columbia on the Coast.

We arrived here yesterday evening after a pleasant passage from North Island. It was dark when we got in but R. went ashore to hunt up our mail, & we had the pleasure of overhauling the first home news we have had for three months back. The latest Montreal, — or rather Metis — dates are Early in July, as there has been no steamer here for some time. I have had bad luck in Sending letters, & find a note written from Masset, to William*, still lying at the H.B. Fort here, no chance having occurred of forwarding it. Thus it is that being quite uncertain how long this may lie here after we leave, that I do not propose now to do more than report our welfare.

We hope to get away tomorrow on our way southward, looking at a few places *en route* & stopping perhaps some time near the north end of Vancouver Island if the weather holds good. Rain we are now quite accustomed to & everything has a dampness about it, so much so that if I put away a pair of boots for a few days, on looking them up again they generally have a coat of mould outside & in.

The Chances are so very infrequent of communication with Victoria from here, that I fear Rankine* may either have to leave very soon, or be too late for his work   I hope to know more about this tomorrow & shall add a note should anything occur. There is quite a large village here,

---

334. See "Photographs," 30 August 1878, GSC269–C2 (PA 44333) and GSC270–C2 (PA 44344).

335. This is Joseph William McKay of the Hudson's Bay Company. The "Chimseyan Ledge," on the hill behind Port Simpson, was, according to Dawson, composed of "pyrrhotite with copper-pyrites in quartz tongue" (Dawson, *Mineral Wealth of B.C.*, [1889], 153).

336. A fort was first built in 1831–32 near the mouth of the Nass River but moved to a location on the Tsimpsean Peninsula in 1834. In 1860, a new fort was built on the same site.

inhabited by Indians under the guidance of a Mr Crosby,[337] a rather imprudent Methodist Missionary. He has a large white church on the slope above the town, which is quite a landmark from far off the harbour.

Please give my best congratulations to William* on his good final Standing.

Aug. 31. Had intended leaving today, but a strong south-easterly gale, with squalls & rain in progress, & judged it better to remain. Went ashore & made arrangements about some additional supplies — Corned beef & butter — Afternoon went round harbour in boat examining rocks, though the strong squally wind, with rain, rendered it very unpleasant, & quite a disagreeable sea had got up toward the north, or outer end. Shot a few small plover[338] on the way back. Wrote up some notes &c. Evg. paid a visit to Mr Mckay* of the H.B. Co, getting on board rather late, & sitting up reading till nearly twelve.

Sept. 1. Weather appearing more moderate, got away this morning, but found a very strong head wind blowing Beat southward slowly, arriving after dark opposite Metla Katla. Weather thick & afraid to run in. Beating about outside all night, with lighter wind.

Sept. 2. Found ourselves early this morning back, about abreast of Ft Simpson. Got a more favourable wind, & reached Metla-katla about 10 A.m. Visited Mr Duncan*, who received us Cordially. Afternoon went round the harbour, examining the rocks, & got photo.[339] of Part of the town. Evg. spent with messrs. Duncan* & Tomlinson.[340] R. decides to stay here to catch first steamer for which Mr Tomlinson* also waiting. Up

---

337. Thomas Crosby (1840–1914), a prominent Methodist missionary to the Tsimshians, came to Fort (Port) Simpson in 1874. For over twenty years, Crosby zealously furthered Methodist missions, establishing a number of outlying stations and initiating a marine mission, as well as developing Port Simpson after the model pioneered by William Duncan. For accounts of his work, see Thomas Crosby, *Up and Down the North Pacific Coast by Canoe and Mission Ship* (Toronto: Missionary Society of the Methodist Church, 1914); and Clarence R. Bolt, "The Conversion of the Port Simpson Tsimshian: Indian Control or Missionary Manipulation?," *BC Studies*, no. 57 (1983): 38–56.

338. Possibly killdeer, *Charadrius vociferus* L.

339. See "Photographs," 2 September 1878, GSC271–C2 (PA 44335).

340. Robert Tomlinson (1842–1913) was an Irish physician who came to British Columbia in 1867 to assist William Duncan. Tomlinson's first posting was to the Nass River, where he founded a mission station at Kincolith. A staunch supporter of Duncan, he lost the Anglican Church's backing when Duncan left the Church Missionary Society. In 1888, Tomlinson founded his own non-denominational mission, Minskinisht or Cedarvale, on the Skeena River. See also Margaret Whitehead, *Now You are my Brother: Missionaries in British Columbia*, Sound Heritage Series no. 34 (Victoria: Provincial Archives of British Columbia, 1981), 6–25.

late getting things packed & arranged.

Sept. 3. Intended to leave this morning but weather turning bad, not withstanding very high barometer, decided to wait. Weather continued to grow worse, gale of wind with very heavy rain showers from the South East. Mr Tomlinson* Came on board, & remained talking till about 4 P.m. Had a visit from a Capt. Madden[341] & a man Called Jones, the latter claiming to be an old acquaintance, having been on the Boundary Commission, in Ashe's Party.[342] Told that the "Grappler" stopped at Inverness (Woodcock's landing)[343] early this morning, & promised to be back on her way to Victoria in three days. Took tea at the mission & spent part of evg. there, leaving R. in hope that we may have early start in morning.

Engaged an Indian boy this morning for extra help in boat &c. Wages to be $20.00 per month, not less than one month paid, & $10. return fare from Victoria in steamer.

Sept. 4. Morning promising fine weather, & South Easterly Gale having ceased, decide to get away. Land to see about barrel of oolachens which I had agreed to purchase, & find R, with Messrs Duncan* & Tomlinson* at breakfast. Get the fish, & shortly afterwards get away, though after leaving the harbour almost constantly in sight of the Village till night fall, as we beat against wind & tide, making very little. The current appears at present to set out Chatham Str.[344] northward at both flow & ebb. This may be owing to the Volume of water discharged by the Skeena, or to the present prevalent South-Easterly winds.

Had the dredge over opposite Metla Katla in about 50 fathoms, & brought it up full of slimy mud, & stones, some several inches in diameter, mostly more or less water rounded, but with occasional angular fragments. In the mud found one living & several dead *Rhynchinellas*, a few *Ledas*, a brittle star,[345] & one or two other shells. Life very scantily represented. Such a deposit as this might almost form a "boulder clay". Have

---

341. Captain William F. Madden, "ship master" of Port Essington.

342. Unidentifiable. William A. Ashe was one of four sub-assistant astronomers.

343. At the Tsimpsean Peninsula at the mouth of the Skeena River where, in the 1860's, William H. Woodcock had established a public inn for the accommodation of miners going to and from the Omineca country via the Skeena River. The site was known as Woodcock's Landing until, with the 1876 establishment of a salmon cannery there, it gradually became known as Inverness, from Inverness Passage.

344. Chatham Sound.

345. The "*Rhynchinellas*" were the brachiopod, *Hemithyris psittacea* (Gmelin); the "*Ledas*" one of the nut clams, *Nuculana* spp., such as Müller's nut clam, *Nuculana pernula* (Müller), or minute nut clam, *Nuculana minuta* (Fabricius); and the "brittle star" the brittle star, *O. lutkeni*.

not before struck similar bottom, & judge it not improbable that the stones may be brought down by floe ice from the Skeena in spring.

Wrote up notes, did some plotting & attended to Several other little matters which have got behind.

Sept 5. Found ourselves this morning off the Skeena, with Inverness in full view, though at a considerable distance. Light baffling winds all day, with heavy tide running out against us most of time. Getting abreast of White-Cliff Island,[346] where some men are trying to open a marble quarry, went ashore for a few minutes to inspect it. Toward evening got a little puff of fair wind, with rain, & distant thunder. This pushed us on nearly to south end of Kennedy Island, when again becalmed. Did a little plotting, reading &c.

Sept 6. Drifted back last night with the tide, which appears to flow in by Ogden Channel at the flood, got into Chalmers anchorage, abreast North End of Kennedy Island. Morning Calm. Went ashore for water, & got additional supply of wood. Light breeze springing up from North or North west between 10 & 11 Am, got away, & have had moderate to light fair wind light astern ever since, making a fair afternoon's run. Did some plotting, wrote up notes, read, & attempted to colour my Sketch of Portland Channel.[347] A very fine day, with much sunshine, & the moon & Jupiter now shining brightly ahead.

[verso]

The Chimseyan Indians are closely related to the Tinne, & have in fact come down from the interior onto the Coast by the Skeena River. The Skeena is not the real Indian name of the river, which is differently pronounced, & the name Chimseyan means simply people from the Skeena.[348] Mr Hall* here at the H.B. post, who knows the Carrier language well finds many Collateral or similar words between it & the Chimseyan. The migration did not take place within the traditional memory of any Indians now living, but may not have occurred more than about 100 years ago. The Chimseyans displaced the Tongas Indians, who now occupy the Coast from the W. side of Portland Inlet to the Stickeen.[349] Their country being Part of that of the Kaigani, or migrated

346. East of Shattock Hill in the entrance to Big Bay.

347. Portland Inlet. The watercolour, dated 29 August 1878, is now in the McCord Museum.

348. Dawson's information in the following was partly reliable. The Tsimshian were not closely related to the Dene nor are their languages related. Tsimshian early history is obscure and controversial, but any migration occurred earlier than the century mentioned by Dawson. Their name is, however, derived from their word for the Skeena, *K-shian* or *ikshean*, river of mists, and thus "people of the river of mists."

349. Stikine River. The Tongas are a Tlingit group.

Haidah Indians. The Haidas have always been in the habit of resorting to the Nasse to fish the oolachen, the Chinseyans allowing them to do so, or rather fearing, or being unable to prevent them.

Haidas. Mr Hall* of H.B. Co tells me that a Custom among them that when a girl arrives at puberty, she goes about for a time in a peculiar Cedar bark Cloak, which conceals the face. Afterwards a feast or time of rejoicing occurs[350]

Pholas borings. North I. In the large bay next north of Parry passage on e. shore, on S. shore of bay. Found distinct pholas borings in Calcareous shales, above present H.W. mark, & {altogether} above the position in which these shells would now live.

Oolachans on the Nasse. The first & great run occurs about the Middle of March, a second smaller run is said to occur in June.

Coal. An indistinct report of Coal on Work's Canal,[351] but appears unlikely to be true.

Distribution of Cervidæ.[352]

Moose.[353] Are found to within about ten miles north of Ft St. James, Stuart Lake, down to Ft. George, & in the whole country North East of the chain of lakes of which Stuart L. is one.

Cariboo very abundant E. of Ft George, also on hills West of the Quesnel & Blackwater trail. Extend to the 49th parallel near Okanagan in winter. Abound about the head & N. side of Francois Lake.

The small red deer,[354] formerly ⟨only⟩ found northward only to Ft George & not common there, now abundant about Ft Fraser, & found also on Stuart Lake near the fort (Ft. St. James).

Grizzly bear,[355] said to be two distinct kinds, large & small, but with uncertainty about specific lines among bears this not of much value.

---

350. For a description of Haida puberty rites, see Swanton, *Haida Ethnology,* 48–50.

351. Work Channel.

352. The deer family. Their distribution has changed considerably since Dawson received his information.

353. British Columbia moose, *Alces alces andersoni* Peterson.

354. It is difficult to know what deer Dawson was describing, since the only species found in the range outlined was the mule deer, *O. hemionus hemionus,* a large deer.

355. The grizzly bear, *U. arctos horribilis.* ''Recent studies have indicated that all these supposed species [of the grizzly bear] refer to individual variations in one species of bear'' (A. W. F. Banfield, *The Mammals of Canada* [Toronto: University of Toronto Press, 1974], 311).

Copper   Shown fine specimens of Copper pyrites & bornite[356] by an Indian. Said to come from a place a little below the Forks of the Skeena, & to exist, of course, in great quantity. Indian believes the locality unknown to whites.

Gold   Capt Madden* has a few small quartz specimens with large pieces of gold scattered through them. He says the ledge is well defined, & he hopes to be able to do something with it. Locality about 60 m. up the Skeena on the left, or south bank. The gold "free" & little pyrites visible.[357]

The several blocks of land separating the mouths of the Skeena {& adjacent channels} with the exception (only?) of Digby Island, are generally high & mountainous, rising steeply, or with a very narrow sloping foot from the water's edge. Kennedy Id. is also of this character, exceedingly bold land, sloping down into Arthur passage at a very steep angle. On this face two great bare "slides", showing solid rock from base to summit {(showing granite apparently)}, one of them connected with a brook. These slides precisely like those seen frequently in the Queen Charlotte Islands.

Grenville Channel opens rather widely at first, but gradually Contracts, the hills immediately bounding it, are at first not very high, are densely wooded, further back, however, both on the Mainland & Pitt Island Mountains still holding extensive patches of last winter's snow, in deep drifts, occur. The summits of these are bare & treeless, & even where they show no snow, whitish, from the almost continuous exposures of granitic rocks. The views up some of the valleys & glens which lead streams from there down into the Channel, singularly wild & beautiful.

[end verso]

Sept. 7. Nearly out of South end of Grenville Channel this morning at breakfast time, having been favoured during the night by breeze & tide. A light head wind springing up, however, set us to beating, & remained beating about mouth of Channel most of day. Even when tide running out strong below, a surface current, probably impelled by the wind, & only a few yards deep, kept dragging us back into the strait. Landed, & got a photo. of Channel from Yolk Point.[358] Anchored for a time in a cove, as we continued to drift back, but finally in the afternoon, getting a fair wind, set off, & now, (8 Pm) have Crossed Wright Sound & are fairly in

---

356. A copper ore mineral.

357. Three months earlier, *The Colonist* had carried a report of Captain Madden's interest in the Skeena quartz ledge, "prospected four years ago" and "believed to be very rich" (*Victoria Daily British Colonist*, 9 June 1878).

358. See "Photographs," 7 September 1878, GSC272–C2 (PA 152369).

⟨Tolmie Channel⟩ McKay Reach

The "California" passed us close, on the way up today. Still no news of the "Grappler" or "Otter".

[verso]

Most of the land about Wright Sound, rises at once steeply, & without beach, from the water, to mountains of considerable altitude. Some of these, especially that on Gill Island, & on south end of ⟨Grenfell⟩ {Hawksbury} Island, are peculiarly picturesque in form. The latter range, ⟨called the Wimbledon Mts. on the Chart,⟩ slopes to the North west, breaking off in a series of abrupt step like escarpments in the other direction, almost as though dependent ⟨on⟩ for form, on bedding of massive strata.

These mountains of the off lying Islands, are however pigmies to the serried & snow burdened ranges which form the axial Summits of the Coast Range. Looking up Douglas Arm,[359] from Wright Sound, tier upon tier of these, glowing in the pale rosy light of a rather cold sunset, appear. Fields of driven snow of great size, & evidently in some places of immense depth, shroud their Summits, while here & there a long ridge, or sharp Crag stands above the white Surface. It would almost appear that some new snow has already fallen this autumn on these unnamed & unmeasured giants.

[end verso]

Sept 8. Beating about, with light baffling winds, in McKay's Reach all night, & a considerable portion of this morning. Could see ahead of us all the time a fine breeze drawing into & down Fraser Reach. Finally, by aid of the sweeps, got into the wind, & have ever since been making good progress Southward, being now, 8 Pm, not far from entrance of Tolmie Channel. Did a little sketching & some reading today though generally lazily inclined. Weather remarkably fine, & the scenery wild & magnificent.

"Grappler" passed us on the way down at 9 P.m.

[verso]

McKay Reach, Fraser Reach & Graham Reach.

The first named, wide, & transverse to the general course of the inland waters about here. Some fine mountains, of which the peaks still hold a little snow, on S. side (see sketch)[360]   Mr McKay* Enformed me that schistose rocks occurred here, but those I have seen from the schooner for the most part evidently granitic, gneissic, or dioritic = massive & white. Fraser & Graham reaches, are really parts of one long narrow passage,

359. Douglas Channel.

360. Probably "Mt. Gill & Whale Passage from Wright Sd.," a watercolour dated 7 September 1878, in the McCord Museum.

which in its character is more rugged than any of those we have yet been in, in coming from the north. The mountains Surrounding the channel, are not very high, but some still hold masses of snow on shady exposures. With the exception of the less height of the mountains, this channel resembles the upper reaches of some of the fiords. Many of the Mountains are almost bare massive blocks of grey granite. Where they are covered with timber it is small. (except occasionally along the water's edge) & scrubby. Cascades fall in on every side, & the roar of a large waterfall fills the quiet mountain fenced passage opposite Work Island.[361] This waterfall is the overflow of a lake,[362] which by the apparent size of the hollow in the mountains must be large. A little further on a second stream[363] of considerable size flows tumultuously out, (also on the W. side) & here a party of Indians were Camped salmon fishing. They Called to us, but did not come off.

Rocks almost everywhere in higher Mts. appear massive granitic. Along shore noted strat. rocks, gneisses or mica schists, in several places, but did not think it worth while to stop to look at them, from their monotonous character. On North West side of Work Island, rocks apparently schistose, & seem to include a bed of brown-weathering limestone.

Glaciation noted as rock rounding & distinct & heavy grooving in many places, in the channels traversed today. This both at the water's edge, & a thousand feet or more up the mountain sides. Direction, as might be expected always parallel to Channel, though frequently grooves slope up, or down, ⟨as regards it⟩ on nearly vertical Surfaces.

The point between McKay Reach & Fraser Reach, is heavily glaciated as though by ice coming out of passage to North.

[end verso]

Sept. 9. Floating slowly along without wind in Klemtoo Passage this morning. Sun bright & perfectly Calm. Went ashore on a small island & took a photo.[364] looking north up the passage; which if it developes should show curious effect of kelps & reflexion of trees in water. Seems, however, rather an act of faith to expose an "Extra sensitive" plate ten or fifteen seconds & expect to carry away a picture! Getting a little wind, at length beat out, & now floating about, again becalmed, in the Centre of Milbank Sound. Ocean all open to the S.W. but scarcely any swell.

361. The waterfall flows into Marmot Cove.

362. The lake is ungazetted.

363. The stream is ungazetted.

364. See "Photographs," 9 September 1878, GSC273–C2 (PA 152368).

A lovely night, full moon & many stars. As last rosy light faded from sky, the clamorous din of sea-fowl on the water, & distant rocks, with the occasional sharp snort of a whale blowing at the surface, or the distant sound of one breaching — combined to give a peculiarly wierd effect. ⟨to the⟩ A distant unvisited haunt of the creatures who congregate where man is not. Sketched out plan of report. Reading &c.

Sept. 10. Nearly becalmed all night, & calm continued with Scarcely a break till noon. Bright sun & smooth water. Drifted a little this way with the tide & that way with the wind, but made no real progress. After noon a nice little wind rising, sailed into Seaforth Channel, & Just about sundown anchored at the Kil-Kite Indian Village of the chart, behind Grief Island. The Indian name of the village is Kā-pa,[365] according to Charley *Ham-Chit*, (the latter being the Indian name. This man is the chief, & Came off to us on our arrival with a neat wreath of red-stained Cedar bark about his head. He seems very intelligent & had a long conversation with me after supper.

Sent a couple of young Indians off to Bella Bella with a note to H.B. Store asking them to keep any letters which may come up in the 'Otter''. Promised them a pound of tobacco for their trouble.

Got the boat on the beach to try to find out where she leaked, but could not succeed in discovering any large break. She begins to be rather frail & strained throught, by much contact with rocks & hard usage.

Sept. 11. Made an early start in the boat, with the Indian above mentioned, & his wife, in a small canoe. The Indian to act as guide to Mr McKays* "Hebrew" mine. Rowed up Ellerslie Channel[366] of the chart a long way getting to the mine about ten o'clock. Examined the little tunnel which has been driven, the ore at its mouth &c. Had lunch, & at noon, set out on return. Strong head wind, Causing us to have a long & heavy row back, getting to the schooner about 6 P.m. A fine day, with a good sailing wind in the afternoon, had we been travelling. Found the Indians who had carried my letter to Bella Bella last night waiting to be paid, also an Indian wishing to Sell a deer — for which he got a dollar — another with some halibut &c. Our guide last night asked me for some old Illustrated news. Today he wants a Cup of flour to make paste to stick them up in his house! Probably Should we wait here tomorrow he will be along asking a brush.

Sept. 12. No wind in the early morning, & very light air for some time

---

365. Now the Kokyet reserve, on the extreme southwest coast of Yeo Island. The Kokyet or Kokyitoch are Heiltsuk-speaking Northern Kwakiutl, closely related to the Bella Bella Heiltsuk speakers.

366. Spiller Channel.

after it began to come in. Beat about the entrance to Ellerslie Channel, but did not get fairly out of it till noon. Then got a good breeze, which pushed us up Seaforth Channel, bringing us to Bella Bella about 5 P.m. Went ashore in boat to leave a few letters, & found a note from R, with a few papers of late dates he had picked up. Looked at some specimens of ore Mr Leighton[367] had, & then set out after the schooner. Light variable winds during early night. A very fine day, quite summer like

G. M. Dawson to Margaret Dawson, 12 September 1878, Bella Bella*

Here we are in the schooner, again at Bella Bella, but this time on the way southward. I have no certainty when this note may go, but as some steamer may pass, will leave it, together with another, written long ago but never sent.

I left Rankine* at Metla Katla, well provided I believe with money to carry him back to Montreal. The "Grappler" on which he was to take passage, passed us in the night some time ago, & is now no doubt in Victoria. R. will miss the steamer of Sept 10, but should get home about October 1st. I requested him not to get off the train & spring on again at the last moment more frequently than absolutely necessary to preserve his mental & bodily health; but noticing that he received all these hints with considerable reserve, believe that he made up his mind to do just as he liked.

The weather is magnificent now, in fact the finest we have had yet. Warm, clear & without any fog. The only drawback is the lightness of the winds, which renders sailing rather slow

I have not yet quite decided exactly how long I may stay at various places on the way to Victoria, but as the season is already so far advanced, judge it best to spend what fine weather remains on the way. There is no time for any separate expedition after return, & I am now provided with everything necessary for work along the Coast.

I do not intend to be very late in returning to Victoria, even in the case of continued fine weather, as I have several things to attend to there which may take some time, & must besides be in Montreal before very long to see about revision of report written last winter, which was left in an incomplete state.[368]

---

367. Unidentifiable.

368. Dawson's reference is to his report on explorations conducted in the 1877 field season in south-central British Columbia. His "Report on the Southern Portion" was not published until 1879.

[verso]

Bella Bella names of stars &c. Stars *To-toa*   Moon *No-si*. Sun
Klik-si-walla   orion's belt, Il-i-wha. Pleides Il-i-wha-so   Great Bear
Klak-tsoo-wis. North Star Pāice (They are unacquainted with the fact that
the north star does not move) Kwa-Kum probably the Dog star. (Sirius)
Milky Way Kum-e-e

When asked as to *origin of Indians* Hain-chit gave me the following.
Very long ago there was a great flood, the sea rose above everything, with
the exception of three mountains.[369] Two of these are very high, one near
Bella Bella, & the other apparently N.E. of it. The third is a low but prominent hill on Don Island Called by the Indians Ko-kwus. This they say rose
so as to remain above the water. Nearly all the Indians floated away on
logs & trees to various places, thus the Kit-Katla's floated to Fort Rupert,
& the Fort Rupert's to Kit-Katla. Some Indians however appear to have
had small canoes, though the making of canoes not very well understood
in these days. These anchoring their canoes, came down when the water
Subsided near home (The story a little confused here & the precise use of
the Mountains not evident) At any rate, ther remained at last of Bella
Bellas just three, two men, a young woman, & a dog. One of the men
came down at the village where we are now anchored, another at a village
site near Bella Bella & the young woman & dog at Bella Bella. The young
woman slept & the dog married her, giving rise to a being half man half
dog. Similar creatures soon multiplied, & these eventually turned into the
Bella Bella Indians.[370]

Fire, first given to the Indians by the deer. This animal it would appear
showed them how to use the fire drill.

When the flood went down, there was no fresh water, & the Indians did
not know what to do. The crow however showed them how, after eating to
chew fragments of Cedar wood, when water came into the mouth. He also
it would seem, by & bye showed them where to get a little water by digging, & soon a great rain Came on, very heavy & very long, which filled all
the lakes & water Courses, so that they have never been dry since. The
water however is still in some way connected with the Cedar, & the Indians
Say if no cedar no water in the country. The reverse at least would certainly hold good

Ham-chit says the Indians are always talking among themselves about

---

369. Flood myths are common among British Columbia Indians.

370. This Bella Bella story appears, without the same ending, in Franz Boas, *Bella Bella
Texts* (New York: Columbia University Press, 1928), 36–45.

their decrease in number.[371] Long ago he Says they were like the trees, in great numbers everywhere. The fought among themselves (as he said the white men men fight among themselves) Some were killed, but always more were born & the whole country teemed with them. Now he says the white men have come & the Indians *Chaco mamaloose,*[372] *Chaco mamaloos,* & Soon there will be none. He pointed out to me the former extent of his village & contrasted its present shrunken Size. Yet he says there is plenty food, plenty fish, & we have various things from the white men which we did not know before. The Indians do not fight among themselves or with the whites, only for a few years was whiskey introduced among them, not long enough to do much harm & yet they die. The Indians he says do not know how to explain it, but as he says — *Klunas saghalie tyee Mamook.*[373]

[end verso]

Sept. 13. Got a good fair wind after getting through Lama passage, sailed down Fitzhugh Sound, finding ourselves in the morning not far north of Safety Cove. Wind falling & then coming ahead, kept us beating most of day. Well outside the point by Sundown, & shortly afterwards a good breeze coming up, Made fine progress for a couple of hours, when again becalmed. A magnificent day. Saw at a distance six large Canoes of Newitti & Ukultaw Indians[374] on their way to Bella Coola to trade Blankets for potatoes. Wrote first part of notes on Haidas.[375]

Sept. 14. Becalmed, & rolling about in the open ⟨between⟩ off Cape Caution, most of day. Light air in the afternoon enabled us to make the land, but strong tide running out obliged us to anchor in Shadwell Passage

A fine & warm day, enjoyable enough but for the Sound of the booms & sails lashing about as the rollers passed under us. Saw several sea lions & a couple of large whales playing about. Boarded this evg. by some Nawitti Indians, made enquiries about coal reported by the Chief *Chip**, who is now off with the Bella Coola party. A magnificent night, bright moon & stars, nearly calm.

Sept 15. Interviewed a couple of Indians about the coal reported near Cape

---

371. Indian populations were declining significantly during the nineteenth century. Introduced diseases were the major cause. For a discussion of the issue, see Duff, *Indian History*, 40-44.

372. Or "chako memaloose," Chinook Jargon for "have died."

373. Chinook Jargon for "I don't know what God is doing."

374. Nawitti Kwakiutl from Hope Island and Lekwitok Kwakiutl from Cape Mudge. Dawson had encountered the Nawitti already, 4 June 1878, and would again, below, 14-15 September 1878.

375. A reference to his survey publication "On the Haida."

Commerell,[376] but as the story indefinite & distance great, — at least twelve miles — & the locality on a very open coast where it might be difficult to effect a landing, decided not to visit it. Waited till about 11 A.m. for tide to turn, got some wood & water on board, & eventually got away, beating up the strait against a westerly wind. Now at 8 P.m. Rolling about a little beyond Cape Commerell & some miles offshore. The wind has brought us so far but left us in *the lurch*.

We moved yesterday evening on the turning of the tide, from our exposed anchorage in Goletas Channel to a snug cove at the Nawitti Indian Village. For several hours this morning the most doleful crying & wailing was kept up by some women in one of the houses. Learned that this the ceremonial mourning for a little child who died a few days ago, & has been some days, buried — or housed — The women were relatives & went on with their work ⟨while⟩ more or less steadily while uttering these heart-rendering cries. A sort of wailing, mingled with interjections, & sentences probably referring to the deceased.

[verso]

Nawitti Indian Village. The houses not built on the old ponderous style, whether that may ever have been in vogue before or not. [*Illus.*] No carving indulged in though rude painting of the flat fronts of the houses has been practised. Now very dim. The best marked design represents two 'heraldic' birds, in black & red fighting, one on each side of the door. One small carved "totem post" in front of the Chief's (*Cheap*)* house. Also one other pole, with a cross stick & two men upon it, intended apparently to represent a mast & yard with two sailors aloft.[377]

[end verso]

Sept. 16. Rolling about all day, drifting a little one way & a little the other with the tide, but not enough wind to fill the sails. Dull gloomy weather. Begin to repent that I ever set out on this Quatsino expedition, which seems about to involve such loss of time, discomfort, & possibly bad weather. Towards evening a good breeze springing up got away again, but no certainty of its continuing. Decide if not much further advanced tomorrow morning to give up the Quatsino expedition

Had the dredge over twice, in about 15 fathoms, but got little of interest. The water shelves away very gradually here, & the rapid tidal Currents appear to keep it quite clean. Composed of gravel & rounded & smoothe stones, with little bryozoon or incrustation. A few shells, mostly dead — &

---

376. Cape Sutil.

377. See Boas, "Houses of the Kwakiutl," for an engraving of Cheap's house and pole in 1886.

many small brown holithurians, sea-eggs,[378] & star fish of common beach varieties.

Sept 17. Got round Cape Scott at 2 A.m. & at 7 A.m. not far from entrance to Quatsino, though some distance off coast. Steered in on recognising the opening, but wind dying away, & then coming ahead it occupied till 4.30 P.m. beating up into North Harbour. When anchor down, went ashore & examined rocks, delighted to find old friends in the "flaggy argillites". Hope now to find out more about their relations with other series. one Indian canoe came off to us, with a man, woman & small boy, but quite unversed in Chinook, & satisfactory communication impossible. A fine day, though probably blowing hard outside. A pretty glow of pink over the purple mountains at sunset.

Sept. 18. Early breakfast, & off in boat up Forward Inlet, examining rocks. Found a locality rich in fossils, of not very attractive appearance, but gathered a number. These belong to the Coal measures, of whatever age, which appear toward head of Inlet. Found Indian Village[379] & got an Indian as guide to the Coal locality, who could speak a little Chinook, but very little. On landing at the village find all the people collected in front of one of the houses & as I Came up all joined in repeated chorus of *Cla-hoya tyee & Klooshe*,[380] the two Chinook terms they seemed to understand. These they repeated over & over again together with much in their own language that I could not understand. They evidently very seldom see strangers & appeared in their manner quite as though apprehensive that I had all the power, & might want to use it, by which they might be anihilated in a moment. The women all have their heads deformed in the manner peculiar to this tribe, having been bandaged up in infancy so as to assume a comical Shape.[381] They appear all very poor, wretched, & dirty, & are about the most miserable & degraded looking Indians I have seen.

---

378. Sea urchins such as the green sea urchin, *S. droebachiensis.*

379. Dawson later noted: "they have also a second little village, of ruder construction, named Te-na-ate (from *ten-ne* meaning 'hone-stone,' and referring to the abundance of sandstone), on the north shore of the upper part of Forward Inlet (Winter Harbour). This may be classed a 'summer village' but is rather an 'autumn village,' in which they reside when the dog-tooth salmon is running up the small streams in its vicinity. The Indians were living here when I first visited the inlet in September, 1878" (Dawson, "Notes and Observations on the Kwakiool People of the Northern Part of Vancouver Island and Adjacent Coasts, Made during the Summer of 1885; with a Vocabulary of about Seven Hundred Words," *Proceedings and Transactions of the Royal Society of Canada* 5 [1887], sec. II, 68).

380. Or "Klahowya tyee," Chinook Jargon for "How do you do, chief," and "Kloshe," Chinook Jargon for "good."

381. The Quatsino and neighbouring Koskimo practised this type of artificial head deformation which led to their being called "roundheads," "longheads," or "sugarloafs."

Most of the men appeared to be away, allowing for these in proportion to the females there should be 35 or 40 people in all belonging to this village. On way back stopped to take a photo. of the natives,[382] but had endless difficulty in getting them to understand what was wanted, to go to the right place, & finally to sit still. The photo. if it turns out visible at all I fear will be a very poor one. Got some reason into them at last by offering them a biscuit all round if they would sit. Two men came down to the schooner afterwards for the biscuits. Found the coal without difficulty, thanks to our guide, had lunch on the spot, & examined it as carefully as possible. Got back to schooner near night fall, with plenty work to be attended to in the way of notes & specimens.

Sept ⟨20⟩ *19.* Off in good time with Charley & Indian Johnny in the boat. Morning dull, overcast, calm & rather foggy Examined north shore nearly to Hecate Cove, when Camped on a narrow & rocky gravelly beach, being overtaken by darkness. The schooner, which was to follow us as soon as possible, got out & having a fair wind got abreast of Camp about 9 P.m. Tooting the horn, under impression that fire might be ours, but did not answer, thinking best if schooner had wind that she should go on to Hecate Cove. Soon, however wind dying away, schooner drifted back with tide, & hearing them at work with the sweeps, I called out & schooner soon anchored in bight opposite Camp. Struck tent packed up & went on board. Visited by a Canoe full of Indians at Koprino Harbour. Most of the tribe now at mouth of river[383] there salmon fishing. The Indians a little forward, but appear good humoured & some of them Can talk good Chinook.

Sept. 20. Awakened this morning by the sound of paddling, then the rubbing of Canoes against the sides of the schooner, the clambering of Indians on deck, & the hub-bub of their talk as they Cooly proceeded to examine everything, & look down into the Cabin, quite blocking up the hatch with their heads. Men women & children. We are it seems only a short distance from the main village,[384] which situated on the E. side of Entrance to Hecate Cove of Chart, & boasts of about 15 houses. Not built in the Same substantial style as those of the Haidas, but large & roomy enough. The Indians here know very little Chinook & are quite unsofisticated. Schooners seldom come into this inlet, probably never so far up as we now are. What trading is done is at Fort Rupert, the trail leading across in about half a day. Went back on work this morning to

382. See "Photographs," 18 September 1878, GSC274–C2 (PA 38146).

383. Koprino River.

384. Quattishe or Koskimo, near the eastern end of the sound.

examine rocks passed over after dark. Then crossed to Limestone I.,[385] & on a small islet near it found some fossil corals, silicified, but in a poor state of preservation. Returned on board schooner, got specimens packed up & other preparations made, though much annoyed by the inquisitiveness & many wants of the Indians, who seem to like nothing better than roorting all over the schooner. One old woman especially troublesome. Knowing a little Chinook she presumed on this to come down into Cabin, had a great deal to say, & wanted to see everything.

Got off after lunch with Williams*, Charley, & an Indian guide, who knows how to row pretty well. Called in at Indian Village to let our gentleman get his pipe. Then rowed up through the narrows[386] & to Coal Harbour, where camped a little before dark, near a small camp of Indians. One of these[387] offered to show me some coal up a small Stream at the head of the harbour. Took me in his Canoe, the boat going on to Camp — & showed me some drift coal in the brook, & some also packed into a bouldery drift, but not *in situ*. Could speak very little Chinook, but his wife, who sat in the bow of the Canoe, & was rather pleasing in appearance but for the peculiarly elongated head, Caused him to employ all the Chinook he knew in asking in succession for every imaginable article, as a *Kultus potlatch* — fish-hooks, needles, thread, pipes, Soap, tobacco &c. &c. The man also requested me not to fire off my gun as it would frighten the salmon, which are now in great numbers in all parts of the inlet, & can be seen jumping whenever a breeze ripples the water. Also requested that we would not have fires on the beach at night, as this also would frighten away the fish! Could hardly comply with the last request, as our Camp on the shore, but made our fires as small as possible. Our guide is a peculiar looking indian, perhaps twenty years old, with a cross eye, a chinese complexion & expression, which is carried out by a pig-tail or que which he wears tied round his head, having given over Cutting his hair in the hope of becomming a "doctor"[388] His costume is simple, consisting (1) of an old woolen scarf bound turban fashion round his head (2) a cotton shirt, (3) half of an old & dirty blanket, originally white. This latter is either worn round the shoulders with a sharp piece of wood pinning it together in front, or bound skirt fashion so as to hang down from the waist. It also Serves as bed & bed covering at night, & as waterproof cloak during

385. Drake Island.

386. Quatsino Narrows.

387. This is Ka-a-let, whom Dawson met again on 20 August 1885.

388. Shamen did not cut their hair, allowing it to grow to great length, though frequently wearing it knotted.

showers. He is rather a dunder-headed individual, not fluent in Chinook, of which his pronunciation is bad. He is heavy on *Nowitka*,[389] but gives it as *Nowitti*. Willing enough to work, collects wood for fires, & appears from time to time in the night to stoke up, especially when it becomes so wet that he cannot sleep comfortably.

[verso]

Sea-otter food. Said by the Indians to consist chiefly of sea urchins, clams, & fish. The Sea-eggs — probably the large kind[390] — are eaten without breaking the shell. The clams are broken, & our guide at Quatsino told me a story, which I could not quite understand, about the otter carrying a "Stone" under his shoulder — below the arm — with which he breaks the Clams. This "stone" the otter does not loose when he dives, nor even when shot & killed. Some of the Indians he says have many of these stones, & if I understood him aright, the "stone" sinks in fresh, but floats in salt-water.

Kō-sk-mo[391] The name of the tribe & region, including the upper part of Quatsino Inlet[392] of the chart. The name is the same as that of these Indians for the Sal-lal bush.

Tobacco   the Koskimos use the roasted leaves of the Sal-lal to mix with tobacco, but also know the Arctostaphylos & would probably use it by preference where it could be found.[393]

Stone-hammer. Found one of the dumb-bell shaped one in actual use among the Koskimo Indians.[*Illus.*][394]

Yew Wedges.[395] Employed in splitting up dead wood for fire-wood, & apparently very effective, especially when applied to half-decayed dry

---

389. Chinook Jargon for "yes."

390. Probably the giant red sea urchin, *S. franciscanus*.

391. According to Dawson, the Koskimo "are still somewhat numerous, and their principal village, which is large and well built, is situated on the point between Hecate Cove and Quatsino Narrows, in Quatsino Sound. They are physically much superior to the Kwa-tsi-no, and better off in every respect. The village is named Hwat-es. A second or 'summer village' is situated on the south side of the Sound, nearly opposite Koprino Harbour, and is named Ma-ate" (Dawson, "Notes on the Kwakiool," 69).

392. Quatsino Sound.

393. Dawson was correct in stating that kinnikinnick, *A. uva-ursi*, was mixed with commercial tobacco. Salal, *G. shallon*, could also possibly have been used.

394. Actually a flat top stone hand maul, as illustrated in Stewart, *Artifacts of the Northwest*, 53.

395. "The heavy, close-grained wood of the yew is well known for its strength and durability. It was prized by all native peoples within the range of the tree" (Nancy J. Turner, *Plants in British Columbia: Indian Technology*, British Columbia Provincial Museum Handbook no. 38 [Victoria, 1979], 117).

Cedar which very often used by Indians. The head of the wedge bound round with withes to prevent it splitting or bushing out when being driven. [end verso]

Sept 21. The Indian camp astir at daybreak & all off in canoes to fish for salmon. This is now done by trolling with a bait. The streams are so low that the fish have not begun to run up them & the fish traps have so far been of no use. Examined Coal on W. side of harbour, & then proceeded westward with examination of Coast, Camping on North shore a few miles from head of arm.[396] Heavy showers & squalls of head wind render work today very unpleasant & irritating. See many Indians Camped about here & there, all at their salmon-fishing grounds. Hear some Indians on the water after dark, but cannot tell what they are about.

Sept. 22. Crossed this morning to S. side of inlet, & finding no more coal rocks, returned along S. shore, examining from point to point. Camped on N. shore a little East of Hankin Pt. of Chart, near a nice little stream, & in the vicinity of plenty good fire-wood, which a desideratum, as we are all wet from the frequent heavy showers.

Sept. 23. Examined coal-rocks which occupy part of north shore of Rupert arm,[397] went up the Creek at its N.E. angle[398] far enough to see beginning of trail to Fort Rupert. Skirted along S. shore, stopping at noon for lunch. Heavy shower & squall coming on, gave the weather a bad 'turn' & it continued raining with Short lucid intervals most of afternoon. Got back on board schooner at about 4 P.m. A lot of Indians immediately appeared with this that & the other to sell, or wanting pot-latches. Bought a couple of cedar mats, & took sketches of some of the deformed heads peculiar to this region. Evening writing up notes. &c.
[verso]

Sept. 23. Visited cave which on W. side of Quatsino Narrows of Chart, near their southern entrance, & only a short distance round point from Indian Village.[399] Cave 40 or 50 feet up a steep cliffy bank from water's edge. In limestone. A rather symetrical broal low entrance as seen from a distance. On entering, the floor at first slopes steeply outwards, but soon becomes more nearly level, & runs back for 35 or 40 feet. The average ⟨broad⟩ width of the cave about 20 feet & the height 8 feet. The roof is heavy with Stalactites, which are all however blunt, old-looking & dirty. Stalagmitic patches or bosses also appear in places on floor, but no sign of

396. Holberg Inlet.

397. Rupert Inlet.

398. Washlawlis Creek.

399. Dawson's Hwat-es, the principal winter village of the Koskimo (Dawson, "Notes on the Kwakiool," 69).

recent drip. The cave used as a burial vault by the Indians, but as I understand my guide none have been put here for a long time, & only men of
importance are accorded a place here.[400] My guide had never seen into the
Cave, & would not come up to look at it. In the innermost recess a mass of
rough boxes — Coffins — of various proportions, but all suited for doubling up the body in the usual Indian style. These made of split cedar
planks, & tied together with cedar bark ropes. Some on the ground, some
on top of these, & some shelved on boards supported by a plank or two.
On the left sid — on entering — several Similar boxes piled together, & on
the right, a few broad boards braced up against a nich probably holding a
single body. All the boxes look moderately ⟨fresh⟩ {new} & strong,
though in this dry place there is no reason why they might not remain so
for an indefinite period. Noticed one small square box probably holding
some property of the dead, & one large wooden dish of peculiar shape.
Something like this, & rudely Carved. [*Illus.*] At the mouth of the Cave a
few poles, to one of which is still attached a ⟨portion of⟩ piece of white
cotton cloth. If the last interment of same date with this, cannot be very
ancient, but not improbable that ornaments erected in honour of dead
here, long after death, as elsewhere practised.

The floor of the Cave, besides the stalagmite already mentioned, is
deeply covered with whitish dry earthy material, on which a few scattered
bones apparently giving evidence of interments still earlier than those
above mentioned. The Cave really a "rock shelter" & would be interesting
to explore with pick & shovel, though this must wait for some future day,
as at present the Indians would doubtless not only object, but forcibly
interfere with any such ⟨measure⟩ process.
[end verso]

Sept. 24. The stars in their courses seem to fight against progress. Had
hoped to get down to mouth of Inlet today, but for the first time Since our
coming here it has remained perfectly Calm, dull, overcast, & showery in
the afternoon. Sails up, but anchor never lifted. Reading &c. with as much
equinimity as the annoyance of the situation allows.

Sept. 25. Off with a good fair wind, which after we got out into the Main
Inlet became very strong. Travelled along at a good rate, with squalls &
showers of rain after us, but found on approaching the mouth of the Inlet
that it was blowing a regular gale from the South East with the barometer
still rapidly falling. Considering it scarcely prudent to go out, ran round

---

400. Burial caves among the Kwakiutl were fairly common. Their use seems to predate the
historical period, though not by much. The normal historical practice was to hang the
boxed remains from trees. Museum collectors raided the caves for skulls and artifacts.
J. A. Jacobsen raided one in the Quatsino vicinity in 1882, but he gives no precise location. See Jacobsen, *Alaska Voyage*, 28, 75.

into North Harbour, getting a lively tossing by the way from the heavy sea which was rolling in from outside, here broken up by reflexion from the rocky shores into steep chopping waves, several of which nearly Came on board. Anchored before noon & remained swinging about since, with heavy wind & showers. Visited by a couple of old Indians & several youngsters in a canoe. Had come down from the village[401] on seeing the schooner come in, bringing their Credentials ("papers") with them. Could speak scarcely any Chinook but *Potlatch Tyee! Clahoya*[402] Seemed amply repaid for their long paddle by a couple of pieces of tobacco Cut off a plug & one or two fish-hooks. P.M. reading, & writing up general note on B.C. Geology.[403]

Sept. 26. Blowing heavily with deluges of rain all night, a state of affairs which continued also the greater part of this morning. In the afternoon the wind moderated, going round to the S.W., & rain did not fall so continuously. A heavy sea still running, however, & the barometer going down. Went up Browning Creek[404] of the map, examining the rocks. Read a little, but have a headache & do not feel particularly well.

Sept. 27. Got away this morning as soon as a little wind came to fill the sails, & found a good S.W. breeze outside, which enabled us to beat out easily. Off Entrance Pt.[405] at 1. P.m. Pm. wind variable & light, made little headway, though much rolling, a heavy sea coming in apparently with wind behind it. Sabiston* wanted to run back into North Hr, & actually turned to do so, but a light wind coming off shore, turned again & kept on our course.

Sept. 28. Morning very fine, light variable winds, but aided by tide made some progress. Afternoon clouded, & then, following a slight fall of barometer — which already low — a South westerly, backing round to South easterly, wind began to blow quite fresh. Made good time, Notwithstanding a very heavy sea rolling in from the westward. Rounded Cape Scott at 4.30, & hauled up along the North Shore, for Goletas Channel. Barometer going down & wind continually freshening, till eventually blowing half a gale, & obliged to take in the fore sail. Weather dark & thick & all appearance of a regular South-easter, which, had it come strong enough might have blown us offshore altogether. Aided by a strong

---

401. Quatsino on Forward Inlet.

402. "Potlatch Tyee," Chinook Jargon for "give chief," and "Cluhoya" or "Klahowya," meaning "How do you do?"

403. George M. Dawson, "Sketch of the Geology of British Columbia," *Geological Magazine*, n.s., decade II, 8 (1881): 156–62, 214–27.

404. Browning Inlet.

405. Probably Cape Parkins.

tide however beat in a few tacks into the Channel, coming through a heavy tide-rip on the bar. Made out entrance to Bull Hr, ran in & anchored at Midnight. Found another schooner, the Kate, here, going to Skeena with coals.

Sept. 29. Blowing a gale all night & morning, but Calming down considerably, with signs of Clearing weather, & a rising barometer, about noon. Wind dead ahead for us, however, & the Ebb tide running all the afternoon so that useless to go out. Working at map, reading & writing. P.m. went in boat to examine rocks about harbour, & also crossed the narrow neck of land at head of Hr — about 300 feet — to Roller bay on the exposed outer coast. The crossing a difficult one as the underbrush consisted of a tangled & extremely dense growth of sal-lal, crab-apple &c. from six to twelve feet high. On gaining the coast however well rewarded for trouble in finding a magnificent sea falling in against the upper, or steeply shelving portion of a shingle beach. The simultaneous advance, rise, & tumultuous break of the great blue seas, as they arched up, fringed with little rainbows as their edges became fretted & misty, truly grand. The impressive Sound of the Stones & pebbles along the whole beach roaring as the broken wave retired brought vividly before one the process of the destruction of continents, & the immense sum of work which must be performed by an agent like this eternally busy. The scene almost realized that of a dream of great waves breaking on a beach, which I remember once to have had. No explanation can be framed of the sentiments Called up by the display of such never ceasing force, Can only fall back on Tennyson's — Break Break Break on thy Cold grey stones oh sea, & I would that my heart could utter the thoughts which arise in me.[406]

The distant roar of the Surf on this island appears to Surround us on every side as we lie in this little land-locked harbour in the still night.

Sept. 30. Ran out this morning intending to beat eastward with the flood tide, but, though Calm enough in harbour, found a fierce South easter blowing outside. Obliged at once to take in foresail, & as no prospect of making anything beating against such a wind, ran back into Harbour. Reading & writing most of day.

Oct. 1. Blew hard from S.W. last night, but this morning moderate. Got away & with fair wind, & fine though Showery weather, anchored in Beaver Hr, opposite Fort Rupert before dark. Mr Hunt,[407] in charge here

---

406. Dawson is quoting the first lines of an untitled Tennyson poem. For the full text, see Christopher Ricks, ed., *The Poems of Tennyson* (London: Longmans, Green and Co., 1969), 602.

407. Robert Hunt (1828–93) came to Victoria from England in the spring of 1850. Hunt later worked for the Hudson's Bay Company at Fort Rupert and, when the company closed their post in 1885, he acquired the property. Hunt remained at Fort Rupert until his

for H.B. Co, came off in canoe with a bag of mail matter, very welcome, containing besides many papers, home letters with good news.

[verso]

Tribes of Indians speaking closely allied languages, & which may be grouped together under the name of the *Kwa-kuhl Nation.*[408]

Name of tribe	Present Chief	Country
Kō-sk-mo	Kwa-h-la	Greater part of Quatsino Inlet of Chart.
Kwat-zi-no	Ow-t	Forward Inlet
N-wittai	Kow-mād-a-Kwa	Hope &c.
	(or "Cheap")*	Islands & extreme North of Vancouver I.
Kwā-Kuhl	ō-ut	Fort Rupert
Nm-Kish	Kla-sho-ti-awl-ish	Nimpkish of Charts
Li-kwil-tah	Yai-ko-tl-is	Cape Mudge
(= Ukulta)	{or wa-mish}	
Mam-il-i-li-a-ka	Ni-kē-dzi	⟨Near Nimpkish (on mainland?)⟩
		{entrance to Knights Inlet}
Kla-wi-tsush	Hum-tzi-ti-kum-a	⟨near Alert Bay on Mainland⟩
		{Lower end of Clio Channel
		Turnour I.}

{also these villages}
Nuk-wul-tuh. Mouth of Seymour Inlet / Tsa-wulti-ē-nūh Wakeman Sd. Tan-uh-tuh Head of Knights Inlet / Met-ul-pai. Havanna Channel {Kwi-'ha on or near Valdez I.[409]
W-wē-kum. Inlet off Nodales Channel.}

Douglas fir. In coming from the north find this tree about the extremity of Vancouver I, though not in great abundance. About entrance to Quatsino Inlet, very few, but abundant, forming extensive groves on upper reaches of the Inlet. Similar distribution obtains, I believe, elsewhere along west coast of Island.

Indians living at Fort Rupert, or Calling it home probably do not exceed 200 in number, according to Messrs Hunt* (HB Co) & Rev.

death.

408. For Dawson's discussion of these tribes and a published list of tribes and localities see his "Notes on the Kwakiool," 65-75. Compare to the lists by Wilson Duff, *Indian History*, 21-22, and by Franz Boas, *Kwakiutl Ethnography*, ed. Helen Codere (Chicago: University of Chicago Press, 1966), 38-41.

409. Quadra Island.

Hall.[410] They appear to be a dirty, ugly, & degraded lot, not better than those of Koskimo, & infinitely worse looking than the Haidas, Chinseyans, or any of the Northern Indians we have seen

Coal. Indian reported to Mr Hunt*. (HB Co. Fort Rupert) that he found seam of coal about 2 feet thick on a river running into Hardy bay.[411] The locality can be reached in a long summer day when the river low. at present season (oct.) would take two days travel to reach the place. Indians says about as near Koskimo as here.

[end verso]

Oct. 2. Morning examined roucks about harbour, collected fossils &c. Afternoon took a couple of photos.[412] Had a talk with Mr Hunt*, & Mr Hall*, the latter a missionary here, but not yet well acquainted with the Indians of this locality. A fine day but some very heavy showers, Coming over from the westward. The "Otter" expected on way South at any moment, wrote note to Father, leaving it in charge of H.B.

G. M. Dawson to J. W. Dawson, 2 October 1878, Fort Rupert

I have to acknowledge several letters from you, & quite a *heap* of "Natures" &c. which I found waiting me here yesterday evening. This is the second mail I have got this season, & brings Montreal dates up to Aug 29! I found here also a letter from Rankine* at Victoria, announcing his safe arrival there & intended immmediate departure for Montreal. He is by this time I hope Safe at home & hard at work.[413] This note is written merely to announce my arrival here, & I shall leave it for the steamer Otter, which is daily expected, to pick up when she comes along.

I have been round at Quatsino Sound on the West Coast of V.I., & having had rather rough disagreeable weather, leading to much delay & lying at Anchor, am not sorry ⟨....⟩ to get back to the inside again.

---

410. Alfred James Hall (1853?–1918) was ordained in England in 1877 and shortly thereafter came to Metlakatla under the auspices of the Church Missionary Society. In 1878, he moved to Fort Rupert where he remained for two years before moving the mission to Alert Bay in 1880. For some thirty years Hall laboured there, establishing a residential school and sawmill. Hall also mastered the Indian language and in 1888 published his "A Grammar of the Kwakiutl Language," *Proceedings and Transactions of the Royal Society of Canada* 6 (1888), sec. II, 59–106. See also Barry M. Gough, "A Priest Versus the Potlatch: The Reverend Alfred James Hall and the Fort Rupert Kwakiutl, 1878–1880," *Journal of the Canadian Church Historical Society* 24 (1982): 75–89.

411. Quatse River.

412. See "Photographs," 2 October 1878, GSC275–C2 (PA 51117) and GSC276–C2 (PA 44336).

413. Rankine arrived in Montreal only the next day, 3 October 1878.

The weather now appears settled & likely to be fine for a while, though heavy & almost continuous rains *may* now set in almost any day. Tomorrow I hope to leave here, & after giving a day or two to the examination of the coast between here & Alert Bay, for the purpose of approximately defining the nature & area of the coal-basin,[414] shall make the best of my way to Comox, where I may have to stay a day or two to look at the Baynes Sound Coal Mine,[415] where they have got into some trouble with faults &c. After this Victoria, which *may* be reached in about ten days, with favourable winds, & should this happen I shall try to get things in train to leave Victoria by steamer Sailing on the 20th of this month. These are the plans for the conclusion of the summer's work.

I am anxious to get back as soon as possible to Montreal as the unfinished state of my last years report demands attention ⟨before⟩ to Avoid delay when the rest of the matter goes to press.[416]

Mr Selwyn* has not favoured me with a line ⟨since⟩ either on the Subject of the report printed before I left, or that which is to come. It is to be supposed he is very busy & probably regards me as beyond Mail Carriers.

Please congratulate William* for me on the success of his essay, & brilliant achievements at the Ecolle. I hope he may succeed in the Toronto Matter,[417] but feel that non-success should be no Cause of surprise, for notwithstanding Capability, he is very young for so responsible a post, where youth is a real disadvantage

Oct. 3. Up before daylight, breakfasted, & off early with Charley & Chimseyan Johnny in boat. Schooner to follow joining us if possible in McNeil Harbour.[418] Examined coast, landing at many places. Lunched at Su-quash & finally, no sign of schooner appearing, camped in McNeil Hr. A very fine warm bright day with light airs only. Several Indian canoes

---

414. Dawson was talking about the Suquash coal fields which were first worked by the Hudson's Bay Company in 1836. Later, in the early 1850's, these deposits were abandoned when the richer finds around Nanaimo became known. See Dawson's description of the Suquash coal in his "Report on a Geological Examination of the Northern Part of Vancouver Island and Adjacent Coasts," in Geological Survey of Canada, *Annual Report, 1886*, n.s., 2 (1887), Report B, 62-70.

415. See below, 13 October 1878.

416. Dawson's report for the 1876 season, "Report on Explorations," which was printed in 1878.

417. Dawson's brother, William Bell, had just returned from completing his course at Paris's Ecole de Ponts et Chaussées. The essay is unidentifiable. He was now seeking a position at the University of Toronto for which he was not successful.

418. Port McNeill.

passed us during day. Saw also a couple of whites in a boat, fishing salmon with seine for West Huston*. They Caught in one haul today about 100 fish. Got a good fire going & find our camp a comfortable one, though weather chilly.

Oct. 4. Off in good time, intending to Coast the South eastern part of Malcolm Island, & then return to Alert Bay to Meet schooner. Found a strong head wind blowing. Ran across to Haddington I. with sail. While examining rocks there saw a young deer on beach, but before rifle obtained it had walked quietly into the woods. Followed it, & catching sight had a shot at it at some distance & in a rather dark place. Missed, as the deer ran away. Followed it again & saw it once more but "on the jump". Ran across from Haddington to Malcolm I. but find wind so strong that Could not proceed along shore against it. Waited remainder of day behind a point, reading several "Witnesses" & dodging the very pungent smoke of a fire, which blew "every-way. Seeing the schooner beating up, made sail & ran down to her. Beat into Alert bay in rain & squally wind, anchoring at 8.30 P.m.

Oct. 5. Morning Calm. Went in boat to visit bluff at entrance to bay, which turned out to be, not sandstone, but grey well strat. clay. Went through the Indian houses, which built in the style sketched on a former page,[419] not So elaborate as the old Haida style. Some of the ridge-poles, however of great size, & the houses also large, several families (related) occupying the different corners.[420] Saw some very large wooden dishes,[421] not unlike those sketched in old Haida house at North Island, but deeper in proportion. Other wooden dishes of various shapes, [*illus.*] not precisely like those of Haidas, but similar. The commonest form here & at Quatsino appears to be this [*illus.*] cut from solid block. Saw two large dishes cut from solid, & standing nearly 2 feet high, in this design, the figures

---

419. See 15 September 1878.

420. Dawson further elaborates: "the houses are generally large, and are used as dwelling places by two or more families, each occupying a corner, which is closed in by temporary partitions of split cedar planks, six or eight feet in height, or by a screen of cloth on one or two sides. Each family has, as a rule, its own fire, with cedar planks laid down near it to sit and sleep on. . . . The household effects and property of the inmates are piled up round the walls, or stowed away in little cupboard-like partitioned spaces at the sides or back of the house. Above the fire belonging to each family is generally a frame of poles or slips of cedar, upon which clothes may be hung to dry, and dried fish or dried clams are stored in the smoke" (Dawson, "Notes on the Kwakiool," 75).

421. The "commonest form" of wooden dish was a canoe-shaped feast dish, indeed a common form. See Audrey Hawthorn, *Kwakiutl Art* (Seattle: University of Washington Press, 1979), fig. 335, 182. The dish with "indians clasping the vessel" was a bowl grasped by two human figures, also a fairly common form. The "large spoon" is more unusual. It is a ladle bearing a frog caught in the mouth of a bird, usually thought to be a kingfisher, and is a motif most commonly associated with the raven rattle.

representing indians clasping the vessel. [*Illus.*] Another about 4′ long was like a large spoon, the end of the handle bent round, & forming a bird's head, which holds a frog (looking also toward the bowl) in its beak. [*Illus.*] Singing going on early this morning, in connection with a potlatch, given by one of the chiefs. Went afterwards into the house, & saw the gentleman counting over & arranging the distribution of blankets in the presence of several of the elders of the tribe. A number of young women employed kneading up dough for bread, which doubtless to form a part of the giving away, which was to be continued, with dancing, in the evening. The song of these people almost exactly in tune (?) & intonation like that heard among the Haidas during a dance.

Westerly wind springing up at noon, got away & made some progress before it died away toward sundown.

Oct. 6. A wasted day. Floated about becalmed in the channel, & eventually carried back beyond our morning position. Anchored in a small cove. Shot a couple of ducks as they swam round the schooner. Heavy rain, which came down as snow not very far up, & when the clouds lifted saw snow on the trees less than 2000′ above us on the mountains

Oct. 7. Got away with morning tide, little wind till noon, then light fair wind [in?] Sundown. Then nearly calm. Made some progress, being now opposite entrance to Havanna Channel. Reading & writing.

Oct. 8. Made with the flood, but against a strong head wind, as far as the west end of Thurlow Island. Got into a little bay[422] there, & remained all night.

Reading & writing, though with such slow progress almost too much anoyed to settle down to anything solid

Oct 9. Off with the flood, & beating up as far as Pender Islands,[423] against an easterly wind. The ebb setting in, the wind fell, & after some trouble we manage to get to an anchorage nearly opposite the islands.

Oct. 10. Anchored this morning for a few hours, during the ebb, & got off again with the flood, a strong south easterly wind blowing up the passage, & raising a tumbling sea. Beat down to Plumper bay, anchoring about 2 P.m., there being too much wind & tide to go through the narrows.[424] Evg. cleared, & became fine & calm. Reading & writing.

Oct. 11. Off about 10 A.m. before the ebb had quite finished running, & got through the narrows almost at slack water. Beat down the passage[425]

---

422. Vere Cove.

423. Walkem Islands.

424. Seymour Narrows.

425. Discovery Passage.

to Cape Mudge against a S.E. wind, which left us, off the cape, to be tumbled about Some hours in a tide rip. Now (7 P.m.) a light N.W. wind pushing us along gaily. A fine bright night.

Arbutus   Saw the first of these trees on the rocks in the narrows. Saw a deer in the woods, at the narrows, but before the rifle could be got, it went off, quietly concealing itself.

Oct. 12. A head wind this morning, but beat down to Harwood Island, which I wished to visit in conformity with request from Mr Sproat* for information on it & neighbouring islands. Went off in boat, coasting the west shore. Examined banks of fine strat. sand, & procured sample of soil. Ran across to Comox with a good breeze, tying up at the wharf about 4 P.m. Found no letters, but got hold of a couple of papers with news to Oct. 2., from Victoria. Reading & writing note on islands for Mr Sproat*.

Oct. 13. All day occupied in getting down to Baynes Sound Mine wharf, in Fanny Bay, a distance of ten miles. A fine day, but light variable winds. Called in on a Mr Watt,[426] who lives on Denman I., opposite the mine, & is in charge of it, now that all work suspended. Arrange with him to accompany me up to mine tomorrow, to show me the various localities. Glimpses of magnificent mountains, heavily snow clad through the lower range near the coast. These belong to a range marked as 6000 to 7000 feet on the chart, of which Mt Albert Edward is the northern summit. The lower tree-clad mountains already covered with some new snow, Watt* says now as far down as it came at any time last winter, which was a remarkably mild one.

Oct. 14. Off early & occupied most of day examining rocks along the railway & about the mines at Baynes Sd. On returning to the coast, took a couple of views[427] of the wharf, & then, there being a strong fair wind got away. Had expected that two days might be required here, but found one sufficient to see everything essential. A fine clear day, but chilly. No rain! Where the rail way to the mine follows parallel to the shore. A cutting has been made in the face of a narrow flat between it & the beach. Here for several hundred yards a great thickness of Indian shell heaps has been exposed. From 12 to 15 feet seen in some of excavations, without bottom being shown. Clams, oysters, (small) mussels, sea-eggs &c. form

---

426. An M. Watt is listed in the *Guide to B.C. for 1877–78*. The workings of the Baynes Sound Coal Company were located on the Tsable River, near Fanny Bay, almost three miles due west from the river's mouth. Organized in October 1875 and working in April 1876, the colliery employed fifty-five men during 1876. By 1 November 1876, some six hundred tons of coal had been produced, but the mine's lifespan was short and, with a falling market for coal in 1877, the company ceased production.

427. Only a single photograph remains. See "Photographs," 14 October 1878, GSC278–C2 (PA 51107).

alternating layers or are mixed together. Some layers Calcined, & many burnt stones scattered through the mass. Appears as though village must have been here, but very long ago, as forest trees several hundred years old grow on the upper layers.[428] More or less Earth mixed with the shells in some layers, & occasionally layers of Earth & gravel with few shells. At End nearest wharf the Shelly deposits are interlocked or "spliced" with the more usual clayey gravels. The explanation of this is that the Soil has been gradually washing down the Slope, in large quantities at certain times, & this has given the spurious appearance of true subaqueous stratification. The structure diagrammatically as below in front view, conjecturally as shown in Cross section — [*Illus.*]

Oct. 15. Got into Nanaimo early this morning. Went about a little business in the town, & then up to find Mr Bryden*, at the Coal mine. Waited long for Mr B, he being underground, but at last finding him, accompanied him to his house, & then walked out to Chase River mine[429] & spent a couple of hours underground examining it. Road back on the engine & returned to schooner, to find all hands but Charley missing. By the time that they were again collected breeze ahead & very light, put off departure till morning. Went up to Hospital to Call on Mr Landale[430] for information about Koskimo, but found him able to give very little. Reading &c. in evening. Had a call from Mr Sutton,[431] who lately carried on assaying in Victoria, now running saw mill at Cowitchin.[432]

Without counting extremes, Mr Bryden* estimates the Douglas Seam in Chase River Mine to range from 20′ to 2′ in thickness. Averages about 5′ of good coal. Scarcely any shaly partings here, though not so infrequent in old workings which on same seam.[433] Small films of calcite but no visible

---

428. Such middens were fairly common along coastal areas.

429. The New Douglas or Chase River Mine, operated from 1875 to 1886 by the Vancouver Coal Mining and Land Company.

430. John J. Landale (1836?-86) was a well-known civil and mining engineer. See his obituary in the *Nanaimo Free Press*, 9 January 1886.

431. William Sutton arrived in British Columbia in 1875 from Ontario, where he had been sheriff of Bruce County. With his three sons, Sutton built a sawmill in 1877 and carried on a considerable logging operation. He was granted a timber lease of 7,069 acres in the Lake Cowichan area in 1879. His enterprises did not prove successful, however, and he later sold the operations.

432. Actually at Genoa Bay on the north side of Cowichan Bay.

433. The "old workings" were the so-called Old Douglas Mine near the centre of the settlement of Nanaimo, first mined in 1852. For a map illustrating the Douglas seam and locations of the two workings, see J. E. Muller and M. E. Atchison, *Geology, History and Potential of Vancouver Island Coal Deposits*, Geological Survey of Canada Paper no. 70-53 (Ottawa: Information Canada, 1971), fig. 12. For a concise outline of the geology of the Douglas seam, see Charles H. Clapp, *Geology of the Nanaimo*

pyrites. Roof & floor of blackish shale, with coarse sandstone or rather fine conglomerate both above & below. The conglom. forms roof & floor without shale in the old mine. Seam locally variable, but with remarkable general, workable, constancy. Strike very variable & dips undulating causing adits to wind. Dips away first at moderate angle, (about 15 degrees say) then suddenly pitches down without break at ⟨300⟩° 30 or in places a little more then begins to flatten out again further down on dip. Slope now down over 400 yards. Very little water, that below the adit (over 300′ below to bottom of mine) being pumped out by force-pump near bottom of workings supplied with steam from Surface. Ventilation by furnace, at bottom of small shaft heightened above by chimney. Very little gass. No safety lamps used except on tours of inspection by *firemen*. Coal blasted out with powder. Several faults already determined in workings, but of Small throw & coal usually easily recovered. Hauling done by wire rope, drum, engine of 90 horse power steam from 4 long round-ended boilers. Roof & floor firm, & comparatively little timbering needed. Double drifts run in along strike, passage & airway, openings between at intervals, but all of those except a few filled up after passages go ahead of them. [Bards?] opened up to rise, & coal cut out in chambers. Pillars for most part taken away before chambers abandoned. Coal brought down to levels below by back balance, fulls hauling up empties. Mr Bryden* does not think any evidence of roots in clay below coal, & fossil plants not find in that above. Believes coal did not grow where now is, but unless so, almost impossible to account for its regularity & purity. [*Illus.*]

Oct. 16. A wet disagreeable morning, with strong head wind. Off at 9.30, reaching Dodd narrows just in time to get through with last of Ebb. Beating down all rest of day making fair progress. Now (9 P.m.) abreast Narrow island.[434] Reading, packing specimens, & writing.

Oct. 17. Made a considerable advance by steady beating during the night, against a strong head wind, being this morning nearly abreast the entrance to Saanich Inlet. Continued beating all day, the wind falling in the afternoon, & leaving up practically becalmed near Trial Island about dark. Drifted on with the ebb tide, however, & finally got a little air to push us into Victoria Harbour. Came up to the wharf from Laurel Pt, with the boat towing ahead. Made fast at 11 P.m. Taking my sponge brush & comb I landed & went up to Driard House, where find all awake. Not Sorry for the present to conclude the Chapter of my ⟨....⟩ marine experiences, Secure a good room & look with admiration on a bed with Clean sheets!

Map-Area, Geological Survey of Canada Memoir no. 51 (Ottawa: Government Printing Bureau, 1914), 110–14.

434. Wallace Island.

[Dawson's journal closed on 17 October and he reverted to his small notebook. While much is routine, the remainder of his stay in Victoria is sufficiently interesting to be reproduced.]

Victoria Oct. 18.

Got all stores specimens &c. out of schooner, having previously made arrangements to have them placed in one of H.B. stores or wharf. Settled accounts with Williams* Charley & Indian Johnny. Attended to various other matters of business. Evg. dined at Judge Greys,[435] Meeting a Dr & Mrs Hanington[436] there.

Oct. 19. To Muirheads to get carpenter send down to take flooring &c. out of schooner. Secured a number of empty boxes for specimens & had them sent down to store. Packing specimens all morning with Charley. Store closing at 1 P.m. — being Saturday — prevented work after lunch. Interviewed several people on mining &c. & took a turn in Chinese quarter to look for China. Dined at Judge Crease's*. A bleak wet stormy day.

Settled with Sabiston* today, & glad to get rid of him.

Oct. 20. Down to Schooner to get Sabiston* to sign a new receipt, the old one being defective. Dr Tolmie* arriving at 10 A.m. went with him to his house, & remained there conversing & working chiefly on Indian Vocabularies most of day. Dinner about 4 P.m. Drove back to Town before 6. Had a cup of tea & set to work on correspondence &c. A fine but cool day.

G. M. Dawson to J. W. Dawson, 20 October 1878, Victoria

I have now been in Victoria three days, having arrived at the wharf, in the "Wanderer" at about Eleven o'clock on Thursday Night. Everything is now out of the Schooner, & much of my stuff packed, men paid off &

---

435. John Hamilton Gray (1814–89) had been a prominent New Brunswick lawyer and politician before coming to British Columbia. A strong advocate of Confederation, Gray represented New Brunswick at the 1864 Charlottetown Conference and served in the House of Commons from 1867 to 1872. Then, realizing he had only a limited political future, Gray sought and obtained a puisne judgeship on the British Columbia Supreme Court in 1872. See "Gray, John Hamilton," *Dictionary of Canadian Biography*, 11: 372–76.

436. Ernest Barron Chandler Hanington (1851–1916) graduated from McGill Medical School in 1875 and acted as medical superintendent at the General Hospital in St. John, New Brunswick, before coming to British Columbia in 1878. On his arrival in the province, Hanington became medical officer to the labourers building the Canadian Pacific Railway in the lower Fraser River. He advanced to chief surgeon at Yale for the railway contractors before leaving in 1885 to enter private practice in Victoria. He had married Ida Tilley Peters of St. John in 1878. See his obituary in the *Victoria Times*, 11 May 1916.

affairs generally in progress towards an end. I shall not be able to leave by tomorrow's steamer, however, — by which this letter goes, — but have not yet decided whether to seek an intermediate boat at Portland, or wait for that of the 30th from this place. The latter date seems a long way off now, but I have a number of things to look after, when my Packing is done, which may detain me too long to allow me to ⟨....⟩ Save anything in time by going *via.* Portland. The latest date from Montreal is your letter of Sept 28th, in which you announce receipt of letters, among others one from Rankine* from Portland. R. has now no doubt been home some time.

The getting from Fort Rupert to this place has been a longer operation than I thought probable, owing to the prevailing South-easterly winds of this season. The weather is now very uncertain & beginning to be very wet, so that the conclusion of field work is not to be regretted.

The railway office has been moved over to New Westminster, & I was told last night that some mail matter is over there belonging to me. These may be letters which have been addressed to care of C.P. Ry, & account for Certain lacunae in home correspondence which appeared to be indicated by letters found here. I have to acknowledge a long letter from William*, but shall not attempt to answer it this time, as there is nothing in particular to write about.

Enclosed you will find a little bill, which reached me at Pt. Simpson, but which seems to be intended for you, as it is for extras of a Paper on Canadian Phosphates.[437]

When I decide on route, I Shall write again, but will not telegraph unless something of special importance turns up.

Oct. 21. Packing specimens &c. & making list of articles left. Removed boxes from room in Custom House to H.B. store. Saw Mr Fawcett[438] & Deans[439] on QCI anthracite. Evg. spent with Mr Woodcock* getting notes on Gold Hr & Omineca country. A steady downpour of cold rain nearly all day.

---

437. J. W. Dawson, "Note on the Phosphates of the Laurentian and Cambrian Rocks of Canada," *Quarterly Journal of the Geological Society of London* 32 (1876): 285–91.

438. Probably Edgar Fawcett (1847–1923) a pioneer who came to Victoria in 1859 and was employed by the customs office for many years. Fawcett wrote extensively about early life in Victoria and British Columbia and was widely acquainted with the region's development. See his *Some Reminiscences of Old Victoria* (Toronto: William Briggs, 1912).

439. James Deans (1827?–1905) had been assistant to James Richardson in his explorations of the Queen Charlotte Islands. Deans also explored for the Queen Charlotte Coal Company and became known as an ethnologist. In 1892, Deans organized a Haida exhibit at the Chicago World's Fair.

Oct. 22. Down to wharf to see about carpenter closing boxes. With Mr McKay* (H B Co) examining specimens. Looking over specimens & plans of Hows Sd Copper Mine[440] with Roscoe* & others. With Messrs Finlayson[441] & Heistermann[442] examining plans &c of Baynes Sd. Mine. At Lands & Works office looking for plans for map. Call at McDonalds* but find no one at home. Looking over plans of Skidegate Coal mine at Fawcetts*.

Oct. 23. At wharf to superintend carpenter closing & addressing boxes. At Lands & Works office getting trace of Okanagan & Spallumsheen region.

After lunch back to L & W office to look over maps & plans there. Find a number which it will be well to have traces of. Call at Judge Greys* & Governor Richards*, & stay to dinner with latter. A mail of papers this evg. from Montreal.

Oct. 24. At Lands & Works making tracings. P.m. with Dr Tolmie* & Haida Mills getting Haida vocabulary   Wrote Hunter* & Robson* on Survey from Duck* & Pringles to Grande Prairie. Authorized former if possible to get work done under $120 to proceed if he can find a surveyor. Asked Robson* for transport from C P Ry.

Evg writing to West Huson* & T.H. Huxley.[443]

440. "The copper deposit which has received most notice, is situated near the head of Salmon Arm of Jarvis Inlet and between that inlet and Howe Sound. This is owned by the Howe Copper Mining Company. The ore is chiefly Bornite or purple copper and the deposit is not far from the coast, but at an elevation of 3000 feet above sea-level. It was discovered about 1874, and was worked at intervals between the years 1877–83" (Dawson, "Mineral Wealth of B.C.," 102).

441. Probably Roderick Finlayson (1818–92) a pioneer Hudson's Bay Company man who came to the Pacific coast in 1839. In 1843, Finlayson supervised the construction of Fort Victoria, commanding the post until James Douglas took over in 1849. Appointed a chief factor in 1859, he supervised the Hudson's Bay Company operations in the British Columbia interior from 1862 until his retirement in 1872. Finlayson also served on the Vancouver Island Legislative Council from 1851 to 1863 and was mayor of Victoria in 1878.

442. Charles Henry Frederick Heisterman (1832–96) owned one of the largest and most profitable real estate businesses in British Columbia. Born in Bremen, Germany, Heisterman settled in England for some years before coming to British Columbia in 1862 and opening his business in 1864.

443. Thomas Henry Huxley (1825–95) was an eminent British natural scientist who had been one of Dawson's teachers at the Royal School of Mines. Best known as "Darwin's Bulldog," he was a renowned scholar and teacher, who wrote extensively in a wide variety of subjects from palaeontology to philosophy, lectured widely, and received numerous awards and distinctions. See *Dictionary of National Biography, Supplement*, s.v. "Huxley, Thomas Henry."

G. M. Dawson to Margaret Dawson*, 24 October 1878, Victoria

Your welcome letter of October 8th, reached me a couple of days ago, & I am glad to know under such late date that all are well at home, but sorry to hear that William* has been disappointed in the Toronto Affair, especially as so much trouble of one sort or another has been taken about it.

I have decided not to leave here till the regular boat sails next Wednesday, finding that by going *via* Portland a day or two sooner I cannot make sure of gaining anything, while by staying here I can get some tracings made in the Lands & Works office & look after other matters.

You ask me in your letter to telegraph on my arrival at Victoria, but as I had already been here some days when I received the letter, & a written notification of my arrival was on the road I thought I might dispense with the Ceremony. Once on the way I shall loose no time in getting to Montreal, & if in good luck may arrive about Novr. 11.

The weather is fine here now, but not really settled. It is begining to be cool, with occasional frosts at night, & all the old inhabitants foretell an early & severe winter —- for this place.

Rankines* description of Victoria contributed to the *Witness* has been reprinted in one of the papers here,[444] but owing to the signature & place from which he dates everyone attributes it to me, & wonders why I have been four years here & only found all that out now!

I may write again before leaving, though it is scarcely probable that letters later than this ⟨can⟩ will reach Montreal before I do.

Please forgive this Scrawl

Oct. 25. Up at 6 Am & down to Esquimalt with Capt Goudy[445] to see Bark Hazelhurst, which about to proceed to China with Chinese passengers, & freight. Breakfast on board & on return go out to Dr Tolmie's*. At work on Indian matters till 5 P.m. Drove back with Dr T.

Oct. 26. At Lands & Works office till after noon tracing maps. After lunch determined sextant index error. About town on various little matters

---

444. "The Pacific Province (From an Occasional Correspondent of the Witness)" appeared in the *Montreal Daily Witness*, 7 October 1878. Dated Queen Charlotte Island, 30 July, it was signed "D." The Victoria paper which reprinted it was probably *The Evening Standard*, of which no issues for October 1878 are extant.

445. Unidentifiable.

Dined at Duponts'* with Mr & Mrs Fellows*, Mr Burns[446] & Miss Martineau.[447]

Oct. 27. Going over things in hotel, packing & making list of what left. P.m. for a walk to Beacon Hill. Evening going over Indian matters & getting list of questions for Mills. Saw Capt. D.E. Sturt[448] of Texada Island Marble quarry.[449] He took me to see samples of the marble in a stone yard on Government Street. Says there is *coal on mainland* inside Texada Island. Sandstones extend about 9 miles along shore S.E. of the Indian Village. Coal seam a mile or so inland & where he saw it 1 foot thick burns well.

Oct. 28. Called on Archdeacon Wright,[450] having understood that he wished to ask about some Indian matters.

Booked for *Dakota* on Wednesday. Got boxes from H.B. taken down to wharf, consular certificates, Bills of lading &c. for them. Found box of specimens from Montreal in bonded warehouse. Paid bills & transacted various business about town. Met Dr Tolmie* after lunch to go over Haida vocabulary but Indian Mills did not turn up. Went down to Indian quarter to look for him, but unsuccessfully.

Met Mr. Fawcett* to discuss Q.C. Anthracite mine.

Evg. writing notes & letters wrote Bowman*, W Duncan* & Rev Mr Collison*.

reading.

Oct. 29. Paid for ticket to San Francisco. Paid various bills. Got boxes down to HB. store, & Blankets returned to C.P. room in Custom House Building. Called at Lands & Works Office. Lunched at McDonalds*. P.m.

446. Thomas J. Burnes (1832–1915) was a pioneer Victorian known throughout the community. Burnes came to the city in 1858 and for many years operated hotels in Victoria. He later left private business and worked in the customs office until his death. See his obituary in *Victoria Daily Colonist*, 21 December 1915.

447. Unidentifiable.

448. Captain D. E. Sturt (d. 1885) was a former British Army officer who had been stationed on the San Juan Islands during the dispute in the 1850's and 1860's with the United States over their ownership.

449. Two marble quarries were eventually opened, one near Vananda at the north end of the island and another at Anderson Bay near the southern tip. Neither proved viable operations and only limited development took place. See R. G. McConnell, *Texada Island, B.C.*, Geological Survey of Canada Memoir no. 58 (Ottawa: Government Printing Bureau, 1914), 96–97.

450. Henry Press Wright (1816–92) was a prominent Anglican clergyman who had been appointed the first archdeacon of the Diocese of Columbia in 1861. Wright resigned his post in 1880 and left North America after continued tension with Bishop Hills. See Donald H. Simpson, "Henry Press Wright: First Archdeacon of Columbia," *British Columbia Historical Quarterly* 19 (1955): 123–86.

Saw Dr Ash,[451] Spencer* on photos, & Dr. Tolmie*.

Dined with At Wards,[452] with Mr [Morglan].[453] Packed up everything. To bed at 12.

Oct. 30. Paid hotel bill Saw Hibben[454] on Reports. Left for Esquimalt in Bowmans buggy[455] at 10.30. Left in S.S. Dakota punctually at noon, passing inside Race Rock light, & abreast Cape Flattery about dark. Magnificent view of Mt. Baker & the serried peaks of the coast range. Clear sunny day, with beautiful glow at sunset on Cape Flattery & Vancouver shore. A slim passenger list & plenty of room everywhere.

[Dawson arrived in San Francisco on the morning of 2 November and departed on the Central Pacific Railway the next day, changing at Council Bluffs for Chicago. Travelling over Detroit, Stratford, and Toronto, he reached Montreal on 10 November 1878.]

451. John Ash (1821?–86) obtained his medical training at Guy's Hospital in London, then practised in England for some years before immigrating to Victoria in 1862. In 1865, Ash was elected to the Vancouver Island House of Assembly and after federation with the mainland was member for Comox until 1882. From 1872 to 1876, Ash was provincial secretary; in 1874 he was appointed the first British Columbia minister of mines. See "Ash, John," *Dictionary of Canadian Biography*, 11: 32–33.

452. Possibly William C. Ward (d. 1922), an eminent member of Victoria's business elite. The manager of the Bank of British Columbia, Ward had been in Victoria since 1864 when he emigrated from England.

453. Unidentifiable.

454. T. N. Hibben & Company was a respected Victoria bookseller and stationary firm, founded by Thomas Napier Hibben in 1858.

455. W. G. Bowman, husband of Sarah Bowman with whom Dawson roomed in the winter of 1875–76, operated a livery stable on Yates Street.

Photographs, 1876–1878

Dawson began field photography in his 1876 season. He used the recently developed dry-plate method which dispensed with the darkroom tent and chest of chemicals previously required for wet-plate field photography. Otherwise little is known of his apparatus.

The following inventory is compiled from catalogue records and from Dawson's lists in his Field Notebooks. Aperture and exposure data, when given, comes from these sources. Dates in square brackets are presumptions from the Field Journal text. GSC numbers are those assigned to the photographs by the Geological Survey of Canada, now superseded by the numbers in parenthesis, which are catalogue numbers assigned by the Public Archives of Canada, National Photography Collection, which holds the collection.

2 July 1876.
Upper Fall Iltasyuko River. GSC132–C1 (PA 51037).

9 July 1876.
Tanya Lakes.[1] [Dawson took four views from near his camp, but only one remains.] GSC133–C1 (PA 37532).

1. Photo-lithographed as "Looking Down Taryabunket Lake," in Dawson, "Report on Explorations in British Columbia, Chiefly in the Basins of the Blackwater, Salmon, and Nechacco Rivers, and on François Lake," in Geological Survey of Canada, *Report of Progress for 1876–77* (1878), opp. 30.

22 July 1876.
Northeast Peaks of Ilgachuz Range.[2] [Dawson took another view but the photograph does not remain.] small stop. 2.5 min. GSC136–C1 (PA 37548).

25 July 1876.
Gatcho Lake and Culla Culla House with Dawson's Camp. small stop. 2.5 min. GSC138–C1, negative missing print in Album Box P–2080. (PA 52370).

3 August 1876.
Looking North from Sinter Knoll Headwaters of Nechako River. GSC139–C1 (PA 51038).

[13] August 1876.
Entiako River turning into Canyon below Entiako Lake. smallest stop. 8.5 min. GSC140–C1 (PA 152387).

[17] August 1876.
Canyon on Entiako River near Fawnie Dome.[3] smallest stop but 1. 8.5 min. GSC141–C1 (PA 37547).

18 August 1876.
Fawnie Dome from the Northeast.[4] GSC142–C1 (PA 37546).

22 August 1876.
Looking North down Nechako River Canyon south of Fort Fraser.[5] GSC143–C1 (PA 37545).

1 September 1876.
Nechako River near Fort Fraser, looking Southward.[6] GSC144–C1 (PA 37544).

10 September 1876.
François Lake looking East. largest stop but 1. 7 min. GSC147–C1 (PA 51051).

2. Photo-lithographed as "Looking across Worn Terrace-Flat at Elevation of 5,200 Feet, Toward Higher Peaks of Il-ga-chuz Range," "Report," *1876–77*, opp. 38.

3. Photo-lithographed as "Canon on Kes-La-Chick, Near Tout-i-ai Mountain (Cliffs of Purple Ash and Agglomerate Rocks)," "Report," *1876–77*, opp. 70.

4. Photo-lithographed as "Toot-i-ai or Fawnie's Mt. from Hills near East End Na-Tal-Kuz Lake," "Report," *1876–77*, opp. 40.

5. Photo-lithographed as "Rapid on Upper Nechacco, South of Fort Fraser (Tertiary Igneous and Sedimentary Rocks)," "Report," *1876–77*, opp. 44.

6. Photo-lithographed as "View at Fort Fraser Crossing of Nechacco River," "Report," *1876–77*, opp. 46.

12 September 1876.
Looking up Nadina River, Head of François Lake. smallest stop. 7.5 min. GSC148–C1 (PA 51050).

28 September 1876 [in Journal as 29th]
Fort Fraser and Fraser Lake. smallest stop but 1. 8 min. GSC145–C1 (PA 51053).

28 September 1876 [in Journal as 29th]
Fraser Lake Looking West. smallest stop but 1. 8 min. GSC146–C1 (PA 51052).

5 October 1876.
Gravel Bank Nechako River below Mouth of Chilako. smallest stop. 8 min. GSC149–C1 (PA 51049).

6 October 1876.
Junction Fraser and Nechako rivers at Fort George. smallest stop but one. 6.5 min. GSC150–C1 (PA 38066 and PA 51048).

6 October 1876.
Fort George and Indian Village. smallest stop but one. 6 min. GSC151–C1 (PA 51047).

[16] October 1876.
Terraces, Blackwater River near Depot. smallest stop but one. 8.75 min. GSC152–C1 (PA 51046).

[16] October 1876.
Terraces, Blackwater River near Depot. smallest stop. 10 min. GSC154–C1 (PA 801278).

[16] October 1876.
Terraces, Blackwater River near Depot. smallest stop but one. 8.5 min. GSC153–C1 (PA 51045).

[29] May 1877.
Between Stump and Nicola lakes Looking South to Nicola. stop no. 2. 7 min. (poor exposure resulted in subsequent overdrawing) GSC155–C1 (PA 152394).

[31] May 1877.
Limestone Outcrop, Hamilton Creek, Nicola Valley. stop no. 4. 7 min. (poor exposure resulted in subsequent overdrawing) GSC156–C1 (PA 152388).

31 May 1877.
Mountain in Angle of Nicola Lake North Side. stop no. 4. 7 min. GSC157–C1 (PA 51044).

31 May 1877.
View up Nicola Lake from Knoll in Hamilton Valley. stop no. 3. 7 min. (light poor). (poor exposure resulted in subsequent overdrawing) GSC158–C1 (PA 152389).

1 June 1877.
Looking down Nicola Valley from South Side of Bridge at Foot of Nicola Lake. stop no. 3. 5.5 min. (poor exposure resulted in subsequent overdrawing) GSC159–C1 (PA 152390).

2 June 1877.
Looking down the Nicola Valley. stop no. 4. 6 min. GSC160–C1 (PA 51043).

7 June 1877.
Looking up Coldwater Valley from Bridge at 48 Mile Point. stop no. 3. 7 min. GSC161–C1 (PA 152391).

9 June 1877.
Looking up Coquihalla River from near Mouth of West Branch.[7] stop no. 3. 6 min. GSC162–C1 (PA 37543).

[11] June 1877.
Silver Peak and Fraser River from Hope. stop no. 4. 6.5 min. GSC163–C1 (PA 51042).

[11] June 1877.
Fraser River and Mountains West of Silver Peak from Hope. stop no. 6. 12 min. GSC164–C1 (PA 51041).

16 June 1877.
Summit of Cascade Range on Hope-Similkameen Trail. stop no. 3. 6.25 min. GSC165–C1 (PA 51040).

16 June 1877.
Summit of Cascade Range on Hope-Similkameen Trail. stop no. 3. 6.25 min. GSC166–C1 (PA 51039).

7.   Photo-lithographed as "View in the Coquihalla Valley, Coast Range," Dawson, "Preliminary Report on the Physical and Geological Features of the Southern Portion of the Interior of British Columbia," in Geological Survey of Canada, *Report of Progress for 1877–78* (1879), opp. 40.

[*20*] *June 1877.*
Looking down Similkameen Valley. stop no. 4. 6 min. (poor exposure resulted in subsequent overdrawing) GSC167–C1 (PA 152392).

[*22*] *June 1877.*
Stratified Mountain from West Side of Hedley Creek. stop no. 4. 8 min. GSC168–C1 (PA 152393).

[*22*] *June 1877*
Striped Mountain East Side of Hedley Creek. stop no. 5. 10 min. GSC169–C1 (PA 51073).

[*22*] *June 1877*
Looking down Similkameen Valley from Same Point. stop no. 4. 6.5 min. (poor exposure of mountains resulted in some subsequent overdrawing) GSC170–C1 (PA 801500).

[*25*] *June 1877.*
Looking down Similkameen Valley below Keremeos. stop no. 4. 9 min. (poor exposure resulted in subsequent overdrawing) GSC171–C1 (PA 801501).

[*26 or 27*] *June 1877.*
Osoyoos Lake from Bench above Bridge. stop no. 4. 6 min. GSC172–C1 (PA 50176).

[*26 or 27*] *June 1877.*
Osoyoos Lake from Same Point. GSC173–C1 (PA 51075).

1 July 1877.
Looking up Okanagan Lake from East Side near Lower End. stop no. 5. 6.75 min. GSC174–C1 (PA 51074).

1 July 1877.
Bluffs of White Silt, Lower End of Okanagan Lake. stop no. 5. 7 min. GSC175–C1 (PA 51066).

6 July 1877.
"The Railway," Kalamalka Lake looking North. stop no. 4. 6 min. GSC176–C1 (PA 51065).

7 July 1877.
Looking East up Coldstream Valley from Boulder Hill. stop no. 4. 8.75 min. (damaged) GSC177–C1 (PA 801502).

14 July 1877
Looking up Cherry Creek from Hill near Mines. GSC178–C1 (PA 152385).

14 July 1877.
Looking up Monashee Creek from Same Point. stop no. 3. 9 min. GSC179–C1 (PA 51064).

17 July 1877.
Camels Hump. stop no. 4. 8.75 min. GSC180–C1 (PA 801503).

20 July 1877.
Westwold [Grand Prairie] from Ingram's. stop no. 4. 6.5 min. GSC181–C1 (PA 51063).

23 July 1877.
Looking up North Thompson River from Kamloops. stop no. 4. 5 min. GSC182–C1 (PA 51062).

23 July 1877.
Looking up South Thompson River from Kamloops. same stop & exposure as 182. GSC183–C1 (PA 51061).

27 July 1877.
South Shore & Part of Upper End of Little Shuswap Lake. stop no. 3. 6 min. GSC184–C1 (PA 51060).

29 July 1877.
Looking down to Outlet of Shuswap Lake. stop no. 4. 7 min. GSC185–C1 (PA 51059).

2 August 1877.
Head of Seymour Arm, Shuswap Lake from Seymour. stop no. 4. 7 min. GSC186–C1 (PA 51058).

2 August 1877.
Looking down Seymour Arm Shuswap Lake from Same Point. stop no. 4. 7 min. GSC187–C1 (PA 51057).

7 August 1877.
Looking up Mara Lake from Mouth of Shuswap River. stop no. 3. 6 min. GSC188–C1 (PA 51056).

8 August 1877.
Looking North up Middle Division of Shuswap Lake. stop no. 3. 6 min. (some

damage) GSC189–C1 (PA 51055).

9–10 August 1877.
Looking up Middle Division of Shuswap Lake. stop no. 4. 15 min. (poor print) GSC190–C1 (PA 152386).

10 August 1877.
Looking up Southwest Arm, Shuswap Lake. stop no. 2. 6 min. (poor print) GSC191–C1 (PA 152379).

26 August 1877.
White Silts at Mouth of Cherry Creek, Kamloops Lake. stop no. 4. 6.25 min. GSC192–C1 (PA 51054).

[27] August 1877.
Lower End of Kamloops Lake at Savona. stop no. 4. 6.5 min. GSC193–C1 (PA 51068).

27 August 1877.
Looking up Kamloops Lake. stop no. 5. 9.5 min. GSC194–C1 (PA 51067).

28 August 1877.
Cherry Creek Bluff from across Kamloops Lake. stop no. 4. 9 min. GSC195–C1 (PA 51072).

[27] September 1877.
Looking down Ravine and across Fraser River. GSC196–C1 (PA 51071).

[28] September 1877.
Peaked Mountain above Fountain Looking West from Lytton. GSC197–C1 (PA 51070).

2 October 1877.
Marble Canyon Looking Eastward. GSC198–C1 (PA 51069).

3 October 1877.
Looking down Hat Creek from Mouth of Marble Canyon. stop no. 3. 6.5 min. GSC199–C1 (PA 51078).

3 October 1877.
Looking into Marble Canyon from East End. stop no. 4. 8.5 min. GSC200–C1 (PA 152380).

[4] October 1877
Limestone Cliff on the North Side of the East Entrance of Marble Canyon. stop no. 4. 8 min. GSC201–C1 (PA 152381).

14 October 1877.
Tufaceous Bluff with Dykes Traversing, Nicola River. stop no. 4. 8.25 min. GSC202–C1 (PA 51080).

[15] October 1877.
Tufaceous Sandstone, Nicola River near Smith's. stop no. 3. 10 min. GSC203–C1 (PA 51079).

[16?] October 1877.
Looking down Nicola Valley from Woodward's. stop no. 3. 9 min. GSC204–C1 (PA 51081).

[20] October 1877.
Typical Fan, Indian Reserve Kamloops. stop no. 4. 12 min. GSC205–C1 (PA 51082).

[20] October 1877.
Mount Paul with Typical Rock Slides from Peterson's near Kamloops. stop no. 4. 12 min. GSC206–C1 (PA 51083).

20 October 1877.
Kamloops, B.C. stop no. 4. 4 min. GSC207–C1 (PA 51086).

21 October 1877.
Kamloops, B.C. GSC208–C1 (PA 51085).

2 June 1878.
Alert Bay and Broughton Strait looking East. ? stop & exp. min. GSC221–C1 (PA 152382).

2 June 1878.
Broughton Strait Looking West, Haddington Island in Centre. 4.5 min. GSC222–C1 (PA 152384).

12 June 1878.
Looking across Houston Stewart Channel from Ellen Island to Mountains about Rose Harbour. stop no. 4. 5.5 min. GSC223–C1 (PA 51097).

12 June 1878.
Looking East down Houston Stewart Channel from Ellen Island. stop no. 4. 5.5

min. GSC224–C1 (PA 152383).

15 June 1878.
Looking up Rose Inlet from Houston Stewart Channel. stop no. 4. 4 min.
GSC225–C? (PA 51090).

26 June 1878.
Dolomite Narrows, Burnaby Strait. stop no. 3. 6 min. GSC226–C? (PA 51091).

28 June 1878.
View from Observation Point. stop no. 4. 4.5 min. GSC227–C2 (PA 152372).

28 June 1878.
View from Observation Point. stop no. 4. 5 min. GSC228–C2 (PA 152370).

29 June 1878.
Ramsay Island from North Shore of Burnaby Island near Section Cove. stop no. 4.
4 min. GSC229–C2 (PA 152371).

29 June 1878.
Looking South into Burnaby Strait from Same Point. stop no. 4. 4 min.
GSC230–C2 (PA 152362).

1 July 1878.
Tar Island and Part of Lyell Island from North Shore of Ramsay Island. stop no.
4. 4 min. GSC231–C2 (PA 51089).

1 July 1878.
Volcanic Agglomerate, North Shore of Ramsay Island. stop no. 4. 4.5 min.
GSC232–C2 (PA 152363).

[2] *July 1878.*
Looking into De la Beche Inlet from South End of Lyell Island. stop no. 5. 4.5
min. GSC233–C2 (PA 152364).

2 July 1878.
Granite Mountains, South Shore of Bigsby Inlet. stop no. 4. 7 min. GSC234–C2
(PA 152365).

4 July 1878.
Grassy Patch Beneath which Hotspring Rises, Hotspring Island. stop no. 5. 3.75
min. GSC235–C2 (PA 51103).

4 July 1878.
Looking up Juan Perez Sound from Hotspring Island. GSC236–C2 (PA 51099).

[*4*] *July 1878*
Echo Harbour Looking South. stop no. 4. 6 min. GSC237–C2 (PA 51100).

[*5?*] *July 1878.*
Mountain above Echo Harbour from Same Point. stop no. 4. 3.5 min. GSC238–C2 (PA 152366).

[*5?*] *July 1878.*
Mountain above Echo Harbour from Same Point. GSC239–C2 (PA 51101).

6 July 1878.
Looking across Crescent Inlet to Redtop Mountain. stop no. 5. 4.5 min. GSC240–C2 (PA 152367).

7 July 1878.
Mountains Above Head of Klunkwoi Bay from North Shore of Logan Inlet. stop no. 5. 4.5 min. GSC241–C2 (PA 51102).

9 July 1878.
Clue's Village or Tanu, Laskeek Bay. stop no. 4. 25 seconds. GSC242–C2 (PA 37753).

16 July 1878.
Cumshewa Indian Village.[8] stop no. 5. 4.5 min. GSC243–C2 (PA 37752).

16 July 1878.
Cumshewa Indian Village. stop no. 5. 5 min. GSC244–C2 (PA 38151).

16 July 1878.
Cumshewa Indian Village. stop no. 5. 4.5 min. GSC245–C2 (PA 38150).

16 July 1878.
Mountains on South Side of Cumshewa Inlet. GSC246–C2 (PA 51104).

17 July 1878.
Mountains on South Side of Cumshewa Inlet Near its Head. stop no. 4. 3.5 min. GSC247–C2 (PA 51105).

---

8.   Photo-lithographed as "Houses and Carved Posts, Cumshewa Village," Dawson, "Report on the Queen Charlotte Islands, British Columbia," in Geological Survey of Canada, *Report of Progress, 1878-79* (1880), opp. 116B.

18 July 1878.
Skedan Indian Village. stop no. 5. 4 to 5.75 min. GSC248–C2 (PA 37754).

18 July 1878.
Skedan Indian Village.[9] GSC249–C2 (PA 44329).

18 July 1878.
Skedan Indian Village. GSC250–C2 (PA 38148).

18 July 1878.
Skedan Indian Village.[10] GSC251–C2 (PA 38153).

23 July 1878.
Skidegate Inlet Looking out. stop no. 5. 4.5 min. GSC252–C2 (PA 51106).

26 July 1878.
Skidegate Indian Village. stop no. 5. 4 min. GSC253–C2 (PA 38152).

26 July 1878.
Skidegate Indian Village. stop no. 5. 4 min. GSC254–C2 (PA 37755).

26 July 1878.
Skidegate Indian Village.[11] stop no. 4. 13 seconds. GSC255–C2 (PA 37756).

9 August 1878.
Rose Point, Mouth of Hiellen River. stop no. 4. 4 min. GSC256–C2 (C 51370).

9 August 1878.
Basaltic Columns, Tow Hill. stop no. 4. 4 min. GSC257–C2 (C 51371).

[9?] August 1878
Basaltic Columns, Tow Hill. GSC258–C2 (C 51369).

10 August 1878.
Masset Indian Village. stop no. 5. 5.25 min. GSC259–C2 (PA 38149).

9. Photo-lithographed as "Houses and Carved Posts, Skedans Village," "Report," *1878–79*, opp. 146B.

10. Photo-lithographed as "Houses and Carved Posts, Skedans Village," "Report," *1878–79*, opp. 146B.

11. Photo-lithographed as "Houses, Carved Posts, and Canoes, Skidegate Village," "Report," *1878–79*, frontispiece.

18 August 1878.
Mission Buildings at Masset. stop no. 4. 5 min. GSC260–C2 (PA 44332).

18 August 1878.
Looking Up Masset Inlet from Indian Village. stop no. 4. 5 min. GSC261–C2 (PA 44327).

20 August 1878.
Looking into Naden Harbour, S33W to S8E. stop no. 4. 4 min. GSC262–C2 (C 51368).

20 August 1878.
Looking into Naden Harbour, S6W to S36E. GSC263–C2 (C 51372).

21 August 1878.
Kung Indian Village, Virago Sound. stop no. 4. 4.75 min. GSC264–C2 (PA 37757).

23 August 1878.
Group of Haida Indians, Including Chief Edenshaw, Second from Left, Standing. stop no. 3. 8 seconds. GSC265–C2 (PA 38154).

23 August 1878.
Edenshaw and Hoo-ya, Chiefs of Yats at Masset. same stop & exposure as 265. GSC266–C2 (PA 38147).

[24] August 1878.
Pillar Rock.[12] stop no. 4. 4.75 min. GSC267–C2 (PA 51118).

24 August 1878.
Dadans Indian Village, North Island. stop no. 4. 6 min. GSC268–C2 (PA 44326).

30 August 1878.
Port Simpson Village and Church. stop no. 4. 5 min. GSC269–C2 (PA 44333).

30 August 1878.
Port Simpson from Hill above Hudson's Bay Post. stop no. 4. 5 min. GSC270–C2 (PA 44334).

2 September 1878.
Metlakatla Church and Mission Buildings. stop no. 4. 6.5 min. GSC271–C2 (PA 44335).

---

12. Photo-lithographed as "Pillar Rock, Pillar Bay, Graham Island," "Report," *1878–79*, opp. 40B.

7 September 1878.
Looking up Grenville Channel from Yolk Point. stop no. 4. 4 min. GSC272–C2.

9 September 1878.
Looking North up Klemtu Passage. stop no. 14. 14 seconds. GSC273–C2.

18 September 1878.
Group of Quatsino Indians, Forward Inlet. stop no. 2. about 12 seconds. GSC274–C2 (PA 38146).

2 October 1878.
Glaciated Rocks and Indian Graves, Shell Island, Fort Rupert. stop no. 4. 7 min. GSC275–C2 (PA 51117).

2 October 1878.
Indian Village at Hudson's Bay Post, Fort Rupert. stop no. 4. 5.5. min. GSC276–C2 (PA 44336).

12 October 1878.
Comox Wharf. stop no. 4. 11 min. GSC277–C2 (PA 51108).

14 October 1878.
Baynes Sound Coal Company's Wharf. stop no. 4. 6.5 min. GSC278–C2 (PA 51107).

Biographical Directory

ALEXANDER, J.M.L., was junior chief trader with the Hudson's Bay Company at Fort Fraser.

ALLISON, John Fall (1825–97) was born in Leeds, England and came to British Columbia from California in 1858. After a short sojourn in Victoria, Allison pre-empted 160 acres at Princeton on the Similkameen River. By the mid 1870's, Allison had expanded his holdings enormously and moved his family to Sunnyside on the west side of Okanagan Lake.

ANDERSON, Alexander Caulfield (1814–84) came to the northwest coast during 1832 in service with the Hudson's Bay Company. Anderson retired from the company in 1854 then moved to Vancouver Island in 1858 to become collector of customs and postmaster at Victoria. Later, he served on the Indian Land Commission from 1876 to 1878 and acted as dominion inspector of fisheries from 1876. Anderson was a competent writer who authored numerous essays and pamphlets.

ANDERSON, Samuel (1839–81) served as chief astronomer to the British North American Boundary Commission.

ARMSTRONG, William J. (1826–1915) was minister of agriculture in the British Columbia government. Armstrong was an early New Westminster settler and merchant who represented that community for many years in the provincial assembly.

BANCROFT, Hubert Howe (1832–1918) was a prominent California publisher and historian interested in the history of the North American Pacific coast.

BARNARD, Francis Jones (1829–89). Born at Quebec City, Barnard travelled to the Fraser River goldfields, then, in 1861, established a mail service from Yale to Victoria, which became, after extending to the Cariboo, the British Columbia and Victoria Express Company and soon the major carrier of the mainland colony. became partners in the F. J. Barnard & Company; in 1880, the British Columbia Express Company was incorporated with his son Frank and brother-in-law George Sargison. He served in the Legislative Council of British Columbia from 1867 to 1870 and as a member of Parliament for Yale from 1879 to 1887.

BELL, H. P. was one of the engineers in charge with the CPRS.

BOSCOWITZ, Joseph (1835?-1923), a pioneer fur trader and entrepeneur who came to Victoria in 1862. Boscowitz organized the Alaska Commercial Company with headquarters in San Francisco to exploit the north Pacific seal trade but soon disposed of the company. Forming his own new firm, Boscowitz proved a severe trial to the purchasers of the Alaska Commercial Company. Boscowitz also owned his own steamship line and, from 1896 to 1912, the old Victoria Theatre.

BOWMAN, Amos (1839-94) began his career as a journalist before spending time with the California Geological Survey. After working with Dawson in 1876, Bowman surveyed and mapped the Cariboo gold fields under Geological Survey of Canada auspices. He later possessed considerable land holdings in the upper Fraser Valley.

BOWMAN, Sarah A. (d. 1900) kept a boarding house on Yates Street in Victoria. Her husband William Gile Bowman (d. 1903) owned a livery stable at Broad and View streets.

BRYDEN, John (1831-1915) was mines manager for the Vancouver Coal Mining and Land Company. Bryden disagreed with Mark Bate's lenient labour policies and management practices and later left the company to work for his father-in-law, Robert Dunsmuir. Rising to the position of managing partner in the Dunsmuir organization, Bryden became one of the wealthiest men in British Columbia.

BURGESS, Thomas Joseph Workman (1849-1926) had been first medical officer to the British North American Boundary Commission. Trained at the University of Toronto, Burgess later became lecturer at McGill and medical superintendent at the Montreal Protestant Hospital for the Insane.

CAMBIE, Henry John (1836-1928) was born in Ireland in 1836; he came to North America in 1852 and to British Columbia in 1874. Cambie was in charge of the Canadian Pacific Railway Surveys in British Columbia from 1876 to 1879 and superintended the Canadian Pacific Railway's construction in the province from 1880 to 1883, then became engineer in charge of its Western Division. He died in Vancouver in 1928.

CAMERON, Donald Roderick (1834-1921), of the Royal Artillery, who had married Sir Charles Tupper's daughter in 1869, was British commissioner on the boundary commission. He later was commandant of the Royal Military College in Kingston from 1888 to 1896, before returning to his native Scotland where he died.

CARRALL, Robert William Weir (1837-79) was a McGill M.D. who served in the American Civil War before coming to British Columbia in 1865. Carrall was an influential figure in British Columbia politics, both as a member of the Legislative Council in the 1860's and, along with J. S. Helmcken, as one of the delegates who negotiated British Columbia's entry into Confederation. In 1871, Carrall was appointed to the Canadian Senate and remained in that position until his death.

CHARTERS, Robert (1837-1904) was an early Nicola region settler.

CHASE, Whitfield (1820-96) was the first settler at the foot of Little Shuswap

Lake. Born in New York, he arrived in British Columbia in 1853, mined in the Cariboo, and worked at various jobs around Kamloops before settling at Shuswap Lake in 1865. Chase not only operated a sizeable ranch but also ran a store and hotel.

CHEAP or CHIP, Chief was a chief at Nuwitty.

COLLISON, William Henry (1847-1922), who was born in Ireland and attended the Church Missionary College at Islington, came to the northern British Columbia coast in 1873 to assist William Duncan. Arriving at Masset on the Queen Charlotte Islands in 1876, Collison later worked on the upper Skeena River with the Gitksan and was archdeacon of Metlakatla from 1891 until his retirement in 1921.

COTTRELL, John Austin lived at Moodyville.

CRAVEN, Elijah Richardson (1824-1908), a Presbyterian minister, was secretary of the trustees at Princeton College for almost fifty years.

CREASE, Sir Henry Pering Pellew Crease (1823-1905) came to British Columbia in 1858 and was joined by his wife and children in 1860. After being called to the bar in 1859, he became attorney general of British Columbia, a position he held from 1861 to 1866. In 1870 he was made a puisne judge. Crease played an important role in British Columbia's entry into Confederation, drafting the Terms of Union in 1870 and opening debate on the subject of Confederation.

CREASE (Lindley), Sarah (1826-1922) was the wife of Sir Henry Pering Pellew Crease, a prominent Victoria judge. On Dawson's visits to Victoria, he spent much time socializing with Mrs. Crease and her family.

DAWSON, Sir John William (1820-99), G. M. Dawson's father, was one of the most prominent figures in nineteenth-century Canadian intellectual and scientific life. After studies at Edinburgh University in the 1840's, Sir William was appointed Nova Scotia's first superintendent of education. Serving for three years, he resigned in 1853 when seeking a position at Edinburgh University. Though unsuccessful in that pursuit, Sir William was unexpectedly offered the principalship of McGill in 1855, a position he held for some forty years, until his retirement in 1893. Under his leadership, that institution emerged as a reputable centre for teaching and research. He was made a K.C.M.G. in 1884. Sir William was always active in a wide variety of intellectual activities. He published the standard text on the geology of the Maritime provinces in 1855, wrote countless other articles on geological and palaeontological topics, and produced several volumes exploring the relationship between religion and science. Throughout his career, Sir William was in the centre of intellectual controversy: a staunch theological conservative, he was embroiled in bitter debate by his denunciation of Darwin's evolutionary theories, and long after most of his geological contemporaries had abandoned the "floating ice" theory of glaciation, Sir William unswervingly held onto the concept.

DAWSON, Margaret Ann Young (Mercer) Dawson (1830-1913) was the youngest of four daughters born to a prominent Edinburgh family. Over the objections of her parents, Margaret married J. W. Dawson on 19 March 1847 and left her native Scotland for life in British North America. Although possessing a retiring nature, Margaret Dawson fulfilled admirably the arduous task of being a university principal's wife and a mother. Deeply religious, Margaret sought to inculcate Christian values and instill a Christian faith in all her children.

DAWSON, Rankine (1863–1913) was George Dawson's youngest brother. He graduated from McGill Medical School in 1882. After spending time as a medical officer for the Canadian Pacific Railway in Manitoba, he left for further training in London. For four years, Rankine acted as surgeon on liners of the P & O Company before settling in London. In 1896, he married Gloranna Coats and they had one child, Margaret Rita. Always prone to depression and instability, Rankine uprooted his family and moved back to Montreal. Never achieving a permanency there, they returned to London where Gloranna left Rankine. Depressed, estranged from his family, and separated from his Montreal relatives, Rankine died in a London nursing home.

DAWSON, William Bell (1854–1944), Dawson's younger brother, also became a prominent scientist though overshadowed for many years by George and his father. William graduated from McGill University in 1874 with his Bachelor of Arts, obtained a bachelor's degree in applied science the year after, then went to Paris to attend the prestigious Ecole des Ponts et Chaussées. Following a three-year course, William returned to Canada and, after unsuccessfully applying for several positions, went into private engineering practice. In 1882, he joined the Dominion Bridge Company as an engineer and stayed until 1884 when he took a position as assistant engineer for the Canadian Pacific Railway Company. William spent ten years designing bridges for the firm, and in 1884 he began what he considered his main professional undertaking: director of the Dominion Survey of Tides and Currents. For thirty years, until his retirement in 1924, he recorded and mapped tides and currents in the harbours and on the major steamship routes of the Canadian coasts. Upon retiring, he spent much energy writing articles and tracts proving the harmony of science with religion, a task not unlike that earlier done by his father. William married Florence Jane Mary Elliott (1864?–1945) and the couple had three sons and a daughter.

DODD, Martin D. was a hotel keeper who lived on the Gorge in Victoria.

DOUGLAS, Dawson's assistant in 1877, was actually Douglas McFarlane.

DOUGLAS, Abel (1841?–1908), a Veteran west coast mariner who captained the vessel used by James Richardson in his geological explorations. Douglas lived in Victoria until 1906, when he moved to Seattle.

DUCK, Jacob was an Englishman who came to British Columbia in 1863 to participate in the Cariboo gold rush but instead headed south to what is now Monte Creek, on the South Thompson River. Duck pre-empted land bordering the river and, with Alex Pringle, operated a well-known roadhouse.

DUNCAN, William (1832–1918) was a prominent Anglican lay missionary who established the Christian Indian village of Metlakatla in 1862, near the mouth of the Skeena River. Duncan took special care to encourage a variety of industries that would further the Indians' economic circumstances. Unfortunately, Duncan's efforts were later marred by bitter strife and, in 1887, he led a band of followers to Alaska to set up a new village.

DUNSMUIR, Robert (1825–89), British Columia's most famous and controversial mine owner, came to Vancouver Island in 1851 under contract as a miner for the Hudson's Bay Company. In 1869 he discovered coal at Wellington, near Nanaimo, and by 1871 had a mine operating. Dunsmuir's operations grew rapidly until their production exceeded that of the older Vancouver Coal Mining and Land Company. Dunsmuir was a ruthless man his mines were continually plagued with labour unrest.

DUPONT, Charles Thomas (1837-1923) was the collector of inland revenue in Victoria. Dupont, like many other British Columbians, was actively involved in the development and promotion of mining schemes.

EDENSHAW, or EDENSAW, Albert Edward (1810?-94) was one of the most prominant Haida of the nineteenth century. He was suspected of complicity in the 1852 plunder of the *Susan Sturgis* off Rose Point Spit. He established Kung in 1853 and Yats (Yatza) in 1875, both on the north shore of Graham Island, Queen Charlotte Islands, before settling in Masset in 1883.

ELLIS, Thomas (1844-1918) was a powerful south Okanagan rancher and land owner. Ellis landed in Victoria from Ireland in 1865 then travelled into the Okanagan Valley, settling at the south end of Okanagan Lake. Along with his friend, Andy McFarland, Ellis bought some land from the nearby Indian reserve then opened a trading post and store in 1866.

ENGELMANN, George (1809-84) was the ablest and best-known scientist in the Mississippi Valley for the fifty years of western American exploration and surveys. After receiving his M.D. from the University of Würzburg, Germany, in 1831, Engelmann came to St. Louis the following year. Even though practising medicine, Engelmann continued his botanical research and wrote several monographs that remain essential references. He was also instrumental in founding the Missouri Botanical Garden which attained an international reputation in systematic botany. Engelmann greatly furthered American botanical research by maintaining close contact with many western explorers and acting as a clearinghouse for their work.

EWEN, Alexander (1832- ?) was a partner in a New Westminster salmon cannery, variously incorporated as Alexander Logie & Company, Ewen & Company and, in the mid 1870's, as Ewen & Wise.

FAWCETT, Edgar (1847-1923), in Victoria since 1859, was employed by the customs office for many years. Fawcett wrote extensively about early life in Victoria and British Columbia and was widely acquainted with the region's development.

FELLOWS, Arthur and Alfred were partners in the Victoria hardware firm of Fellows and Roscoe.

FISHER, Andrew was deputy purveyor to the CPRS.

FISHER, William was a prominent New Westminster businessman who operated a dry goods, provisions, and wine store in partnership with Henry Holbrook.

FORTIER, Charles E. worked for the Hudson's Bay Company in the 1860's around Kamloops before settling up the North Thompson River, near the mouth of the Clearwater River. He was later drowned when the rope broke on the ferry at Savona, B.C.

FOSTER, Frederick William (1831-1915) came to British Columbia around 1860 to participate in the gold rush. Reaching Lillooet, Foster opened a store. When the Yale wagon road was constructed, he moved his business to Clinton then opened a branch at Ashcroft. Along with his mercantile activities, Foster also was a participant in mining ventures in the Clinton area.

GAMSBY, C. H. was an engineer in charge with the CPRS.

GLASSEY, John served as deputy purveyor for the CPRS and later operated a hotel in Ashcroft.

GOOD, Charles (1832–1910?) was both deputy minister of mines and deputy provincial secretary in the provincial government.

GRANT, G. R. was a clerk with the Geological Survey of Canada.

HALL, Alfred James (1853?–1918) was ordained in England in 1877 and shortly thereafter came to Metlakatla under the auspices of the Church Missionary Society. In 1878, he moved to Fort Rupert where he remained for two years before moving the mission to Alert Bay in 1880. For some thirty years Hall laboured there, establishing a residential school and sawmill. Hall also mastered the Indian language and in 1888 published his "A Grammar of the Kwakiutl Language," *Proceedings and Transactions of the Royal Society of Canada* 6 (1888), sec. II, 59–106.

HALL, Robert H. Hall was a Hudson's Bay Company clerk at Fort Simpson who had previously served at Stuart Lake.

HAMILTON, Gavin (1835–1909) was the Hudson's Bay Company factor at Fort St. James on Stuart Lake. Hamilton had arrived in Victoria in 1853 and entered the service of the Hudson's Bay Company at Fort Langley. After briefly leaving the company in 1857, Hamilton returned until 1879 when he retired and erected a sawmill and grist mill on the Cariboo Road.

HARRINGTON, Anna Lois (Dawson) (1851–1917), Dawson's oldest sister, was also his closest friend and confidant. Even after her marriage to Bernard Harrington in 1876, Anna continued to share an intimate and rich relationship with George. They corresponded regularly and George recurringly offered assistance to his sometimes beleaguered sister, who had nine children. Anna remained in Montreal for her entire adult life, eventually dying of a lung tumour.

HARRINGTON, Bernard James (1848–1907), who married Anna Dawson in 1876, was born at St. Andrews, Lower Canada, and educated at McGill and Yale universities. Harrington was appointed lecturer in mining and chemistry at McGill in 1871 and was on the staff there for thirty-six years. From 1872 to 1879 he also served with the Geological Survey of Canada. Along with a large number of scientific articles, Harrington wrote a biography of William Logan, the founder of the Geological Survey of Canada, *The Life of Sir William E. Logan* (Montreal: Dawson Brothers, 1883).

HARRIS, Dennis Reginald (1851–1932), a civil engineer, was employed by the CPRS.

HARVEY, Frank was a Kamloops packer.

HAYNES, John Carmichael (1831–88) emigrated from Ireland to British Columbia in 1858 and joined the British Columbia Police as a constable. In 1860, he became deputy collector of customs at Rock Creek then, in 1862, took charge of the district and moved to Osoyoos. Haynes grew to be a powerful regional figure; his duties included assistant gold commissioner and magistrate, county court judge and member of British Columbia's Legislative Council. Haynes also possessed major land holdings covering some twenty-two thousand acres.

HELMCKEN, Dr. John Sebastian (1824–1920) was one of Victoria's best-known residents. Helmcken arrived in the settlement in March 1850 and served as medical officer and later surgeon to the Hudson's Bay Company. Actively involved in politics, he was speaker of the Vancouver Island Assembly in the colonial period and, in 1870, was one of three delegates sent to Ottawa to negotiate British Columbia's entry into Confederation. Subsequently, Helmcken devoted himself to private medical practice and was instrumental in founding Victoria's hospital system.

HEYES, S. W. was an American who settled at Princeton in the 1860s and became a partner of John Fall Allison in a cattle ranching operation.

HIND, Henry Youle (1823–1908), while professor at the University of Toronto, was employed by the Canadian government as geologist on the Red River expedition of 1857 and the Assiniboine and Saskatchewan expeditions of 1858. He published his two-volume *Narrative of the Canadian Red River Expedition of 1857, and of the Assiniboine and Saskatchewan Exploring Expedition of 1858* (London: Longman, Green, Longman and Roberts) in 1860.

HOMFRAY, Robert (1824?–1902) was born in England and trained in engineering. After spending time in California, Homfray came to Victoria where he was a civil engineer.

HOOKER, Joseph Dalton (1817–1911) was one of the foremost botanists of the nineteenth century. Author of numerous papers and monographs, Hooker was director of the Royal Botanic Gardens, Kew, from 1865 to 1885. He made several noteworthy field expeditions, including a visit to western North America in 1871 with his friend, Asa Gray. Though publishing in a wide range of fields, Hooker's enduring interest was in taxonomy and plant geography.

HORETZKY, Charles George (1839–1900) was a photographer with the CPRS. Though a competent photographer who took many invaluable photographs of British Columbia topography, Horetzky was extremely difficult to work with and fought constantly with his associates.

HUGHES, Josias Charles (1843–86), a native Upper Canadian, came to British Columbia in 1862 and settled in Moodyville when S. P. Moody bought the sawmill. After being in charge of clerical duties there, Hughes moved to New Westminster where he became provincial government agent. Before his premature death, Hughes also served in the British Columbia legislature and worked as a real estate broker and Indian agent at Metlakatla.

HUMPHREYS, Thomas Basil (1840–90) was finance minister in the provincial government of A. C. Elliott.

HUNT, Robert (1828–93) came to Victoria from England in the spring of 1850. Hunt later worked for the Hudson's Bay Company at Fort Rupert; when the company closed their post in 1885, he acquired the property. Hunt remained at Fort Rupert until his death.

HUNTER, Joseph (1842–1935) became one of the most recognized surveyors and engineers in British Columbia. Hunter had come to the Cariboo in 1864 as a miner and surveyor and was elected to the provincial legislature. In 1872, he joined the CPRS and conducted some of their most memorable explorations, including trek through the Pine River Pass in 1877. In 1883 he was the chief engineer in charge of building the Esquimalt and Nanaimo Railway, then general superintendent and vice-president of the line until retiring in 1918.

HUSON, Alden Westley (1832?-1913) was born in New York and came from California to the Cariboo in 1858. In the early 1860's he settled on the British Columbia coast where he operated a trading schooner along the east side of Vancouver Island, opened a store at Suquash, and then in 1881 went into the cannery business with S. A. Spencer and Thomas Earle at Alert Bay. Huson later sold his share of the cannery and worked a stone quarry.

INGRAM, Henry (d. 1879) was an American miner and packer who worked in the Cariboo then bought land at Grand Prairie (now Westwold) in the early 1860's.

JELLY, H. F. served as an axeman on R Division of the CPRS during the summer of 1875.

JENNINGS, W. T. was in charge of one of the divisions of the CPRS.

KEEFER, George Alexander (1836-1912) was a surveyor and engineer in the employ of the CPRS. Keefer began his career in eastern British North America as engineer for various railway lines before joining the CPRS in 1872. He remained with the Canadian Pacific Railway until 1886, supervising construction of the difficult Fraser Canyon section of the line. Later he was consultant on the construction of the Vancouver waterworks system and resident engineer for the Canadian Department of Public Works.

KEITH, J. C. was a ledger keeper for the Bank of British Columbia.

KIRKPATRICK, Andrew J. (d. 1891), along with his wife Agnes, ran a farm at Grand Prairie (Westwold) and also operated a renowned stopping place for travellers.

LAIRD, David (1833-1914) had been appointed federal minister of the interior and superintendent general of Indian affairs in November 1873. Laird retained that position until October 1876, when he was appointed lieutenant-governor of the North West Territories.

LE JACQ, Father Jean-Marie (1837?-99) came to British Columbia in 1862 and worked for some years at St. Joseph's Mission near Williams Lake. In 1873, Le Jacq, in company with his fellow priest, Georges Blanchet, went to Fort St. James to establish a permanent mission station in the more northerly region. That mission, Our Lady of Good Hope, was the centre from which the two priests reached out into the other districts of north-central British Columbia.

LOUIS or HLI-HLEH-KAN (1828-1915) was chief of the Kamloops Indians from about 1855 until his death. He guided his people through the difficult transition stage when the region was settled by large numbers of Euro-Canadians. Louis represented British Columbia Indians several times in Ottawa and also went to England as a delegate to Queen Victoria.

MACDONALD, Senator William John (1829-1916) came to British Columbia from Scotland in 1851 and, after working for the Hudson's Bay Company, went into business for himself. He was a member of Vancouver Island's Legislative Assembly from 1860-63 and of the Legislative Council of the United

Colonies from 1867 to 1868, and one of three British Columbia senators from 1871 until 1915.

McKAY, Joseph William (1829-1900) was a long-time Hudson's Bay Company employee in British Columbia. In the early 1850's, he led explorations which established the coal reserves at Nanaimo. Later appointed a chief factor, McKay spent time at Kamloops and Victoria before retiring in 1879, when he took the position of Indian agent at Kamloops, then Indian superintendent for British Columbia.

MACKENZIE, Alexander (1822-92) was prime minister of Canada from 1873 to 1878. He came to power on the fall of Sir John Macdonald, forming a Liberal administration that was troubled by economic depression, internal division, and the problem of building the Canadian Pacific Railway. Delay of the railway brought constant difficulties with British Columbia.

McKINLAY, Archibald (1810-91) came to British North America from Scotland in 1831 to work for the the Hudson's Bay Company. He served in the Red River area, in New Caledonia, as chief trader at Fort Walla Walla, and at Oregon City. McKinlay retired in 1851 because of failing eyesight, but set out for the Cariboo gold fields when his health improved in the 1860's. In 1863 he settled at Lac La Hache and later served as provincial government representative on the Commission on Indian Land from 1876 to 1878. He later moved to Savona.

McLEAN, Alexander. There were three McLeans employed by the CPRS; this is probably, Alexander McLean, a North Thompson packer.

McMILLAN, D. was an engineer in charge with the CPRS.

McPHADDEN, Donald (1847-1918) came to Victoria in 1865, moved to Kamloops in 1870, left for the Omineca country in 1871, and then returned to Kamloops, where he operated a store and hotel.

MACOUN, John (1831-1920) was born in Ireland; he emigrated to Canada in 1850 and became a farmer. In 1868, Macoun accepted a position as professor of natural history at Albert College in Belleville, Upper Canada. Later, Macoun accompanied Sandford Fleming on his expedition of 1872 and, in 1879, took a job as explorer in the Department of Interior. By 1881, he was promoted to botanist for the Geological Survey of Canada. In 1887, Macoun attained the position of assistant director and naturalist to the survey.

MADDEN, Captain William F. was "ship master" of Port Essington.

MAX or Maximillien Michaud operated a hotelry on the south shore of Burrard Inlet.

MEREDITH, Edmund Allen (1817-98) was born in Ireland and came to Canada in 1842. From 1847 to Confederation he was assistant provincial secretary of Upper Canada. In the new federal government, he served first as secretary of state for the provinces then, in 1873, became the first duputy minister of the new Department of the Interior. He retired from the public service in 1878, although he remained active on the Canadian Prison Board.

MONTEITH, William (1850?-1920) was a Scot who came to Victoria in 1870 in the employ of Janion, Rhodes and Company.

MURPHY, Charles and James. The Murphy brothers lived two miles above Hope on the opposite side of the Fraser River. In the late 1870's they struck gold in paying quantities on Union Bar Flat near their residence.

NATHAN, Henry (1842–1914) was a Victoria wholesale merchant, active in politics. Nathan was elected to the British Columbia Legislature in 1870 as representative for Victoria and to the Canadian House of Commons in 1871. Nathan served as a member of Parliament until 1874, returned to Victoria for several years, then left for London in 1876.

NELSON, Hugh (1830–93) was vice-president and manager of the Moodyville Saw Mill Company owned by the firm Moody, Dietz and Nelson. Nelson also was an active politician, having served in British Columbia's Legislative Assembly before Confederation, in the House of Commons from 1871 to 1874, and in the Senate from 1879 until 1887. He was appointed British Columbia's lieutenant-governor, serving 1887 to 1892.

O'REILLY, Peter (1828–1905) was an Anglo-Irishman who came to British Columbia in 1859. Shortly after, he was appointed stipendiary magistrate for Langley District then for Fort Hope District. He later served as magistrate and gold commissioner in a variety of other mainland areas. In 1863 he was appointed a member of the British Columbia Legislative Council, serving until 1871. He became Indian reserve commissioner for British Columbia in 1881 after the resignation of Gilbert Malcolm Sproat.

OFFUT, Martin H. established the Hudson's Bay Company's Masset post in 1870 and retired in December 1878, though a Mr. A. Cooper replaced him from 1871 to the fall of 1874. Offut was not an old company man, apparently joining the service recently, perhaps only for the Masset posting.

OGDEN, Charles was a clerk with the Hudson's Bay Company at Fort George.

PERRAULT, Joseph Xavier (1836–1905) was secretary-treasurer to the Canadian Commission for the Philadelphia Centennial Exposition.

PERRY, C. E. was an engineer in charge with the CPRS.

POOLE, Francis was a mining engineer who investigated copper reports in 1862 on behalf of the Queen Charlotte Mining Company of Victoria. He abandoned his mines in 1864 after shafts had been sunk on Burnaby and Skincuttle islands. He published *Queen Charlotte Islands: A Narrative of Adventure in the North Pacific*, ed. John W. Lyndon (London: Hurst and Blackett, 1872).

POOLEY, Charles Edward (1845–1912) arrived in Victoria in 1862 and, after a few months in the Cariboo, secured a clerical position with the government, eventually becoming registrar of the British Columbia Supreme Court. He was admitted to the bar in 1877 and had a partnership with A.E.B. Davie. Elected to the legislature in 1882, he remained a member for twenty-two years.

POWELL, Dr. Israel Wood (1836–1915) was active in many facets of Victoria life. After graduation from McGill University in 1860, Powell came to Victoria in 1862, established a busy medical practice, and became heavily involved in politics. From 1863, he sat in the Vancouver Island House of Assembly until he lost his seat when the colony amalgamated with British Columbia. In 1872, he was appointed B.C. superintendent of Indian affairs by the Canadian government.

He later profited handsomely from real estate investments in Vancouver during the 1880's.

PRICE, Barrington moved to Keremeos in 1873 after selling his store in Osoyoos, which he had owned and operated since 1871. Price then established a prosperous farm by pre-empting 640 acres in 1873 and adding more in following years.

RAMSAY, Sir Andrew Crombie (1814-91) was director-general of the British Geological Survey. One of the most distinguished nineteenth-century geologists, Ramsay had an enviable reputation as a field geologist and innovative theoretician. Like so many others, Dawson was heavily influenced by Ramsay's geological postulations and sought to apply his concepts to the British Columbia situation.

RAYMUR, Captain James Arnold (1823-82) was born in Halifax, Nova Scotia, and spent several years on vessels in the West Indian trade before coming to British Columbia in 1864. Initially employed by Anderson & Company of Alberni, Raymur later took over management of the Hastings mill and stayed in that capacity throughout the 1870's.

REID, James (1839-1904) was born in Wakefield, Lower Canada, and came to British Columbia in 1862. After mining in the Cariboo for several years, Reid opened a large store in Quesnel. Later, he was active in a variety of other business interests such as mines, steamers, and sawmills. He was a member of Parliament from 1881 to 1888 and senator from 1888 until his death.

RHODES, Henry of Henry Rhodes & Company, was a Victoria merchant and commission agent.

RICHARDS, Albert Norton (1822-97) was appointed lieutenant-governor on 20 July 1876. Earlier, Richards practised law in Brockville, Upper Canada, before sitting in the House of Commons from 1872 to 1874. Richards was appointed police magistrate in Victoria in 1888.

RICHARDSON, James (1810-83) was a geologist with the Geological Survey of Canada for some thirty-six years. Richardson came to North America early in life and farmed in Beauharnois County, Lower Canada, until he joined the survey in 1846 on the urging of Sir William Logan. Richardson's expeditions to British Columbia, conducted every season from 1871 to 1875, formed the basis of his pioneering work on British Columbia coal fields.

ROBERTSON, Duncan was a Quesnel blacksmith.

ROBSON, John (1824-92) played a prominent role in the life of nineteenth-century British Columbia. From 1875 to 1879, he served as paymaster and purveyor to the CPRS. He had founded *The British Columbian* newspaper in 1861, served in the provincial legislature and ministry, and in 1889 became premier.

ROSCOE, Francis James (1831-78) came to British Columbia in 1862 and settled in Victoria, where he operated an iron and hardware business. In 1873 he was elected to the House of Commons but declined renomination for the 1878 election.

ROSS, A. W. was employed with the CPRS.

ROWE, Valentine Francis (1841-1920), an officer with the Royal Engineers, had joined the boundary commission as an assistant astronomer in the spring of 1873 to take charge of a special survey of the Lake of the Woods.

RUSSELL, Thomas (1836–1912) was born in Scotland and came to Victoria to work for the Hudson Bay Company's Craigflower farm. In 1870, he superintended the Queen Charlotte Coal Mining Company's Cowgitz mine. He later served as Victoria city treasurer.

SABISTON, John (1853?–98) was the son of John Sabiston, a prominent Nanaimo pilot from 1867 until 1896. He captained the *Wanderer*, Dawson's schooner during the 1878 field season. The younger Sabiston later died of brain disease in New Westminster.

SCUDDER, Samuel Hubbard (1837–1911) was one of the great figures in American entomology. He was especially interested in fossil insects and carried out extensive, pioneering work in the field. In his lifetime, Scudder produced some 791 scientific articles and several large treatises.

SELWYN, Alfred Richard Cecil (1824–1902) was director of the Geological Survey of Canada from 1869 to 1895, when Dawson assumed the position upon Selwyn's retirement. Under Selwyn's direction, Dawson and his contemporaries began the immense task of surveying the western portion of British North America.

SEYMOUR, Charles was a miner who had worked in the Omineca district and elsewhere in British Columbia before leaving for the South African diamond fields in 1880.

SKEDAN (also Skedans or Skedance) was chief of Koona village on the Queen Charlotte Islands. The name was hereditary.

SMITH, Marcus (1815–1904) was the engineer in charge of the CPRS in British Columbia. An outspoken champion of a Pine River-Bute Inlet route, Smith was often embroiled in conflict with those advocating other routes. In 1876, when he became chief engineer for the survey after Sandford Fleming left for England for two years, Smith continued to stir up controversy by his unrelenting advocacy of the Bute Inlet route. In spite of Smith's strenuous efforts, the Canadian government eventually chose an alternate route through the Fraser Canyon to Burrard Inlet.

SMITH, J. McB., together with William Sterling, had established an oilworks to extract oil from dogfish livers in 1876.

SPENCE, Thomas (1826?–81) arrived in British Columbia in May 1858 and proceeded to the Cariboo gold fields. After mining for several years, he won one of the contracts to build the Cariboo Road from Boston Bar to Lytton. In 1865, he built a bridge across the Thompson River at the location that now bears his name. In that same year Spence was appointed the first civilian superintendent of public works for the colony of British Columbia.

SPENCER, Stephen Allen (1829?–1911) came to Victoria in 1858 and was in business for some years as a "daguerreian artist" before disappearing from view for several years then re-emerging in Barkerville in 1871. Spencer subsequently returned to Victoria in 1872 where he operated a number of photographic establishments. In the 1880's, he entered into the cannery business at Alert Bay in partnership with West Huson and Thomas Earle.

SPROAT, Gilbert Malcolm (1834–1913) was born in Scotland and came to Vancouver Island in 1860 under the employ of Anderson & Company, operators of a sawmill near Alberni. After returning to London, where he was agent-general for British Columbia, Sproat came back to British Columbia and was appointed joint commissioner on the Indian Land Commission in 1876. Upon resigning in 1880, Sproat spent much time in the Kootenay region in various capacities such as gold commissioner and assistant commissioner of lands and works.

TEIDEMANN, Herman Otto (1821–91) was employed in 1975 as a topographer for for the CPRS. He was also known as a civil engineer and designed British Columbia's first legislative buildings, the "Birdcages."

TOLMIE, Dr. William Fraser (1812–86) was one of Victoria's pioneer citizens. Tolmie joined the Hudson's Bay Company in 1832 and was assigned to Fort Vancouver on the Columbia River, arriving in 1833. In 1859, he came to Victoria to manage the farms of the Puget's Sound Agricultural Company. Tolmie also was a member of the Legislative Assembly on Vancouver Island and later the representative for Victoria in the provincial legislature. Upon his retirement in 1870, Tolmie spent much time on his own eleven-hundred acre Cloverdale Farm.

TOMLINSON, Robert (1842–1913) was an Irish physician who came to British Columbia in 1867 to assist William Duncan. Tomlinson's first posting was to the Nass River where he founded a mission station at Kincolith. A staunch supporter of Duncan, he lost the Anglican Church's backing when Duncan left the Church Missionary Society. In 1888, Tomlinson founded his own non-denominational mission, Minskinisht or Cedarvale, on the Skeena River.

TORRANCE, J. Fraser, a Montrealer was a British Columbia gold commissioner who later worked for the GSC.

TREW, Dr. Charles Newland (1837?–87), who resided in New Westminster, was surgeon to the New Westminster jail, the British Columbia Penitentiary, and the British Columbia militia.

VERNON, Charles (1840–1906) came to the Okanagan Valley with his brother Forbes and Charles Frederick Houghton in the early 1860's. The Vernons eventually acquired a large amount of land that formed the nucleus of the Coldstream Ranch. Along with his interest in the ranch, Charles Vernon also engaged in mining activities and merchandising and for a number of years served as gold commissioner, land commissioner, and justice of the peace.

VERNON, Forbes George (1843–1911) was chief commissioner of lands and works in the British Columbia government from 1876 to 1878. Vernon spent most of his early years in the province acquiring land and building up the Coldstream Ranch, but after the ranch was sold in 1891 he became agent-gencral for British Columbia in London and remained there until his death.

WALKEM, George Anthony (1834–1908) was premier of British Columbia from 1874 to 1876 and again from 1878 until 1882. After legal training at McGill, Walkem came to British Columbia in 1862, was called to the bar in 1864, and served in the colonial Legislative Council from 1864 to 1870. Upon leaving politics in 1882, Walkem was appointed a British Columbia Supreme Court judge.

WALKEM, William Wymond (1850–1919) was a Queen's medical graduate who came to the province in 1875. Walkem moved to Nanaimo where he established a general practice and was medical officer for the East Wellington Company. He subsequently became coroner and in 1894 was elected a member of the provincial legislature.

WALLACE, A. was a leveller with the CPRS.

WATSON, Adam (1824?-80) was a miner and blacksmith in Victoria.

WATT, M. was responsible for the Baynes Sound Coal Company, near Fanny Bay.

WEBSTER, Arthur W. was a topographer with the Geological Survey of Canada who was employed from 1868 to 1882 and then, briefly, in 1902.

WHITEVES, Joseph Frederic (1835-1909) came to Canada in 1862 and was at this time curator of the museum operated by the Montreal Natural History Society. In 1876 he succeeded Elkanah Billings as palaeontologist to the Geological Survey of Canada.

WOODCOCK, William H. established Woodcock's Landing on the Skeena.

YATES, William (1832-1917) began his service with the Hudson's Bay Company at York Factory in 1849. Later he moved to New Caledonia and, in 1854, came to the British Columbia coast. In 1856, he assumed his position at Fort Hope, where he was in command for many years.

Publications, 1870–78

"On Foraminifera from the Gulf and River St. Lawrence." *Canadian Naturalist and Quarterly Journal of Science* n.s. 5 (June 1870): 172–80.

"Note on the Occurrence of Foraminifera, Coccoliths, etc., in Cretaceous Rocks of Manitoba." *Canadian Naturalist and Quarterly Journal of Science* n.s. 7 (April 1874): 252–57.

"The Fluctuations of the American Lakes and Development of Sun Spots." *Nature* 9 (30 April 1874): 504–6.

Report on the Tertiary Lignite Formation, in the Vicinity of the Forty-Ninth Parallel. Montreal: Dawson Brothers, 1874.

"The Lignite Formations of the West." *Canadian Naturalist and Quarterly Journal of Science* n.s. 7 (April 1874): 241–52.

"On Some Canadian Species of Spongillae." *Canadian Naturalist and Quarterly Journal of Science* n.s. 8 (November 1875): 1–5.

"On the Superficial Geology of the Central Region of North America." *Quarterly Journal of the Geological Society of London* 31 (November 1875): 603–23.

Report on the Geology and Resources of the Region in the Vicinity of the Forty-ninth Parallel (British North American Boundary Commission). Montreal: Dawson Brothers, 1875.

"Notes on the Locust Invasion of 1874 in Manitoba and the North-West Territories." *Canadian Naturalist and Quarterly Journal of Science* n.s. 8 (1876): 119–34.

"Mesozoic Volcanic Rocks of British Columbia and Chile: Relation of Volcanic and Metamorphic Rocks." *Geological Magazine* n.s. 4 (July 1877): 314–17.

"Note on the Economic Minerals, and Mines of British Columbia: First List of Localities in the Province of British Columbia, Known to Yield Gold, Coal, Iron, Copper and Other Minerals of Economic Value." Appendix R in *Report on Surveys and Preliminary Operations on the Canadian Pacific Railway up to*

January, 1877. Ottawa: MacLean, Roger & Co., 1877.

"Note on Agriculture and Stock Raising, and Extent of Cultivable Land in British Columbia." Appendix S in *Report on Surveys and Preliminary Operations on the Canadian Pacific Railway up to January, 1877.* Ottawa: Maclean, Roger & Co., 1877.

"Note on Some of the More Recent Changes in Level of the Coast of British Columbia and Adjacent Regions." *Canadian Naturalist and Quarterly Journal of Science* n.s. 8 (April 1877): 241–48.

"Notes on the Appearance and Migrations of the Locust in Manitoba and the North-West Territories, Summer of 1875." *Canadian Naturalist and Quarterly Journal of Science,* n.s. 8 (April 1877): 207–26.

"Report on Explorations in British Columbia." Geological Survey of Canada, *Report of Progress for the Year 1875–76.* Montreal: Dawson Brothers, 1877. [Report on 1875 Field Season.]

"Erratics at High Levels in North-Western America: Barriers to a Great Ice-Sheet." *Geological Magazine* n.s. 5 (May 1878): 209–12.

"General Note on the Mines and Minerals of Economic Value of British Columbia, with a List of Localities, with Appendix." Geological Survey of Canada, *Report of Progress for 1876–77.* Montreal: Dawson Brothers, 1878.

"Notes on the Locust in the North-West in 1876." *Canadian Naturalist and Quarterly Journal of Science* n.s. 7 (April 1878): 411–17.

"On the Superficial Geology of British Columbia." *Quarterly Journal of the Geological Society of London* 34 (February 1878): 89–123.

"Report on Explorations in British Columbia, Chiefly in the Basins of the Blackwater, Salmon, and Nechacco Rivers, and on Francois Lake." Geological Survey of Canada, *Report of Progress for 1876–77.* Montreal: Dawson Brothers, 1878. [Report of 1876 Field Season.]

"Report on Reconnaissance of Leech River and Vicinity." Geological Survey of Canada, *Report of Progress for 1876–77.* Montreal: Dawson Brothers, 1878. [Report of Part of 1876 Field Season.]

"Travelling Notes on the Surface Geology of the Pacific Coast." *Canadian Naturalist and Quarterly Journal of Science* n.s. 8 (February 1878): 389–99.

"Notes on the Glaciation of British Columbia." *Canadian Naturalist and Quarterly Journal of Science* n.s. 9 (March 1879): 32–39.

"On a Species of Loftusia from British Columbia." *Quarterly Journal of the Geological Society of London.* 35 (February 1879): 69–75.

"Preliminary Report on the Physical and Geological Features of the Southern Portion of the Interior of British Columbia." Geological Survey of Canada, *Report of Progress for 1877–78* Montreal: Dawson Brothers, 1879. [Report on 1877 Field Season.]

"Sketch of the Past and Present Condition of the Indians of Canada." *Canadian Naturalist and Quarterly Journal of Science* n.s. 9 (July 1879): 129–59.

"Memorandum on the Queen Charlotte Islands, British Columbia." Appendix No. 9 in *Report and Documents in Reference to the Canadian Pacific Railway.* Ottawa: MacLean, Roger & Co., 1880.

"Report on the Queen Charlotte Islands." Geological Survey of Canada, *Report of Progress for 1878–79*. Montreal: Dawson Brothers, 1880. [Report on 1878 Field Season.]

"On the Haida Indians of the Queen Charlotte Islands." Appendix A in Geological Survey of Canada, *Report of Progress for 1878–79*. Montreal: Dawson Brothers, 1880.

"Vocabulary of the Haida Indians." Appendix B in Geological Survey of Canada, *Report of Progress for 1878–79*. Montreal: Dawson Brothers, 1880.

"Meteorological Observations." Appendix F in Geological Survey of Canada, *Report of Progress for 1878–79*. Montreal: Dawson Brothers, 1880.

Published Maps, 1875-78

Map 120. "Map of a Portion of British Columbia between the Fraser River and the Coast Range." Scale 8 miles to 1 inch.

Map 127. "Map of Portion of the Southern Interior of British Columbia." Scale 8 miles to 1 inch. Geological Survey of Canada, *Report of Progress for the Year 1877-78*. Montreal: Dawson Brothers, 1879.

Map 139. "Map of Queen Charlotte Islands." Scale 8 miles to 1 inch.

Map 140. "Plans of Harbours, Queen Charlotte Islands." Scale 2 nautical miles to 1 inch.

Map 141. "Map of Skidegate Inlet, Queen Charlotte Islands." Scale 1 nautical mile to 1 inch. Geological Survey of Canada, *Report of Progress for 1878-79*. Montreal: Dawson Brothers, 1880.

Diaries and Notebooks, 1873–78

McGill University, Rare Books & Special Collections; George M. Dawson Papers.

CARTON 2:

File 19
 a. Diary (5 May–1 June 1873)
 b. General diary & observation book, H. M. North American Boundary Commission (NABC) (1 June–26 June 1873)
 c. Catalogue of specimens, NABC (June 1873)

File 20
 a. Private diary, NABC (27 June–1 September 1873)
 b. Geological & topographical notebook, NABC (18 June–30 August 1873)

File 21
 a. Private diary, NABC (3 September–26 November 1873)
 b. Geological notes, NABC (5 September–16 October 1873)

File 22
 a. Diary (6 April–19 May 1874)
 b. Reference list of specimens, NABC, May 1874

File 23
 General diary & note book, NABC (20 May–16 October 1874)

File 24

    Note book (10 August–23 October 1875)

File 25

    Diary 1875 (19 August 1875–9 May 1876, 10–19 May 1876)

File 26

    a.   Glaciation, Indians & West Coast, 1876
    b.   Note book, New Boundary, 1876

CARTON 3:

File 1

    Diary & general note book (26 May–20 October 1876)

File 2

    Diary & general note book (28 May–26 October, 27 October–13 November 1877)

File 3

    a.   Diary (24 April–27 May 1877)
    b.   Note book, Murray Bay Terraces (10 August–16 August 1877)

File 4

    Queen Charlotte Islands (27 May–17 October 1878)

Field Notebooks, 1875-78

Public Archives of Canada, RG 45, Geological Survey of Canada.

2790, vol. 134.
23 August–30 October 1875
Interior Plateau, B.C., between the Fraser River and the Coast Ranges and between 52° and 54° North Latitude

2791, vol. 134.
December 1875
Vicinity of Victoria, B.C.

2793, vol. 134.
18–23 April 1876
Expedition from Victoria, B.C. to Leech River via Gold Stream and return by Sooke River and Sooke Road
11–16 May 1876
Expedition from Victoria, B.C. to Bute Inlet on Steamer *Sir James Douglas*
16 May–19 July 1876
Interior Plateau, B.C., between the Fraser River and the Coast Ranges and Between the Bella Coola Valley and François Lake

2794, vol. 134.
20 July–1 September 1876
Interior Plateau, continued

2795, vol. 134.
7 September–17 October 1876
Interior Plateau, continued

3044, vol. 134.
22 October–3 December 1876
Interior Plateau, continued

2796, vol. 134.
28 May–30 June 1877
Southern Interior Plateau, B.C., between 49° and 51° 30′ North Latitude
and between 119° and 121° 30′ West Longitude

2797, vol. 134.
1 July–11 August 1877
Southern Interior Plateau, continued

2798, vol. 134.
13 August–30 September 1877
Southern Interior Plateau, continued

2799, vol. 134.
1–19 October
Southern Interior Plateau, continued

2803
(missing)

2805
(missing)

2800, vol. 134.
13 June–27 July 1878
Queen Charlotte Islands, continued

2801, vol. 134.
31 July–25 August 1878
Queen Charlotte Islands, continued

2804, vol. 134.
6 July–21 August 1878
Queen Charlotte Islands, continued

2802, vol. 134
28 May–5 August 1878
Queen Charlotte Islands, continued

Index